I0796842

Court Poetry and the Culture of Learning in Japan

Harvard East Asian Monograph Series 485

Court Poetry and the Culture of Learning in Japan

Ariel Stilerman

Published by the Harvard University Asia Center
Distributed by Harvard University Press
Cambridge (Massachusetts) and London 2026

Published by the Harvard University Asia Center, Cambridge, MA 02138

The Harvard University Asia Center publishes a monograph series and, in coordination with the Fairbank Center for Chinese Studies, the Korea Institute, the Reischauer Institute of Japanese Studies, and other facilities and institutes, administers research projects designed to further scholarly understanding of China, Japan, Korea, Vietnam, and other Asian countries. The Center also sponsors projects addressing multidisciplinary, transnational, and regional issues in Asia.

The Harvard University Asia Center gratefully acknowledges the generous support of the Reischauer Institute of Japanese Studies at Harvard University, whose funding contributed to the publication of this book.

Library of Congress Cataloging-in-Publication Data
Names: Stilerman, Ariel author
Title: Court poetry and the culture of learning in Japan / Ariel Stilerman.
Description: Cambridge, Massachusetts : Harvard University Asia Center, 2026. | Series: Harvard East Asian monograph series ; 485 | Includes bibliographical references and index.
Identifiers: LCCN 2025027089 (print) | LCCN 2025027090 (ebook) | ISBN 9780674303416 hardcover | ISBN 9780674304307 epub
Subjects: LCSH: Japanese poetry—1185–1600—History and criticism | Learning and scholarship—Japan—History | Literature and society—Japan—History | Waka—History and criticism | Kyōka—History and criticism | LCGFT: Literary criticism
Classification: LCC PL733.3 .S75 2026 (print) | LCC PL733.3 (ebook)
LC record available at https://lccn.loc.gov/2025027089
LC ebook record available at https://lccn.loc.gov/2025027090

Index by David Prout

Printed by Books International, 22883 Quicksilver Drive, Dulles, VA 20166, USA (www.booksintl.com). The manufacturer's authorized representative in the EU for product safety is LOGOS EUROPE, 9 rue Nicolas Poussin, 17000, La Rochelle, France (e-mail: Contact@logoseurope.eu).

Contents

Acknowledgments

Writing up this project took long years during which I was blessed by the friendship and support of countless people. The journey from dissertation to book began in Tallahassee, where I was fortunate to receive support and inspiration from Junko and James Brudenell, Kristina Buhrman, Michael Carrasco, Beth Coggeshall, Matthew Goldmark, Bop and Annie Hewes, Aaron Lan, Laura Lee, Jenny Morton, Chiho and Junko Nishida, Mark Pietralunga, Gary and Gerry Rickard, Rob Romanchuk, Jeannine Spears, Corbin Treacy, Silvia Valisa, Lisa Wakayama, Jimmy Yu, and others.

Similarly wonderful friends and colleagues awaited me in Palo Alto: Marty Breidenbach, Jeremy Bulow, Richard Dasher, Shane Denson, Sebastián and Mercedes Di Tella, Rowan Dorin, Ron Egan, Charlotte Fonrobert, Boris Glants, Roland Greene, John Groschwitz, Tom Hare, Blair Hoxby, Tom Jack, Min Jung and Greg Buchak, Roanne Kantor, Regan Murphy Kao, Alexander Key, John Kieschnick, Matt Kohrman, Richard Lebakos, Haiyan Lee, Indra Levy, Bryant Lin, Momoyo Kubo Lowdermilk, Hideo Mabuchi, Yoshiko Matsumoto, Kathi Matsuura, Cyril Millendez, Craig Milroy, Ekaterina Mozhaeva, Reviel Netz, Brad and Becky Osgood, Jim Reichert, Aaron Roodman, Gabriella Safran, David and Joan Stevenson, Jeanne Su, Chao Sun, Joe Wager, Ban Wang, Kären Wigen, Yiqun Zhou, and Dafna Zur.

Beyond Florida State and Stanford, I found support and friendship at Columbia University, thanks to Haruo Shirane, David Lurie, and Tomi Suzuki; at Waseda University, thanks to Jinno Hidenori, Kanechiku Nobuyuki, and Toeda Hirokazu; at the University of California, Los Angeles, thanks to Torquil Duthie, Michael Emmerich, and

Satoko Shimazaki; and at the Nichia Gakuin Institute in Buenos Aires, thanks to Paula Hoyos Hattori.

I am profoundly grateful to the language instructors who guided me early in my journey: Kawada Nobue in Madrid, Wada Akie in Buenos Aires, and Nazukian Fumiko in New York. Likewise, Arimidzu Emiko, Doi Yoko, Kimura Sōkei, and Nojiri Michiko shared their knowledge of the tea ceremony, ultimately preparing me for a transformative year of study at Urasenke Konnichian in Kyoto.

Among those I met while still a student and now proudly count as friends and colleagues are David Atherton, Erin Brightwell, Andrea Castiglioni, Matías Chiappe, Gosia Citko-DuPlantis, Matt Feldt, Joshua Frydman, Tom Gaubatz, Jenny Guest, Nan Hartman, Malena Higashi, Paul Kreitman, Ashton Lazarus, Michael McCarty, Mariko Naitō, Pau Pitarch, Daniel Poch, Kristopher Reeves, Josh Rogers, Nate Shockey, Shiho Takai, Luke Thompson, Rob Tuck, Kei Umeda, Tyler Walker, Anri Yasuda, Christina Yi, and Hitomi Yoshio.

In Buenos Aires, New York, Tallahassee, and Palo Alto, I found inspiration and support in many students. Among them are Tyrhen Cameron, Yan Chang, Bingrui Chen, Po Linn Chia, Jacqueline Fong, Rosaley Gai, Calvin Grant, Alex Heron, Christian Ho, Luo Jia, Sijia Li, Caitlin McCann, Gustavo Mercado, Avery Michael, Andrew Nelson, Eric Suen, William Varteresian, Emily Wan, Lin Meng Walsh, Katherine Whatley, Victoria Wilson, Natt Wojas, James Wronowsky, and ZiFan Yang.

This book would not have been possible without institutional support from Florida State University's First-Year Assistant Professor, Committee on Faculty Research Support, Bradley, A&S Faculty Travel, and Provost Travel grants; the Stanford Humanities Center Fellowship and Manuscript Review Workshop; a Stanford Freeman Spogli Institute Japan Fund grant; the University of Edinburgh's PAIXUE Project; Japan Foundation grants and programs in Tokyo, Madrid, and Mexico; the Shincho Fellowship; and Waseda University's Overseas Researcher Program.

I am particularly grateful for the insights on early drafts offered by David Atherton, Steven Carter, Torquil Duthie, Regan Murphy Kao, David Lurie, and Haruo Shirane. Special thanks to the Publications Committee of Harvard University Asia Center and to the two anonymous readers for their invaluable feedback; to Kristen Wanner for her steadfast belief in this project; to Daniel Lee for expertly guiding it through review and preparation, and for suggesting the cover image. I also want to acknowledge Irene Pavitt and Julie Hagen's meticulous copyediting, Penelope Perkins's rigorous proofreading, Regina Starace's elegant cover design, and Suzanne Harris's skillful composition and typesetting. John Carpenter generously discussed with me the background for the poem on the cover (and provided the image from the Met archive).

Finally, I would like to mention friends and colleagues around the globe who, with their unwavering affection and intellectual curiosity, made the toil of writing sweeter and lighter: Alfonso Amat, Luciano Asian, Alejandro Chaskielberg, Juan Pablo Coletti, Adelqui Del Do, Pat Fogarty, Kumagai Yūki and Maiko, Crispín Maldonado, Xavier Ortells, Ben Johnson, and Guido Herzovich.

In our family, my thanks go to Cely; Ira and Mindy; Ari and Isaac and Iona; Yael and Scott; Meghan and Tsultrim; Sarah and Emma; Jorge and Ana; Marta and Beto; Andrea; Daniel and Gabi; Anita and Oliver; to my in-laws, Frank and Gretchen; and to my parents, Dalia and David; and to my wife, Tracy, and our daughter, Valentina, for nothing sustained me more than knowing that at the end of a long day their love and joy awaited me.

To all of you, thank you.

Note to the Reader

Japanese personal names appear in the order of family name followed by given name in the main body of this book but follow each individual's practice in the Acknowledgments. After the first reference in the text to a historical person, I follow the customary practice of using given or Buddhist names instead of family names, such as Toshiyori for Minamoto no Toshiyori. Romanization of Japanese words follows the modified Hepburn system. All translations, unless otherwise noted, are my own.

Set of Utensils for the Tea Ceremony, by Kubo Shunman (Japanese, 1757–1820). Edo period, 1810s. Woodblock print (*surimono*); ink and color on paper, 13.8 × 18.4 cm. The Metropolitan Museum of Art, H. O. Havemeyer Collection, Bequest of Mrs. H. O. Havemeyer, 1929 (JP1974). www.metmuseum.org.

On the Cover of This Book

This *surimono* print bears the seal of Kubo Shunman 窪俊満 (1757–1820). It features a *kyōka* poem.

ON THE DAY SPRING ARRIVED, AT A TEA GATHERING.

ōbuku ni	In a large bowl
tatsuru chanoyu no	for good luck, making tea
kuchikiri ya	to mark a beginning:
toshi no temae ni	Ahead of the new year
haru wa ki ni keri	spring has arrived!

A large bowl (*ōbuku*) of tea (*cha*), prepared (*temae*) using the first water drawn, is part of the auspicious (*ōfuku*) celebrations at the beginning of the year (*toshi*) by practitioners of the tea ceremony (*chanoyu*). However, tea practitioners would have already marked their own "new year" earlier (*temae*) in the winter, when they cut the seals (*kuchikiri*) on ceramic jars to begin using tea leaves stored in summer and autumn.

The poem is signed "Kokin no Nakanari," likely a nom de plume created just for this occasion, to play on the title of the first imperial anthology of court poetry, *Kokinshū* (Collection of poems ancient and modern, 905). The final two lines allude to the first *waka* poem in *Kokinshū*, which similarly plays on calendric discrepancies.

COMPOSED ON A DAY WHEN SPRING HAD ARRIVED DURING THE OLD YEAR.

toshi no uchi ni	Before the year's end
haru wa kinikeri	spring has arrived:
hitotose wo	Of these twelve months,
kozo to ya iwamu	shall we say "last year"?
kotoshi to ya iwamu	Shall we say "this year"?

In the solar calendar, the new year begins with spring, whereas in the lunar calendar it begins with the second new moon after the winter solstice. The poem highlights an event—occurring every two or three years—when the first day of spring precedes the new moon.

The camellias in the illustration, like the new year, can bloom in the winter or the spring.

The emblem on the tea caddy pouch indicates that this *surimono* was commissioned by the Gogawa 五側 collective of *kyōka* poets, led by Rokujuen 六樹園 (1753–1830), who were bitter rivals of the Yomo 四方 collective led by Shikatsube no Magao 鹿都部真顔 (1753–1829).

The image encapsulates some of the central themes of this book. The feuds among poets—despite their shared foundations—is reminiscent of the rivalries among professional *waka* specialists discussed in the first chapter. The complex relationship of *kyōka* poems to the *waka* tradition is explored in the third chapter. And the connections between poetic pedagogy and the study of the tea ceremony feature prominently in the epilogue.

INTRODUCTION

What we call the classical poetry of Japan, known in Japanese as *uta* 歌 or *waka* 和歌, is characterized by its brevity and its contrived diction. We find accounts of its performance in the earliest historical chronicles, in aristocratic court narratives of the classical period (894–1185), in tales of war and destruction from the medieval era (1191–1573), on the Noh stage during the late medieval years, and in every genre of popular fiction from the early modern centuries (1600–1868). Since the nineteenth century, poets have composed similar poems (now known as *tanka* 短歌) to laud Japan's imperial expansion, lament the ensuing military disaster, celebrate the economic resurgence, and mourn social malaise. By contrast, the practice of poetry in the Chinese style, known as *shi* 詩 (Ch. *shī*), which accompanied *waka* through all its history, did not survive modernization and exists today only as an academic exercise.[1] The *waka* form remains available, accessible, and engaging to speakers of Japanese at home and abroad.[2]

Waka as a form remained intact, but in its social functions—its cultural existence, which is the focus of this book—it experienced sweeping changes. *Waka* was an aristocratic (*kuge* 貴族) practice that expanded first to elite warriors (*bushi* 武士), then to their non-elite retainers and servants from the regions around the new city of Kamakura, and later to urban merchants (*machishū* 町衆) in the capital (Kyoto), in the trading centers, such as Sakai (Osaka), and in the provinces. In each of these instances, *waka* transformed to incorporate new interests and shed what had become less relevant. For the most part, these transformations do not register at the level of the canonical genres sponsored by the elites: the imperially commissioned anthologies of *waka* and the classical court narratives. They can be traced only through an examination of other works, other genres, and other social spaces.

This book looks at a diversity of writing about poetry from late classical (1086–1185) to early modern Japan to make a new argument about how and why poetry came to matter widely, particularly to non-elites and, even more crucially, to nonpoets. Reconstructing the centuries-long arc traced by the practice of *waka* as it moved across social spaces beyond the aristocracy inevitably involves linking a diverse assortment of texts and genres across disparate time periods. We find a precedent for such an analysis over many centuries in Ogawa Takeo's *Bushi wa naze uta wo yomu ka: Kamakura shōgun kara sengoku daimyō made* (Why do warriors compose poems? From Kamakura's shoguns to Warring States lords), which focuses on poetic composition by the nascent warrior elite and their descendants.[3] We have research also on the literary dimension of the relationship between the new warrior leadership and the general population of early medieval Japan, such as Gomi Fumihiko's "Shi to setsuwa" (History and brief narrative).[4] But we still lack a systematic attempt to uncover how non-elite warriors and other commoners found themselves in contact with *waka* for the first time. The approach of this book—which moves across both time and genres—stems from the sources themselves, which connect in unexpected ways and without any direct references or open gestures to one another. When we explore how medieval collections of brief narratives (*setsuwa-shū* 説話集) repurposed material from late classical scholarly poetry treatises (*karon* 歌論 / *kagaku* 歌学) that later, in turn, became the target of parody in fictional tales for urban commoners (*otogizōshi* 御伽草子), it becomes apparent that poetry transcended class divisions, in great part thanks to its capacity to serve as a vehicle for the production and transmission of knowledge.

This knowledge could be of many kinds—from local geography to linguistics to history—but over time what came to matter most was knowledge about the culture of the court, particularly for a constituency without access to it. These were practitioners of *waka* in the widest sense, as most of the lower-level warriors and rising urban commoners discussed in this book would never have dreamed of becoming famous poets, let alone professional poetry specialists. For them, learning about *waka* was a chance to learn about the court, at a moment when the habits and preferences of the aristocracy were becoming the standard of high culture for all classes.

Beyond the Ivory Tower

In "Los teólogos" ("The Theologians," 1947), a short story set in early medieval Europe, Jorge Luis Borges recounts the tale of two theologians who compete for the patronage of Rome as they make a career out of the condemnation of heresy. Aureliano is a learned, meticulous composer of lengthy commentaries, footnotes, and marginalia. Juan de Panonia's arguments, by contrast, are rivetingly succinct and incisive. In Aureliano's mind, the virtues of the other are a vitiation of his own. He is jealous of his rival and, in a moment of weakness, suggests that a long-forgotten volume by Juan de Panonia is akin to the writings of the heretics. Juan de Panonia is soon burned at the stake. Years later, as Aureliano is wandering away from Rome in the hope of understanding (or perhaps of atoning for) his life, lightning strikes the hinterlands he is passing through and he dies in a fire. At this point, Borges writes,

> The end of this story can be referred to only through metaphors, since it takes place in the kingdom of heaven, where there is no time. Perhaps it could be said that Aureliano conversed with God, who is so little interested in religious differences that He took him for Juan de Panonia. This, however, would suggest a confusion in the divine mind. It would be more correct to say that in paradise Aureliano learned that, for the unfathomable divinity, he and Juan de Panonia (orthodox and heretic, abhorrer and abhorred, accuser and accused) were one single person.[5]

The elite poetic circles of medieval Japan had their own Borgesian "theologians." The composition, evaluation, and circulation of poems were commandeered by a handful of households of hereditary professional specialists. The Rokujō and the Mikohidari, at first; then two branches of the latter, the Nijō and the Kyōgoku; and further down the line, the Reizei and the Asukai. Like Aureliano and Juan de

Panonia, these poetry specialists denounced one another as unorthodox, careless, and ignorant as they vied for the patronage of the mighty. The highest honor was to receive a commission to compile an anthology of poems for the emperor. For individual poets, the inclusion of even one poem in such a collection meant immediate canonization. For hereditary specialists, the privilege of editing a once-in-a-generation poetry anthology brought unmatched power to their camp for centuries.[6]

There was more to poetic practice than the activity of these hereditary professionals, however. When introducing a study of the overlooked aspects of modern design and urban environments, Roman Mars and Kurt Kohlstedt write,

> The world is full of amazing things. Walk around any major city and you will find soaring skyscrapers that inspire awe, bridges that are marvels of engineering, and lush parks that provide respite from the concrete landscape. There are travel guides for all of that. This, however, is a guide to the overlooked and ordinary: the boring stuff. The truth is that the mundane objects we pass by without noticing or trip over without thinking can represent as much genius and innovation as the tallest building, the longest bridge, or the most manicured park. So much of the conversation about design centers on beauty, but the more fascinating stories of the built world are about problem-solving, historical constraints, and human drama.[7]

To borrow Roman Mars's language, elite poets were the buildings that towered over the medieval poetic landscape, the bridges that connected the mighty to the prestigious, and the lush parks that were rich in the lyrical flora and fauna of the poetic past. While their poems varied in style, their commentaries to classical works varied in approach, and their scholarship varied in quality, these families were not as dissimilar from one another as they assumed. Their sour rivalries, like that of Aureliano and Juan de Panonia, were the product of a hypersensitivity to minor differences that only deeply shared commonalities can engender.[8] All of these professionals were men of aristocratic pedigree, scions of hereditary households of specialists based in the imperial capital, Kyoto, and invested in a medieval worldview that looked back to the classical period as the exclusive source of cultivation and precedent. They represent the most visible facet of medieval poetics, yet their work accounts for only a fragment of the story of how *waka* came to be experienced at all levels of society.[9]

Since its very inception, *waka* was intimately connected with social functions and cultural roles.[10] In the aristocratic milieu of the tenth and eleventh centuries, the point in time and space from which this book departs, composing *waka* could serve to signal access to court culture, woo an amorous partner, secure the patronage of a social superior, embellish a banquet or ceremonial occasion, and—as a form of communication free from the honorifics required in speech—connect sites of unequal power.[11] Eventually these functions waned, and by the late classical period, members of elite poetry circles increasingly sought to please the judges of taste who presided over lavish competitive poetry gatherings, a development that has been celebrated as signaling the end of *waka*'s social functions. Kuboki Tetsuo, for example, has argued that unleashing the creative potential of *waka* as a form required that poems be released from the constraints imposed on them by their role as a social medium.[12] I argue otherwise, that the social functions of *waka* did not disappear but morphed as *waka* expanded into social spaces beyond elite salons and as poetic practice became a vehicle for cultural transmission. In a way that would have shocked mid-classical poets, *waka* came to be a way for many outside the court to learn about history, society, and the world.

The Social Uses of Poems

The paradigmatic instance of *waka* practice in the mid-classical period involved an exchange of poems between two aristocrats in one of a handful of conventional social settings, such as wooing, celebrating, mourning, requesting, and so on. These exchanges appear in all courtly narrative prose, from *Ise monogatari* 伊勢物語 (The tales of Ise, mid-tenth century) to *Genji monogatari* 源氏物語 (The tale of Genji, early eleventh century), in personal diaries, in private collections of poems, and in historical tales, as well as in the most canonical genre: the imperially commissioned collection of poems.[13] The following exchange, for example, is from the second imperial collection, *Gosen wakashū* (*Gosenshū* 後撰集 [Later collection], 951). It appears in this anthology together with a brief headnote added by the compilers:

> Sent after having withdrawn to her home to mourn the passing of her mother, and in response to a letter from the former emperor, by the Ōmi imperial concubine:
>
> | | |
> |---|---|
> | *samidare ni* | My sleeves, |
> | *nurenishi sode ni* | wet since the summer rains, |
> | *itodoshiku* | are now |
> | *tsuyu okisofuru* | soaked even more with the dew: |
> | *aki no wabishisa* | the sadness of autumn. |
>
> The emperor's reply:
>
> | | |
> |---|---|
> | *ōkata mo* | Autumns are in general |
> | *aki wa wabishiki* | a sad season, |
> | *toki naredo* | yet I feel particularly |
> | *tsuyukekaruramu* | for the sleeves |
> | *sode wo shi zo omou* | no doubt soaked in dew.[14] |
>
> 母の服にて里に侍けるに先帝の御文たまへりける御返ごとに近 江更衣　五月雨に濡れにし袖にいとゞしく露をきそふる秋のわびしさ　御返し　延喜御製　おほかたも秋はわびしき時なれど露けかる覧袖をしぞ思

The emperor mentioned here is Daigo 醍醐 (885–930, r. 897–930), a patron of *waka* who had commissioned the first imperial anthology, *Kokin wakashū* (*Kokinshū* 古今集 [Collection of poems ancient and modern], 905). His concubine is Shūshi 周子 (Chikako, d. 935), who bore him eight children. Shūshi was the daughter of Minamoto no Tonō 源唱 (n.d.), a courtier of the fourth rank, and thus not a particularly powerful personage by lineage. Like Daigo, Shūshi was a patron of *waka* and a host of poetry contests.[15]

The poems by Shūshi and Daigo deploy concrete images and conventional seasonal associations, such as the summer rains of the Fifth Month (*samidare* 五月雨) and the dew (*tsuyu* 露) of autumn. Autumn was conventionally associated with sadness. Wet sleeves, similarly, was a fairly standard metonym for tears. In this exchange, the poets are showing off their poetic talents. But they are also negotiating a pressing issue: the length of Shūshi's stay away from court. According to the headnote, the context for this poem was the passing of the concubine's mother. In these circumstances, she would have been expected to spend forty-nine days away from the court to avoid defiling the emperor. The sadness that started in the summer and continued well into the autumn corresponds with this leave of absence, and her poem seems to be saying that although this period has ended and she is now expected to return, she is still feeling too sad to resume her duties. As is conventional, the emperor incorporates the natural images from Shūshi's poem to offer a reply, in this case sending his condolences and expressing his love and understanding. In practical terms, this translates into an authorization to stay away from the court for a longer period.

One way to look at this complex interaction is through Caroline Levine's theory of form. According to this theory, the shape that an exchange will take is the product of the collision of a number of different forms. In the poems by Shūshi and Daigo, some of these are the poetic form of *waka* itself; the specific patterns of heterosexual exchanges of poems (as opposed to heterosocial and homosocial exchanges); the poetry of love and longing (with its tropes and rhetorics and blind spots); the ritualized dialogue between ruler and subject, shaped by Chinese notions of virtuous governance; the aristocratic aversion to bringing attention to bodily fluids (tears being an exception, accepted exclusively as a synecdoche for excessive affect); the anxieties about defilement and attendant practices of prophylaxis; and the politics of marriage, among others. Levine's approach is helpful in that it allows us to understand, for example, how in an imperial collection of poetry the emperor is presented at the same time as a lover, a patron, and a virtuous ruler, and how both poets—all the poets in the collection, in fact—are simultaneously enabled and constrained in their expression by preexisting patterns of interaction.[16]

This poetic interaction can be examined in terms of the Ōmi concubine's strategic positioning when engaging with a lover who is also a patron and a ruler. The form that an exchange between lovers takes is, by convention, adversarial: the first poem encodes in natural images a complaint, and the reply poem retorts by subverting the same images to mean the opposite. An exchange between subject and ruler, by contrast, tends to be harmonizing: the first poem encodes in natural images an expression of praise or alliance, and the reply poem uses the same images to confirm a sense of mutual trust. To use a concept central to Levine's system, these two forms of engagement have different *affordances*. In the first case, the exchange affords a witty repartee that negotiates mutual mistrust; in the other, it affords a reassuring confirmation of community. As Levine states, "In practice, we encounter so many forms that even in the most ordinary daily experience they add up to a complex environment composed of multiple and conflicting modes of organization—forms arranging and containing us, yes, but also competing and colliding and rerouting one another."[17] On the one hand, the Ōmi concubine's poem emerges from the free play of available forms. On the other, there is something in the poem that feels *crafted*, purposeful. The poem skillfully plays the affordances of different forms against each other to produce an artifact that forces the emperor to make a choice between the unreasonable wishes of a lover and the responsibilities of a ruler.

The Switch to Poetic Topics

It is possible to trace a shift in the roles that *waka* played in society to the turn of the twelfth century, which marks the beginning of the late classical period. Until then, as I have noted, the paradigmatic practice had been the recitation and exchange of poems as part of public and private interactions. Starting in the late classical period, attention turned to the composition of poems for poetry gatherings (*utakai* 歌会) and for poetry contests (*utaawase* 歌合)—in which poets competed to earn the praise of an expert judge. These events had been common since at least the tenth century, but as Hashimoto Fumio has argued, they became the dominant driver of poetic practice around the time of the compilation of the fourth imperial anthology, *Goshūi wakashū* (*Goshūishū* 後拾遺集 [Later collection of gleanings], 1086).[18] As poets now anticipated that their poems would be assessed for their technical qualities by a designated judge, the ability to match the conventional associations and expectations of a poetic topic (*dai* 題) assigned by the organizers of an event became more important than their capacity to deliver a social message in poetic form. Professional specialists and their treatises emerged in this context of practice during the late classical period.

This turn away from social dialogues and toward standardized poetic topics is often understood as a sign that *waka* had finally become a fully developed, mature literary genre. Kubota Utsubo, for example, has posited a distinction between practical (*jitsuyōhin* 実用品) and literary (*bungeihin* 文芸品) uses of poetry.[19] Inoue Muneo, drawing on Kubota, has postulated that since subsequent editors of imperial anthologies favored poems produced for their literary value rather than for utilitarian reasons, we should understand those compositions as representing the "proper style" (*shōfūtei* 正風体) of *waka*.[20] And as mentioned, Kuboki similarly argued that poems freed from their traditional role as a social medium could now embrace the creative (*sōsaku* 創作) dimension of *waka*.[21] It is unquestionable that after the compilation of *Goshūishū* and until the last imperially commissioned collection in the late medieval period, all official anthologies of poems reflected the work of poetry circles that were focused on topical composition.

Topical poetry had been practiced throughout the classical period, but only as a relatively minor element in a complex system of practice. Edward Kamens has called this system "*waka* culture." It encompasses the "traditions and practices of making, reproducing, receiving, circulating, and preserving classical Japanese poems in a variety of settings and media through time" and, crucially, includes the "various forms of teaching, critiquing, editing, and commenting that thrive in tandem with these practices and their results."[22] Kamens applies this analysis not only to texts but also to material objects, such as standing screens (*byōbu* 屏風) and the scale models of the dwellings of ancient immortals (*suhama* 洲浜) used to decorate banquets celebrating the accession of a new emperor. As topical composition moved from being one of many modes of engagement to becoming the central concern of elite poets and their instructors in late classical Japan, and as imperial anthologies from *Goshūishū* onward became populated predominantly with topical poems, social groups other than aristocrats and professional poets entered the realm of *waka* culture and shaped with their interests, needs, and activities the ways in which poems would exist socially beyond the elites.[23]

Reaffordances

The notion of affordances is particularly helpful in understanding the trajectory of *waka* in the postclassical period as well as the classical. The exchange of poems between the Ōmi concubine and Emperor Daigo was preserved in *Gosenshū*, together with a brief narrative headnote. This is the form in which poetry exchanges appear in classical works, such as *Ise monogatari* and *Genji monogatari*. In them, poems are always embedded in a narrative frame. Isolated poems are hard to connect with social occasions; it is only thanks to these narrative vignettes that we know about the diverse affordances of classical poems as a form of social dialogue.

The narrative vignette as a form proved particularly enduring. It went on to play a key role in the transmission of knowledge about *waka* to social spaces beyond the aristocracy and the court. Vignettes of this type appear in all the works that are the main focus of this book: late classical poetry treatises (*karon/kagaku*), early medieval collections of brief narratives (*setsuwashū*), and fictional tales (*otogizōshi*) written between the late medieval period and the beginning of the early modern period. Narrative vignettes perdured not only in form but often in content as well: a passage taken from a classical imperial collection or poetic tale could be repurposed first in a late classical poetry treatise, then in a medieval collection of narratives, and finally in a fictional tale as a target of parody. The same is true of their affordances. As Levine states, forms "carry their affordances with them as they move across time and space."[24] In these vignettes coexist several affordances, and in each of their new iterations we find a new balance of weight among them. Affordances that had remained latent or dormant for a long time often came to the foreground, and other, hitherto dominant affordances receded into the background.

This iterative process of "reaffordance" is driven by historical changes in readership. In the late classical poetry treatises written by aristocratic professional poets for their noble and elite-warrior patrons, poetic vignettes provided the historical, geographical, and linguistic knowledge necessary to compete at a poetry gathering and win the approval of expert critics. In the early medieval collections of brief narratives compiled for non-elite warriors, the same vignettes afforded a glimpse into the culture of the aristocracy for an audience without direct access to it and with little prospect of becoming serious poets. The later fictional tales of the late medieval period offered the urban merchant class parodic renditions of the culture of the aristocracy as seen through the eyes of an emerging popular culture—yet by inverting the content while preserving the form of the poetic vignette, these tales simultaneously maintained and transmitted core aspects of aristocratic culture. Something analogous happens with the poems in these humorous tales. Known as *kyōka* 狂歌 (absurd poetry), they preserve the *waka* form while subverting its content for comedic effect in a way that both passes on and makes fun of the culture of the aristocracy.

The noun "affordance" is now widely used—thanks chiefly to Levine's theory and, before that, to the work of designers and psychologists. I have coined the term "reaffordance" to describe the repurposing and reframing of a literary object (a form, a genre, or a text) by foregrounding affordances that have remained latent and downplaying those that had until then defined its social circulation. In a few extreme cases, this involves creating new affordances out of an old object. A type of reaffordance specific to the manuscript culture of late classical and medieval Japan consisted in the repurposing of passages from a variety of existing works to compile a new text, a process which I refer to as diffusion.[25] When thinking of individual texts, it is possible to draw a distinction between their initial round of circulation (let's call it their inception) among their intended readers and a secondary circulation (dissemination) among socioeconomically similar circles. Late classical poetry treatises, for instance, were created for specific patron-students (inception), but they soon found a readership among other aristocratic patrons, poets, and specialists (dissemination). In these two types of circulation, a manuscript was typically reproduced as a whole and copied with a painstaking eye for accuracy and integrity. We can say that the work was passed down, tracing a vertical lineage of transmission from its putative origin—although in most cases that origin is lost to us, and all we have are the copies produced during its dissemination. By contrast, when early medieval authors borrowed passages from these treatises for the new readership of non-elite warriors, they did so without any reference to the source of the material, even if it stemmed from the most prestigious genres. This liberal collation of material from different texts and genres happened horizontally—disconnected from a point of origin and unconcerned with issues of authorship or textual authority.

The process of diffusion involves movements of fragmentation and reconstitution, and thus can be considered a type of reception. A key to reception is the diversity of paths that a work can follow. Haruo Shirane has explored a productive distinction between popularity and canonicity.[26] Canonicity refers to the efforts to preserve intact and to interpret a text considered to have cultural authority or importance. Canonized texts become the object of extensive commentary and exegesis, while popular texts do not. Popular texts are, instead, altered through (or with the assistance of) new media and visual technology that make them accessible to new audiences. A parallel distinction can be made between "readerly" reception (by which a text is read, interpreted, and taught) and "writerly" reception (by which it becomes the source of allusive variation, parody, pastiche, digests, adaptations, and translations). A single text can undergo both processes, as Shirane discusses in connection with *Genji monogatari*, and Richard Bowring explores in his analysis of *Ise monogatari*.[27]

The paths of canonicity and popularization have a common interest in consistency. They seek, in Bowring's words, "to provide, create, or identify a principle of coherence that could be used to order a more satisfying reading."[28] In the case of popularization by means of writerly reception, the source text can be digested for readers with less linguistic competence, parodied for a skeptical audience, adapted to reflect new sociocultural preferences, or translated into other languages. In all these cases, the success of the new work depends on its ability to reproduce or suggest the coherence of the original. By contrast, the notion of diffusion I propose refers to attempts to detach a passage from the coherence of the source text (severing its ties to it) and provide it with a new frame of coherence. Diffusion thus involves reaffordance because this new frame highlights affordances of the borrowed material that were not foregrounded in the source text.

Another useful way to understand the process of diffusion is in contrast to the concept of replacement. Michael Emmerich has introduced this idea to supersede that of reception and the attendant centrality of the notion of a "text."[29] Replacement can refer to the emergence of new works that enable the consumption of an (often imagined) old work, and to the act of newly "placing" an (often imagined) old work in a contemporary context. In the case of canonized works such as *Genji monogatari* and *Ise monogatari*, the material circumstances of the early forms of circulation are lost to later generations and a series of historically and materially determined new configurations come to bear the load of negotiating the relationship of text and reader. A work of poetry or prose sometimes could be condensed into iconic visual patterns on fabric, wood, or lacquer—as happened to both the *Genji* and the *Ise* texts during early modernity. Also during this period, woodblock printing replaced calligraphic manuscripts, only to be superseded, in turn, by typeset editions in the modern period. The texts were later translated (becoming new replacements of previous replacements) into a host of other languages (including modern Japanese) and were turned into films, into manga, and into video games. In replacement, as in canonization and popularization, the title of the work and the name of the author are of paramount importance, and in extreme cases, they are the only features of the original text that are present (or hinted at) in the replacement.

Diffusion refers to the inverse process—that is, the severing of the ties to the source text and the creation of a new frame of reference as a way to signify new or unexplored affordances. Consider a poem by an old man, a local official in Ōsumi Province who was accused of a crime and is about to receive physical punishment for it.

oihatete	Grown fully old
yuki no yama woba	the snow covering
itadakedo	topping the mountain, and yet
shimoto miru ni zo	when I look at whipped frost
mi wa hienikeru	I am left chilled.[30]

老いはてゝ雪の山をばいたゞけどしもと見るにぞ身は冷えにける

In the imperially commissioned classical anthology *Shūi wakashū* (*Shūishū* 拾遺集 [Collection of gleanings], 1006), the poem appears with a brief narrative frame recording that, thanks to the poem, the man was pardoned.[31] This vignette subsequently would appear in late classical poetry treatises, such as *Toshiyori zuinō* 俊頼髄脳 (Toshiyori's essentials of poetry, 1111–14) and *Ōgishō* 奥義抄 (Digest on deep principles, ca. 1124–44). And it would be borrowed from the former work and included in early medieval collections of brief narratives, such as *Uji shūi monogatari* 宇治拾遺物語 (A collection of tales from Uji, early thirteenth century) and *Jikkinshō* 十訓抄 (Ten-lesson digest, 1252).[32] These early medieval compilations do not make any reference to the source text, *Shūishū*, in spite of its cultural authority, nor to the officially sanctioned status of the genre to which it belongs, the imperial anthology. The editors of these collections treat sources such as *Shūishū* as mere repositories and feel free to place the poetic vignette within a new conceptual frame—for example, collating it with other stories in which poems bring about similar advantages. The vignette afforded this reading from the very beginning, but in classical anthologies this possibility was not emphasized; it came to the fore only later.

Writing as Design

The dominant affordance of Levine's theory—and of the New Formalist enthusiasm it has sparked—is also its main constraint. In Levine's view, "No form, however seemingly powerful, causes, dominates, or organizes all others. This means that literary forms can lay claim to an efficacy of their own. They do not simply reflect or contain prior political realities."[33] Because forms bring their affordances with them as they move across time and space, and as collisions and competition with other forms determine which affordances come to the fore in any given historical moment, literary forms cannot be reduced to expressions of relationships of power, such as domination or resistance. In other words, no form can single-handedly organize others, and no historical agent or structure can commandeer the free play of forms and their affordances. But this is not how affordances had been understood before Levine. Her theory rested, in fact, on a theoretical intervention that reafforded this notion.

Levine's intervention, which amounts to the theoretical foundation stone of New Formalism, is discussed explicitly only in passing and is relegated to a note in her seminal work, *Forms: Whole, Rhythm, Hierarchy, Network*. That note acknowledges the origins of the notion of affordances in the work of cognitive psychologist James J. Gibson and designer Donald Norman, and at the same time substantially modifies it: "Most design theorists emphasize the relations between an object and its users; I am more interested in the ways that affordance allows us to think about both constraint and capability—that is, what actions or thoughts are made possible or impossible by the fact of a form."[34]

In Levine's system, affordances are properties of an object, which in the case of literary studies is form. Thus to speak of affordances is to inquire into the actions that are made possible or impossible, likely or unlikely, appealing or unappealing by a given form—regardless of who is interacting with it, when this happens, and where form and agent find themselves, since forms "are not outgrowths of social conditions; they do not belong to certain times and places."[35] Levine's redefinition can be understood as the reaffordance of Gibson's and Norman's notions of affordances to a new context, that of forms. They had emphasized the relational nature of affordances because they were thinking about artifacts and environments, not about literary objects or forms.

Norman wrote for an audience interested in creating artifacts of utility for diverse users—many of them invested in effective solutions to issues of accessibility. He defined an affordance fundamentally as a "relationship between the properties of an object and the capabilities of the agent that determine just how the object could possibly be used."[36] Gibson, who coined the term "affordance," had similarly argued for dynamic relationships. Thinking about his empirical research on how organisms interact with their visual field, Gibson wrote,

> The affordances of the environment are what it offers the animal, what it provides or furnishes, either for good or ill. The verb to afford is found in the dictionary, but the noun affordance is not. I have made it up. I mean by it something that refers to both the environment and the animal

> in a way that no existing term does. It implies the complementarity of the animal and the environment.[37]

In this formulation, the animal can be human or nonhuman. Later, Gibson would clarify, for example, that "what other persons afford, comprises the whole realm of social significance for human beings."[38] Similarly, the illustration that Gibson offered in this context applies to both environments and artifacts, because his interest is in what the agent can and cannot do with them:

> If a terrestrial surface is nearly horizontal (instead of slanted), nearly flat (instead of convex or concave), and sufficiently extended (relative to the size of the animal) and if its substance is rigid (relative to the weight of the animal), then the surface affords support. It is a surface of support, and we call it a substratum, ground, or floor. It is stand-on-able, permitting an upright posture for quadrupeds and bipeds. It is therefore walk-on-able and run-over-able. It is not sink-into-able like a surface of water or a swamp, that is, not for heavy terrestrial animals. Support for water bugs is different.
>
> Note that the four properties listed—horizontal, flat, extended, and rigid—would be physical properties of a surface if they were measured with the scales and standard units used in physics. As an affordance of support for a species of animal, however, they have to be measured relative to the animal. . . . Different layouts afford different behaviors for different animals, and different mechanical encounters.[39]

What Norman calls the object, Gibson calls the environment, and what Gibson means by the animal, Norman refers to as the agent.[40] Their thinking is analogous in their rejection of an analysis concerned exclusively with the isolated characteristics of artifacts or environments. Norman and Gibson conceptualize an affordance as the coming together of agent and object, and of animal and environment. They created the notion of affordances to focus precisely on that very interaction. By contrast, Levine defines affordances as actions or thoughts that are made possible or impossible by a form that is independent of those who interact with it. My notion of reaffordances is thus closer to Gibson's and Norman's emphasis on interactions, relationships, and interdependence. To say that the iterative process of reaffordance is driven by historical changes in readership is equivalent to saying that the affordances of a form belong to a time and place, and that for a form to transcend that context of use it must be reafforded—that is, made ready to be used by other agents in other places for other purposes. Of particular help is Norman's concept of signifiers, which refers to the ways in which a maker can direct a user to perceive the affordances of the object (what can be done with it and how).[41] It enables us to explore the various affordances of a text (or genre) beyond the limited circle of affordances explicitly signified by its title or in its preface.

How are these theoretical and methodological distinctions relevant to a study of *waka*? This project grew out of a simple moment of cognitive dissonance. I started with the assumption that I would be able to trace the transformation of a lively court habit—elegant classical poetic dialogues—into a literary art—late classical topical composition—and then into early medieval narratives that recorded the spread of this aesthetic pursuit to poets outside the aristocracy, such as provincial warrior lords. But the texts that I was reading were suggesting, one after another, a clear pedagogic dimension. What is worse, they did not present learning as the initial stage of the process of becoming a poet. Learning stands as the logic that structured the whole field of practice. I found that there are no extant treatises that were not created by a specialized instructor for a student—young or old, male or female, amateur patron or professional heir. Medieval narrative collections, by analogy, can all be traced to educational arrangements, as their authors did not write for peers—as in many other traditions—but for students. There is a vertical orientation of transmission in all these texts, which suggests that the ultimate form of medieval scholarship was pedagogic. This realization I would later extend to late medieval fictional tales, and in particular to works that can be entertaining but also informative.

As modern scholars, we are perfectly entitled to mine these texts for aesthetic systems, religious rituals, and strategies for political dominance and resistance. Yet the historical fact is that all these texts were crafted and preserved at least partially for their instructional affordances. They are artifacts of a pedagogic apparatus, part of a social dialogue between a teacher and a learner that exceeded the realm of the text but also left its marks on it.[42]

This realization is compatible with the classical formalist approach. In "The Intentional Fallacy," the article that founded the Formalist movement that New Formalism reaffords, W. K. Wimsatt and M. C. Beardsley famously argue:

> Judging a poem is like judging a pudding or a machine. One demands that it work. It is only because an artifact works that we infer the intention of an artificer. . . . Poetry succeeds because all or most of what is said or implied is relevant; what is irrelevant has been excluded, like lumps from pudding and "bugs" from machinery. In this respect poetry differs from practical messages, which are successful if and only if we correctly infer the intention. . . . But even a lyric poem is dramatic, the response of a speaker (no matter how abstractly conceived) to a situation (no matter how universalized).[43]

If all literary objects are a response of a speaker to a situation, they are not far from what Mikhail Bakhtin understood as dialogic discourse. This is the notion that discourse has a natural orientation toward the already uttered and the already known, and that it simultaneously exists in a dialogue as a living rejoinder to it.[44] What Wimsatt and Beardsley call "dramatic" and what Bahktin calls "dialogic" intersect in their interest for the embeddedness of an utterance, a text, a genre, or a form in a social circumstance. They are always *for* someone. This is not to say that we should go back to focusing on reconstructing the "intentions" of an "author"—the argument that Wimsatt and Beardsley offered against this approach still carries weight—but that we cannot analyze a text, a work, or a form independently of the tensions that structured the situations for which it was created.

The Reaffordance of Classical Learning

Until the late classical period, there was no articulated pedagogic apparatus for *waka*. Aspiring poets learned from a handful of bare-bones technical treatises and lists of poetic terms. About the social uses of poetry they could learn intuitively, as they grew up at court and in provincial aristocratic enclaves, witnessing their elders perform poems at public gatherings and recite them in private dialogues. Although *waka* had no pedagogic framework, Sinitic learning did. To create their educational arrangements, the new professional *waka* specialists borrowed from the long-established institutions that had supported the acquisition of literacy and scholarly training with Sinitic texts.

The male aristocrats who populated the imperial administration of ancient and classical Japan saw in Chinese practices a model for proper government. In the Sinitic political, historiographical, and critical corpus, they sought ideological support for the legitimacy and authority of the court. And in the Sinitic writing system, they found the appropriate language for legal and administrative exchanges.[45] Since at least the seventh century, the institution that had provided and regulated access to Sinicizing learning, known as the Daigakuryō 大学寮 (State Academy of Literacy and Letters), offered training to young aristocratic men in preparation for their entrance into the imperial bureaucratic system of office and rank. The establishment of the Daigakuryō represented the consummation of a long process of engagement with continental forms of learning.[46]

Over the centuries, the Daigakuryō was shaped by changes in the imperial administration and in aristocratic life. For the purposes of this discussion—focused on the legacy of the institution as a model for cultural learning—it is helpful to consider a schematic description of its structure.[47] Formal training began after applicants passed an entrance examination that required them to expound on one of four areas of study: classics (*myōgyōdō* 明経道), law (*myōbōdō* 明法道), numbers (*sandō* 算道), and records (*kidendō* 紀伝道). The last path was also known more informally as "writings" (*monjōdō* 文章道). The dormitories in which the students resided frequently offered supplementary instruction, which could start as early as the period of preparation for the entrance examination. Further examinations (for the *kidendō* track, for example, involving a task such as composing a poem in Chinese inspired by a given classical quotation) led to the ranks of provisional academic (*gimonjōshō* 擬文章生) and, eventually, regular academic (*monjōshō* 文章生). While ritualized lectures did take place at the Daigakuryō, the main pedagogic device was individual mentoring, in which a graduate, now serving as an instructor (called professor of writing [*monjō hakase* 文章博士] in the *kidendō* track), offered firsthand, in-person guidance to a matriculated student.

As sociopolitical circumstances changed, the practical significance of the Daigakuryō deteriorated. By the tenth century, academic meritocracy had given way to family connections in appointments to the uppermost ranks and offices of the imperial bureaucracy. From the perspective of those in the higher echelons of the aristocracy, this recasting of roles and expectations made engaging private tutors preferable to seeking entrance into a state institution. The Daigakuryō lost influence but survived the privatization of elite learning, which preserved for the most part the Daigakuryō's pedagogic approach.

After official education and certification lost their practical value for many aspiring bureaucrats and the upper aristocracy ceased to rely on the Daigakuryō for the instruction of their sons, the newly dominant practice of private instruction came to reproduce the Daigakuryō's method of ritualized lectures and personalized mentoring. A male child started his education at the age of five by receiving a brief but dignified semipublic lecture on a Chinese classic, followed by a celebratory banquet. The instructor could be a relative, or he could be a graduate of the Daigakuryō who had distinguished himself publicly and was now selected by the family to enter into a private patron-client arrangement. The initial learning of classical Chinese was mediated by studying imported primers and commentaries, such as *Qiānzì wén* 千字文 (Jp. *Senjimon* [Thousand character classic]), a poem in which each of one thousand logographs are used once in a series of rhyming stanzas that offer information on Chinese cosmology, history, and ethics. Another commonly used primer, *Méng qiú* 蒙求 (Jp. *Mōgyu* [Child's treasury]), is a collection of mnemonic verse summaries of episodes in the history of China. Commentarial editions, in which the main text is interspersed with explanatory notes, offered the instructor and the advanced student both cultural and lexical context, since this pedagogic method considered historical and cultural education to be inseparable from functional literacy. As in the Daigakuryō, the standard approach of private tutoring with Chinese texts involved the sophisticated practice of *kundoku* 訓読 (reading by gloss), by which the student learned to associate the logographs of Chinese origin with Japanese expressions, to rearrange them to conform to the expected Japanese order, and to add the missing Japanese particles and supplementary verbs.[48] He learned to compose strings of logographs in accordance with Chinese grammar that when glossed by *kundoku* produced a sentence in Japanese, as this was the writing system employed by the imperial court and bureaucracy.

The switch from state-sponsored education to private arrangements also brought changes in the production of knowledge. As Brian Steininger shows, while the instructors at the Daigakuryō assigned exclusively Chinese texts, private tutors began to create primers for their elite students.[49] In contrast to Chinese primers, which offer no information on topics specific to Japan, these domestic pedagogic artifacts cover geography, local lore, and customs, as well as the system of rank and office in the imperial bureaucracy. One of these compendia is *Kuchizusami* 口遊 (Singing to yourself, 970), compiled by a graduate of the *kidendō* track, Minamoto no Tamenori 源為憲 (d. 1011). The work was commissioned to him by Fujiwara no Tamemitsu 藤原為光 (942–92), a powerful and ambitious courtier. At the time, he had just been appointed as Imperial Adviser (*sangi* 参議), but he would eventually rise to the office of prime minister (*daijōdaijin* 太政大臣) in 991. *Kuchizusami* was written for Tamemitsu's seven-year-old son, Sanenobu 誠信 (Shigenobu, 964–1001). It organizes essential knowledge into nineteen thematic categories called gates (*mon* 門). These include solemn public topics, such as heavenly phenomena (*kenshō* 乾象) and bureaucratic offices (*kanshoku* 官職), and also more quotidian ones, such as food and beverages (*inshoku* 飲食) and birds and beasts (*kinjū* 禽獣).[50] Each of the entries, called tunes (*kyoku* 曲) because the student was expected to sing them to himself as a way to facilitate memorization, is followed by a brief explanation and often some supplementary information (under the heading "Discussion" [*kon'an* 今案]). The work was written in *kanbun* 漢文 (literally, "Han writing"; literary Sinitic) and assumed either reasonable literacy on the student's part or the presence of a tutor who could offer considerable scaffolding.

A work related in many ways to *Kuchizusami* is *Wamyō ruijūshō* 倭名類聚抄 (Categorical miscellany of Yamato names, ca. 931–38). It was created by Tamenori's teacher, Minamoto no Shitagō 源順

(911–83), a scholar of both Chinese writings and *waka*. Shitagō was, for example, one of the compilers of *Gosenshū*, the second imperial anthology of *waka*. Princess Kinshi 勤子(908–38), a daughter of Emperor Daigo, commissioned Shitagō to compile *Wamyō ruijūshō* after the death of her father. Shitagō produced an encyclopedic work organized into disparate thematic categories, from heaven and earth (*tenchi* 天地) to disease (*shippei* 疾病) to farm animals (*gyūba* 牛馬). Each individual entry offers an expression's Sinitic and vernacular pronunciations, plus a citation from a Chinese text or some explanation of its meaning, or both. In the preface, the compiler praises his patron and cites her request that he produce a work that could dispel the confusions that arise when writing.[51] The entries are not arranged by the shape of the characters, as in contemporary logographic dictionaries, but by category, affording Kinshi and her descendants both a primer and a reference work on the vernacular uses of Chinese logographs.[52] The commonalities between *Kuchizusami* and *Wamyō ruijūshō* suggest that they were created to address related pedagogic and cultural needs. They emerged from the relatively new arrangement in which a powerful and wealthy patron engaged the labor of an academically distinguished instructor. They show a keen awareness of the precedent set by similar works brought from China, yet respond to the needs created by the natural lacunae in imported texts, which contained no information on issues particular to Japan.

Texts such as *Kuchizusami* and *Wamyō ruijūshō* bear witness as well to how sociohistorical changes in pedagogic practices (the switch from public to private instruction at the elite level) could affect the wider production of knowledge, as these texts began to circulate beyond the initial context of creation (inception) and immediate readership. These two works eventually became standard primers, widely known and used by what can be theorized as a secondary layer of readership (dissemination). This secondary circulation, and the process of manuscript reproduction that it required, involved the introduction of changes (other than the common copying mistakes): often the texts were abridged into digest versions, expanded with updated information, or reframed to suit new needs. *Wamyō ruijūshō*, for example, was preserved in two significantly different versions.[53] Another way in which the switch to private pedagogy changed the patterns of knowledge circulation was that it allowed the tutor-pupil relationship to extend beyond the age at which a pupil would have graduated from the Daigakuryō. After coming of age, a private student could continue to engage his tutor as a consulting scholar.

Analogously, the primer created for a young student could continue to serve him beyond his initial course of training.[54] In Shitagō's *Wamyō ruijūshō* and Tamenori's *Kuchizusami*, we find two different sets of affordances for two different types of users. They could function not only as textbooks for a child under the tutelage of a private instructor but also as reference works for a fully literate adult. Their "reference work" affordance was enabled by their meticulous, systematic organization into categories and subcategories, and thus would have been available only to a fully trained user who was capable of navigating the index and the headings and subheadings to locate a specific desired section. By contrast, a student with emergent literacy who was working on his (and later, her) own would be limited to the sequential access for which primers were usually structured (the "primer" affordance). The *waka* treatises of late classical Japan, like these domestic Chinese-influenced primers, would be produced by specialists engaged in private tutoring arrangements with student-patrons, and similarly were designed so that they could be used by different kinds of users. If *Wamyō ruijūshō* and *Kuchizusami* reafforded the form of the Chinese primers to support learning practices specific to Japan, *waka* treatises reafforded the approach of those domestic Chinese-influenced primers to create pedagogic artifacts to support the systematic, comprehensive study of poetry.

The Organization of This Book

Given the broad time frame under discussion in this study, some form of periodization is necessary. There are compelling reasons to adopt the standard European historiographical divisions of ancient, classical, medieval, early modern, and modern. One is relatability. This scheme affords the presentation of historical events, gradual developments, and *longue durée* arcs in a way that is approachable for readers who specialize in other fields and regions. It also maps relatively easily onto the shifts in the geographic seat of power in Japan—assigning the Heian period (894–1185) to the classical era, defining the Kamakura and Muromachi periods (1191–1573) as early and late medieval, and designating the Edo period (1600–1868) as early modern.[55] But this practical consideration faces a number of problems, such as the risk that it will be read as suggesting it is possible to synchronize the history of Japan with European or global history. Other problems stem from the fact that—like all periodization schemata—it is inevitably arbitrary, teleological, retroactive, and at best only partially faithful to the complexity of historical changes and continuities.

The second reason this periodization is compelling has to do with its power to organize events into categories that are specifically coherent and meaningful to this book's aims and interests. I found a precedent in how the authors of the works I analyzed organized and conceptualized time according to their own narrative and historiographical goals. Instead of relying solely on the common practice of following imperially sanctioned eras—such as Engi (ca. 901–22) and Hōgen (ca. 1156–58)—they sought and deployed categories that had more analytical promise for the purposes of their works. The *waka* specialist Fujiwara no Shunzei 藤原俊成 (Toshinari; 1114–1204), for example, in one of the earliest attempts at what we would call a literary history (see chapter 1), organized historical developments into the distant (*jōko* 上古, our eighth century), middle (*chūko* 中古, up to the turn of the eleventh century), and contemporary (*matsudai* 末代) periods. Fellow poetry instructor Kamo no Chōmei 鴨長明 (ca. 1155–1216) further introduced a distinction between the recent past (*nakagoro* 中頃) and the present moment (*kindai* 近代).[56] Their approach would resurface as the underlying principle in the selection and chronological organization of a collection of brief narratives compiled by the court culture specialist Tachibana no Narisue 橘成季 (ca. 1205–before 1273; see chapter 2).

This book throws light on the progressive spread of poetic practice beyond the aristocratic elites and their preferred canonical genres. Its expansion across social spaces acknowledges three stages, which can be traced first to the twelfth century, in which the authority of the imperial court received its earliest serious challenge; then to the thirteenth century, when the new warrior elites began to consolidate their grip on power and their retainers and attendants came into regular contact with the culture of the court; and finally to the fifteenth and sixteenth centuries, when urban expansion and an emerging market economy resulted in the economic and cultural rise of the merchant-commoner class.

Referring to the culture of the twelfth century as late classical emphasizes the importance that it would have for the writers of subsequent centuries, who tended to regard it as a watershed and to interpret everything that had come before it as having established the foundations of their civilization.[57] Starting in the mid-thirteenth century and continuing through the eighteenth, authors and editors looked back at Heian society and culture as a model, a source of precedent, and a frame of reference for their own contemporary society—in effect, treating Heian Japan as what we understand as a "classical" period and the target of "classicizing learning."

Similarly, considering the thirteenth century to be early medieval highlights the impact of warfare and incipient social mobility on Japan's social and cultural fabric.[58] The fifteenth and sixteenth centuries are the period of transition to early modernity in the sense that they were still marked by extended military violence, but they also saw developments that would lead to the market economy that characterizes the early modern period.[59] Thus, organizing this book into three chapters—the first on late classical, the second on early medieval, and the third on late medieval or, rather, the transition to early modernity—allows us to visualize the connections among wider historical processes and the different stages in the expansion of court poetry and court culture to other social spaces.

The three chapters relate to one another in a number of different ways. In terms of fundamental primary sources, the first chapter looks at four of the earliest comprehensive poetry treatises (*kagaku-sho* 歌学書): *Toshiyori zuinō*, *Fukurozōshi* 袋草紙 (Bag book, 1159), *Korai fūteishō* 古来風躰抄 (Poetic styles from the past, 1197–1201), and Mumyōshō 無名抄 (Untitled notes, 1211). The second chapter considers three early medieval collections of brief narratives (*setsuwa-shū* 説話集): *Jikkinshō*, *Kokonchomonjū* 古今著聞集 (Collection of tales written and heard in the past and present, 1254), and *Shasekishū* 沙石集 (Collection of sand and pebbles, 1283). In the third chapter I discuss three anonymous fictional tales (*otogizōshi*) from the late medieval period: *Monokusa Tarō* 物くさ太郎 (Lazy Tarō), *Saru Genji sōshi* 猿源氏草子 (The tale of monkey Genji), and *Nakagoro no koto* 中ころの事 (Not too long ago), known today as *Menoto no sōshi* 乳母草子 (The nursemaid's book). All these works can be considered writings about *waka*—even those that do not focus exclusively or even primarily on poetic practice—as they all engage with *waka* poems, poets, and events. And they connect, each in their own way, the learning of poetry with a wider process of cultural transmission across social spaces.

The different chapters also allow for an exploration of the shifting relationships among three internally diverse social spaces. The poetry treatises were created for an intended readership of aristocrats—who ranged from young women about to enter the competitive arena of the court to young men training to become professional poetry specialists—as well as members of the emerging warrior elite, who intended to raise their children at court as aristocrats. The collections of narratives arguably were designed for non-elite warriors, mostly midlevel officials and liaisons in the new military bureaucracy, who did not enjoy direct access to the court but still had to acquire knowledge about the culture of the aristocracy. The fictional tales reveal an intended readership of sophisticated merchant commoners interested in learning about the high culture of the aristocracy and, at the same time, in celebrating new values and modes of being connected with their own urban social and cultural experiences. In each chapter, a new set of configurations emerges between different strata within these groups: the higher aristocrats of the capital and the province-bound aristocratic intellectuals, the warrior elites and their retainers and security forces, the city merchants and the rural producers, the wildly rich tycoons and the small-time merchants and peddlers of the urban centers, and so on.

A significant portion of the texts analyzed in this book were either intended for female readers or focused on the education of young women. For instance, the treatise *Toshiyori zuinō* was written specifically for Kunshi 勲子 (1095–1155), a young member of the influential Fujiwara clan who later enjoyed a distinguished court career. In contrast, *Korai fūteishō* was created for Shokushi 式子 (ca. 1153–1201), an imperial princess in her late forties who had already retired from public life. Drawing from the injunctions of an early medieval aristocrat for her young daughter, the late medieval tale *Nakagoro no koto* stages a satirical contrast between two young women, one taught to compose poems that conformed to this elite model, and another encouraged to explore the interests of the nascent culture of urban merchants. These texts consistently emphasize knowledge of poetry as a key factor for courtship and marriage eligibility, a theme that also appears in narratives like *Saru Genji sōshi* and *Monokusa Tarō*, where poetic prowess promises to transform commoner men into polished gentlemen fit to marry into elite society. Other works further illustrate how writers adapted their material and presentation to their readership: *Fukurozōshi* was prepared for a few elite men, *Kokonchomonjū* addressed a wider male audience, *Jikkinshō* targeted young men aspiring to careers in service, and *Shasekishū* spoke to monastics. In each case, I will examine how writing style, thematic focus, specialized vocabulary, and intertextual references reflect how intended readerships shaped decisions about what readers needed to learn about poetry and from poetry.

Yet another way to look at the scope of this book is through the gradual emergence of a discourse on the potencies of poetry. Some of the narrative vignettes in the poetry treatises display an interest in the use of poetry to achieve practical ends, from making rain to healing illness to advancing one's career. Anecdotal evidence for this resurfaces in the narrative collections, which served as the central element in a system that explicated *waka*'s role as a shared emotional language during a period of extreme social transformation. Poems that elicited an affective response (*kan* 感) from a figure of authority—human or divine, aristocrat or elite warrior, military or administrative bureaucrat—showed that those in power not only spoke one's own language but also actually *cared*. This discourse on the power of *waka* to integrate a society resurfaces in inverted form in the fictional tales. These narratives for commoners parody the idea that educating nonaristocrats in the ways and preferences of the imperial court could bring social cohesion. They also satirize the commoners who pinned on this cultural education their own hopes of upward social mobility. Inspired by the way parodic *kyōka* poems could bring together the standard *waka* form with absurd and humorous variations, I approach these satiric and parodic versions through the notion of the *kyōka*-esque. This term refers to a structural imbrication of *waka* with its related practices—*kyōka*, *renga* 連歌 (linked verse), *haikai* 俳諧 (popular linked verse), and so on—that emerged in the transition to early modernity and remained operative throughout the rest of the period. Not even the intellectual debates of the so-called National Learning (*Kokugaku*) scholars challenged the structure of a field in which one form of practice was defined by its juxtaposition to the others.

Court Poetry and the Culture of Learning in Japan concludes by revisiting the place of *waka* practice in the culture and society of Japan from two new vantage points. One is the transformation of the field of cultural production in the late nineteenth century away from the *kyōka*-esque array of related poetic practices. This arrangement had been particularly enduring, but it eventually gave way in the 1890s to sudden pressures to reconfigure *waka* as an exclusively literary artifact. Out of this reconfiguration emerged what is known as *tanka* (modern *waka*), which took its limited social and cultural meaning from its place within the general edifice of literature and, more generally, the arts or the aesthetic realm. The now-common view that *waka* from the late classical *Goshūishū* onward were exclusively literary artifacts has its roots in this period of modernization.

The other position from which to take stock of the place of poetry issues from the practice that eventually would replace *waka* as a societywide cultural organizer. This is the tea ceremony (*chanoyu* 茶湯, or *sadō* 茶道) of Japan. The early tea masters of the late medieval period modeled their pedagogic activity after that of poetry specialists, shaped their aesthetic systems by borrowing poetic notions, and adapted the *waka* form to teach their elite patron-students. Throughout the early modern period the tea ceremony remained relevant to the elites in Edo (Tokyo) and the provincial castle towns, and it progressively expanded to groups in other social spaces, particularly to urban commoners. When *waka* shed its cultural cachet and social relevance to become modern *tanka* in the nineteenth century, the tea ceremony moved to the center as the prime vehicle for the transmission of cultural knowledge and as a venue for the ideologies of nationalism, empire, and colonialism. As part of this process, thinkers such as Yanagi Sōetsu 柳宗悦 (1889–1961) and Hisamatsu Shin'ichi 久松慎一 (1889–1980) discussed tea culture as a "synthetic culture system" (*sōgo teki bunka taikei* 総合的文化体系), representative of the totality of the culture of the Japanese Empire—both the metropole and the colonies in East Asia—and as a gateway for learning about all other cultural practices, from ceramics and architecture to poetry and cuisine, as well as religion, ethics, philosophy, and more. The modern notion of a "synthetic culture system" has its roots in the centrality of *waka* in premodern Japanese society, and in the emphasis on learning over performance that had shaped the practice of poetry since the late classical period.

CHAPTER ONE

The Knowledge of *Waka*

The poetry treatise (*zuinō* 髄脳) is the most significant genre for understanding medieval poetic practice.[1] The many personal anthologies produced by famous poets and the twenty-one imperially commissioned compilations were crucial in producing a canon of poems, but they contain practically no critical discourse. New poems were often made public in the context of poetry contests (*utaawase*), and many transcriptions of the judges' decisions were preserved. These brief comments offer insight into contemporary critical discourse, but they are by their very nature fragmentary and unsystematic. The aesthetic systems, standards of quality, and linguistic boundaries that a poet could grasp only after decades of perusing anthologies and records of contests were, however, described in explicit detail in the treatises produced by the most influential poets of each generation.[2]

Poetry treatises are, as well, a unique source of information on the relationships among poets, patrons, and students. While poetry anthologies and *utaawase* records were often created for open circulation, treatises were written with a specific individual in mind and as part of pedagogic relationships. This is of great significance in the context of a poetic practice in which study and training were gradually displacing public gatherings and private poetry exchanges as the main focus of activity. Moreover, many passages intended to provide information on the practice of *waka* for elite students were later repurposed in works in other genres for non-elite readers who were interested in learning about the life and values of the court. (This process, referred to in the introduction as *diffusion*, is discussed in detail in chapter 2.) Consequently, for centuries a lot of what the people knew about the court came from poetic treatises, particularly those written in the twelfth century.

The Professionalization of *Waka*

Until the twelfth century, there had been no stable professional household of *waka* specialists and no articulated, systematic pedagogy for *waka*. Aside from reading the canonical anthologies, young men and women had been expected to pick up the practice of *waka* mostly as part of the wider processes of their enculturation and socialization into aristocratic society. Each of the treatises discussed in this chapter represents a critical stage in the emergence of a new pedagogic model for *waka*. *Toshiyori zuinō* 俊頼髄脳 (Toshiyori's essentials of poetry, 1111–14), by Minamoto no Toshiyori 源俊頼 (1055–1129), belongs to an era of flux in which *waka* specialists were not yet fully organized into stable households. *Fukurozōshi* 袋草紙 (Bag book, 1159) was created less than half a century later by Fujiwara no Kiyosuke 藤原清輔 (1104–77), the third-generation head of the first poetry household, the Rokujō. *Korai fūteishō* 古来風躰抄 (Poetic styles from the past, 1197–1201) was written by Fujiwara no Shunzei 藤原俊成 (Toshinari; 1114–1204), the founder of the Mikohidari, the poetry household that would dominate the field of elite *waka* for centuries. Finally, *Mumyōshō* 無名抄 (Untitled notes, 1211) was written by Kamo no Chōmei (ca. 1155–1216), a court poet well connected but not affiliated with either the Rokujō or the Mikohidari.

The changes in the practice of *waka* that came to the fore during the twelfth century have been explained elsewhere in connection with two historical processes: the shift from social poetry to topical composition and the ascendance of specialist lineages (along with the concomitant development of rivalries among them).[3] As the treatises illustrate, although *waka* lost its centrality as a form of sophisticated dialogue in everyday aristocratic society, it began to play a new but still-practical role as the core of a process of transmission mediated by professional poets. They reveal the emergence of an explicit, systematic, and professionalized instructional apparatus for *waka* that also had ramifications for other spheres of knowledge.

Throughout the twelfth century, the world of *waka* developed into a field whose structure was both vertical (with relatively stable lineages) and horizontal (marked by bitter rivalries).[4] The authors of the treatises analyzed in this chapter were at the heart of this structural transformation. Minamoto no Toshiyori, for example, was the son of an accomplished poet, Tsunenobu 経信 (1016–97).[5] Toshiyori took after his father in competing fiercely against rival specialists, notably Fujiwara no Mototoshi 藤原基俊 (ca. 1056–1142). An imperial commission—the ultimate official accolade and one that rarely came more than once in a poet's lifetime—had escaped Tsunenobu. The honor had gone to a younger rival, Fujiwara no Michitoshi 藤原通俊 (1047–99), whom Retired Emperor Shirakawa 白河 (1053–1129, r. 1073–86) commissioned to compile the fourth imperial anthology, *Goshūi wakashū* (*Goshūishū* 後拾遺集 [Later collection of gleanings], 1086). Tsunenobu reacted by writing the critical *Nan goshūi* 難後拾遺 (Criticism of the *Goshūishū*, 1086), which censures eighty-four of the poems included by Michitoshi in the anthology.

Tsunenobu came from a powerful family: both his father, Michikata 道方 (968–1044), and grandfather Shigenobu 重信 (922–95) had reached the upper crust of the aristocratic hierarchy. But his son Toshiyori went no further than junior fourth rank, upper grade, and, after resigning from his post as head of palace carpenters (*moku no kami* 木工頭) in 1111, fell into the rocky category of "courtiers with rank but without office" (*san'i* 散位).[6] Toshiyori had been an active and influential member of the literary salon of Emperor Horikawa 堀河 (1079–1107, r. 1087–1107), which dissolved with the ruler's death. As Komine Kazuaki discusses, it is likely that until the establishment of a new literary salon hosted by the powerful Fujiwara no Tadamichi 藤原忠通 (1097–1164), Toshiyori experienced anxiety about the fate of *waka* specialists.[7] This sense of uncertainty, however, did not last; ten years after composing *Toshiyori zuinō*, Toshiyori prevailed over his rival Mototoshi and received from Shirakawa the commission to compile the fifth imperial anthology, *Kin'yō wakashū* (*Kin'yōshū* 金葉集 [Collection of golden leaves], 1127).[8]

Although Toshiyori achieved courtly success, he did not produce an heir through whom his family could take shape as a stable household of hereditary *waka* specialists. Two of Toshiyori's sons were accomplished poets and potential heirs who might have consolidated the Minamoto as a lineage of poets. *Toshiyori zuinō* features poems by one of them, Toshishige 俊重 (n.d.), who was active in poetry circles, but did not manage to build a reputation comparable to his father's. The other son, the much younger Shun'e 俊恵 (1113–ca. 1194), was only sixteen when Toshiyori died, in 1129. After losing his father he left the court, taking the tonsure and entering Tōdaiji Temple 東大寺 in Nara. Two decades later he returned to the capital, becoming a member of courtly poetry circles and transmitting his knowledge about the practice of *waka* to the next generation of poets, foremost among them Kamo no Chōmei. Yet in the interim, two other households had moved to positions of dominance, and neither Shun'e nor his disciple, Chōmei, was able to position himself as acting head of an established household.[9]

Those two households, the Rokujō and the Mikohidari, came to dominate the world of *waka* during the second half of the twelfth century. Practitioners of *waka* included female poets and some members of elite warrior families, but those who were considered *waka* experts were without exception the male scions of aristocratic houses.[10] The founder of the Rokujō lineage was Fujiwara no Akisue 藤原顕季 (1055–1123). His son Akisuke 顕輔 (1090–1155) inherited the role of household head and passed it down to his son Kiyosuke, the author of *Fukurozōshi*. Akisuke brought the house prestige and authority when he was commissioned by Emperor Sutoku 崇徳 (1119–64, r. 1123–42) to compile the sixth imperial anthology, *Shika wakashū* (*Shikashū* 詞花集 [Collection of verbal flowers], 1151). The rival Mikohidari lineage was founded by Fujiwara no Shunzei and led later by his son Teika 定家 (1162–1241). Rival poets and households came head to head in poetry gatherings and in contests hosted by powerful personages, where contenders competed by composing poems on a series of predetermined topics. In 1193, for example, the prominent courtier Fujiwara no Yoshitsune 藤原良経 (1169–1206) hosted a contest for twelve of the foremost poets of the time. Known as the *Roppyakuban utaawase* 六百番歌合 (Poetry contest in six hundred rounds), its participants included Mikohidari-house affiliates such as Teika and Fujiwara no Ietaka 藤原家隆 (1158–1237), as well as leading Rokujō-school poets such as Kenjō 顕昭 (ca. 1130–ca. 1210). Shunzei acted as the judge for the contest.[11]

Professional *waka* specialists enjoyed the support of a group of powerful aristocratic patrons. The pool of potential patron-students then expanded during the second half of the twelfth century with the rise of warrior households at court.[12] In 1156, a dispute about succession between rival branches of the imperial house led both sides to engage the help of clans of warriors. Four years later, the warriors clashed again. The winning side was led by Taira no Kiyomori 清盛 (1118–81), who sought to occupy the position previously held by aristocratic regents by marrying his daughter Tokuko 徳子 to Emperor Takakura 高倉 (1161–81, r. 1168–80) in order to become grandfather to the next crown prince, Tokihito 言仁 (later known as Antoku 安徳, 1178–85). As part of this project of upward social mobility, his family members sought training in court culture. Kiyomori engaged Shunzei as *waka* tutor for his younger brother Tadanori 忠度 (1144–84). The Genpei War (1180–85) led to the downfall of the Taira and the creation of a warrior government in Kamakura led by the Minamoto and Hōjō households. They as well, aspiring to acquire the cultural prestige of the aristocracy, sought training in poetry.[13] Minamoto no Sanetomo 源実朝 (1192–1219, r. 1203–19), the son of Genpei War victor Minamoto no Yoritomo 源頼朝 (1147–99, r. 1192–99) and Hōjō Masako 北条政子 (1157–1225), became the third shogun of the Kamakura period in 1203. After Shunzei passed away the following year and Teika became household head, Sanetomo engaged him in a formal and explicit pedagogic relationship. In this way, the Mikohidari household was able to outlive the cataclysmic political changes by securing the patronage of the period's ruling families.

Discord among the descendants of the third household head, Fujiwara no Tameie 藤原為家 (1198–1275), led to the split of the Mikohidari house, with its legacy of prestige and its pool of patron-students, into three separate households: the Nijō 二条 of Tameuji 為氏 (1222–86) and his son Tameyo 為世 (1251–1338); the Kyōgoku 京極 of

Tamenori 為教 (1227–79) and his son Tamekane 為兼 (1254–1332); and the Reizei 冷泉 of Tamesuke 為相 (1263–1328) and more than two dozen generations of descendants reaching to the modern day. All three households explicitly traced their lineage back to the three Mikohidari patriarchs.

The ultimate victory of the Mikohidari over the Rokujō and the division of the Mikohidari into rival households in the thirteenth century have been extensively examined by Robert Huey in the context of the "medievalization" of the practice of poetry.[14] According to Huey, the two most salient features of medieval *waka* practice were exclusivity and factionalism. By exclusivity, Huey refers to the steady supersession of semipublic, inclusive poetry contests by contests exclusive to one household of specialists. As he shows, by the turn of the fourteenth century all contests were exclusive to either Nijō-schooled or Kyōgoku-schooled poets. With regard to factionalism, Huey contrasts open clashes, such as Tsunenobu's scathing attack on Michitoshi's *Goshūishū*, with an earlier presumed consensus that was lost as *waka* moved "from social expression, about which people in a hierarchical environment are likely to agree, to art, about which people in a more factionalized medieval setting are apt to disagree."[15]

In identifying the shift toward exclusivity and factionalism as products of *waka*'s maturation as an art form, Huey's argument accords with the interpretations of Hashimoto Fumio and Kuboki Tetsuo.[16] It also comports with an earlier conceptualization by Robert Brower and Earl Miner, who describe the rivalry between the Rokujō and the Mikohidari as a clash between, respectively, parochial conservatism and artistic freedom.[17] This approach lends itself to the assumption that poetry treatises were venues for purely intellectual and artistic exploration—that is, they are artifacts of discourse rather than practice. Working under a similar assumption, in her history of poetry treatises Hilda Katō describes *Toshiyori zuinō* as a work in which the author was "mainly concerned with the technical aspects that interested him as a poet."[18] A more recent, prolonged consideration of *Toshiyori zuinō* by Saeko Shibayama argues, in the same vein, that it reflects an "open-mindedness" and a "non-utilitarian, near-romantic" approach to poetry.[19] Understanding the changes in the practice of *waka* during the twelfth century requires acknowledging that poetry treatises were not the detached musings of free spirits, but were fine-tuned tools created for pedagogic purposes.

One good indication that treatises were artifacts of a pedagogic practice is that they were often tailored for specific individual readers. These readers would be either powerful patrons and their families, or professional heirs to one of the poetic houses, who would have to compete against other *waka* specialists for patronage. This is true for all of the treatises, regardless of their approach, structure, or content. Toshiyori's *Toshiyori zuinō* was commissioned by a powerful aristocrat for his daughter, who was about to enter the court. Kiyosuke's *Ōgishō* 奥義抄 (Digest on deep principles, ca. 1124–44) was written for Emperor Sutoku and later presented to Emperor Nijō 二条 (1143–65, r. 1158–65). Shunzei's *Korai fūteishō* was composed for a princess who had retired from court and taken Buddhist vows. Teika's *Kindai shūka* 近代秀歌 (Supreme poems of our time, 1209) was intended for an elite male reader from a powerful warrior house, and his *Eiga no taigai* 詠歌大概 (Essentials of poetic composition, 1213–19) for an imperial prince.

In contrast to most of the treatises that have reached us, Kiyosuke's *Fukurozōshi* was created for a colleague and successor, the future head of his professional household. Treatises produced for in-house use were closely guarded, and most are no longer extant. We do not have, for example, any treatise written by a head of the Mikohidari for his heir, although it is highly likely that these texts existed and were kept within the household. We can be grateful that Kiyosuke's patrons pressured him to provide copies of the treatise, and that—through channels unknown to us—some eventually circulated more widely and thus survived, since this treatise offers a rare glimpse into how pedagogy changed when the recipient was a fellow professional.

From the treatises analyzed in this chapter, we can learn how poetic skill was displayed and understood, as well as how it was acquired, transmitted, and preserved. More crucially, these works enable us to retrace the trajectory that *waka* described as its foremost practitioners became professionals and as the field of *waka* as a whole evolved into a hub of cultural knowledge and social memory.

A Comprehensive Curriculum

Throughout the twelfth century, professional poets experimented with the form, structure, and content of the poetry treatise. The first attempt at redefining the scope and approach of the treatise was *Toshiyori zuinō*.[20] Minamoto no Toshiyori's project was highly ambitious, and its guiding principle seems to have been comprehensiveness. For this reason, *Toshiyori zuinō* packs more knowledge and detail than all other extant previous treatises combined. The little we know about the early instructional practices for *waka*, before the emergence of professional households in the twelfth century, stems from a few surviving texts. The earliest of these *waka* treatises focused exclusively on issues of style, setting down "rules" (*shiki* 式) for poetic composition modeled on Chinese Six Dynasties (220–589) critical thought, making repeated references to Chinese canonical prose, and discussing poems that were considered anomalous—including those that exhibited "poetic diseases" (*kahei* 歌病), "poetic irregularities" (*satei* 査体), or "miscellaneous styles" (*zattei* 雑体). These categories were illustrated with example poems, and brief commentaries were provided to elucidate obscure expressions. Such is the case, for example, with the earliest extant treatise, *Kashiki* 歌式 (Code of poetry, 772), composed and presented to Emperor Kōnin 光仁 (709–81, r. 770–81) by Fujiwara no Hamanari 藤原浜成 (724–90).[21]

In the following centuries, poetry treatises became more numerous and began to offer systems of classification and to postulate specific aesthetic ideals for *waka*, together with the consideration of "poetic diseases," a concept that had by then become familiar. Two examples of early treatises that include a system of classification are *Waka teijisshu* 和歌体十種 (Ten styles of *waka*, early eleventh century), attributed to Mibu no Tadamine 壬生忠岑 (n.d.), and *Waka kuhon* 和歌九品 (Nine levels of *waka*, ca. 1008), by Fujiwara no Kintō 藤原公任 (966–1041). Kintō also authored a treatise that offers specific aesthetic ideals, *Shinsen zuinō* 新撰髄脳 (New selection on the essence of poetry, n.d.).[22] Inventories of poetic terms, particularly of "poetic places" (*utamakura* 歌枕), were another source of information for poets. The priest Nōin 能因 (Tachibana no Nagayasu 橘永愷; b. 988) compiled in *Nōin utamakura* 能因歌枕 (Nōin's poetic places, mid-eleventh century) lists of poetic places and of alternative names (*imyō* 異名) for individual poetic terms. The dictionary of poetic terms *Kigoshō* 綺語抄 (Digest of ornate expressions, 1107–16), by Fujiwara no Nakazane 藤原仲実 (1057–1118), provides brief elucidations of terms and exemplary poems taken from major anthologies such as *Man'yōshū* 万葉集 (Collection of myriad leaves, after 759) and *Kokin wakashū*. Increasingly complex commentaries on style and diction can also be found in the records of semipublic poetry contests (*utaawase*), which describe the grounds for many of the judges' decisions. The oldest poetry contest on record was the *Zai minbukyō ie utaawase* 在民部卿家歌合 (Poetry contest at the house of the Minister of People's Affairs [Ariwara no Yukihira], 884–87). The first to include critical comments were *Teiji-in utaawase* 亭子院歌合 ([Retired Emperor Uda's] Poetry contest at the Teiji Palace, 913) and *Tentoku dairi utaawase* 天徳内裏歌合 ([Emperor Murakami's] Poetry contest of the Tentoku period at the Imperial Palace, 960).

When considered in light of these precedents, *Toshiyori zuinō* was a watershed in the history of *waka* instruction. A lengthy treatise, it was the first text that attempted to provide a thorough course of study in one volume. In many ways, it drew from precedent. Like previous treatises (such as *Kashiki* and *Shinsen zuinō*), *Toshiyori zuinō* discusses "poetic diseases." It also quotes the *Kokinshū*'s kana preface, written by Ki no Tsurayuki 紀貫之 (ca. 866–ca. 945), as the classic source of *waka* criticism. It gives specific advice on composition, records the judgments of *utaawase*, and includes lists and discussions of place-names and their poetic significance as well as poetic terms used as synonyms. Yet it also transformed knowledge about *waka* into a means of cultural preservation and placed it at the center of a wider process of education that provided information, for example, on the history and customs of the court and the provinces. Together with instruction for *waka* composition, *Toshiyori zuinō* transmits the culture of *waka* and of the court.

Toshiyori's text opens with a presentation of *waka* as a practice that began in the age of the gods, as famously stated in the preface to *Kokinshū*. Toshiyori then breaks with precedent, arguing that prior treatises had tended to focus mostly on poetic diseases, and thus were of little use to a person intent on actually learning about *waka*. He next launches into a structured discussion of subgenres—from the by then standard 5-7-5-7-7 form to the 5-7-7-5-7-7 form (*sedōka* 旋頭歌, common in *Man'yōshū* poems) to the acrostic-poem form (*oriku* 折句). With regard to humorous poems (*haikaika* 誹諧歌), Toshiyori remarks that they have not been studied properly. He then reviews the notion of poetic diseases, again arguing that simply avoiding such mistakes will not guarantee a successful poem.

In the sections that follow, Toshiyori painstakingly imparts the kinds of knowledge that he deems to be required for success as a poet. There are sections on the different types of people who compose *waka* (from gods and emperors to children and lowly beggars); the utility of poems (for example, in appeasing gods or inciting them to action); the composition of poems based on set topics; examples of excellent poems; standard poetic techniques, such as the use of visual metaphors (*nisemono* 似物, or what we would now call *mitate* 見立て) and of traditional place-names, or poetic places; and a list of synonyms, or alternative names, for more than one hundred poetic terms.[23] After this list of alternative names, the themes and treatment change considerably, which has led modern scholars to divide the work into two parts.[24]

The second part of *Toshiyori zuinō* begins with an extensive and detailed examination of the origins and proper use of many poetic terms. Toshiyori traces their etymology and, in the process, refers to a diverse range of texts and relates numerous anecdotes. Taking a similar approach, the next section analyzes twenty-odd poems of obscure meaning or intention. Then Toshiyori turns to very brief elucidations of poems composed as part of the practice of verse-capping (*renga* 連歌), in which a poet offers part of a poem for another poet to complete.[25] After a brief section on expressions that could lead to confusion (such as the words *tsuma* and *seko*, which could refer to either a man or a woman), Toshiyori devotes another lengthy section to tracing poems to their narrative subtexts, which range from Chinese stories to episodes in the lives of the poets. The treatise closes with a discussion on miscellaneous topics of interest to practitioners of poetry, among them the importance of being able to compose poems on the spot, as well as anecdotes about poets who showed a particular devotion to *waka*. In summary, while *Toshiyori zuinō* is not meticulously divided into chapters, it does reflect an interest in thematic organization and in the goal of providing a comprehensive education in the practice of *waka*.

Although the text does not mention explicitly for whom it was written, Toshiyori's pedagogic choices, as well as colophons to the manuscripts and external evidence, suggest that *Toshiyori zuinō* was created for a specific individual, Kunshi (later known as Taishi), the daughter of the powerful regent Fujiwara no Tadazane 藤原忠実 (1078–1162).[26] Kunshi had a remarkably successful career at court. She initially entered the palace of Emperor Toba 鳥羽 (1103–56, r. 1107–23) as a lady-in-waiting. In 1123, Toba abdicated in favor of Sutoku, becoming retired emperor, and in 1134 he made Kunshi his official consort. She received from him the appellation Kaya-no-in 高陽院 in 1139 and took Buddhist vows in 1141. Around the time Toshiyori composed his treatise, Kunshi was in her late teens and was training to enter the court.[27] At court, ladies-in-waiting were constantly challenged to prove their knowledge, and Toshiyori seems to have created *Toshiyori zuinō* with a mind to covering all the bases for his student.

Because treatises contained valuable information, they were often copied and shared by a broad circle of readers. *Toshiyori zuinō* circulated widely at court, very quickly and through channels unknown to us. Kiyosuke quotes from Toshiyori's treatise repeatedly in *Fukurozōshi*, as do Shunzei in *Korai fūteishō* and Kenjō in *Shūchūshō* 袖中抄 (Pocket notes, 1185–89). In all likelihood, other *waka* specialists of Kiyosuke and Shunzei's generation also obtained copies of it. By the middle of the thirteenth century, Toshiyori's work had achieved the status of a classic.[28] As is common in a manuscript culture, *Toshiyori zuinō* survived in a variety of manuscript versions that can be organized into separate lines of transmission. An added source of variation stems from the fact that even when two extant manuscripts are textually identical, they may have arisen from different reading practices. For example, in his analysis of the manuscript history of *Toshiyori zuinō*, Umeda Kei identifies two different strategies of reproduction. While some manuscripts were copied under the assumption that they would be read sequentially from beginning to end, others show a systematic use of indentation to separate paragraphs in what seems to have been an attempt at producing a copy that would be useful as a casual work of reference.[29]

For these reasons, it is important to distinguish among a work's initially intended readership (referred to in the introduction as its "inception," or primary circulation) and the audiences to which it was later circulated (its "dissemination," or secondary circulation) as well as those it would indirectly reach (through "diffusion," or tertiary circulation).[30] *Toshiyori zuinō* was created with a very specific reader in mind, a young woman who was entering the court in the hope of becoming an official consort to the emperor and ultimately even mother of the crown prince. The usefulness of the treatise—its affordances—was apparent to other readers in her world, and she, her father, or Toshiyori himself provided copies to those in other circles. Key to this process of dissemination—and a main difference from the later process of diffusion—is that the manuscript would have been copied with an eye to preserving its integrity, its connection with the moment of inception (often connected to its authorship and expressed in colophons stating, for example, "This is the treatise Toshiyori made for Tadazane's daughter Kunshi"), and in some cases even a stable title, although that was not the case with *Toshiyori zuinō*, which lacked one and was often referred to as *Toshiyori mumyōshō* 俊頼無名抄 (Toshiyori's untitled notes).

Toshiyori zuinō benefited from diffusion as well, as other authors borrowed whole passages, removing them from the coherence of the source text and providing them with new frames of coherence, without any mention of Toshiyori or his treatise. This tertiary circulation of material from *Toshiyori zuinō* to wider audiences targeted, in particular, the brief narrative passages that offer rare glimpses of the culture of the aristocracy and the court.

Waka *and Narrative*

A groundbreaking and distinctive feature of *Toshiyori zuinō* is its use of concise narrative passages to relate anecdotes that lie behind specific poems and poetic expressions. Take, for example, Toshiyori's discussion of a poem from the earliest anthology of *waka*, *Man'yōshū*:

iwashiro no	At Iwashiro
hamamatsu ga e wo	I tie the branches
hikimusubi	of the pine;
masashiku araba	if things go well
mata kaerikomu	I will be able to return.

いはしろの浜松が枝をひきむすびまさしくあらばまたかへりこむ

When the sovereign known as Emperor Kōtoku was about to abdicate, his appropriate heir should have been Prince Arima. But the sovereign saw that Prince Arima did not look like he would keep the throne safe, so he decided not to turn it over to him. Prince Arima protested and set off to wander in the wilderness. At a place called Iwashiro, he tied the branches of a pine tree and composed this poem.[31]

これは孝徳天皇と申しけるみかど位をさり給はむとしける時有間の皇子に位をゆづり給ふべきをえたもつまじきけしきをご覧じてゆづり給はざりければうらみ申して山野にゆきまどひ給ひて岩代といへる所にいたりて松のえだを結びて詠み給へる歌なり。

The anecdote related by Toshiyori throws light on the meaning of the poem. In Toshiyori's account, Prince Arima 有間 (640–58) composed it when he went into self-imposed exile in the Iwashiro 岩代 region (in present-day Wakayama Prefecture) after having been denied the throne by his father, Emperor Kōtoku 孝徳 (596–654, r. 645–54). When the poet speaks of returning, he means going home to the imperial capital and the center of power, which he has abandoned. Toshiyori then quotes other poems from *Man'yōshū* that combine the words *musubu* (to tie), *matsu* (pine), and Iwashiro, and sums up his argument:

People nowadays ignore that there is an actual place called Iwashiro. They take the expression *iwashiro* to refer to the burial mound of a deceased person. And the expression *musubi matsu* [tied pine tree] as referring to a tree planted there as a marker. They say that for this reason, [these expressions] should not be used in poems composed for congratulatory occasions.[32]

このごろの人は岩代といふ所のあるとは知らでうせたる人の塚なりむすび松といへるはしるしに植ゑたる木なりされば祝ひの所にては詠むまじきよしをいへる。

Toshiyori argues that the poetic expression *musubi matsu* actually originated with the anecdote about Prince Arima. In light of that story, tying the branches of a pine tree signaled a desire to return safely to the capital. By searching for the original context of Prince Arima's poem, Toshiyori connects a technical issue of composition—whether and how a particular expression is to be used in *waka*—to an episode in the history of the court. Toshiyori's account of Prince Arima's exile, however, is not taken from *Man'yōshū*. The headnote in that collection does not mention key details, such as the name of the place of exile, Iwashiro.[33]

It is not clear what sources Toshiyori used for the story of Prince Arima, son of Emperor Kōtoku. One possibility is *Nihon shoki* 日本書紀 (Chronicles of Japan, 720), but there the story includes a passage in which Arima, after his father's death, revolts against his aunt, Empress Saimei 斉明 (r. 655–661), who had reigned before as Kōgyoku 皇極 from 642 to 645), and is then executed.[34] As Toshiyori does not mention this final piece of information, it is possible that he consulted a later, derivative text, such as a commentary on *Nihon shoki*.[35] At the same time, it is also possible that in relating this anecdote, Toshiyori eliminated the elements that would not have been acceptable to a late Heian audience, since by the end of the Heian period aristocrats were seldom sentenced to death.[36]

In the second passage, Toshiyori is connecting a poetic expression to a poem in an old anthology and revealing the subtext of the poem. In other narratives, he connects poems to provincial customs, ancient rites, and folk etymologies. For example, concerning a poetic exchange from the third imperial anthology, *Shūi wakashū* (*Shūishū* 拾遺集 [Collection of gleanings], 1006; poems 535–36), that talks about confusing a horse with a deer, Toshiyori tells the story of Zhào Gāo 趙高 (d. 207 BCE), a minister during the Qin 秦 dynasty (221–206 BCE) who plotted against the second Qin emperor, Húhài 胡亥 (n.d.). To test the emperor's support at court, Zhào Gāo brought an animal with him, insisting that it was a horse. Although the emperor countered, rightfully, that it was a deer, many of those present agreed with Zhào Gāo to call it a horse, and soon the emperor was deposed.[37]

Similarly, Toshiyori takes up poems that include the expressions *tsuyu no inochi* (dewlike transient life), *kusa no ne* (plant roots), and *tsuki no nezumi* (mouse of the month, or moon), explicating them with reference to a passage from a sutra. In the excerpt that he quotes, the fleeting quality of life is presented as an impending menace through the metaphor of a person chased by a tiger (representing sin) who hides in a hole, only to find a crocodile (representing hell), and then quickly grabs the roots of a plant to stop his fall just as a mouse (representing the passage of time) comes to gnaw at the plant, loosening his grasp.[38] *Toshiyori zuinō* includes many similar passages that reveal subtexts from classical sources of history and religion, as well as subtexts connected to local customs and ancient rites.[39] Toshiyori's decision to incorporate this material into his pedagogic treatise suggests that an awareness of such subtexts had become necessary to understand *waka*. This had the effect, conversely, of transforming the study of *waka* into an opportunity to acquire historical, cultural, religious, and linguistic knowledge.

Toshiyori zuinō does more than simply provide such an education. The treatise also recounts many recent events that the author either witnessed firsthand or heard about from his father, Tsunenobu, or other elders. These anecdotes depict how *waka* were performed at court, discussed, criticized, and otherwise circulated. For example, the discussion of the expression *iwashiro* quoted earlier is followed by an account of how Fujiwara no Sukenaka 藤原資仲 (1021–87) more recently had composed a poem for a poetry contest. The poem used the term *iwashiro* and was pitted against a poem by Priest Nōin that contained a reference to Kasuga 春日 Shrine:

> There are these poems from the poetry contest of the ninth day of the eleventh month of Eishō 4 [1049], during the reign of Emperor GoReizei [後冷泉, 1025–68, r. 1045–68].
>
> 後冷泉院の御時永承四年十一月九日の歌合に詠める歌.

POEM OF THE LEFT, BY PRIEST NŌIN:
左　能因法師

kasuga yama	On Kasuga Mountain,
iwane no matsu wa	by the foot of a big boulder,
kimi ga tame	the pine tree looks after my lord
chitose nomi kawa	not just one thousand years,
yorozu yo ya hemu	but myriad generations to come.

春日山いはねの松は君がためちとせのみかはよろづ世やへむ

POEM OF THE RIGHT, BY CONTROLLER SUKENAKA:[40]
右　資仲の弁

iwashiro no	On the mountaintop
onoe no kaze ni	of Iwashiro,
toshi furedo	the wind blows as years go by,
matsu no midori wa	but the green of the pine
kawarazarikeri	remains unchanged.

岩代のをのへの風に年ふれど松のみどりはかはらざりけり

The regent at the time [Fujiwara no Norimichi] was present and before the judge announced his decision said, "The poem that is about Kasuga, how could it lose? This is self-evident." Because of this, and without further discussion, it was announced as the winner. As it was a powerful member of the Fujiwara household who had spoken thus, they concurred and left it at that. The poem by the right mentioned the pine of Iwashiro, but nobody said anything about it during the contest, and they left it at that. Counselor Akizane,[41] the son of the poet [Sukenaka], said that afterward someone was appalled [that this infelicitous expression had been used in a congratulatory poem] and that his father [had] retorted, "That's what people call not knowing anything!"

I was taught that even if "the pine of Iwashiro" does not mean a tree planted to mark someone's burial mound, it makes one think of the awful events that led to the wanderings of Prince Arima, and thus it should not be used in poems for poetry competitions.[42]

これを大二条殿と申しし関白殿のその座にさぶらはせ給ひていまだ判者の定め申されぬさきに春日と詠まれたらむ歌はいかが負けむ沙汰にも及ぶまじ

と申させ給ひければ、さる事とてまた沙汰する事もなくて勝ちにけり。藤氏の長者にて申させ給ひければめでたき事にてやみにけり。右の歌は岩代の松詠まれたれどその座には沙汰する人もなくてやみにけり。後に人のかたぶきければようもしらぬ事いふなりとぞ作者申されけるとその人の子の顕実の宰相申されし。岩代の松はうせたる人の塚の木にはあらずとも有間の皇子のよからぬ事によりてまどひあるき給ひけることのおこりを思へば歌合には詠までもありぬべしとぞうけたまはりし。

Toshiyori makes a point that was very important to the court poet: a lack of relevant knowledge can have social implications, sometimes even dire consequences. This is demonstrated, first, when the powerful minister Fujiwara no Norimichi 藤原教通 (996–1075), son of Michinaga 道長 (966–1027), interrupts the judging to declare Nōin the winner of the round, arguing that a reference to Kasuga Shrine, the tutelary shrine of his family, could not lose. It is also apparent when Sukenaka stands accused of having been irresponsible in making reference to a place like Iwashiro, with its history of misfortune and exile. Through accounts such as these, Toshiyori provides poets with an expansive education, selecting and cataloging events from the court's recent past and connecting them to more distant cultural and historical memories.

The connections that *Toshiyori zuinō* makes between knowledge of *waka* and knowledge across the wider spectrum of culture, history, and language place it on common ground with texts in other pedagogic genres. Among them are *ōraimono* 往来物—compilations of exemplary correspondence used as primers in the education of courtiers—which became more widespread in the medieval period.[43] Toshiyori's extensive use of concise narrative passages also recalls the format of collections of brief narratives, thematically diverse texts grouped today in the genre known as *setsuwa-shū* (anecdotal collections). Among these is *Konjaku monogatari shū* 今昔物語集 (Collection of tales of times now past, after 1120), a monumental compendium of brief narratives structured into three parts corresponding to India, China, and Japan. In contrast to long-winded fictional tales such as *Genji monogatari*, which are now seen as part of the *tsukuri monogatari* 作り物語 (fictional narrative) genre, these collections of short narratives were considered truthful accounts. The organization of these works into discrete narrative units facilitated their wide diffusion (tertiary circulation), as later authors borrowed and recontextualized individual episodes for new purposes and new readerships.[44]

The differences between *Toshiyori zuinō* and the earlier poetry treatises can also be explained in connection with two intellectual and historical developments, as Komine Kazuaki has argued. First, the early twelfth century was marked by a turn toward putting in writing knowledge that until then had been transmitted in through the oral tradition (*kuden* 口伝).[45] This can be seen in the example of *Gōdanshō* 江談抄 (A selection of Ōe no Masafusa's conversations, 1104–16), a collection of anecdotes recorded by Fujiwara no Sanekane 藤原実兼 (1085–1112) at the behest of the scholar of Chinese learning Ōe no Masafusa 大江匡房 (1041–1111). After his eldest son and prospective heir, Takakane 隆兼, died in 1102, Masafusa, already an old man, feared that his household would cease to exist and thus his knowledge would be lost. Aside from the differences in intended readership, *Toshiyori zuinō* can be regarded with *Gōdanshō* as a product of a wider intellectual interest in preserving knowledge for future generations in written rather than oral form.

The second, related movement was the annotation and explication of classical works (*koten* 古典). Komine conceptualizes this as an attempt to overhaul the reading of old texts to meet current social circumstances and needs. Masafusa, for example, worked on the glossing (*kundoku*) and interpreting (*chūshaku* 注釈) of works written in classical Chinese and produced an annotated version of *Wakan rōeishū* 和漢朗詠集 (Collection of Chinese and Japanese poems for singing, ca. 1013). Distinguishing fact from fabrication is one of the main tasks in annotating texts, and as Toshiyori attempted to provide reliable commentaries to poems, he was faced with making choices about oral transmissions and subtexts from classical works that were likely to be untrue. In Toshiyori's decision to include such materials in his treatise and simply mark them as unreliable or likely fictional, Komine sees the emerging tension and syncretism that, in his analysis, would mark the relationship of *waka* and narrative until the end of the medieval period.[46]

Placing *Toshiyori zuinō*, as Komine does, in the context of concurrent trends toward the recording of oral transmissions and the annotation of classical texts helps to highlight the intellectual challenges that *waka* specialists faced at the turn of the twelfth century. At the same time, it is important to stress that Toshiyori was not concerned with preserving knowledge in the abstract; he was invested in the practical aspects of its transmission to specific individual students. In other words, the use of narratives as pioneered by Toshiyori was not an intellectual necessity but a pedagogic device. Seen in light of the shift from sophisticated poetic dialogue as an everyday form of interaction to the topical composition described by Hashimoto and the rise of lineages and rivalries outlined by Huey, the pedagogic use of narrative passages emerges as a fitting response to the intellectual, institutional, and practical parameters that had come to structure *waka* as a field.[47]

Lineage and Pedagogy

Toshiyori's achievements did not translate into the creation of a stable household of hereditary *waka* specialists. As mentioned, his son Shun'e left the capital after the death of his father and returned later to find the literary circles dominated by the Rokujō and Mikohidari. Shun'e, however, had a prominent student in Kamo no Chōmei. The work of Chōmei illustrates how poetry treatises were shaped by the recently developed institution of the professional poetic houses and the new focus on pedagogy.

Chōmei is widely known for his essay *Hōjōki* 方丈記 (The ten-foot-square hut, 1212), considered a masterpiece of recluse literature. This has colored the reading of his poetry treatise *Mumyōshō*, obscuring the ways in which it was carefully crafted to support a career in *waka*. One concern raised by modern scholars is the work's perceived disorganization. Kubota Jun, for example, has pointed out that although the beginning and the end of *Mumyōshō* do consist of lessons seemingly aimed at an inexperienced student of *waka*, the bulk of the treatise contains discussions of Chōmei's views on the interesting and challenging aspects of *waka* composition, interspersed with anecdotes about recent and contemporary poets, all strung together randomly. In Kubota's argument, this lack of systematic organization sets Chōmei's work apart from earlier poetry treatises.[48] Another interpretation of the work highlights Chōmei's apparent disinterest in the court. Katō argues, for example, that Chōmei adopted "the point of view of an observer who watches with detached interest" and that, as someone whose access to the court was limited by his lack of pedigree, "it should not have taken him long to realize that he did not miss much, considering the shallowness of court life. He was constantly torn between the ideal world he imagined and the reality around him."[49] However, an emphasis on Chōmei as a hermit, wanting to live in solitary tranquility and jotting down random thoughts, risks missing what *Mumyōshō* can tell us about the practice of poetry at court.

Many episodes in *Mumyōshō* describe Chōmei's triumphs at court. It might be tempting to write this off as casual vanity, yet his descriptions of success are meticulously deployed. About the poem he contributed to the seventh imperial anthology, *Senzai wakashū* (*Senzaishū* 千載集 [Collection of a thousand years], 1187), for example, he remarks, "I lack pedigree, I lack skill. And I am not one of those respected enthusiasts [*kōshi*]. So that I nevertheless had one poem included [in *Senzaishū*] is nothing short of an extraordinary distinction."[50] This might look like the usual self-deprecation that hides one's pride, but his lack of lineage, in particular, posed a serious problem for Chōmei. He refers in similar terms to his appointment to the court's Waka-dokoro 和歌所 (Bureau of Japanese Poetry), led by Retired Emperor GoToba 後鳥羽 (1180–1239, r. 1183–98). With this affiliation came access to the most exclusive circle of poets, which included the foremost poet of the time, Fujiwara no Teika 藤原定家 (1162–1241), head of the Mikohidari line. Other names Chōmei casually mentions are Fujiwara no Yoshitsune, heir to a line that had included regents since the tenth century; Priest Jien 慈円 (1155–1225), a son and brother of regents; and Fujiwara no Ietaka, a courtier of the second rank.[51] It would be obvious to any of Chōmei's readers (in both primary and secondary circulation) that he was the only one in this group to have earned that access exclusively through his hard work and skill.

By Chōmei's time, elite aristocratic and military circles granted their patronage—and their attendant financial and political support—almost exclusively to poets of distinguished poetic lineage. Those chosen to inherit the role of household head were particularly likely to be engaged as *waka* tutors by the patrons and their offspring. Chōmei, by contrast, grew up in a family that had traditionally been employed as wardens (*negi* 禰宜) of the Lower Kamo Shrine (Shimogamo Jinja 下鴨神社). As befitted his family's position, when Chōmei was a child he received training in the composition of *waka* and the playing of the biwa, or lute. After the early death of his father, however, Chōmei failed to be appointed successor to his father's position and was left without financial or institutional support. In his late teens and early twenties, he grew progressively impoverished but found encouragement in his relationship with his *waka* instructor, Toshiyori's son Shun'e. Under the tutelage of Shun'e, Chōmei's rise as a court poet was extraordinary. Not only was one of his poems included in *Senzaishū* when he was only in his early thirties, but in his late forties he was appointed to the Waka-dokoro. A few years later, when the *negi* position at the Lower Kamo Shrine again became available, Retired Emperor GoToba himself supported Chōmei's bid openly and forcefully. But Chōmei was ultimately unsuccessful, and he took holy vows at the age of fifty. He continued engaging with poetry circles; he had ten poems included in *Shin Kokin wakashū* (*ShinKokinshū* 新古今集 [New collection of poems ancient and modern], 1205); and through the mediation of fellow Waka-dokoro member Asukai Masatsune 飛鳥井雅経 (1170–1221), in 1211, at the age of fifty-seven, he traveled to Kamakura to meet the third shogun, Minamoto no Sanetomo, who was a patron and student of Teika.

During 1211 and 1212, Chōmei produced *Mumyōshō*, together with the prose works for which he is known: *Hōjōki* and *Hosshinshū* 発心集 (Collection of awakenings of faith, ca. 1211), a collection of brief narratives with a Buddhist theme. Just as his sustained networking and pursuit of new and more reliable patronage belies the reclusive persona seemingly behind these two works, his treatise *Mumyōshō* suggests a continued engagement in *waka* pedagogy. Chōmei quotes from a number of widely circulating treatises, but his main pedagogic model seems to have been *Toshiyori zuinō*, which he references explicitly.[52] On the one hand, this gesture toward the work of his teacher's father can be regarded as an effort to suggest his affiliation with the lineage. On the other, many elements in Chōmei's work suggest that its purport was fundamentally similar to Toshiyori's.

Mumyōshō was carefully shaped to maximize the student's learning. Chōmei's preferred pedagogic device is analogy. To explain the conventional epithets we today call *makura kotoba* 枕詞 (pillow words), Chōmei draws a parallel with the *hanpi* 半臂, a sleeveless layer of fabric worn between a sleeved outer layer (such as a formal *hō* 袍, or robe) and an undergarment (*shitagasane* 下襲). Chōmei quotes his teacher, Shun'e:

> Used in the first line, they add no interest. Placed in the third line, they introduce a pause, bringing out the best qualities of the poem and serving as an accomplished ornament. People of old called this "the *hanpi* line." *Hanpi* have no purpose, but when worn as part of the formal court attire [*shōzoku*] they play a decorative role.[53]
>
> されど始めの五文字にてはさせる興なし。腰の句によく続けて言葉の休めに置きたるはいみじう歌の品も出できふるまへるけすらひともなるなり。古き人これをば半臂の句とぞいひ侍りける。半臂はさせる用なき物なれど装束の中に飾りとなるものなり。

The main function of an epithet was to offer an imposing introduction to an image, such as the moon or a mountain. The issue that Shun'e addresses is the placement of an epithet in the third line of a poem instead of in the first line, where it would fit naturally as an introduction. Like the *hanpi*, this third-line epithet serves no apparent function but adds to the overall effect of the ensemble.

Chōmei then offers another analogy, this time with a tune from court music (*gagaku* 雅楽) called *sogō* 蘇合, in which just before the finale there is a passage that is not danced but only tapped with the feet to the beat, and thus serves as a pause. That passage is exclusively ornamental, just like a vest covered by other clothes or an epithet in the third line of a poem. Chōmei concludes by suggesting that the *sogō* should be called the "*hanpi*-line dance," and poems with a third-line epithet should be known as the "*sogō* style of poetry."[54] As Toshiyori had done, Chōmei incorporates into *Mumyōshō* knowledge about other fields to enrich his lessons on *waka*.

At the same time, Chōmei is breaking with this precedent. In *Toshiyori zuinō*, Toshiyori had included relevant information about history, geography, provincial customs, Buddhist lore, and so on—whenever it was immediately necessary to the understanding of a poetic expression or a literary reference. In *Mumyōshō*, however, other fields of knowledge are brought into the discussion to illuminate an abstract point about the practice of *waka*. This can be seen, for example, in Chōmei's discussion of a fierce contemporary debate that was going on within poetry salons. One faction embraced exclusively the style of the recent past (*nakagoro*), while the other pushed the "modern" (*kindai*) style of contemporary poets such as Teika. In *Mumyōshō*, Chōmei likens this to sectarian controversies, saying that "this debate will never be settled because it is of the same kind as a religious debate."[55] He continues by explaining that the more conservative poets usually call their rivals the "Daruma faction" (*daruma shū* 達磨宗), thus drawing a parallel with the skeptical view held by the established Shingon and Tendai of the new Chan/Zen sect, which they regarded as a heretic upstart. Further analogies are offered in two passages in which Chōmei quotes Shun'e's teachings:

> A poem that is good in an unexceptional way is like fabric in which the weft blends into the background [*katamon* 固文]; a poem of striking refinement is like looking at fabric in which the weft is woven into relief, as if it floated in the air.[56]
>
> 世の常のよき歌はたとへば固文の織物のごとし。よく艶すぐれぬる歌は浮文の織物などを見るがごとく空に景気の浮かべるなり。

> [In a poem,] in fact, even a string of good expressions, if sought too deliberately, should be taken as a failure. . . . This is analogous to a person decorating with stones, who, unable to put in place a good stone, seeks smaller stones, and combines them well, yet this can never be better than a truly big stone; so looking like one is trying too hard only leads to failure.[57]
>
> ただしよき言葉を続けたれどわざと求めたるやうになりぬるをばまた失とすべし。 . . . これはたとへば石を立つる人のよき石をえ据ゑずして小さき石どもを取り集めてめでたくさし合はせつつ立てたれどいかにもまことの大きなる石には劣れるやうにわざとびたるが失にて侍るなり。

These comments, which appear interwoven with illustrative examples, clearly exploit analogies with fabric and stone as a pedagogic device.

Chōmei draws in these passages from the fields of court attire, court music, fabric design, and landscaping. Not much in the way of detail is provided about any of these fields, which suggests that his intended reader (at the level of inception and even anticipated immediate dissemination) was conversant with them and thus able to profit from the analogies. Toshiyori, on the other hand, had assumed little knowledge of other fields in his reader and thus provided detailed explanations. The way in which Chōmei boasts about his appointment to the Waka-dokoro and his access to the court makes it unlikely that his intended reader was Retired Emperor GoToba or any other high-ranking aristocrat. A figure like Sanetomo—or someone from the shogun's immediate entourage—is more distinctly possible. The differences in organization and treatment between the treatises of Chōmei and Toshiyori mask a commonality of approach whereby each *waka* specialist adapted his teaching style to the knowledge and interests of his intended reader. Chōmei's steady production of new poems, scholarship, and pedagogic material for patron-students places him far from the detachment conjectured by Katō. An added advantage of conceptualizing poetry treatises as artifacts of practice is that it enables us to regard Chōmei's sustained attempts at self-promotion as an integral part of his professional project, rather than as a personality quirk. Self-aggrandizement can be a purposeful way to compensate for a competitive disadvantage when working in social circles in which pedigree is paramount.

The Transmission of Profession

Treatises created by *waka* specialists for nonspecialists, such as students and patrons, tended to find their way into wider circulation. This is the process of dissemination, or secondary circulation. By contrast, treatises written to pass down scholarship and procedural knowledge to a professional heir were kept secret, and thus were more likely to be lost if the household eventually was discontinued or dispersed.

Fukurozōshi, by Fujiwara no Kiyosuke, is a fortunate exception and an invaluable source of information on in-house pedagogic practices. *Fukurozōshi* needs to be understood first and foremost as an intramural document that was at first exclusive to the Rokujō household. Kiyosuke wrote it as part of his effort to provide the knowledge that would be necessary for future household heads. He was the grandson of the founder of the Rokujō lineage, Fujiwara no Akisue, and the son of the second-generation head of the household, Akisuke. It is not clear whom Kiyosuke had in mind as his own eventual successor, but it is possible that he wrote the treatise for his younger half-brother Fujiwara no Suetsune 季経 (1131–1221), who in fact became the head of the household after Kiyosuke's death. Another possibility is Kenjō, his brother by adoption, who was about twenty-five years his junior.

The Transmission of Household Knowledge

Preparing documents for one's scions had a long tradition among the aristocracy. For centuries, male aristocrats had kept household diaries. Some also kept "precedent guides" (*yūsoku kojitsu* 有職故実) that covered diverse aspects of court life, from regulations to etiquette to attire.[58] For example, *Kujō dono no yuikai* 九条殿遺誡 (Teachings of Lord Kujō, after 947), by Fujiwara no Morosuke 藤原師輔 (908–60), describes the etiquette and procedures for many events in the everyday life of the aristocracy. Written in a style close to classical Chinese (*hentai kanbun* 変体漢文), these diaries and precedent guides preserved knowledge about the official proceedings, customs, and history of the court, and could thus serve as references for heirs and other descendants.[59]

Until the twelfth century, there were no treatises on *waka* that served as precedent guides. Kiyosuke's *Fukurozōshi* is the first work that can be considered close to performing this function in terms of its structure and content, and its stylistic and lexical choices. *Fukurozōshi* stands as both a continuation of and a departure from the precedent set by Toshiyori, of which Kiyosuke was keenly aware—*Toshiyori zuinō* had been disseminated widely at court by then. *Fukurozōshi* combines the detailed technical information on etiquette and procedure typical of household diaries with the topical (rather than chronological) organization of a *waka* treatise such as *Toshiyori zuinō*. *Fukurozōshi* is also similar to *Toshiyori zuinō* in its content and its incorporation of commentary and narrative. Yet *Fukurozōshi* is in many ways a very different kind of treatise, as it was meant for a male reader who would, in turn, become a professional *waka* expert. For example, Kiyosuke composed *Fukurozōshi* in the *hentai kanbun* style of precedent guides and household diaries, not in the more accessible style that Toshiyori had used in *Toshiyori zuinō*.[60]

Household treatises tended to be closely guarded and seldom shared with outsiders. This meant keeping them away from all strangers—in particular, professional rivals but also patrons, who could potentially leak the works to competitors. Such exclusivity was hard to achieve if the patrons were very powerful individuals, such as emperors or regents. It is likely that Kiyosuke himself initially facilitated the secondary circulation of his text by making copies for patrons. Most extant manuscripts of *Fukurozōshi* end with a passage, positioned as a colophon (*okugaki* 奥書) and dated 1191, in which the unnamed copyist notes that he once asked Regent Kujō Kanezane 九条兼実 (1149–1207) about the origins of this treatise. Kanezane explained that Kiyosuke had written and presented the text to Emperor Nijō. After the emperor passed away, the treatise went to his empress, Fujiwara no Muneko 藤原宗子 (1146–73), who, in turn, gave it to Kanezane. Kanezane told the copyist that he had also received a copy of *Fukurozōshi* from Kiyosuke, but that it was lost in a fire. The copyist closes the text with the admonition that *Fukurozōshi* is a treasured secret and should not be made public.[61] The emphasis on secrecy is also seen in other contemporaneous contexts. Notable, for instance, is the interest in esotericism, oral transmissions, and initiation rituals prevalent among medieval Buddhist lineages, as analyzed by Mark Teeuwen.[62] Susan Klein has likewise discussed a culture of secrecy in medieval poetic treatises that involved the fabrication of artificial secrets to be used as economic and political bargaining chips.[63]

In *Fukurozōshi*, Kiyosuke was arguably attempting to protect valuable knowledge from professional competitors. It is likely that in making copies of the treatise for his patrons, he was acting under coercion. Some of the extant manuscripts continue onto another colophon, dated 1296, that records a more detailed account of the copy's origin. According to this colophon, Emperor Nijō had summoned Kiyosuke to court many times and repeatedly insisted on being shown the manuscript. Kiyosuke eventually yielded. Once the emperor had read the text, he gave Kiyosuke a stack of paper and ordered him to make a fair copy, which Kiyosuke presented to the emperor in 1159. Also according to this account, Kiyosuke was displeased with having been pressured into making a copy because he did not want outsiders to see his treatise.[64]

If this story is true, it should be noted that Kiyosuke produced a copy for the emperor only a few years after his father had passed away and he had become the acting head of the family. Conceivably, a more experienced Kiyosuke would have been better equipped to fend off the emperor's insistence. But these colophons were written long after Kiyosuke wrote *Fukurozōshi* and are, in part, recorded as hearsay. They do not provide indisputable evidence that Kiyosuke himself was invested in keeping his work secret. They do show, however, that as early as the last decade of the twelfth century, fifteen years after Kiyosuke's death, manuscript holders regarded the knowledge contained in *Fukurozōshi* as useful and in need of safeguarding from prying eyes. There seems to have been an expectation that households such as the Rokujō would make a clear distinction between texts intended for circulation and those meant only for household members. This expectation proved unrealistic, for material from *Fukurozōshi* eventually found its way into thirteenth-century collections such as *Jikkinshō* and *Kokonchomonjū*, just as occurred with *Toshiyori zuinō*.[65]

There is another way in which the transition from inception to dissemination of *Fukurozōshi* is obscure. At some point, the transmission of the manuscript bifurcated, leading to two separate lineages. To be more precise, the modern scholarly consensus is that two texts with separate histories of transmission stem from a single manuscript that was lost, in which they had been collated as volume 1 and volume 2.[66] To make things more confusing, the two colophons are found only at the end of volume 1. And to complicate matters still further, there is evidence that one of Kiyosuke's successors (either Suetsune or Kenjō) may have introduced modifications and additions to the text we have today.[67] Rather than being viewed as a work created by a single author for a single reader, as *Toshiyori zuinō* was, *Fukurozōshi* is better understood as part of an ongoing dialogue that a lineage of specialists conducted with itself over time. The details of this dialogue, which took place through the medium of manuscripts and copying, have, unfortunately, been lost to us. For the sake of simplicity, I discuss this treatise as if Kiyosuke were the only author; it would be more precise to say that it was written collectively by several generations of the Rokujō household, in ways unknown to us.

It is certainly possible that the rival Mikohidari household engaged in a similar iterative process of collectively developing in-house treatises. The absence of an equivalent document among their extant treatises could suggest that the Mikohidari were more successful than the Rokujō in safeguarding their house's intellectual property—or that this document was simply lost at some point. However, it could also imply the opposite: that the Mikohidari, having learned from Kiyosuke's cautionary example, deliberately avoided producing comprehensive in-house treatises, fearing that a patron might compel them to hand them over. The head of the Mikohidari house, Fujiwara no Teika, did pass down to his heir, Tameie, the diary *Meigetsuki* 明月記 (Record of the clear moon, 1180–1235), but this text is not comparable to *Fukurozōshi* in structure or content. For these reasons, *Fukurozōshi* remains an invaluable document for understanding professional poetic practice—and perhaps even a source of clues to what may have been lost.

An Education for Professionals

Waka pedagogy for patrons seeking instruction for themselves or their children incorporated knowledge of history, literature, religion, and geography as well as social skills. For a professional poet in training, that learning would be necessary but insufficient. If *Toshiyori zuinō* established a new standard of comprehensiveness for patron-students, *Fukurozōshi* complemented it with the training required by future professional who belonged to a hereditary household of *waka* specialists.

Following the model established by Toshiyori, Kiyosuke offers plenty of practical advice in *Fukurozōshi* on composition, including how to borrow lines from old poems (a technique known as *honkadori*

本歌取り) and how to make small adjustments to a poem to polish it, as well as examples of how poetic merit often hinges on the choice of a single sound. Yet he devotes much of his treatise to more erudite considerations. For example, his discussion of canonical texts—such as *Man'yōshū*, the imperial anthologies, the poem-tales *Ise monogatari* and *Yamato monogatari* 大和物語 (Tales of Yamato), both mid-tenth-century works, and the topical anthology *Kokin rokujō* 古今六帖 (Collection of poems ancient and modern in six books, late tenth century)—focuses on the process of compilation, the manuscript history, and variant manuscripts for each of these texts. Kiyosuke also includes a list of poets who appear in older texts such as *Man'yōshū* and the first four imperial anthologies, sometimes adding biographical information, and follows it with detailed entries on the more famous of these figures. Similarly, he offers a long list of official court titles and ranks, presented in kanji with their corresponding readings in kana. For example, Kiyosuke provides for 典薬寮 the reading *kusuri no tsukasa* クスリノツカサ (Office of Medicine).[68] These topics and their presentation suggest that Kiyosuke considered the role of *waka* specialist to be not simply a creator of peerless poems but also an authority with an exhaustive and detailed command of *waka* scholarship, particularly concerning procedural, historical, and linguistic issues.

At the same time, *Fukurozōshi* combines discussions of these academic matters with what we would today call "professional" issues. This instruction, not necessarily needed by the patron-students who sought to master poetry because of its role in the aristocracy, was of crucial importance to a professional *waka* specialist. For example, Kiyosuke devotes a section of the text to the details of orchestrating a poetry contest, including the responsibilities of each role, the preparation of the required documents, the inscription of poems on paper (each written in three lines, with the last three characters at the end as a short fourth line), and the way to deal with certain unusual situations. A contest organizer might encounter, for instance, one poet submitting the same poem for two or more set topics, or another becoming paralyzed with fright and fleeing the room without submitting a poem. There are also passages on how to compose congratulatory poems and poems for an imperial enthronement ritual (*daijōe* 大嘗会),

as well as how to select poems for an imperial anthology (do include powerful people, advises Kiyosuke, even if they are bad poets, and do not include lowly people, even if their poems are good). This is all information vital to the head of a poetry household who is competing at court for patronage.

Kiyosuke's interest in matters that concerned professional specialists can be seen, in particular, in the importance he gives to "proof poems" (*shōka* 証歌) and to avoiding being discredited in public. In a subsection titled "Zōtan" 雑談 (Miscellaneous conversations), consisting of brief narrative passages similar to those in *Toshiyori zuinō*, Kiyosuke includes the following anecdote:

> During that period, around the time of the year when clothes are beaten at the fulling block, Kanemori composed a poem for a folding screen that said, "I wonder if the time has come when they beat clothes on the fulling block" [*koromo utsu beki toki ya kinuramu*].[69] When Ki no Tokibumi was about to inscribe this poem on the screen, as he took the brush, he stopped and asked, "He sees the clothes being beaten in front of his eyes and still says, 'I wonder if the time has come when they beat clothes on the fulling block?' How can this be?" When people asked Kanemori about this, he responded, "Did not Tsurayuki compose on the topic of 'Horse-Welcoming,' on a folding screen of the Engi period [901–23], a poem that went, 'I wonder if right now they are pulling the tribute horses from the Full Moon stables' [*ima ya hikuran Mochizuki no koma*]?[70] Did he make a mistake, too? How can this be?"
>
> This left Tokibumi at a loss for words.[71]
>
> 其時御屏風歌擣衣所ニ兼盛詠コロモウツベキトキ時ヤキヌラン紀時文件色紙形ヲ書之時抑筆云見在ニ擣衣ヲミテ衣可打時ヤキヌラント詠之条如何。仍被問兼盛之処申云貫之延喜御時屏風駒迎所ニイマヤヒクラン望月ノ駒ト詠有此難歟如何。干時時文閉ロ云云。

This passage is highly condensed, leaving much unsaid. Here, Taira no Kanemori 平兼盛 (d. 990) is criticized by Ki no Tokibumi 紀時文 (n.d.) for misusing in a poem the expression *ramu*, which modern grammarians would describe as an auxiliary verb used to indicate speculation about the present.[72] Tokibumi says that *ramu* cannot be used for an event that is evident and in plain sight. Kanemori, on the verge of public humiliation, rallies by providing proof that it has been used in this way before. He cites as evidence a poem by an established poet of the past, Ki no Tsurayuki, chief editor of *Kokinshū*. With this proof poem, Kanemori defeats Tokibumi and saves his reputation as a poet.

This anecdote skillfully combines two different forms of instruction. First, it contains an important lesson for any poet: the expression *ramu*, though generally associated with speculation, can still be used even when a situation leaves no room for doubt. But, second, there is more to it. In this passage, Kiyosuke recounts a type of social interaction that appears in several other anecdotes in *Fukurozōshi*. The common denominator is that someone is criticized in public and to shake off the attack, quotes a poem composed by an established poet or included in an imperial anthology. The criticism tends to concern the correctness of the poem rather than its artistic merit. There is a fundamental lesson here that is particularly useful for a professional heir to a poetry household: a specialist should expect to be challenged and to have his own challenges swiftly countered. In this cutthroat environment, command of precedent is crucial to success. The emphasis on proof poems redefined the role of memorization in *waka* pedagogy. Committing a vast number of poems to memory was not sufficient for a professional. Linguistic and critical discernment were equally important to identify and offer a suitable proof poem.

By contrast, in the education of aristocratic women—who were not eligible to become professionals—rote memorization remained the dominant practice. In *Makura no sōshi* 枕草子 (The pillow book, 1002), for example, the lady-in-waiting Sei Shōnagon 清少納言 (ca. 966–1017 or 1025) recounts an anecdote passed down by her patron, Empress Teishi 定子 (977–1001), and set at least half a century earlier. According to Teishi, the powerful Fujiwara no Morotada 藤原師尹 (or Moromasa, 920–69) advised his daughter Hōshi 芳子 (d. 967) as she prepared to enter the court:

> First, you must study calligraphy. Next, practice until you are the best at the seven-stringed *kin* harp. Then, you must memorize all the poems in all twenty volumes of *Kokinshū*.[73]

一つには御手を習ひたまへ。次には琴の御琴を人よりことに弾きまさらむと おぼせ。さては古今の歌二十巻をみな浮かべさせたまふを御学問にはせさせたまへ。

Teishi then recounted how some time after Hōshi had become consort to Emperor Murakami 村上 (926–67), the emperor tested her by demanding that she produce the poems in the order they appear in the *Kokinshū* (which had been commissioned by his father, Emperor Daigo). When Morotada heard about this he panicked and commissioned prayers, but his daughter was able to meet the challenge. Hōshi's success came from her ability to replicate sequences of sounds. Her comprehension of the poems and her capacity to assess them critically were left untested.[74]

Kiyosuke's passage on proof poems, also set during Murakami's court, highlights how a male specialist must know many more poems than just those in *Kokinshū* and, moreover, must be able to recall them to defend lexical and technical choices made in other contexts.[75] In other words, he needs to be able to analyze poems down to their linguistic constituents, identify those that can serve as precedents for the use of abstruse expressions, and deploy them as proof, on the spur of the moment. Tokibumi, moreover, was Tsurayuki's son, and thus arguably the earliest hereditary specialist. His mistaken critique of Kanemori serves, then, to historicize the role of the hereditary *waka* specialist and to remind Kiyosuke's heir to avoid Tokibumi's inexcusable mistake, since no precedent could be more important than that set by one's ancestors.

There are indications that Kiyosuke was speaking from experience when he emphasized the importance of proof poems. Kamo no Chōmei recounts in *Mumyōshō* an anecdote in which Kiyosuke was criticized in public for having used an expression incorrectly in one of his poems:

During the time Emperor Nijō was fond of poetry, when Okazaki Third Rank [Fujiwara no Norikane] was serving as the emperor's tutor, Lord Kiyosuke was summoned to court because of his high reputation in the field of *waka*. Something very interesting happened then. At some point during a poetry gathering, Kiyosuke used the expression "here and

> there" [*konomo kanomo*] when composing a poem about a mountain, I don't remember which. Third Rank criticized him, saying, "The expression 'here and there' applies exclusively to Mount Tsukuba. You can't use it for any other mountain." When he saw himself thus criticized, Kiyosuke muttered, "It goes without saying that it applies to Tsukuba. But it can be used more generally, even for rivers." Third Rank sneered at him, "Show me a proof poem." Kiyosuke replied, "When Mitsune wrote the preface to the poetry gathering by the Ōigawa River, he wrote 'Here and there in the Ōigawa River.' This is a fact." After he said this, everybody kept their silence, and that was the end of the matter. One should not criticize others rashly.[76]
>
> 二条院和歌好ませおはしましける時岡崎の三位御侍読にて候はれけるにこの道の聞こえ高きによりて清輔朝臣召されて殿上に候ひけり。いみじき面目なりけるをある時の御会に清輔いづれの山とかこのもかのもといふことを詠まれたりければ三位これを難じていはく筑波山にこそこのもかのもとは詠め。おほかた山ごとにいふべきことにはあらずと難ぜられければ清輔申していはく筑波山までは申すべきならず。川などにも詠み侍るべきにこそとつぶやきければ三位あざ笑ひて証歌をたてまつれと申されけるに清輔のいはく大井川の会に躬恒が序書ける時大井川のこのもかのもと書けることまさしく侍るものをと言ひ出でたりければ諸人口を閉ぢてやみにけり。荒涼にものをば難ずまじきことなり。

In this passage, when Kiyosuke insisted that his poem was correct, Fujiwara no Norikane 藤原範兼 (1107–65) challenged him to provide a proof poem, which Kiyosuke did, thus saving himself from public humiliation and cementing his reputation as a scholar of *waka*. The proof that Kiyosuke brings up, interestingly, is not a poem but a prose preface written by the poet Ōshikōchi no Mitsune 凡河内躬恒 (early Heian period), one of the compilers of *Kokinshū*. Yet the structure of the exchange—the public challenge and the quick response—is identical to that of proof poems. In *Mumyōshō*, Chōmei frames this event as a cautionary tale about the risk of being aggressive toward a fellow poet. In *Fukurozōshi*, Kiyosuke takes a rather defensive stand, connecting proof poems to the anxiety that one might be challenged. The former is writing for a patron-student; the latter, for a junior colleague.

Proof poems are only one means among many for eluding public embarrassment, which was perhaps Kiyosuke's biggest concern in

Fukurozōshi. In the following passage, for example, he emphasizes more generally the importance of prudence in dealing with others:

> Someone said, "Tomofusa, the governor of Mikawa Province, composed a poem, and Controller Koreie, greatly impressed, praised him by saying 'Well done!'[77] Tomofusa flew into a rage and said, 'Outside of *shi* poetry, I am no match for you. At *waka*, you beat me by far. Having to hear something like this is outrageous. From now on, I will not compose *waka* again.'" One must be careful even with one's words of praise.[78]
>
> 或人語云三河守知房所詠之歌伊家卿感歎云優読給ヘリト云々。知房立腹云予ハ非詩事は非敵。而和歌頗劣彼。如此被仰云尤奇怪也。自今以後不可読和歌云云。優詞可用意事歟。

This vignette illustrates the importance of tactfulness to avoid making a gaffe. The lesson is not specific to poetry, but applies to court life in general. *Fukurozōshi* contains many similar lessons on how to negotiate the challenges of court life—among them how to decline a challenge and how to provide constructive feedback. There are cautionary passages about how poets often receive sarcastic sobriquets after composing poems that revealed their ignorance, as well as an episode relating how one poet tricked and exposed another who was secretly relying on a ghostwriter. Kiyosuke tells as well of a father who scolds his son for wasting a good poem on an unimportant occasion instead of saving it for a more consequential event, such as being called into the presence of the emperor. Such narrative passages record events intended to serve as proof of precedent—and, as such, are not unlike proof poems. These cautionary tales codify and transmit the types of social skills and professional ethos required of specialists in poetry.

Another of Kiyosuke's objectives in writing *Fukurozōshi* was to impress on his potential successor the benefits of serving as the head of a household of poetry specialists. For this reason, along with cautionary tales, *Fukurozōshi* includes more cheerful narrative passages that encourage the reader to pursue *waka* as a career. To stress poetry as a potential path to rank and office, Kiyosuke narrates how he received the junior fifth rank, upper grade, from Emperor Toba, thanks to the sponsorship of the regent Fujiwara no Tadamichi; later received the senior fifth rank, lower grade, from Retired Emperor Sutoku; and, finally, after many unsuccessful attempts, received the fourth rank, from Toba. Kiyosuke relates Toba's remark on the poem included in his application (*mōshibumi* 申文): "Even descendants of many generations of famous poets sometimes reveal insufficient skill, but this is a poem of unsurpassed style." Later in the same passage, Kiyosuke adds, "Isn't this the highest honor? I have many shortcomings, but thanks to the way of poetry I have received honors repeatedly. This must be the result of years of practice and effort."[79] This is an instance of self-promotion similar to those discussed in connection with Chōmei's *Mumyōshō*. It is unlikely that Kiyosuke wrote it with a feeling of self-satisfaction; while his father, Akisuke, had reached the senior third rank, Kiyosuke never got beyond fourth. To the contrary, the emphasis here, as is true for the whole of *Fukurozōshi*, is on the benefits of the study and practice of *waka* as a professional activity.

The production of works such as *Fukurozōshi* that could serve as guides for the descendants of professional *waka* poets was a major milestone in the world of poetry. These texts were instrumental in turning *waka* experts into professional specialists organized as households and in transforming a living court praxis into a field of closely guarded knowledge. Kiyosuke, just like Toshiyori, served at court and in a powerful household as poetry consultant, master of ceremonies of poetry contests, editor of poetry anthologies, and so on. However, *Toshiyori zuinō* and *Fukurozōshi* were written for readers of different genders, ages, and career expectations. It is in these circumstances that we can locate the source of their different approaches to *waka* pedagogy, the ways in which they compare to their predecessors, and their significant commonalities—in particular with respect to the incorporation of commentary and narrative.

Professionalism and Zeal

Kiyosuke was aware that the professionalization of the role of *waka* specialist was a recent development. He attempted, for example, to historicize its emergence and demarcate its boundaries.[80] In *Fukurozōshi*, he presents the emergence of professional households as a response to a new social need for reliable instructors, whose numbers were few. Kiyosuke traces their origins in this way:

> In *waka*, from the distant past there had been no instructors. The first instance was when Nōin took Nagatō, the governor of Iga, as his instructor.[81] Just before that time, Nōin had started to become known as the Higo Graduate.[82] Nōin was on his way to run errands when his carriage's wheel was damaged, right in front of Nagatō's residence. He sent for another carriage and in the meanwhile entered the house and met Nagatō for the first time. Nōin had meant to make himself useful to Nagatō at some point, and now as he was casually driving by, this happy accident occurred. They discussed this and entered into a mutual contract [*keiyaku*]. "How should one compose *waka*?" Nōin asked. Nagatō responded, "In this way:

yama fukami	Deep in the mountains
ochite tsumoreru	autumn leaves pile up,
momijiba no	desiccated
kawakeru ue ni	and, on top,
shigure furu nari	a wintry drizzle falls."[83]

> Following that, Nōin took Nagatō as his instructor [*shi*]. This is why in *Gengenshū* there are many poems by Nagatō.[84]

> 和歌ハ昔ヨリ無師。而能因始長能(伊賀守也)ヲ為師。当初肥後進士ト云ケル時物へ行間於長能宅前車輪損之。乃車取遣之間入彼家始面会。雖有参仕之志自然過之間幸有如此事。其由ヲ談相互契約ス。能因云和歌者何様可読哉。長能云山フカミオチテツモレル紅葉ゝノカハケル上ニシクレフルナリ。如此可詠云々。自此為師。仍玄々集ニ多ク入長能歌也。

Key to this new practice were explicit pedagogic contracts (*keiyaku* 契約) between a student and an instructor (*shi* 師) from outside the student's household, or even from a different social circle. In *Mumyōshō*, in the context of a discussion of his connection with his teacher, Shun'e, Chōmei refers to this new social practice as an "exchange of vows between teacher and disciple" (*shitei no chigiri musubi*).[85] In Kiyosuke's anecdote, Nōin and Fujiwara no Nagatō 藤原長能 (Nagayoshi; ca. 949–ca. 1009) had no common acquaintances who could arrange for a more formal introduction, and Nōin needed a lucky coincidence as an excuse to introduce himself. What *Fukurozōshi* traces is the emergence of a new social type: the professional *waka* instructor. These were individuals who were recognized in some formal sense as experts and who engaged in this pursuit as a remunerative occupation, rather than a leisure-time activity.

The passage also touches on the issues of lineage and patronage. The practice of master-to-disciple transmission (*shishi sōshō* 師資相承) had a long tradition in Buddhist institutions, but not in the world of *waka*. In the field of Sinitic learning, scholars were affiliated with the Daigakuryō or served as private tutors, as discussed in the introduction. Nōin had graduated from the Daigakuryō and had served in the imperial bureaucracy. But in his midtwenties he took Buddhist vows, rendering himself ineligible to receive official appointments, thereby acknowledging that his career at court was foundering. Before taking Buddhist vows, Nōin had supplemented his income by acting as a purveyor of horses for fellow low-level officials (*zuryō* 受領) and by selling off his property in the capital.[86] Nagatō, however, was a successful court poet. He was a close associate of the foremost patron of *waka* at the time, Retired Emperor Kazan 花山 (968–1008, r. 984–86). It is very likely that Nagatō was central to the process of compiling the third imperial *waka* anthology, *Shūishū*. Once Nōin became part of Nagatō's lineage, the Buddhist vows that had prevented him from receiving official appointments now allowed him to cross social boundaries and associate more freely with higher-level courtiers who could become his patrons.[87] Nōin soon succeeded in the world of *waka*, becoming a mentor to the next generation of poets—in particular, a group of *zuryō*-level bureaucrats who identified themselves as the Clique of Six (*rokunintō* 六人党) and enjoyed high-level patronage from powerful figures close to Regent Fujiwara no Yorimichi 藤原頼通 (992–1074).[88]

Kiyosuke's efforts to find a historical precedent for the professional *waka* instructors who were now emerging as a new social type are related to his interest in proof poems. Both speak to the main theme of *Fukurozōshi*: the need for knowledge of earlier events, which Kiyosuke regarded as guides to appropriate action when faced with similar circumstances. It is distinctly possible that Kiyosuke included the passage on Nagatō and Nōin in a similar spirit. With it, he provides a verifiable precedent for, and thus lends legitimacy to, the pedagogic activity, social status, and claims to authority of professional poetry lineages, such as his own Rokujō.

From the perspective of the head of a professional household, the emergence of the *waka* instructor and the pedagogic contract posed both a promise and a threat. On the one hand, instructor-student bonds were the foundation of the patronage relationships that supported the Rokujō. On the other, pedagogic contracts, in which instructor and student could freely choose each other, presented a challenge. If any accomplished poet could serve as an instructor, how could the Rokujō members differentiate their practice from that of other, nonhousehold, self-appointed poetry experts?

To position himself and his household advantageously within the emergent professionalization of *waka* practice, Kiyosuke turned to the figure of the "enthusiast" (*sukimono*). Variously written with the characters 数寄 or 好 for *suki* and 者 or 物 for *mono*, the word *sukimono* had a long history and had been used to refer to persons (usually men) with an inclination toward either elegance or sensuality.[89] In the context of twelfth-century *waka* practice, how one understood *sukimono* depended on one's affiliation. Specialists who did not come from a long lineage of poets, such as Nōin and Chōmei, used the term in a highly positive way (as in Chōmei's use of the related expression *kōshi* 好士 when he wrote, "I lack pedigree, I lack skill. And I am not one of those respected enthusiasts [*kōshi*]").[90] In *Fukurozōshi*, by contrast, Kiyosuke ridicules what he presents as extreme enthusiasm. He considers the *sukimono* to be a foil for the seriousness and propriety of the lineage specialists whom Kiyosuke himself stood for. He offers this illustration of the kinds of attitudes that *sukimono* had toward *waka*:

> Kakuya Tokinobu, the head of the crown prince escort, was an enthusiast [*sukimono*].[91] When he met Nōin for the first time, they impressed each other. Nōin said, "To mark our meeting, I have something that you will want to see," and took out of the fold of his robe a small bag made

> of brocade. Inside the bag, there were wood shavings. Showing them, he said, "This is my treasure. These are wood shavings from when the bridge over the Nagara River was built." Tokinobu was extremely pleased and took a wrapped object out of the fold of his robe. Upon opening it and taking a look, it turned out that this was a dried-up frog. "This is a frog from Ide," he said. They were both moved and admired, and each put his object back in his robe and said good-bye. People today would call them fools [*woko*]![92]

> 加久夜長力節信ハ好奇物也。始テ逢能因相互有感緒。能因云今日見参ノ引出物ニ可見物侍トテ自懐中錦小袋ヲ取出。其中ニ鉋屑一筋有。示云是ハ吾重宝也。長柄橋造之時鉋クツ也ト云云。于時節信喜悦甚テ又自懐中紙ニ裹物ヲ取出。開之見ニカレタルカヘル也。是ハ井堤ノ蛙ニ侍ト云云。共感歎シテ格懐之退散。今世人可称嗚呼哉。

The bridge over the Nagara River (in present-day northern Osaka) was a famous poetic place (*utamakura*); so was Ide, a location poetically associated with frogs.[93] By carrying these tokens on their persons, Tokinobu and Nōin displayed their zeal for the poetic tradition. Kiyosuke continues by recounting how Nōin usually advised students in this way: "You should be fond [*suku*] of poetry. If are fond of it, you will compose great poems."[94] In Kiyosuke's presentation, the verb *suku* and the noun *sukimono* are markers of hyperbolic zeal.[95]

Kiyosuke found enthusiasm foolish precisely because it set a bad precedent for future generations. He recounts, for example, how once, when Toshiyori was about to ride by the old house of a poet of the past, he suddenly dismounted and walked his horse, and was then imitated by everybody in his party. Kiyosuke also points to the precedent (*senshō* 先蹤) set by Nōin when he alighted from a carriage and walked for blocks when approaching the old house of the poet Ise no Go 伊勢の御 (Lady Ise; active early tenth century).[96] Kiyosuke explains the consequences of this attitude:

> When Chamberlain Takeda Kuniyuki went to Michinoku Province, the day he was to cross the Shirakawa Barrier he wore especially formal clothes and smoothed his hair with water. Someone asked him, "Do you have a reason to do this?" He replied, "This is the place that Nōin sung in his poem that says 'arrived at Shirakawa Barrier with the autumn

> winds' [*akikaze zo fuku Shirakawa no seki*], so how could I cross it in everyday clothes?" What a strange thing!
>
> Nōin actually hadn't traveled to Michinoku Province. Because he had composed this poem, he secretly sequestered himself at home and later made the poem public, saying that he had composed it while he had been away from the capital. It is recorded as composed during his second trip away from the capital, but didn't he go there only once?[97] This was recorded in *Yaso shima no ki* [Records of the eighty islands].[98]
>
> 竹田大夫国行ト云者陸奥ニ下向之時白川関スクル日ハ殊装束テミツヒムカクト云々。人問云問等故哉答云古曾部入道ノ秋風ゾフク白河関トヨマレタル所ヲハカテケナリニテハ過ント云々。殊勝事也。能因実ニ不下向奥州。為詠此歌窃ニ籠居シテ下向奥州之由を風聞云々。二度下向之由カケリ。於一度者実歟。書八十島記。

In this passage, Kuniyuki shows for Nōin the same exaggerated respect that Nōin himself had shown for poets of the past. The irony, Kiyosuke points out, is that the trip that Kuniyuki memorialized actually never happened: Nōin was in the capital when he composed a poem about a famous site in Michinoku Province; he pretended to have been away to present the poem as a travel composition. In describing Kuniyuki's dramatic gesture, Kiyosuke appears to suggest that while Nōin's foolishness and dishonesty may have been inoffensive, they produced more ridiculous fools and more confusion. In an earlier passage, moreover, Kiyosuke provides an extreme illustration of the dangers of excessive attachment to the practice of *waka* (*michi wo shū suru* 道執). He recounts that after Nagatō was criticized in public for one of his poems, he became so dejected that he stopped eating and soon died.[99]

What Kuniyuki, Nōin, and Nagatō had in common was that they were *waka* specialists working outside the institutional framework of the lineage-based professional household. The choice of these poets as the subjects of cautionary tales is, by implication, a suggestion that Kiyosuke himself and his Rokujō house offered a healthier and more balanced relationship to poetic practice, one in which serious commitment did not degenerate into obsession. Toshiyori, by contrast, does not ridicule the figure of the enthusiast or emphasize the risks of excessive attachment to the field. In *Toshiyori zuinō*, he narrates the death of Nagatō in terms similar to those in *Fukurozōshi* but adds, as a moral of the story, simply that "I recorded this incident as an example of how it is better not to criticize someone who takes things to heart this much, even if there are valid grounds for the criticism."[100] Fujiwara no Teika referred to these events in a long letter to one of his patron-students, as an illustration of how "a person committed to this way [*michi* 道] shouldn't even for an instant lose the spirit of attachment [*shū suru* 執する] and recklessly compose a poem."[101] The difference in the stances of these specialists could not be starker. Yet it is important to keep in mind that they stem from works for substantially different audiences. Toshiyori, like Teika, was writing for a patron-student, while Kiyosuke was training a prospective professional heir. One type of reader would benefit from encouragement; the other, from caution and restraint.

Another way to explain this divergence is to point out that Toshiyori was concerned about the future of the practice of *waka*. As Hashimoto Fumio argues, Toshiyori's generation had cause for alarm. After the compilation of the third imperial collection, *Shūishū*, eighty years went by without a new imperial anthology; the fourth, *Goshūishū*, compiled by Fujiwara no Michitoshi for Retired Emperor Shirakawa, was part of the efforts to restore the cultural significance of *waka*, but on its own would not guarantee their success.[102] Kiyosuke, by contrast, perceived the composition of *waka* as an established practice. For him, what was at stake was the survival not of this tradition but of the institutions that would control and regulate it to secure the patronage of powerful students. Teika, whose household was a direct rival to the Rokujō, possibly may have agreed with Kiyosuke's negative evaluation of the *sukimono*, but the absence of treatises written for Mikohidari heirs makes this assessment impossible to corroborate. As mentioned, Chōmei, who had no hope of establishing a dominant professional lineage, saw *waka* enthusiasts in a much more positive light. In summary, these different views on the issue of the *sukimono* should be understood positionally, particularly in terms of each writer's outlook on lineage and professionalism.

The Future of the Poetry Treatise

Understanding *Toshiyori zuinō*, *Mumyōshō*, and *Fukurozōshi* as artifacts of a new social practice centered on the professional poetic household and dependent on explicit contracts between students and instructors provides an opportunity to reevaluate the textual legacy of the Mikohidari school and its offshoots: the Nijō, Kyōgoku, and Reizei households. The Mikohidari have been the focus of the majority of research in the field in English and of translations into English, as modern scholars over the years mined their treatises for clues about each poet's understanding of what made a good poem, how poets from rival households regarded one another, and how these communities of practitioners conceptualized poetic beauty.[103]

We have critical studies and translations of most of their extant works, such as Fujiwara no Teika's personal collection, *Shogaku hyakushu* 初学百首 (One hundred poems by a beginner, 1181), his treatises *Kindai shūka* and *Eiga no taigai*, his wide-ranging *Maigetsushō* 毎月抄 (Monthly notes, 1219), his contributions to the eighth imperial anthology *ShinKokinshū*, and his Buddhist poems.[104] *Teika jittei* 定家十体 (The ten styles of Teika, 1213), traditionally attributed to Teika, is now suspected to have been created later by a different writer.[105] Among the writings of Teika's descendants are *Eiga no ittei* 詠歌一体 (The foremost style of poetic composition, ca. 1261–64) by his son Tameie; the many texts written by Tameie's wife, Nun Abutsu 阿仏尼 (1225–83), such as *Izayoi nikki* 十六夜日記 (Diary of the sixteenth night moon); *Wakashō* 和歌抄 (Notes on poetry, ca. 1285–87) by Tameie's grandson Kyōgoku Tamekane (1254–1332); and *Shōtetsu monogatari* 正徹物語 (The Tales of Shōtetsu, 1448–50), by Priest Shōtetsu 正徹 (1381–1459), a student of Tameie's great-grandson Reizei Tametada and a huge Teika admirer.[106] These works have received careful attention, no doubt thanks to the institutional and professional success of the Mikohidari households throughout the medieval period.

Until the rise of the Mikohidari, the history of *waka* practice had seen a long list of individual poets ascend to the top of the field because of their poems and their knowledge. Many of them trained their offspring in the hope of producing a comparable or even more successful heir who would continue the family trade. Toshiyori, for example, compiled an imperial anthology, *Kin'yōshū*, a commission that had escaped his father, Tsunenobu. Conversely, while Akisuke compiled another imperial anthology, *Shikashū*, his son Kiyosuke did not. The first to succeed in securing stable patronage were Shunzei and Teika. Two hundred fifty years had gone by since Tsurayuki and Tokibumi had compiled, respectively, *Kokinshū* and *Gosen wakashū* (*Gosenshū*)—the first and second imperial collections—during the first half of the tenth century. Shunzei compiled the seventh imperial anthology, *Senzaishū*. Teika led a group of compilers for the next collection, *ShinKokinshū*, and was later the sole editor of the ninth imperial anthology, *ShinChokusen wakashū* (*ShinChokusenshū* 新勅撰集 [New imperial *waka* collection], 1235), making their Mikohidari family the first enduring lineage of *waka* professionals. Their descendants split into three rival households—the Nijō, Kyōgoku, and Reizei—and went on to compile the remaining eleven official anthologies (the practice was discontinued after 1439). For more than two centuries, all the compilers of imperially commissioned *waka* anthologies claimed descent from Shunzei. Shunzei had been trained by the highly respected poet Fujiwara no Mototoshi, to whom he was not closely related (while both poets belonged to the Northern Fujiwara group of aristocratic families, they descended from separate lineages; Shunzei from the Mikohidari and Mototoshi from the Naka-Mikado). Shunzei's progeny, by contrast, would be trained in house, by descendants of the Mikohidari lineage.

Aside from the brief justifications of his rulings that Shunzei left behind after serving as a judge of poetry competitions (*utaawase*), the main text in which Shunzei systematized and established his conception of *waka* was his treatise *Korai fūteishō*, which enjoys a unique place in the intellectual history of medieval Japan.[107] In modern scholarship, this treatise has been hailed as the earliest attempt to show that the ways of *waka* and of the Buddhist law were one and the same. This is a theme that would gain importance in later medieval texts, such as *Shasekishū*, a development discussed in detail in chapter 2. *Korai fūteishō* is the earliest work to touch explicitly on the affinity of *waka* and Buddhism, laying out the issue of their apparent incompatibility and proposing an approach to overcome it. It is possible to interpret this posture as originating in Shunzei's own religious inclinations and as an early indication of the general direction in which the whole field would soon move.[108] We know, for example, that Shunzei had taken holy vows about two decades before he finished this treatise. But we also know that, like *Toshiyori zuinō*, *Korai fūteishō* was created for a patron-student, Princess Shokushi, who had by then taken Buddhist vows.[109] It is possible, then, to conjecture that the Buddhist references in this treatise were a pedagogic appeal to the inclinations, concerns, and previous knowledge of this specific patron-student.

Shunzei addresses the relationship between poetry and Buddhist practice from the beginning. He presents his argument early in the text, stating that *waka* poetry is difficult to understand, and that drawing a parallel with Buddhist teachings can simplify its comprehension. After acknowledging the great number of available scholarly works produced by different specialists—from treatises (*zuinō*) to lists of poetic expressions and poetic places (*utamakura*) to explications of confusing issues—he states,

> Still, there are very few people capable of succeeding at the extremely difficult task of explaining how to tell the good (good like the mountains of Yoshino) from the bad (bad like the reeds of Naniwa Inlet).[110] However, at the beginning of the text known as *Tendai shikan*, his eminence Zhāng'ān wrote, "The clarity and tranquility of meditation [*shikan*] are unheard to previous generations," and as they admiringly say that upon hearing this, one can fathom a deep, boundless, advanced sense, I thought of how the good, the bad, and the deep gist [*kokoro*] of *waka* poetry can be understood, so in order to explain what is hard to put into words, I have here resorted to drawing parallels [*yosohe-te*] to make it possible to, similarly, imagine it.[111]

> たゞこの歌の姿詞におきて古野川善しとはいかなるをいひ難波江の蘆の悪しとはいづれを分くべきぞといふことのなかなかいみじく説き述べ難く知れる人も少かるべきなり。しかるにかの天台止観と申す文のはじめのことばに止観の明静なること前代も未だ聞かずと章安大師と申す人の書き給へるがまづうち聞くよりことの探さも限りなく奥の義も推し量られて尊くいみじく聞ゆるやうにこの歌の善き悪しき深き心を知らんこともことばを以て述べ難きをこれによそへてぞ同じく思ひやるべき事なりける。

Here, Shunzei refers to one of the central texts in the Tendai canon, the treatise *Móhē zhǐguān* 摩訶止観 (Jp. *Maka shikan* [The marvelous calm-and-contemplation], 594). This work was based on the lectures of the third patriarch, Zhìyǐ 智顗 (Jp. Chigi; 538 –97), as put in writing by his disciple Guàndǐng 灌頂 (Zhāng'ān 章安; 561–632).[112] In the *Móhē zhǐguān*, Zhìyǐ proposed that his students understood the practice of *móhē* (meditation) as a threefold process: the notions that everything is empty (*kōng* 空; Jp. *kū*) and that everything exists provisionally (*jiǎ* 假; Jp. *ke*) might seem incompatible, but they come together and are transcended by the middle way (*zhōng* 中; Jp. *chū*) of the doctrine of nondualism (*wúèr* 無二; Jp. *muni*). Shunzei discusses these notions once he has made it clear that in that same way that a secular work can convey sacred truth, a Buddhist teaching can aid in the study of *waka*:

> In fact, the former [Buddhist teachings] are endowed with profound meaning that stems from the golden mouth of the Buddha himself. The latter [*waka*] might look like the jesting of frivolous words and fancy expressions,[113] but they manifest a deep significance [*mune*] and thanks to this connection, they can even convey [*kayowasa-mu*] the way of the Buddha, and it is for this reason that we learn from the Lotus Sutra that "if a secular classic [from the Confucian canon] . . . expounds on how to lead one's life, we should accept it as properly teaching the [Buddhist] truth," and from the Fugen Bodhisattva Sutra, "What is sin? What is fortune? Nothing is inherently sinful or fortunate. Our mind [*kokoro*] is naturally empty [*kū*]." Thus, now, even when I refer to the depth of the way of *waka* poetry, because of its similarities [*ni-taru*] to the three truths—emptiness [*kū*], the provisional [*ke*], and the middle way [*chū*]—I adopt this manner to convey it [*kayowashi-te*].[114]

> ただしかれは法文金口の深き義なり。これは浮言綺語の戯れには似たれどもことの深き旨も顕はれこれを縁として仏の道にも通はさんためかつは煩悩即ち菩提なるが故に法華経には若し俗間の経書 . . . 之を略す . . . 資生の業等を説かば皆正法に順はんといひ普賢観には何者かこれ罪何者かこれ福罪福主無く我が心自ら空なりと説き給へり。よりて今歌の深き道を申すも空仮中の三諦に似たるによりて通はして記し申なり。

Although this is nowhere made fully explicit in the text, *Korai fūteishō* is clearly inviting the reader to map onto the three dimensions of the practice of *móhē* meditation—emptiness, provisionality, and the middle way—the three concepts that Shunzei presents as central to the practice of *waka*—poetic gist (*kokoro* 心), diction (*kotoba* 詞), and style (*sugata* 姿). The idea that diction corresponds to the provisional and style to the middle way becomes clear later in the treatise, when Shunzei argues,

> For this reason, since expressing in writing this way's deep gist [*kokoro*]—as I parted the groves of leaflike diction and dipped my brush in a sea [of ink]—is very difficult, I have simply drawn from the poems in the *Man'yōshū* of the ancient period, in the *Kokinshū*, *Gosenshū*, and *Shūishū* of the middle period, and the more recent compositions since the *Goshūishū*. As the times change, so have the style and the diction of poems, as can be seen in the successive poetry anthologies. A bit of this I have recorded here. Thus, since the style [*sugata*] and gist [*kokoro*] of *waka* are so difficult to discuss, I sought to convey [*kayowashi*] them through the Buddhist way, likening [*yose-te*] them to the Buddhist scriptures.[115]
>
> しかるをこの道深き心なほことばの林を分け筆の海を汲むとも書き述べんことは難かるべければただ上万葉集よりはじめて中古古今集後撰拾遺下後拾遺よりこなたざまの歌時世の移りゆくに従ひて姿もことばも改まり行く有様を代々の撰集に見えたるを端々記し申すべきなり。それによりて歌の姿心申し述べ難しとてもことに仏道に通はし法文に寄せて申しなすことなり。

As in the other two passages quoted, here Shunzei uses the expressions *kayowasu* 通はす (to convey, to communicate) and *yosu* 寄す (to liken, to draw an analogy) to explain his use of Buddhist references for teaching *waka*. Through his insistence that he is incorporating scripture and commentary only as a pedagogic device, Shunzei makes it clear that he is by no means suggesting an identity or even equivalency between poetry and Buddhist practice. That notion would surface only toward the end of the thirteenth century in the collection *Shasekishū*. Instead, faced with the task of teaching subject matter that is hard to explain, he draws analogies to a field of knowledge that would have been familiar to his student, Princess Shokushi. A daughter of Emperor GoShirakawa 後白河 (1127–92, r. 1155–58), Shokushi was appointed in 1159 (that is, at the age of six) to the post of high priestess (*sai'in* 斎院) of Kamo Shrine, but ten years later she quit owing to illness and, while her father was still alive, took Buddhist vows. Her older brother, Prince Shukaku 守覚 (1150–1202), was both a priest at the Shingon-sect temple Ninnaji 仁和寺 and a scholar of *waka*.[116]

Given this family background, and the fact that Shokushi trained under Hōnen 法然 (1133–1212), the Tendai-educated founder of the Pure Land sect, it is safe to assume that she was abundantly familiar with the teachings of the *Móhē zhǐguān* (Shunzei refers to it simply as *Tendai shikan*). She was forty-five years old when Shunzei wrote *Korai fūteishō* for her, and the fact that he had included ten of her poems in *Senzaishū* suggests that he saw her both as a student and as a patron. The pairing of critical concepts from *waka* with Buddhist thought is a felicitous and auspicious find, but in the treatise, it serves ultimately as a practical, pedagogic analogy. As discussed earlier in this chapter, analogy played a key role in the work of Chōmei as well. Within ten years of the completion of *Korai fūteishō*, Chōmei would pepper his treatise *Mumyōshō* with analogies to the fields of court attire, court music, fabric design, and landscaping. That Chōmei chose secular analogies while Shunzei preferred sacred ones must be understood in connection with the differences between the patron-students for whom these two works were originally created.

The main focus of *Korai fūteishō* as a whole is the craft of *waka*. The discussion of *waka* poetics in light of *shikan* appears in only the first few paragraphs of the work. The rest is devoted to *waka* practice, which Shunzei regarded as a twofold process; consequently, he divided his treatise into two parts. In the first part, he addresses the legacy of centuries of composition and numerous generations of poets. Here, Shunzei discusses in detail the history of the compilation of the canonical anthologies, dividing it into the ancient (*jōko*, dominated by *Man'yōshū*), middle (*chūko*, up to *Shūishū*), and contemporary (*matsudai*) periods. He also offers a selection of exemplary poems from *Man'yōshū*, accompanied by cultural and linguistic commentary.[117] In this part of the work, *Korai fūteishō* reflects the philological influence of Shunzei's teacher, Mototoshi, who had done work on the annotation and interpretation of poems from *Man'yōshū*, and the scholarly approach of Toshiyori, whose treatise also contains detailed discussions of poems and their background—and often offers measured deliberations on the respective values of competing theories or explanations. Shunzei examines as well the work of earlier authors of rule books (*shiki*), treatises (*zuinō*), and lists of poetic expressions (*utamakura*), such as Fujiwara no Kintō, Priest Nōin, and Toshiyori.

The initial paragraphs of the first part of *Korai fūteishō* contain a few isolated forays into poetic prose, but as Shunzei takes stock of the field's history and accumulated knowledge, he maintains a measured and scholarly tone. By contrast, the second part opens with a spirited celebration of poetic language, written in paratactical prose and incorporating copious poetic expressions in a fast-moving journey through the four seasons. Shunzei follows this with a lengthy list of exemplary poems from the seven imperial anthologies, from Tsurayuki's *Kokinshū* to Shunzei's own *Senzaishū*. The poems are laid out in the same order in which they appear in the collections and thus reproduce the seasonal and topical arrangement that inspired the opening paragraphs of *Korai fūteishō*'s second part.

Shunzei does not discuss explicitly how the reader is to understand the relationship between these two dimensions of *waka*, the hermeneutical and the generative. If the first part of *Korai fūteishō* provides a conceptual framework and offers a research guide to bibliographic sources for the scholar interested in the history of *waka* as a linguistic and social practice, the second part facilitates the composition of new poems by providing archetypal examples for each established topic.[118] These two dimensions of *waka* practice are inseparable in previous treatises, part of an integrated, comprehensive approach to the transmission of knowledge about *waka*. By separating them into two distinct modules, Shunzei is suggesting that, however complementary, they reflect two different sets of attitudes, methodologies, and practices. *Korai fūteishō* covers both, but the two-part structure offers the possibility of transmitting only one of them to a patron-student while reserving the other for professionals.

During Shunzei's lifetime, a new group of patron-students emerged. Kiyosuke's main patrons had been emperors and top-ranking aristocrats. Although Shunzei and his heir, Teika, worked for aristocrats such as Shokushi, they sought the patronage of elite warrior families as well. Shunzei taught the powerful Taira no Kiyomori's younger brother Tadanori. Teika taught the third Kamakura shogun, Minamoto no Sanetomo. When Sanetomo was seventeen years old, Teika wrote for him the treatise *Kindai shūka*.[119] Among Teika's aristocratic students was Retired Emperor GoToba's son Prince Sonkai 尊快 (1204–46). When Sonkai was fifteen years old, Teika wrote for him the treatise *Eiga no taigai*.[120] Both *Kindai shūka* and *Eiga no taigai* are similar to the second part of *Korai fūteishō*, as they open with a few expository paragraphs but turn immediately to a long list of exemplary poems. In their brief prose sections, Teika briskly discusses conceptual and technical issues regarding the composition of poems. The lengthy, scholarly discussions that appear in the first part of Shunzei's *Korai fūteishō* are absent from both *Kindai shūka* and *Eiga no taigai*.

This suggests that in Teika's estimation, his students Sanetomo and Sonkai did not have to understand the history of *waka* to write good poems. Both men became successful court poets. Sonkai had a poem included by Teika's son Tameie in the tenth imperial anthology, *ShokuGosen wakashū* (*ShokuGosenshū* 続後撰集 [Later collection, continued], 1251), and another in the eleventh, *ShokuKokin wakashū* (*ShokuKokinshū* 続古今集 [Collection of poems ancient and modern, continued], 1265); one more appears in *ShokuShūi wakashū* (*ShokuShūishū* 続拾遺集 [Collection of gleanings, continued], 1278), the twelfth imperial collection, compiled by Tameie's son Tameuji. Sanetomo had twenty-five of his poems included by Teika in *ShinChokusenshū*, the ninth imperial compilation; more than sixty appear in subsequent collections. He also left an anthology of his poems: *Kinkaishū* 金槐集 (Collection of the Kamakura Minister of the Right, 1213). Neither student had intended to start his own household of *waka* specialists, and the training that Teika gave them reflected that expectation.

As in *Korai fūteishō*, Teika keeps narrative to a minimum in his treatises for patron-students, since the emphasis is not on contextual knowledge (as it had been in the case of Toshiyori and Chōmei), but on how such knowledge has been referenced in the poems of the past. For this purpose, lists of poems suffice. In an extreme version of this pedagogic approach, the treatise *Teika jittei*, attributed to Teika but now considered likely to be the work of a later poet, consists of a selection of poems grouped to illustrate ten different approaches to composition, without any commentary.[121] If *Teika jittei* is indeed not by Teika, it stands as a useful illustration of how the Mikohidari template of instruction was so influential that it was adopted to give a later work the appearance of legitimacy. Something similar happens with *Maigetsushō*, which takes the shape of a letter sent to a student when returning a list of practice poems that the student prepared for the instructor to mark.[122] That poet has been interpreted to be either Sanetomo or Fujiwara no Ieyoshi 藤原家良 (Kinugasa Ieyoshi 衣笠家良, 1192–1264), another of Teika's students. While this treatise has also been traditionally attributed to Teika, several modern scholars have argued otherwise.[123] Shunzei's and Teika's tendency to forgo narrative is reflected in passages of *Maigetsushō* where events of the past that Toshiyori or Kiyosuke would have told of in full, colorful detail appear instead in schematic summaries from which all nonessential information has been omitted. As an illustration, consider the death of Nagatō, which, as discussed earlier, receives ample space and careful attention in *Toshiyori zuinō* and *Fukurozōshi*, and which *Maigetsushō* recounts simply as, "I heard of a man who, after receiving strong criticism, died of distress."[124] As with *Teika jittei*, *Maigetsushō* is a testament to the eminence of the perceived style of a house's pedagogy.

Teika's leading role in the compilation for GoToba of the eighth imperial anthology, *ShinKokinshū*, and his single-handed compilation of the ninth, *ShinChokusenshū*, for Emperor GoHorikawa 後堀河 (1212–34, r. 1221–32) further strengthened the prestige that the Mikohidari had earned under Shunzei.[125] Teika's son Tameie succeeded him as head of the household in 1241, and was soon successful in obtaining patronage through instruction and in earning an imperial commission to compile an official *waka* anthology (and a few years later, another one). The treatises that Tameie created for his students include *Eiga no ittei*.[126] This is an introductory handbook that covers the basic attitudes and techniques of composition in a schematic way. The work's simple structure and elementary content suggest that it was intended to be presented to a patron-student in the relatively early stages of the pedagogic relationship. In it, Tameie follows his household's established custom of avoiding narrative. He lays out the treatise as a series of brief expository commentaries interspersed with exemplary poems. As in the extant treatises by Teika, the emphasis is on the composition of poems rather than on the comprehensive mastery of the field of *waka* practice.

The treatises of the twelfth century are marked by their incorporation of comprehensive cultural knowledge, ranging from history to linguistics to court life and provincial customs, into *waka* instruction, and by the supplementation of this knowledge with lessons specific to the needs of patron-students and future experts who would be in their employ. For this reason, the treatises contain narrative passages that recount events of the court from the very recent past. In *Toshiyori zuinō*, written by Minamoto no Toshiyori for the daughter of a patron, these events are usually simple, everyday interactions between poets that illustrate for the student the general social skills expected of a court poet. In *Fukurozōshi*, created by Fujiwara no Kiyosuke, the head of the Rokujō poetry household, to educate a capable heir to succeed him, many anecdotes focus on the new, specific challenges and duties of the professional *waka* specialist. Similarly, it features the procedural knowledge required to perform the public functions expected of the head of a house, such as organizing and judging carefully orchestrated formal poetry contests. This professional and procedural knowledge is absent from the extant treatises of the Mikohidari, which, like *Toshiyori zuinō*, were created for patron-students instead of for professionals.

Toshiyori was just as invested in teaching poetics and poetic language as were Fujiwara no Shunzei and his son and grandson, Teika and Tameie, but in *Toshiyori zuinō*, he combines technical advice and exemplary poems with an interest in cultural knowledge that extends beyond its representation in the poems. Toshiyori uses brief anecdotes to provide information about fields such as history and geography, as well as about the way poems were deployed socially in a context where etiquette and social skills were of great importance. In *Fukurozōshi*, Kiyosuke also relies extensively on brief narrative passages to convey the knowledge necessary for the professional *waka* poet. The later treatises of the rival Mikohidari house moved against this precedent. They emphasize lists of exemplary poems and dispense with any cultural context for them. Teika summed up this new approach in the very brief preface to his treatise *Eiga no taigai*—which is fundamentally a curated list of poems—by writing, "In *waka* poetry, there are no instructors. We simply make old poems into our teachers. If they take the gist [*kokoro*] of the styles of old and learn from the words [*kotoba*] of those who came before, who would be unable to create poems?"[127]

The emergence of the Mikohidari treatise—streamlined, cleansed of extraneous information, reliant almost exclusively on model poems—can be understood as analogous to a process of speciation. In the life sciences, speciation refers to a gradual process of differentiation, in which initially small differences coexist with major commonalities. Even if the limited number of extant texts makes this analogy only partially justified, we can say that in the case of poetry treatises, this process started with Toshiyori's comprehensive pedagogic approach. He liberally combined brief narrative passages with expository passages. Kiyosuke included narrative passages in *Fukurozōshi*, as did Kamo no Chōmei in *Mumyōshō*, but they had different intended readers and produced different texts. In an earlier treatise, *Ōgishō*, Kiyosuke had tentatively used narrative to explicate some poems, but this work is by and large a series of commentaries on a long list of poems.[128] This is an approach that another Rokujō poet, Kenjō, took even further in *Shūchūshō*, which focuses on clarifying difficult poetic expressions.[129] In his primer *Waka shogakushō* 和歌初学抄 (First studies in *waka*, 1169), Kiyosuke provides an introduction to poetic expressions, poetic places, and traditional themes, together with examples of poetic precedents from *Man'yōshū*, the imperial anthologies, and the poem-tale *Ise monogatari*. *Ōgishō* and *Waka shogakushō* represent the philology that modern scholars commonly associate with the Rokujō house, but Teika adopts a similar philological focus in *Kenchū mikkan* 顕注密勘 (Secret inquiry into Kenjō's Commentary, 1221), his subcommentary to Kenjō's *Kokinshū chū* 古今集註 (Commentary on *Kokinshū*, 1191).[130] Each of these treatises emphasizes different aspects of *waka* knowledge, sometimes overlapping with one another and sometimes veering away.

Driving this process of speciation was the role of treatises in pedagogic relationships. This is encapsulated in the notion of artifacts of practice, which calls attention to the ways in which poems and treatises had not just literary uses but also very specific practical ones. Created to address the practical needs of both beginning and advanced students, each treatise reflects the interests, knowledge, and linguistic competence of its specific intended reader. The treatises of the twelfth century, along with the professional poets who created them and the poetry households that organized—and limited—their circulation, were shaped by competing attempts to respond to those needs. Taken together, the works reveal how *waka* specialists experimented to expand the affordances of their writings. And they show how, toward the end of the century, the newly dominant Mikohidari house, led by Shunzei and Teika, limited the type and amount of information that it would make available to students, with the effect of both streamlining and restraining the use of *waka* as a vehicle for the transmission of other types of knowledge. The contexts in which this affordance of *waka* survived, in genres other than the poetry treatise, are the focus of the next chapter.

CHAPTER TWO

The Powers of *Waka*

The non-elite warriors of early medieval Japan engaged with *waka* in ways that differed not only from those of aristocrats but also from those of the upper echelons of the emerging warrior class. The elite members of the Minamoto and Hōjō households—like the aristocratic poets and instructors they emulated and from whom they learned—polished their creations and engaged in poetry contests with a view to having their poems included in imperially sanctioned anthologies. The many retainers, clerks, and personal secretaries serving them, by contrast, did not have access to poetry contests, and their poems were not usually considered for inclusion in imperial anthologies. They sought knowledge of *waka* primarily for its connection with the culture of the court and the aristocracy. Consequently, works that discussed *waka* for non-elite warriors tended to refrain from offering instruction on composition, and instead covered what we could call the cultural life of poetry.

In this chapter I examine three early medieval texts that discuss *waka* poetry (but do not focus primarily on it) to make the argument that close analysis reveals they were aimed at a readership of midlevel warriors. This analysis faces a number of obstacles that were, luckily, absent from the examination of late classical treatises, such as *Toshiyori zuinō* 俊頼髄脳 (Toshiyori's essentials of poetry, 1111–14) and *Fukurozōshi* 袋草紙 (Bag book, 1159), in chapter 1. First, the authors of the earlier period were aristocrats about whom we have court records, mentions in private diaries, and cameos in historical (and semihistorical) narratives. We also can rely on detailed evidence of their poetic activity from personal and official anthologies (some of which they themselves compiled), as well as from the proceedings of poetry contests (of which they sometimes served as judges). This wealth of documentation is not available for most of the authors discussed in this chapter. What little we know about them is thanks only to painstaking research, cross-checking of obscure sources, and educated guesses. In one crucial case, the name of the author is still a mystery. Second, we know the identity of the patrons and students for whom those poetry treatises were written (that is, their intended readers or *primary* layer of circulation or *inception*), as well as the groups among whom they were soon read and cited (their *secondary* layer of circulation, or *dissemination*). All of the readers were aristocrats or elite warriors, about whom, again, we have detailed historical records. This information is not available for nonelite warrior readers. Analyzing the works created for them calls for a different methodological approach.

This scarcity of external information is compounded by the derivative nature of the texts, which borrow extensively from preexisting works, such as poetic treatises of the previous period. The borrowing follows the pattern described in the introduction as *diffusion* (a *tertiary* layer of circulation). In this process, the borrowed material is severed from its original rhetorical framework and recontextualized within a new frame, allowing it to serve new functions for new audiences (what I refer to as its *reaffordance*). Unlike instances of *replacement*, which also reimagine a work for a new audience, sometimes through new media, but preserve the coherence and identity of the original work, diffusion involves an inherent degree of fragmentation. This fragmentation and subsequent reaggregation characterize early medieval collections of brief narrative texts.

In this chapter I look at three voluminous collections of brief narratives: *Kokonchomonjū* 古今著聞集 (Collection of tales written and heard in the past and present, 1254), compiled by an obscure aristocrat named Tachibana no Narisue 橘成季 (ca. 1205–before 1273); *Jikkinshō* 十訓抄 (Ten-lesson digest, 1252), compiled anonymously, arguably by a peer or an acquaintance of Narisue; and *Shasekishū* 沙石集 (Collection of sand and pebbles, 1283), compiled by a priest of warrior lineage known as Mujū Dōgyō 無住道暁 and, in some sources, as

Ichien 一円 (1226–1312).[1] All three collections are collations of brief narrative passages from preexisting works. Although no passage is explicitly attributed or cited, it is evident that *Toshiyori zuinō* and *Fukurozōshi* were among the sources. In line with their derivative approach, the medieval collections obtain their rhetorical force from the way they frame preexisting content through editorial prefaces, organize it into different chapters, and lay it out in specific and starkly different configurations. My methodological approach relies on an analysis of these rhetorical strategies, which vary substantively from text to text.[2] The aim of this analysis is to provide a rare glimpse of the very first moments of the (hitherto unexplored) engagement of non-elite warriors with the aristocracy, with poetry, and with the culture of the court at large.

The Powers of Early Medieval *Waka*

Before we begin the analysis proper, it might be useful to summarize my findings. Beyond their remarkable differences, and the fact that *waka* is not their primary focus, *Kokonchomonjū*, *Jikkinshō*, and *Shasekishū* coincide in presenting the poetry of the court as a practice that was available to and appropriate for persons in other social spaces, from elite warriors to non-elite warriors to Buddhist monastics. What brought these spaces together was the capacity of *waka* to serve as a shared emotional language available and intelligible to persons regardless of their lineage or experience, provided they were familiar with the culture of the court and the aristocracy. The three collections restate or endorse the view that *waka* originated as the language of the gods of Japan—*Shasekishū*, in particular, emphasizes its universality and finds parallels in Indic and Sinitic practices—and narrate how poems were created, circulated, and discussed among elite practitioners almost exclusively. This allows us to revisit a thorny and confusing feature of medieval writing about *waka*: the insistence that *waka* has a special potency (*toku* 徳) that translates into social, material, and spiritual benefits for poets.[3] In contrast to modern scholarship that has approached this potency as a predominantly religious phenomenon (that is, as a form of incantation), an examination of the different narrative instances reveals that in the vast majority of cases, a poem is offered by someone of lower status to someone of higher status. Drawing from affect theory and performance studies, we can interpret these narratives as assertions of a social value of *waka* as a shared emotional language capable of mediating or negotiating differences in power.

The following episode illustrates these points. Because accounts of non-elite warriors composing and reciting poems are extremely rare, this passage is of interest also for the social background of its protagonist. It appears with small variations in all three collections. Here it is in the *Jikkinshō* version:

> When a warrior had first introduced himself at the residence of the Hanazono minister, he had stated in the front matter of his application, "Skills: Composition of *waka* poems."
>
> At the beginning of autumn, the minister was in the Southern Hall, and as he was fond of the cries of the *hataori* grasshoppers, toward dusk he ordered, "Put down the lattice, and have the people come!"
>
> He was told, "The chamberlains of the fifth rank are all away. Not one man is serving."
>
> Since that warrior was around, turning to him he said, "Then you put them down, boy." And, as he approached, "You said you were good at poems, no?" Then, when he was respectfully lowering the blinds, "Can you hear these grasshoppers? Compose us a poem."
>
> He began to recite the first line, "Leafy green willows . . ."[4] But the ladies-in-waiting in attendance burst out laughing—perhaps because they thought that the poem did not match the season.
>
> "What sense is there in laughing before hearing the whole poem?" remonstrated the minister. And added, "Say it quickly!"
>
> | | |
> |---|---|
> | *aoyagi no* | Leafy green willows |
> | *midori no ito wo* | like verdant strings of yarn |
> | *kurikae-shi* | stretched out |
> | *natsu he-te aki zo* | through the summer and into the autumn: |
> | *hataori wa naku* | Thus sing the grasshoppers. |
>
> He recited this poem, and the minister had a robe with a bush clover design brought out and given to him.[5]

花園大臣の御許にはじめて参りたる侍の名簿の端書に能は歌よみと書きたりけり。殿の秋の初めに南殿に出でて機織の鳴くを愛しておはしけるに暮れければ下格子に人参れと仰せられける。蔵人の五位たがひて人も候はぬと申してこの侍の参りたるをただおのれ下ろせとありければ参りたるに汝は歌よみとなとありければかしこまりて格子下ろしさして候ふにこの機織をば聞くや一首つかまつれと仰せられければ青柳のと五文字を出したるを候ひける女房たち折に合はずと思ひたりげにて笑ひ出でたりけるをものを聞きはてず笑ふやうやあると仰せられてとくつかまつれと仰せられければ青柳の緑の糸をくりかへし夏へて秋ぞ機織は鳴くとよみたりければ萩織りたる直垂を押し出してたまはせてけり。

In this episode, a mid-rank warrior who is serving in a powerful household composes a poem on command and receives a reward.[6] His employer, the "Hanazono minister," is Minamoto no Arihito 源有仁 (1103–47), minister of the left, who was an expert in court etiquette and precedent, Sinitic prose and poetry, *waka*, and calligraphy. When the ladies in attendance laugh at the warrior, he faces public humiliation in a situation analogous to the ruthless public challenges between professional specialists in connection with proof poems.[7] He rallies with a technically accomplished poem, sophisticated perhaps to the point of exaggeration—a tendency to hyperbole being another salient feature of early medieval writing about *waka*—but this actually makes narrative sense as a way to underscore the ladies' derision.[8] The minister's reaction, the granting of a material reward, is also typical of these narratives in which the figure of authority displays a form of emotion or affect.

Elite Poetic Practice in Early Medieval Japan

During the early medieval period, the two most powerful households, the Minamoto and the Hōjō, enjoyed direct access to the court and engaged in the traditional prerogatives of the hitherto ruling aristocratic families—the imperial household and the northern branch of the Fujiwara.[9] Among these privileges were the sponsorship of lavish cultural activities—such as banquets, poetry contests, and musical performances—as well as the building of temples and shrines.[10] Elite warriors of the time practiced *waka* alongside elite aristocrats, and their practice was similarly shaped by changes to *waka* practice during the twelfth century—the shift from social poetry to topical composition and the rivalries between lineages of hereditary professional specialists.[11] The activities of their elite literary salons and circles has been the exclusive focus of research conducted on medieval Japanese poetry, such as Ogawa Takeo's *Bushi wa naze uta wo yomu ka: Kamakura shōgun kara sengoku daimyō made* (Why do warriors recite poems? From Kamakura's shoguns to Warring States' lords). In his discussion of early medieval poetics, Ogawa shows, for example, that the activity of elite warrior poets had a direct impact on the themes and treatment considered appropriate in the most canonical genre of *waka*, the imperial anthology.[12]

Among the changes identified by Ogawa is a reassessment of the poetic topography of the realm. For centuries, *waka* had reflected the aristocratic culture centered on the five central provinces.[13] From this point of view, the eastern provinces were remote and rustic territories.[14] The following anonymous poem from *Kokin wakashū* (*Kokinshū* 古今集 [Collection of poems ancient and modern], 905) illustrates this conception of the eastern territories as distant and isolated:

kahi ga ne wo	Through the peaks of Kai Province
ne koshi yama koshi	over mountains and over peaks
fuku kaze wo	blows the wind:
hito ni mogamo ya	Wish it were a person
kotozute yaramu	that I could entrust with a message.[15]

かひかねをねこし山こし吹く風を人にもがもや事つてやらむ

In this poem, the wind blowing toward the east from the capital (modern Kyoto) and across mountain ranges foregrounds the remoteness of Kai Province (present-day Yamanashi Prefecture). The poem combines two established poetic conventions: the insurmountable obstacles to communication that is common in poems of longing, or unrequited love (*koi uta* 恋歌), and the emphasis on physical distance that is a feature of travel poems (*kiryo-ka* 羈旅歌).[16] A poem composed more than three centuries later, in the middle of the Kamakura period, similarly assumes the capital as the center of reference, but now the eastern provinces appear in a different role:

ahusaka ya	At Ōsaka
seki no to akete	opening the mountain checkpoint
tori no naku	the birds are singing:
azuma yori koso	It is from the east
haru wa kinikere	that spring has come.[17]

逢坂や関の戸あけて鳥のなく東よりこそ春はきにけれ

The Ōsaka checkpoint was located in the mountains immediately east of the capital, on the boundary between Yamashiro and Ōmi Provinces. In the poetic tradition, it symbolized the beginning of the long road that led to the eastern provinces. Since ōsaka (written *ahusaka*) could mean "hill of encounter," as it included the sounds *ahu* (to meet), over the centuries aristocrats had mentioned this checkpoint in love and travel poems. While in the poem from *Kokinshū* the wind is blowing from the capital toward the east, the wind in the later poem is blowing from the east and moving westward across the checkpoint and into the capital, to bring home the long-awaited spring.[18]

This second poem was composed by Prince Munetaka 宗尊 (1242–74), the eldest son of Emperor GoSaga 後嵯峨 (1220–72, r. 1242–46). Ogawa argues that this poem is representative of the process of development of the first poetry salon in the eastern city of Kamakura. In 1252, the shogunal regent, Hōjō Tokiyori 北条時頼 (1227–63), chose the ten-year-old Munetaka to serve as the sixth Kamakura shogun. As befitted an imperial prince, Munetaka had received a standard elite *waka* education from Shinkan 真観 (Fujiwara no Mitsutoshi 藤原光俊, 1203–76), a student of Fujiwara no Teika, who later served as one of the compilers of *ShokuKokin wakashū* (*ShokuKokinshū* 続古今集 [Collection of poems ancient and modern, continued], 1265). GoSaga had presided over a renaissance of aristocratic culture in the capital, hosting numerous banquets with poetry, music, and kickball (*kemari* 蹴鞠). Munetaka took the same approach during his stay in Kamakura, establishing and leading a group of practitioners of courtly disciplines. Their practice of *waka* centered on topical composition for highly structured and performative poetry gatherings and contests.[19] Ogawa's research succeeded in shifting scholarly attention away from poetic technique and moving it toward a consideration of medieval *waka* as a social practice. Moreover, GoSaga and Munetaka were influential figures in the salons that guided elite culture precisely at the time *Kokonchomonjū*, *Jikkinshō*, and *Shasekishū* were created. In my analysis I aim to complement Ogawa's by exploring works that carried knowledge about the practice of *waka* to an audience that did not belong to the grand aristocratic and military elites.

Readers and Writers in Early Medieval Japan

The Emergence of a New Readership

The first step in an exploration of how non-elite practitioners began to engage with *waka*, aristocrats, and court culture in early medieval Japan is determining the makeup and internal heterogeneity of this social group. During the late classical period, the capital was socially and culturally diverse. At the top were the heads of powerful aristocratic households, including the imperial family, and the aristocratic head priests of powerful temples.[20] Serving them was a tier of lower-rank aristocrats, among them administrative clerks (*ietsukasa* or *keishi* 家司), who dealt with bureaucratic matters, and personal guards (*musha* 武者), who provided security. The main distinction within the aristocracy was between the upper nobility (*kugyō* 公卿), about two dozen men of the first three ranks, and the lower nobility (*tenjōbito* 殿上人), up to a hundred men of the fourth, fifth, and sixth ranks who had permission to enter the court (*seiryōden* 清涼殿) but no real political influence. This lower tier included the resident provincial administrators (*zuryō* 受領), who traveled to the provinces as deputy governors to oversee administrative activities in lieu of the slightly higher-level *yōnin* 遥任, the holders of the office of provincial governor (*kami* 守), who often stayed behind in the capital.

In the capital, too, lived people whom we would call urban commoners. They were young retainers serving in powerful households, staff at shrines (*kamibito* 神人), artisans, and merchants. Below them were peasants who had recently arrived from the provinces. The populace also included mendicant traveling Buddhist priests (*hijiri* 聖), musicians, dancers, and other artistic performers, as well as outcasts (*hinin* 非人). Finally, the most recent additions to the urban population were provincial warriors. Starting in the late Heian period, warriors from the provinces traveled to the capital to serve as a police force. Organized under the Ōbanyaku 大番役 (Office of Watchmen), these security guards (*ōbanshū* 大番衆) provided protection for the imperial palace, the residences of retired emperors, and other official facilities. They worked under a system of alternate service, in which longer-serving members rotated out, so this police force was always partially manned by men who had only recently arrived in the capital.

The number of provincial warriors in the capital increased significantly from the late twelfth through the thirteenth century. When the Genpei War (1180–85) between the Minamoto and Taira warrior households ended with the establishment of a warrior government (*bakufu* 幕府) in Kamakura, the first Kamakura shogun, Minamoto no Yoritomo 源頼朝 (1147–99, r. 1192–99), strategically left the imperial court bureaucracy in place in the capital.[21] Three decades later, after the failure of the Jōkyū Disturbance (1221) led by Retired Emperor GoToba 後鳥羽 (1180–1239, r. 1183–98), the *bakufu* again let the imperial bureaucracy survive and retain administrative functions.[22] This time, however, to keep a close eye on the court, a stronger warrior presence was instituted in the form of a branch office of the *bakufu* government in Rokuhara 六波羅 (in the southeast of the capital). At the head of the Rokuhara office were two shogunal deputies (*tandai* 探題), always chosen from among the male members of the Hōjō clan. The office was staffed by men connected to the *bakufu* who served administrative, policing, and military functions. As Ishii Susumu has argued, while this office was a social space exclusive to warriors from the eastern provinces, its functions, in particular that of providing security, brought its staff into constant and close contact with the other residents of the capital at all levels.[23]

The structure of society outside the capital was changing as well. The efficacy of the new bureaucracy developed by the Minamoto and

Hōjō in Kamakura depended on its ability to keep its stakeholders under control and to exert influence over faraway territories. In response to these circumstances, the central *bakufu* regime turned to a system of clientelism, converting the men who had fought on its side during the Genpei War into hereditary vassals (*gokenin* 御家人) and thus direct retainers of the shogun. These men, a couple thousand residents of the eastern provinces, were made eligible for two new offices. One was estate steward (*jitō* 地頭), or administrator of land. The land the stewards were appointed to control could be private estates (*shōen* 荘園) that belonged to absentee landlords (holders of transferrable rights to revenue, known as *shiki* 織), such as aristocratic households or Buddhist temples, or they could be public lands (*kokugaryō* 国衙領) that were the property of the imperial state.[24] The appointment of a *jitō* did not lead to a change in ownership, but since *jitō* were accountable to the *bakufu*, not the court, this progressively shifted to Kamakura some control over the revenue produced by land owned by aristocratic institutions. The other new office was military governor (*shugo* 守護). Replicating the model of the traditional absentee provincial governors (*kuni no kami* or *kokushu* 国守) and their *zuryō* deputies appointed by the court, the *shugo* usually did not reside in their assigned provinces but governed through deputy governors (*shugodai* 守護代). Although *shugo* appointments were not hereditary, they tended to be granted to *gokenin* loyal to the Hōjō family, and they involved responsibility over the *gokenin* living in the province. It was through these two new offices that the *bakufu* controlled and rewarded its *gokenin* stakeholders.

Hereditary vassals were not the only warriors who were active during the Kamakura period. In his examination of the efforts by Emperor GoDaigo (1288–1339, r. 1318–39) in the late summer of 1333 to restore imperial rule, Andrew Goble has proposed that we must understand "warrior" as a category that was not necessarily connected to military activity or the agenda of the Kamakura *bakufu*.[25] Rather, Goble emphasizes that, throughout the medieval period, men accustomed to bearing weapons engaged in a variety of occupations, in areas from commerce to scholarship to land management.[26] As Goble points out, moreover, many warrior clans lacked a direct association with the *bakufu* and often saw in the Kamakura administration a continuation of the oligarchic government by aristocratic elites.

Warriors who were unaffiliated with the *bakufu* tended to organize themselves into networks. As Lorraine Harrington has shown, while the groups of free-floating warriors never coalesced into a rebel army, they could still destabilize the *bakufu*, counteract its policies, and ultimately disrupt its ability to exercise social control.[27] These bands of warriors usually were referred to in legal documents as *akutō* 悪党 (evil bands). As Morten Oxenboell discusses, while this term had existed before, it came to be used more frequently between the mid-thirteenth and mid-fourteenth centuries, when it appeared widely in legal disputes that requested the intervention of the *bakufu* in conflicts between absentee proprietors and an estate's residents.[28] In these documents, the term *akutō* was often used derogatorily, as part of a rhetorical strategy to persuade the *bakufu* to intervene against unaffiliated warriors. Both Harrington and Oxenboell emphasize that the bands that were generally labeled *akutō* by their rivals were generally very diverse in their regional and social composition.

Another group of men who took to bearing arms in their occupations were lower-ranking aristocrats. They were, for the most part, men of the *zuryō* class. As Karl Friday points out, these men belonged to three traditional families: the Seiwa Genji 清和源氏 (bearing Minamoto surnames), the Kanmu Heishi 桓武平氏 (bearing Taira surnames), and the northern Fujiwara (Fujiwara hokke 藤原北家). They regarded bearing arms as a vehicle for career advancement, providing security to more powerful aristocrats, whom they served as bodyguards, and serving as a police force in the capital and the provinces in exchange for support in securing office and rank appointments.[29] By the early eleventh century, *zuryō* had entered into alliances with nonaristocratic local warriors in the provinces to which they were posted as a way to gain military power and better perform their duties on behalf of their patrons. The local warriors saw in the *zuryō* a way to obtain access to the court and, through this gateway, perhaps to gain the patronage of aristocrats who were more powerful than the *zuryō*.[30]

The great diversity of warriors who were active during the Kamakura period—the *gokenin*, the nonaffiliated so-called *akutō*, and the *zuryō*—can be theorized in a number of ways. One approach is to place them in the context of a process of privatization (the economic approach). Friday has argued that since the middle of the tenth century, as part of a general tendency to have key government functions performed through private channels, public conscription and training had given way to an arrangement by which policing and soldiering became more and more the responsibility of private individuals.[31] In this sense, we can speak of warriors as a professional group. Since private-client arrangements tended to be hereditary, warriors can also be looked at in terms of lineage (the diachronic approach). In addition, since individual warriors tended to join wider networks, it is possible to examine warriors as a primarily collective phenomenon (the synchronic approach), in which warrior activity is inseparable from community making. Finally, we must consider warriors in terms of their cultural literacy (the sociological approach). A trait common to nonaristocratic, non-elite warriors—that is, the *gokenin* and the *akutō*—was the need to learn how to interact successfully with aristocrats (*zuryō* and others).

The production and circulation of *Kokonchomonjū*, *Jikkinshō*, and *Shasekishū* can be understood as a response to this need. Contact with aristocrats and the court bureaucracy could be a source of both friction and gain for the non-elite warriors of the Kamakura period. As Hongō Keiko has argued, the *bakufu* was never able to govern the land without recourse to the bureaucratic structure (*kan'i* 官位; literally, "rank and office") controlled by the court and the system of rules and formal etiquette (*girei* 儀礼) that the bureaucracy embodied. Even the most politically powerful *gokenin* found they needed to apply to the court for rank and office appointments in order to be able to govern efficaciously.[32] Similarly, in a context marked by land disputes and legal challenges, the ultimate success of less powerful *gokenin*, as well as of the *akutō*, often depended on their interactions with two legal systems: one run by aristocrats in the capital, and the other built in Kamakura and modeled in many respects after the precedent set at the court.

These circumstances required from warriors the ability to anticipate the expectations, prejudices, and habits of aristocrats. The aristocrats to whom mid-rank warriors had the most immediate access were at the *zuryō* level, employed as clerks and police at court and in powerful aristocratic households, and as deputy governors and military officials in the provinces. Warriors and *zuryō* sometimes found themselves at cross-purposes, but it was mainly from the *zuryō* that non-elite warriors were able to acquire the cultural literacy needed to engage with the aristocracy, its institutions, and its traditions.

Editors as Points of Contact between Social Spaces

The creator of *Kokonchomonjū* signed the name Tachibana no Narisue at the end of that work, next to a Sinitic expression that was conventionally applied to courtiers of the junior fifth rank, upper grade.[33] He was, in other words, a *zuryō*-level aristocrat. Narisue studied the biwa under Fujiwara no Takatoki 藤原孝時 (Hōshinbō Takatoki 法深房孝時), a chamberlain like his father, Fujiwara no Takamichi 孝道.[34] And he learned *waka* from Takasuke 隆祐 (n.d.), the son of Fujiwara no Ietaka 藤原家隆 (1158–1237).[35] Narisue is an otherwise elusive figure, but luckily scholars such as Ōmori Shirō, Nakajima Etsuji, Nagazumi Yasuaki, and Nishio Kōichi have collated external sources and references to create a relatively rounded picture of his life.[36] A key finding is that throughout his life, Narisue had contact with not only elite warriors but also the kind of non-elite warriors I have described. He was, in other words, uniquely positioned to serve as a channel between two social spaces that until then had been unconnected.

The image we have of Narisue is that of a middle-rank aristocrat who had direct access to the imperial court and its everyday workings. Born around 1205 into the Tachibana family, he enjoyed a noble lineage but lacked real political clout, and he was never appointed to a prominent office or granted high rank.[37] His highest office was captain of the Right Gate Guard (*uemon no jō* 右衛門尉), a third-tier position in the Right Gate Guard (Uemonfu 右衛門府), which secured the perimeter at the imperial palace. Realizing that he had little prospect of promotion at court, Narisue sought employment in the service of the powerful regent Kujō Michi'ie 九条道家 (1193–1252) from as early as 1230, while in his twenties.[38] Michi'ie's later political troubles, and his death when Narisue was in his forties, put an end to this patron-client relationship. It was during this period of uncertainty that Narisue produced *Kokonchomonjū*. He died in 1272, two decades later.[39]

To better understand Narisue's position at court and in service, it is helpful to consider that courtiers of the fifth rank who did not provide security in the Uemonfu or its counterpart, the Saemonfu 左衛門府 (Left Gate Guard), were usually appointed to the office of *kurōdo* 蔵人 (chamberlain). The chamberlains (eight in all) were officials of the fifth and sixth ranks; they worked in the chamberlains' office (*kurōdo-dokoro*) under the supervision of two heads of the office (*kurōdo no tō* 蔵人頭) and were assisted by many lower-level workers (*hikurōdo* 非蔵人 or *kurōdo no minarai* 蔵人の見習). The *kurōdo* had important administrative duties but no hope of promotion. Their bosses, the *kurōdo no tō*, could expect an appointment to *sangi* 参議 (imperial adviser) and a promotion to the third rank or even higher—that is, to the higher nobility. But a *kurōdo* of the fifth rank was usually appointed, at best, to the position of *ben* 弁 (controller) or *zuryō* and might attain at most—and often posthumously—the fourth rank. *Kurōdo* of the sixth rank were in an even harsher position and could expect to receive only the fifth rank. Regardless of whether their appointment was connected to military or civil service, or whether they had served in the provinces, these men are now usually referred to as members of the *zuryō* class, since they had similar or equivalent hierarchical positions and career prospects within the court system and thus tended to associate among themselves.

Narisue's relationship with Michi'ie was paradigmatic of the tensions and opportunities of the early medieval period.[40] Michi'ie was the head of a household that played a central role in the dual system that followed the founding of the shogunate.[41] On his father's side, Michi'ie was a scion of a lineage of powerful aristocrats; on his mother's side, he was related to Minamoto no Yoritomo, the first shogun.[42] His wife, similarly, was the daughter of an aristocrat who had sided with the *bakufu* in the Jōkyū Disturbance.[43] After the assassination of the third shogun, Sanetomo, Michi'ie was asked to send his third son, the two-year-old Mitora 三寅, to Kamakura to become the fourth shogun, under the name Yoritsune 頼経 (1218–56, r. 1226–44). Yoritsune's son Yoritsugu 頼嗣 (1239–56, r. 1244–52), born in Kamakura, would become the fifth shogun. In other words, the Kujō household was an ideal place of employment for a sophisticated *zuryō* like Narisue, as it was able to give him political backing, financial support, and cultural prestige. But Michi'ie soon lost his influence and, in 1252, died. The same year, the Hōjō accused Yoritsune of treason and forced Yoritsugu out of the office of shogun. Four years later, both father and son died, like Michi'ie, in adversity. Narisue's compilation of the monumental *Kokonchomonjū* can be interpreted, then, as an effort to engage a new network of patronage.[44]

A number of candidates have been proposed for the identity of the anonymous editor of *Jikkinshō*. The manuscript that is considered the most reliable, now held by the Imperial Household Agency, contains a colophon attributing it (from hearsay) to a person called Rokuhara Jirōzaemon Nyūdō 六波羅二臈左衛門入道 (the Lay Practitioner Jirōzaemon from Rokuhara).[45] There are competing theories about the identity of this person. Nagai Yoshinori identified him as Yuasa no Munenori 湯浅宗業 (b. 1195), a warrior from Kii Province (present-day Wakayama Prefecture) who was noted for his scholarship.[46] Inui Katsumi and Shimura Kunihiro, by contrast, identified him as Sugawara no Tamenaga 菅原為長 (1158–1246), a graduate of the Daigakuryō and the expert on court precedent, Sinitic writings, and *waka* who compiled the dictionary of characters *Jikyōshū* 字鏡集 (A mirror of characters, n.d.).[47] Gomi Fumihiko proposed instead Tamenaga's grandson Sugawara no Munenaga 菅原宗長 (n.d.).[48] Asami Kazuhiko argued for Gotō no Mototsuna 後藤基綱 (1181–1256), a powerful *gokenin* who served in roles such as security (*keibiishi* 検非違使), climbed to the fifth rank at court, and had direct access to the cultural salons of the early Kamakura shoguns.[49] Until further evidence is unearthed, the editor of *Jikkinshō* will remain anonymous. Nevertheless, a pattern emerges from these candidates: a man with knowledge of court culture, access to aristocratic circles, familiarity with Sinitic and vernacular scholarship, and direct connections with and investments in warrior circles.

We find a similarly liminal figure, with overlapping social networks and the ability to connect disparate social spaces, in Mujū Dōgyō, the compiler of *Shasekishū*. Mujū was the grandson of a powerful military leader, Kajiwara Kagetoki 梶原景時 (d. 1200).

Kagetoki was a member of a military household from Sagami Province (present-day Kanagawa Prefecture) in the east. He had earned the trust of Yoritomo in 1180 at the beginning of the Genpei War and gone on to become one of the first shogun's closest retainers. After the war, Kagetoki was elevated to high office and granted control of several provinces. Later, in the context of political tension with the Hōjō following the death of Yoritomo, Kagetoki left Kamakura to regroup before attempting to take the city. He died in battle in 1200 while on the way to Kamakura with his troops.

Kagetoki's grandson Mujū was born in Kamakura and raised by relatives in the provinces of Shimotsuke (Tochigi Prefecture today) and Hitachi (Ibaraki Prefecture). After taking Buddhist vows at the age of eighteen and becoming an unaffiliated monk (*tonsei* 遁世) at twenty-eight, he studied at Shingon and Tendai temples in Nara, in the capital, and in Kamakura. When he was thirty-seven years old, Mujū was appointed abbot (*jūshoku* 住職) of Chōboji Temple 長母寺 in Owari (present-day Nagoya). Chōboji had been founded in 1179 by the warrior leader Yamada Shigetada 山田重忠 (d. 1221) as a Tendai temple. Mujū transformed it into a Rinzai Zen temple, the Buddhist sect favored by the Kamakura warrior elites. Mujū stands out in the cultural landscape of early medieval Japan for the variety and detail of his writings. During his time at Chōboji, he produced a number of works that include depictions of the everyday lives of warriors and other commoners, among them *Shasekishū*; *Zōtanshū* 雑談集 (A collection of miscellaneous conversations, 1305), a ten-volume compilation of brief Buddhist narratives; and *Shōzaishū* 聖財集 (A collection of sacred assets, 1299), a more doctrinally oriented treatise on Buddhism in three volumes.

The Rhetorics of Derivative Writing

Early medieval collections of brief narratives were designed to be persuasive and impactful. This is not how they have been commonly interpreted in modern scholarship, however. They have been connected with an archival or a descriptive interest. About *Kokonchomonjū*, for example, Yoshiko Dykstra has written that "by recording stories and episodes about art, music, and poems, the compiler obviously wished to put on record the elegance of the aristocratic life that was rapidly disappearing."[50] Similarly, Ōsumi Kazuo has argued that *Kokonchomonjū* reveals a yearning for the restitution of the past glory of the court and an encyclopedic approach to its preservation.[51] The broad-ranging view adopted by the editor of *Jikkinshō* has led John Brownlee, for example, to write that it lacks any programmatic approach or ideology and is simply a "guide to making practical advantage in daily life, no more and no less."[52] Similarly, in Keller Kimbrough's reading, *Shasekishū* is an attempt to conceptualize *waka* "in the terms of medieval syncretic philosophy."[53] These scholars are correct: Narisue does adopt a nostalgic tone in his introduction to *Kokonchomonjū*; the topics of the ten lessons in *Jikkinshō* range from Buddhism to Confucianism to down-to-earth practicality; and in *Shasekishū* Mujū discusses Buddhist doctrine in the most technical and precise ways. But another, complementary, way to read these texts is revealed when we consider how they discuss *waka* at a time when interest in the practice was expanding and knowledge about *waka* was becoming crucially relevant to an ever-widening number of people.

The creation of a discourse on *waka* for a non-elite audience cannot be separated from the practice of transmitting knowledge about the imperial court and the aristocratic class. *Jikkinshō*, compiled anonymously, offers ten lessons for a young man considering employment in the service of a powerful figure; but throughout, it also constructs and argues for a new place for *waka* and court culture in society. Narisue's *Kokonchomonjū* is structured as an encyclopedia of court culture, yet careful analysis reveals beneath the veneer of erudition a similarly complex cultural project. *Shasekishū* is a treatise on Buddhism written by a priest of warrior extraction who was invested in showing that *waka* was compatible with doctrine, but the narrative material it repurposed from other works tells a more complicated story about the place of poetry in monastic life.

These three collections of brief narratives share a salient feature: the way they regard *waka*. This is significant, in particular, when considered relative to other established classical courtly practices, such as composing *shī* (poetry in the Chinese style) and performing music.[54] In *Kokonchomonjū*, we find 54 *shī* poems and 253 *waka* poems (a 1:5 ratio).[55] There are also 43 poems that look like *waka* but use nonstandard language or images—poems of the type called *haikai* 誹諧 (nonstandard verse) in *Kokinshū* and later known as *kyōka* 狂歌 (absurd poetry), as well as 15 verse-capping exchanges (today known as *tan-renga* 短連歌) and 3 "modern-style" songs (*imayō* 今様) of the kind Emperor GoShirakawa anthologized in *Ryōjin hishō* 梁塵秘抄 (Secret selections to make the dust on the beams move, after 1169).[56] This amounts to an average of about one *waka* or *waka*-related poem in every other episode.[57] In *Jikkinshō*, we find 144 *waka* and 74 *shī* (a 2:1 ratio) in about three hundred episodes.[58] In *Shasekishū*, there are about 200 *waka* and less than a handful of *shī*.[59] These aggregates and ratios speak to the important role of *waka* in these works. To understand the nature of their significance, we need to look at the way these collections frame, organize, and lay out the narratives about the poems that they incorporate from other texts.

Frames (Prefaces and Postfaces)

An "original assumptive authorial preface"—that is, a prefatory passage deemed authentic and assumed to have been included by the author—has two aims, according to Gérard Genette: to ensure that the text is read and that it is read properly.[60] Genette was writing about the nineteenth-century European book, but some of the elements that he identifies as structural to prefaces are helpful for our discussion of these early medieval collections of narratives. Many of the prefaces he analyzes discuss the inception of the work, its intended readership, its inscription within a genre, its general structure, and the meaning of its title, and sometimes they include a statement of intent.[61] Even when pretending to describe a set of circumstances or aims, the preface (or postface, as in *Kokonchomonjū*) is inevitably prescriptive.[62] Genette's analysis is particularly relevant for our discussion because the works we are considering consist, for the most part, of derivative material. Often, the same material (for example, the narrative about a warrior writing about "Leafy green willows" in the autumn) appears in all three collections, but we must read the material differently in each work. Key to this differential reading is what can be conceptualized as the "frame" (in the sense of "boundary," but also of "frame of reference") constructed in a preface or postface with the aim of giving new meaning to old narratives.

A good place to begin is Narisue's general preface to *Kokonchomonjū*, as it covers most of these points. To give a sense of the nature of this passage, I quote it in full:

> This *Chomonjū* [Collection of tales written and heard] is a successor to the Uji Major Counselor's skillful writings and comes in the wake of Governor General Ōe's lofty discussion. I was born to the great Tachibana lineage, and even when I look back on my unaccomplished incompetence, I have received training in the biwa from a wise master. By sheer chance, I got to learn the six techniques and the six pitches of musical performance. Painting is for me a hobby I merely dabble in. Every once in a while, it brings contentment to my heart for a day or an hour at a time. Ah, I feel how easy it is for excellent melodies to harmonize with the singing of the spring warbler under the [plum] blossoms and the cries of the autumn geese in front of the moon.[63] Refined emotions follow the ways of nature. All creation fulfills the actions of heaven. I believe that all this should be reflected by the painting brush. In this way, sometimes I join the musicians and secretly enjoy the music of the reign; at some other times, I commission painters to show the marvelous landscapes of antiquity. Perhaps since I started to have more leisure time, because of the years I have spent in retirement, I have come to think about these two [music and painting] and thus sought to explore many different affairs relating to them. I compiled them and organized them into thirty chapters, arranged them into twenty scrolls, and gave them the title *Kokonchomonjū*.
>
> Even though it is a work grand in conception but very haphazard in execution, to some extent it serves also as a faithful record of historical events. I have not consulted the Chinese classics and histories at all; this work was created from the manners and customs of the world. Its scope is the past and the present of Japan. It consists in gossip and rumors about events. Now, the ignorance and narrow-mindedness of its omissions and excesses are shameful. It invites the derision of those actually knowledgeable. Now I don't want to leave this tiny room at all. It will mistakenly be compared to the great works.
>
> The time is the middle of the Tenth Month of the sixth year of the Kenchō era [1254]. I, Useless-Throwaway-Timber Tachibana no Nan-En

> [Narisue], have willfully forced the young that surround me to put in writing this chaotic outline.[64]

> 夫著聞集者、宇縣亜相巧語之遺類、江家都督清談之余波也。余稟芳橘之種胤、顧瑮材之樗質、而琵琶者賢師之所傳也。儻辨六律六呂之調。圖畫者愚性之所好也。自養一日一時之心。於戲春鶯囀花下、秋雁之叫月前、暗感幽曲之易和。風流之随地勢、品物之叶天為、悉憶彩筆之可寫。繇茲或伴伶客、潜楽治世之雅音、或誂畫工、略呈振古之勝槩。蓋居多暇景以降、閑度徂年之故、據勘此両端、搜索其庶事。註緝為三十篇。編次二十巻。名曰古今著聞集。頗雖為狂簡、聊又兼實録。不敢窺漢家經史之中。有世風人俗之製矣。只今知日域古今之際、有街談巷説之諺焉。猶愧淺見寡聞之疎越。偏招博識宏達之盧胡。努不出蝸廬。謬比鴻寶。于時建長六年應鐘中旬。散木士橘南袁。愁課小童猥叙大較而已。

The wistful tone, the discussion of courtly pastimes, and the presentation of this collection as a work of leisure suggest that it is the product of nostalgia and an attempt at conservation. This, as noted, is how *Kokonchomonjū* has often been read by modern scholars. It is also possible to construe this preface as a performative display of professional legitimacy and competence. Narisue starts by inscribing his work within what we today conceptualize as a specific literary genre, which he delineates by citing well-known texts. One is by Minamoto no Takakuni 源隆国 (1004–77), *Uji dainagon monogatari* 宇治大納言物語 (A collection of tales from the Uji major counselor). This work is not extant, but we can get a sense of its character from *Uji shūi monogatari* 宇治拾遺物語 (A collection of tales from Uji, early thirteenth century), which was created as a continuation of or sequel to *Uji dainagon monogatari*. The other is *Gōdanshō* 江談抄 (A selection of Ōe no Masafusa's conversations), a record of oral teachings (*kikigaki* 聞書) by the specialist in Sinitic writings Ōe no Masafusa 大江匡房 (1041–1111). These two collections of brief narratives collate material presented as historically and factually accurate.[65] By connecting his own work to that of Takakuni and Masafusa, Narisue is it making clear that his collection contains narratives, but is not a work of speculation or fiction.

By the same gesture, Narisue presents himself as a member of a lineage of professional specialists. Both Takakuni and Masafusa descended from households of specialists in Sinitic writings and court protocol. Takakuni's paternal grandfather was Minamoto no Taka'akira 源高明 (914–82), the author of *Saikyūki* 西宮記 (Records of Lord Nishi-no-miya, n.d.), a precedent guide to the practices for official business at the court. Masafusa's paternal ancestors had been scholars of Sinitic learning for generations, as was his maternal grandfather, Tachibana no Takachika 橘孝親. These two authors, whom Narisue mentions at the very outset, are exemplary cases of individuals whose success at court was owed to knowledge and expertise. Takakuni had served as *kurōdo-no-tō* (head of the chamberlain's office) and then reached *gon-dainagon* 権大納言 (acting major counselor); Masafusa served as *kurōdo* and reached *gon-chūnagon* 権中納言 (acting middle counselor). Toward the end of the preface, Narisue adopts a self-effacing tone, as is customary in prefaces and interactions among aristocrats. This is phatic, however, and should not distract us from the compiler's carefully crafted self-presentation as a competent and legitimate specialist in court culture.

Texts produced by specialists during the twelfth and thirteenth centuries were often closely guarded. This was particularly important for documents produced for reference and the education of younger scholars. One such example is Fujiwara no Kiyosuke's *Fukurozōshi*, a compendium of knowledge useful to professional *waka* specialists that the Rokujō household passed down, expanded, and amended, while attempting to restrict any wider circulation in the face of demands from powerful patrons (as discussed in chapter 1). In a postface to *Kokonchomonjū*, Narisue presents his work in a similar way:

> To begin with, this collection is not to be shown to other people. If one of my descendants violated this mandate and exposed this work to outsiders, then he cannot consider himself my descendant. The guardian-god of our family will surely add further punishment. However, permission should be decided on a case-by-case basis. The circumstances must be considered. Closest acquaintances and intimate friends should occasionally be allowed to see it.[66]

> そもそもこの集においては他見をゆるすべからず。若し子孫の中にこの鑑誡をそむきて閫外にいだすものあれば我が子孫たるべからず。氏の明神かならず照罰を加へ給ふべきものなり。但し人によりて許否あるべし。事にしたが

ひて思惟をいだすべし。繊芥のへだてなく等閑の儀あさからざらむには聞これをゆるすべし。

Narisue's strict injunction against allowing the text to be circulated is followed by a pragmatic acknowledgment that some form of dissemination may be necessary. Narisue himself took steps to raise public awareness of his new work, as is evident in the postface, where he records the details of a banquet that he offered to celebrate the completion of the work. Narisue mentions that the party "was modeled after completion banquets," likely meaning those given for imperial anthologies of *waka*.[67] This lavish event, held in the winter of 1254, involved the performance of *shī*, *waka*, and music and the making of offerings in front of images of the *Man'yōshū*-era *waka* poet Kakinomoto no Hitomaro 柿本人麻呂 (662–710), the Tang dynasty poet Bái Jūyì 白居易 (772–846), and the Tang dynasty biwa master Lián Chéng Wǔ 廉承武 (Jp. Renshōbu), as well as readings from *Kokonchomonjū* and toasts.[68] This combination of secrecy, pragmatism, and publicity—all three, to some extent, performative and purposefully reported in detail by Narisue himself—are an indication that *Kokonchomonjū* is an artifact created in the context of constructing a practice of cultural transmission modeled on that of Sinitic- and *waka*-specialist households.

The general prefaces to *Jikkinshō* and *Shasekishū* are very similar in length and tone to that of *Kokonchomonjū*. With this in mind, instead of quoting them in full, I will limit the discussion to the more relevant passages.

It should be noted that Mujū wrote his preface in literary Sinitic (*kanbun*), just as Narisue had, but the editor of *Jikkinshō* wrote his preface in the same mixed style (so-called *wakan konkōbun* 和漢混交文 [medieval "mixed style"]) that all three collections use for the body of the text. The preface to *Jikkinshō* is also noteworthy because it contains a rare explicit discussion of the work's intended readership. This appears in the opening passage:

The people of this world behave in many different ways, but in all cases, regardless of whether they are mighty or humble, the wise gain much and

> the foolish lose much. I have chosen from what I have seen and heard—with the tales of the past and of the present as seed, and myriad words as leaves—instances of both, to encourage the good and to reprove the bad, and thus help build the character of young people who haven't yet received instruction in this path [*michi*], and I have tentatively divided them into ten chapters and given it the title *The Ten-Lesson Digest* [*Jikkinshō*]. It is presented in three scrolls for perusal at the three times of leisure.[69]

> それ世の中にある人ことわざしげき振舞につけて高き賤しき品をわかず賢なるは得多く愚なるは失多し。しかるにいまなにとなく聞き見るところの昔今の物語を種としてよろづの言の葉の中よりいささかその二つのあとをとりて良きかたをばこれをすすめ悪しきすぢをばこれを誡めつついまだこの道を学び知らざらむ少年のたぐひをして心をつける便となさしめむがためにこころみに十段の篇を別にて十訓抄と名づく。すなはち三巻の文として三余の窓に置かむとなり。

Jikkinshō is framed in this passage as a collection of tales that have been chosen to illuminate the kinds of attitudes and behaviors that lead to worldly success. The editor argues that people succeed or fail on the basis of their abilities, not their social class or status (their being "mighty or humble" by birth), a notion with a long tradition in the Confucian canon. He similarly stresses the importance of study and preparation. For this reason, Hirao Yūko has described *Jikkinshō* as a "manual of Confucian virtue."[70] It was against this interpretation that Brownlee suggested that *Jikkinshō* lacks any programmatic approach or ideology. The "intention" of the editor might be hard to know for sure, but the identity of his intended readership is clear. From the preface, we learn that the work was created for young men; from the organization into titled chapters and the layout of episodes within each chapter, we will learn that these young men could only have been non-elite warriors with the prospect of a career in the service of powerful lords.

Like *Jikkinshō* and Narisue's *Kokonchomonjū*, Mujū's *Shasekishū* is a compilation of preexisting material from diverse sources, among them stories about aristocrats taken from poetry treatises. Its main theme, the truth of Buddhism, calls for an effort to justify the inclusion of these worldly tales, and Mujū offers a doctrinal justification in the opening passage of the preface to the collection:

> Coarse words and soft phrases all come from the First Principle [of Absolute Truth]. Neither life nor work is at cross-purposes with the truth. For these reasons, I strive to make the playful idleness of "crazy words and fancy expressions" into an auspicious connection to spread the splendid way of Buddhism, and to draw examples [*tatohe*] from the lowly shallowness of worldly affairs to offer entrance into the deepest and most meaningful truth.[71]
>
> それ麁言軟語みな第一義に帰し治生産業しかしながら実相にそむかず。然れば狂言綺語のあだなる戯れを縁として仏乗の妙なる道を知らしめ世間浅近の賤きことを譬として勝義の深き理に入れしめむと思ふ。

The passage is heavily laden with technical language, but the key seems to be the phrase translated as "crazy words and fancy expressions" (*kyōgen kigo* 狂言綺語). Its origin is not in Buddhist scripture, but in a line from a poem by Bái Jūyì, in which the poet prays that his engaging in (*shī*) poetry will result in Buddhist merit.[72] In Japan, since at least the late twelfth century, this term had come to embody an ambivalence about the status of *waka*: the concern that poems were idle language and the hope that they could still lead to merit.[73] In the preface to *Shasekishū*, which is structured as a series of parallels (a common style in Sinitic prose and poetry), Mujū employs the concept of "crazy words and fancy expressions" to justify his decision to draw material, or examples (*tatohe* 譬), from secular narratives.

All three prefaces offer reasons why a person should read the works and—as Genette theorized in his model—suggest how to approach them properly. These reasons and approaches vary starkly from text to text. Narisue frames *Kokonchomonjū* as a reflection of the life of the court; *Jikkinshō* is offered as exemplary narratives for career success; *Shasekishū* presents its secular narratives as a gateway to Buddhist truth. Still, beyond these differences in theme, treatment, and intended readership, all three prefaces draw connections to the practice of poetry. Narisue insists on his interest in music and painting but modeled his work on the poetry anthology *Kokinshū*, added injunctions reminiscent of those of poetry specialists, and recorded a celebratory banquet that he organized in front of images of the poets Hitomaro and Bái Jūyì. In *Jikkinshō*'s preface, the line "with the tales of the past and of the present as seed, and myriad words as leaves" is a direct and easily recognizable allusion to the kana preface to *Kokinshū*. In *Shasekishū*, Mujū found, in the uneasiness about the compatibility of poetry and truth, a simile for the problematic status of secular narratives in a discussion of Buddhist doctrine.

Organization and Layout

The more than seven hundred brief narrative episodes in *Kokonchomonjū* are organized into thirty thematic chapters distributed across twenty scrolls (table 2.1). The chapters are ordered hierarchically, beginning with lofty topics (such as religion, governance, scholarship, poetry, and music) and slowly progressing toward the humble (such as food, plants, and animals). This connects Narisue's collection with the Sinitic genre of *leishu* 類書 (Jp. *ruisho* [topical encyclopedias]). One of the most prominent topical encyclopedias, the *Yìwén lèijù* 藝文類聚 (Jp. *Geimon ruijū* [A compendium of literary writings], 624), is organized into forty-six categories over one hundred scrolls, in hierarchical order: it begins with heavenly matters, moves on to cultural and social issues, and finally reaches birds, beasts, fish, and insects.[74] This thematic and hierarchical organization had appeared as well in the classic lexicographic guide *Ěryā* 爾雅, before the second century BCE.[75] A quick glance at the organization of the thirty chapters of *Kokonchomonjū* will reveal how closely Narisue was working within this Sinitic precedent.

Chinese encyclopedias had a remarkable impact on the aristocratic worldview in Japan. In examining the role of these encyclopedias in the founding of the imperial state in Japan, Torquil Duthie has highlighted how continental precedent was not only instrumental in the education of members of the imperial bureaucracy, but also the source of models for new texts, such as legal codes, histories, and poetry anthologies such as *Man'yōshū* and *Kaifūsō* 懐風藻 (Fond recollections of poetry, 751).[76] Minamoto no Shitagō, for example, followed the model of *Yìwén lèijù* and *Ěryā* when he organized the lexicographic guide *Wamyō ruijūshō* into thematic sections arranged in order of decreasing status—starting with the natural and social constraints on humans and ending with insects and plants.[77] In organizing the

Table 2.1. Contents of *Kokonchomonjū*

1. Gods (*jingi* 神祇)
2. Buddhism (*shakkyō* 釈教)
3. Politics and Loyalty (*seidō chūshin* 政道忠臣)
4. Public Matters (*kuji* 公事)
5. Learned Texts in Chinese (*bungaku* 文学)
6. Classical Japanese Poetry (*waka* 和歌)
7. Music and Dance (*kangen kabu* 管弦歌舞)
8. Calligraphy (*nōsho* 能書)
9. Medical and Occult Conjurations (*jutsudō* 術道)
10. Filial Piety and Affection (*kōkō on'ai* 孝行恩愛)
11. Eroticism (*kōshoku* 好色)
12. Military Courage (*buyū* 武勇)
13. Archery (*kyūsen* 弓箭)
14. Horsemanship (*bagei* 馬芸)
15. Fighting and Physical Strength (*sumō gōriki* 相撲強力)
16. Painting (*gato* 画図)
17. Kickball (*kemari* 蹴鞠)
18. Gambling (*bakueki* 博奕)
19. Theft (*tōtō* 偸盗)
20. Celebratory Words (*shūgen* 祝言)
21. Sorrow (*aishō* 哀傷)
22. Entertainment (*yūran* 遊覧)
23. Attachment (*shukushū* 宿執)
24. Quarrels (*tōjō* 闘諍)
25. Witticism (*kyōgenrikō* 興言利口)
26. Mysterious Events (*kai'i* 怪異)
27. Apparitions (*henge* 変化)
28. Eating and Drinking (*onshiki* 飲食)
29. Plants and Trees (*sōmoku* 草木)
30. Fish, Insects, Birds, and Beasts (*gyochū kinjū* 魚虫禽獣)

chapters of *Kokonchomonjū* hierarchically, Narisue claimed for his work the comprehensive coverage and cultural authority of the Sinitic *leishu* genre and of related works created in Japan.

While the overall structure of the work relies on the *leishu* genre, within each chapter Narisue appeals to the precedent of historical writing. One of the most important Japanese historiographical works, by Sugawara no Michizane 菅原道真 (845–903), is *Ruijū kokushi* 類聚国史 (Catalog of the six national histories, 892), which collates information from the official histories known collectively as *Rikkokushi* 六国史 (Six national histories). Michizane reorganized material from these sources into categories and arranged the episodes within each category in chronological order. By adopting this same approach, Narisue gave his collection the appearance of a compendium of documented events. But whereas Michizane had conformed to the tradition of relying exclusively on the written word—an approach shared by histories and *leishu*—Narisue included material that until then had been transmitted orally. Here is where *Kokonchomonjū* is closer to the works in the *kikigaki* genre that Narisue mentions in his preface—*Uji dainagon monogatari* and *Gōdanshō*—a choice reflected in his use of the expression *chomonjū* in the title of the collection, as it literally means "collection of the written and the heard." Thus *Kokonchomonjū* presents itself as incorporating the comprehensiveness and cultural authority of the Sinitic *leishu*, the truthfulness and accuracy of domestic historical writing, and the relevance and timeliness of recent records of oral transmission.

However, the more than seven hundred brief narrative episodes that make up this collection often veer away from their lofty framing. Many of them add little to an encyclopedic coverage of a topic, hold minimal historical interest, and are otherwise irrelevant—unless a reader looks at them for what they teach about the culture of the aristocracy, in which *waka* played a central role. An illustration of this mismatch can be found in chapter 19, "Theft" (*tōtō* 偸盗), in which a preface announces: "Theft is a crime punishable by law with imprisonment. The wicked and violent are relentless, recklessly seeking drifting wealth, always using the cover of night to bring loss and suffering. Theft should never cease to be prohibited in the capital and the provinces."[78] What follows, though, is not an examination of diverse criminal practices and the efforts of the authorities to curb them. Among accounts of thieves and the fates they meet, we find a series of episodes in which the focus is not on the thief, the crime, or the punishment, but on poetry. This is one of them:

Someone said that a person who was going to worship at Kurama ran into thieves at dusk, right after passing Ichiharano, had his clothes stolen, and was hurt. Upon hearing this, Keisan composed:

yūgure ni	At dusk
ichiharano nite	in Ichiharano
ohu kizu wa	to be hurt:
kura magire to ya	Shall we call it
iubekaruran	the dark chaos of Kurama?[79]

鞍馬まうでの者の夕暮に市原野をすぎけるに盗人に行きあひてきたる物はぎとられて剰へきずを負ひて侍ると人の語るを聞きて慶算がよみ侍りける
夕暮に市原野にて負ふきずはくらまぎれとやいふべかるらん。

Keisan was an aristocrat, the son of a provincial governor, and a well-known poet. His poem is witty, hinging on a tongue-in-cheek pun on *kura magire* (to be confused in the dark) and *kurama gire* (to be cut at Kurama). Arguably, learning about this poet's reaction—however frivolous it may seem at first—would be more immediately useful to a non-elite audience than a learned discussion about criminal law and its application. Narisue may have organized and framed *Kokonchomonjū* in ways that evoked a series of established, authoritative genres, such as *leishu* and historical writings, but the main affordance of his work is as an introduction to the culture of the court.

Like *Kokonchomonjū*, *Jikkinshō* is arranged in chapters, presented as ten thematic "lessons." Each lesson opens with a preface that prescribes a desirable attitude—from avoiding arrogance and developing patience to showing loyalty and exercising care when communicating with others. Each preface is followed by a series of episodes that illustrate the maxim (table 2.2). A quick look at the subject of each of the ten lessons may suggest an eclectic attitude focused on practical outcomes. Lesson 6, "One Must Be Loyal and Honest," for example, refers to moral values such as loyalty (*chū* 忠) and honesty (*jitsu* 実) that stem from Confucian learning. Lesson 9, "One Must Refrain from Desire," by contrast, expounds on Buddhist teachings against attachment (*konmō* 懇望). Episode counts, however, show that by far the bulk of the attention was devoted to the last chapter, lesson 10: "One Must Aspire to Develop Knowledge and Skills." The skills

Table 2.2. Contents of *Jikkinshō*, with Approximate Numbers of Episodes

1. One Must Grant Benevolence to People (*hito ni megumi wo hodokosu-beki koto* 可施人恵事)[a] (57 episodes)
2. One Must Avoid Arrogance (*kyōman wo hanaru-beki koto* 可離憍慢事) (5 episodes)
3. One Must Avoid Despising People (*jinrin wo anazurazaru koto* 不侮人倫事) (16 episodes)
4. One Must Be Prudent with Other People (*hito no ue wo imashimu-beki koto* 可誡人上事) (19 episodes)
5. One Must Choose One's Friends Carefully (*hōyū wo erabu-beki koto* 可撰朋友事) (18 episodes)
6. One Must Be Loyal and Honest (*chūchoku wo zonjiru-beki koto* 可存忠直事) (38 episodes)
7. One Must Be Thoughtful and Careful (*shiryō wo mopparani su-beki koto* 可専思慮事) (32 episodes)
8. One Must Be Patient in All Situations (*shoji nite kan'nin su-beki koto* 可堪忍于諸事事) (18 episodes)
9. One Must Refrain from Desire (*konpō wo todomu-beki koto* 可停懇望事) (8 episodes)
10. One Must Aspire to Develop Knowledge and Skills (*saigei wo shoki su-beki koto* 可庶幾才芸事) (about 100 episodes)

[a] In one of the manuscript variants, known as the *Kokkai toshokan* (previously *Kunaichō*) MS, the title of the first chapter reads instead "One Must Be Firm in One's Thoughts and Behavior" (*shinsō furumai wo sadamu-beki koto* 可定心操振舞事).

covered in this lesson are *shī*, *waka*, court music, and the like, and the narrative episodes in lesson 10 are offered as evidence of the importance of acquiring them. In other words, *Jikkinshō* contains nothing in the way of advice such as that offered in poetry treatises: nothing on composition, on scholarship, on the hosting of poetry events, or on the compilation of poetry anthologies, but only arguments for the importance of practicing courtly disciplines.

The rhetorical nature of this presentation—that it advocates for, even insists on, the importance of the culture of the court—eliminates aristocrats and elite warriors from the list of likely intended readers, since they were already deeply invested in the customs of the court. Mid-rank warriors were the only social group in early medieval Japan that existed in the zone defined by contact with the court without full access to its workings, and in a place to profit from a text that offered knowledge about the court. Consistent with this view is the fact that lesson 10 is structured as two complementary parts. The first focuses on the culture of aristocrats, and the second, much briefer than the first—likely for lack of precedent and material—explicitly encourages warriors at all levels to imitate aristocrats. The brief preface of lesson 10 argues a similar point, glossing the lesson's title, "One Must Aspire to Develop Knowledge and Skills":

> There are people who say that this applies as a matter of course to those who from the very beginning were born to households of specialists in a specific discipline [*so no michi michi no ie ni umarenuru*], but also those who weren't will still need skills [*nō*], each according to his station in life. In some cases, men who inherit a family name that enjoys renown will neglect developing skills and ultimately prove to be unable to carry on their lineage. Even those who have no connection with a specific discipline should develop skills and—since a discipline [*michi*] has potency [*toku*]—strive to continue their own lineage and make a name for themselves in each of the different disciplines.[80]
>
> ある人いはくもとよりその道々の家に生れぬるはさることなりさなきたぐひもほどほどにつけては能は必ずあるべきなり。なかにも氏をうけたる者芸おろそかにして氏をつがぬたぐひあり。道にあらざるたぐひ能によりて道にいたる徳もあれば氏をつがむがため道にいたらむがためにかれもこれもともにはげむべし。

This passage impresses on the reader that the traditional skills of the court aristocracy are desirable, appropriate, and accessible to all, regardless of family origin or social status. The hundred or so episodes that follow in lesson 10 offer evidence of the advantages of courtly skills. These episodes are not lumped indiscriminately or arranged in chronological order (as in *Kokonchomonjū*) but are carefully grouped into meaningful clusters. Individual clusters are nested within broader bundles, which come together to reflect the logic (rather than the chronology) of the expansion of court culture to spaces outside the aristocracy. The concept that pulls these diverse narratives together and embodies this logic is the notion of *toku* (potency).[81]

The editor of *Jikkinshō* borrowed the notion of *toku*, some of the narratives that illustrate it, and the arrangement of episodes into nested clusters from the poetry treatises of the late classical period, chief among them those by Minamoto no Toshiyori and Fujiwara no Kiyosuke. *Toshiyori zuinō*, for example, has an episode in which an old man is about to be punished, but thanks to a poem is pardoned. The poem appeared originally in the third imperial anthology, *Shūi wakashū*, followed by the editorial remark, "Thanks to this poem, he was pardoned."[82] Toshiyori glossed this remark as "Thanks to this potency of poems [*ko no uta no toku*], a pardon was obtained."[83] In *Ōgishō*, Kiyosuke listed it after a poem by a court official in exile, and suggested that the two poems illustrated the capacity of poetry to placate (*nadamu*) anger in both public and private life.[84] The editor of *Jikkinshō* incorporated and significantly developed these connections. This is episode 39 in lesson 10:

> This happened when Sakurajima no Tadanobu left the capital to serve as the governor of Ōsumi Province. Among the district administration officials there was a white-haired old man who had committed a wrongdoing, and when they were about to punish him,
>
> | | |
> |---|---|
> | *oihatete* | Grown fully old |
> | *yuki no yama woba* | the snow covering |
> | *itadakedo* | topping the mountain, and yet |
> | *shimoto miru ni zo* | when I look at whipped frost |
> | *mi wa hienikeru* | I am left chilled.[85] |
>
> He recited this poem and was pardoned. And this is not an isolated case. *Waka* poems are intermediaries that soften the relationships of husband and wife. For this reason, it is written that "those who seem passionate [*iro meku*] use it as a flowery and feathered messenger" and also that others "use it as a bridge to travel across this destitute world." Its potencies [*toku*] are numerous.[86]

桜島忠信が大隅守にて下りけるに郡の司に頭の白き翁ありけるをとがありて召し勘へんとしたりければ　老いはてて雪の山をばいただけどしもと見るにぞ身はひえにける　とよみてゆりにけり。かやうのことのみならず歌は妹背の中を和らぐる媒なるによりて　色めく類これを花鳥の使とすとも　ありあるいはまた　貧しき世を渡る橋とす　とも見えたり。その徳かたがた多かるべし。

The statements that close the passage are taken from the *kana* and *mana* 真名 prefaces to *Kokinshū*. The kana preface, by Ki no Tsurayuki, reads, "What without effort drives heaven and earth, affects the invisible gods and demons, softens the relationships of men and women, and calms the heart of fierce warriors is *waka* poems."[87] And the *mana* preface, credited to Ki no Yoshimochi 紀淑望 (d. 919), notes, similarly, that "persons of an amorous disposition [*kōshoku*] use them as flowery and feathered messengers; and beggars use them as a means to earn a living."[88] Tsurayuki and Yoshimochi were following the model of the "Great Preface" (Dàxù 大序; Jp. *daijo*) to the *Shījīng* 詩經 (Jp. *Shikyō* [Book of songs]).[89] The passage from *Jikkinshō* seems to incorporate Toshiyori's notion of *toku*.[90] It also appears to extend the specific potency illustrated by the passage (pardon) to the full list, as enumerated in *Kokinshū*.[91]

This passage contains important clues, as well, to the system of nested clusters that structures *Jikkinshō* and serves as the foundation for its rhetorical strength. We do not have the original manuscript, but it is likely that it was a continuous text without breaks or episode numbers.[92] Most extant manuscripts parse episode 39 as discussed earlier. However, because it is preceded by episodes on pardons (35–38) and followed by episodes on husband-wife relationships (40–47), it is apparent that the passage is intended to serve as a transition between clusters. The same applies to episode 47, which contains the transition between the cluster on husband-wife relationships (40–47) and another on material gains (47–49).[93] In other cases, several episodes are combined into one. If we set aside the received parsing and numbering of episodes, and use the editorial comments as guides to cleave the text, a complex structure emerges, as illustrated in table 2.3.[94]

Lesson 10 is divided into three main parts. The first shows the potencies of the culture of the court. In this part, the notion of a potency of poetry is extended to music and prose writing. The second part extends the concept to the world of warriors, covering practices such as archery. The third part is a miscellaneous repository of odds and ends; interestingly, *kemari* (kickball), played by aristocrats, is included here. In the first part, the narratives are grouped into three main categories: gods, humans, and buddhas. Within each of these

Table 2.3. Structure of Lesson 10 in *Jikkinshō*, with Episode Numbers

- Introduction
- Tales about general literacy and *kanbun* (1–5)[a]
- Part I: Aristocrats
    - With gods
        - Potencies of *shī* (6–7)
        - Potencies of *kanbun* (8–9)
        - Potencies of *waka* (10–16)
        - Potencies of music (17–27)
    - With humans
        - Potencies of *shī* and *kanbun* (28–33)
        - Potencies of *waka* (34–50)
            - Office and rank (34)
            - Pardon (35–39a)
            - Love and sex (39b–47a)
            - Material goods (47b–49)
            - Social status (50)
        - [Potencies of music probably originally here, now in episode 57b]
    - With buddhas
        - Potencies of *imayō* [popular songs] (51)
        - Potencies of *shī* (52)
        - Potencies of *waka* (53)
- Part II: Warriors
    - Potencies of *shī* (54)
    - Potencies of *waka* (55a)
    - Potencies of *kanbun* (55b)
    - Potencies of archery
        - Sinitic precedent (55c)
        - Domestic events (56)
            - Archery and *waka* (verse-capping)
            - Archery and *shī*

(continued)

categories, they are grouped by discipline (prose writing, *shī*, *waka*, classical music, and popular songs). A similar approach structures the second part and, to some extent, the third. Poetry emerges from this system as the organizing principle for understanding the culture of the court, the prime gateway for its acquisition, and the model for understanding the culture of other social spaces.

Table 2.3 *(continued)*

- Part III: Miscellaneous and supplementary episodes
    - Music
        - Potencies of music (57)
        - Cautionary tales about music, *shī*, and *waka* (58–59)
        - Domestic lore (60–62)
        - Sinitic precedent (63–67), involving ascetics and divine beings
            - Calligraphy (68)
            - Potencies of *kemari* [kickball] (69)
        - More lore and cautionary tales about music (70–72)
        - More tales about music, *shī*, and *waka* (73, comprising many episodes)
- Conclusion (end of 73)
- Later additions
    - Tales about crime and punishment (74–79, comprising many episodes)

Note: The episode numbers refer to modern annotated editions.

[a] These tales include accounts of two aristocratic polymaths famous for their skill in *shī*, *waka*, and music: Fujiwara no Kintō and Minamoto no Tsunenobu, who was Toshiyori's father.

The editor of *Jikkinshō* does not say where he got the idea to aggregate and structure preexisting narratives in ways that make them rhetorically effective. In modern scholarship, the structure of lesson 10 itself has received no attention. Nevertheless, it might be possible to trace it back to sections in *Toshiyori zuinō* and *Fukurozōshi* that display a similar approach in embryonic form. In *Toshiyori zuinō* we find a section about different kinds of poets (see table 2.4), bracketed by a review of "poetic diseases" (*kahei* 歌病) and a discussion of topical composition (*daiei* 題詠). Toshiyori introduces the section with this statement: "Generally speaking, starting with the gods and buddhas, the emperors and empresses, and all the way down to the lowliest mountain beggars, all beings with a heart, without exception, compose *waka* poems."[95]

The narrative episodes in this section cover people in different social positions, in order of decreasing status: from emperors,

Table 2.4. Structure of a Section in *Toshiyori zuinō*

- Introductory remarks
- Poem by an emperor
- Poem by an empress
- Poems by buddhas
- Poems exchanged by priests
- Poems by gods (and poems by court ladies on similar themes)
- Three poems with potency
    - Izumi Shikibu at Kibune
    - Ki no Tsurayuki at Aridōshi
    - Priest Nōin at Mishima
- Quotation from kana preface to *Kokinshū*
- Poems by seven old men
- Poems by children
- Poems by beggars
- A poetic exchange between a woman's husband and her lover
- Poems by thieves and alleged thieves
- Poems by people on their deathbed

empresses, buddhas, legendary priests, and gods to old men, children, beggars, and thieves.[96] They are divided into two groups. The first focuses on divine and semi-divine poets and includes the gods, buddhas, and members of the imperial household; the second features the human poets, beginning with old men composing in the mode known as *jukkai* 述懐 ("to express one's feelings" or "to vent one's frustrations," commonly recited as appeals for higher office or rank). In between the clusters on deities and humans, we find a cluster of three stories that Toshiyori presents as a digression.[97] As in *Jikkinshō*, modern annotated editions parse these episodes in a way that obscures how they relate to one another.[98] In all three stories, a poet offers a poem to a god. In the first, the poet Izumi Shikibu 和泉式部 (turn of the eleventh century) presents a grief poem at Kibune Shrine 貴船神社 (in present-day Kyoto) right after she is abandoned by her husband, Fujiwara no Yasumasa 藤原保昌 (958–1036), and a voice from inside the shrine responds with a poem expressing sympathy.[99] In the second, Tsurayuki appeases the wrath of the god at Aridōshi 蟻通 with a poem.[100] In the third, the priest Nōin 能因 (b. 988) appeals successfully for rain to the god at Mishima Shrine in Iyo Province.[101] Later in *Toshiyori zuinō*, two contiguous stories are about poems addressed to humans. In one of them, the poet is a servant accused of theft; the other is the aforementioned account of an old man who escapes punishment because of a poem.[102]

By placing these episodes within a larger section on the different types of poets, Toshiyori is connecting the potency of poems with the universality of poetic practice. Kiyosuke incorporated and expanded on this approach in a section of *Fukurozōshi*, which is similarly structured according to the various kinds of poets. In *Fukurozōshi*, Kiyosuke parses the different clusters using brief thematic headings and places the whole section under the title "Kitai no uta" 希代の歌 (Exceptional poems); see table 2.5. He significantly augmented the number of narrative episodes offered as evidence of the types of poets as well as of the potencies of *waka*, but otherwise reproduced Toshiyori's framework. Among the additions is a story about a Sinitic prose preface by Masafusa to be recited during a banquet at Michizane's mausoleum in Anrakuji Temple 安楽寺, to which the spirit responded with a signal.[103] That no mention of the potencies of Sinitic writing appears in *Toshiyori zuinō* likely has to do with its intended reader, a young female student, while Kiyosuke wrote for a male professional specialist. Relatedly, Toshiyori does not discuss poems intended as formal requests for office, but Kiyosuke does, recounting the success of his own application for appointment to the fourth rank submitted to Retired Emperor Toba.[104] Thus while Kiyosuke makes no mention of a *toku* of *waka*, in terms of its material and organization, *Fukurozōshi* stands as an expansion of the discussion of the potencies of *waka* in Toshiyori's work.

We find another indication of the influence of Toshiyori's work in *Ryōjin hishō*, an anthology of *imayō* compiled by Retired Emperor GoShirakawa.[105] Known also as *imayō-uta*, they shared the *waka* meter but were commonly sung, and often took on Buddhist themes. In his accompanying treatise *Kuden-shū* 口伝集 (Oral transmission), GoShirakawa explicitly followed the model of Toshiyori, including brief narrative episodes and describing the events in them as a product of *onchō no toku* 音調之徳 (the potency of tunes).[106] *Kuden-shū* is

Table 2.5. Structure of the Subsection "Exceptional Poems" in *Fukurozōshi*

- Poems by gods (*shinmei no ōn-uta* 神明御歌)
- Poems by buddhas (*hotoke no ōn-uta* 仏御歌)
- Poems by heavenly people (*ten'nin no uta* 天人歌)
- Poems by ascetic people (*sen'nin no uta* 仙人歌)
- Poems by holy people (*shōnin no uta* 聖人歌)
- Poems that elicit an affective response from gods and buddhas (*busshin kannō no uta* 仏神感応歌)
  - Ki no Tsurayuki at Aridōshi
  - Akazome-emon at Sumiyoshi
  - Priest Nōin at Mishima
  - Minamoto no Tsunenobu's poem extends the life of the emperor
  - Poem by a Kumano pilgrim
  - Poem presented at Sumiyoshi
  - Poem presented at Kitano by a woman suspected of a crime
  - Poem presented at Kitano by Fujiwara no Akisuke
  - Poetic preface in *kanbun* presented by Ōe no Masafusa at the shrine to Sugawara no Michizane at Anrakuji Temple
- Poems by dead people (*bōsha no uta* 亡者歌)
- Poems by dying people (*rinji no uta* 臨時歌)
- Poems by children (*yōji no uta* 幼児歌)
- Poems by poor people (*senpu no uta* 賤夫歌)
- Poems by begging monks (*kissha no uta* 乞者歌)
- Poem spells (*jūmon no uta* 誦文歌)

roughly contemporary with *Fukurozōshi*, and it is unclear whether the editor of *Jikkinshō* was consulting it when he discussed the *toku* of music.[107] In a cluster of episodes on music performed for gods, for example, the editor of *Jikkinshō* included an account of a band of pirates who attack a ship but then, when they hear a musical performance, decide to spare it:

> "Consoling the heart of fierce warriors" is not limited to *waka* poetry. These [stories] are all about the potency of music [*kangen no toku*]. This [last] instance was not a case of "affecting the gods and demons," but since it was about how lives were magnificently saved, I still have recorded it here.[108]

猛きもののふの心をなぐさむること和歌には限らず。これらみな管絃の徳なり。またこのことは鬼神の所感にあらざれども命を助くること厳重によりてついでにしるし申す。

This passage appears in the first part of lesson 10, which also features narratives about *shī* and *waka* that prompt the response of buddhas and bodhisattvas, and, more generally, aid in reaching enlightenment. When considered as a whole, this part is a systematic and well-organized extension of Toshiyori's notion of *toku* to the culture of the court (represented by its main disciplines or skills: *waka* and *shī*, Sinitic prose, and classical music).

The second part of lesson 10 reproduces the approach and structure of the first part, but extends them to the world of warriors. It opens, as does the first part, with a discussion of Chinese precedent:

> Originally born to a household of warriors [*takeki hito*], Yǎng Yóujī inherited the trade and Lǐ Guǎnglì carried on the family name, and although they had no need to acquire any other skills, they still studied writings and enjoyed poetry, a most remarkable feat.[109]

またもとより猛き人の家に生れぬる養由が芸をつぎ李広が跡を伝ふるほかなにごとをかは学む習はむと思へどもそれしも文を兼ね歌を好むたぐひいとどいみじくこそ。

In the episodes that follow is a mention of an unnamed father and son who served as generals in Kamakura and had their poems included in imperial anthologies. This is most likely a reference to the shoguns Minamoto no Yoritomo and his son Sanetomo:

> Generally speaking, at times when warriors [*bushi*] act to restore order to the chaos of this world, they give priority to this, and thus achieve no distinction in writing [*bun*]. At court, literary and military arts [*bunbu*] are split as two separate ways, like the two wings of a bird. It is believed that where there is literary learning, military prowess will follow.[110]

およそ武士といふは乱れたる世を平らぐる時これをさきとするがゆゑに文にならびて優劣なし。朝家には文武二道をわきて左右のつばさとせり。文事あれば必ず武備はる謂なり。

The idea that warriors generally "restore order to the chaos of this world" (*midaretaru yo wo tahiragu*) seems in this context to refer to the wars of the twelfth century, which ended with Yoritomo's founding of the *bakufu* in Kamakura. Ideally, the second part of lesson 10 would have followed this contention with numerous accounts of warriors practicing courtly skills and benefiting from their potencies, but the editor had started to run out of material. An indication of this is the next account, about Minamoto no Shitagō, who had already appeared at the beginning of the first part as a paragon of courtly skills. Shitagō may have shared his family name with Yoritomo and Sanetomo, and at one point he went by the formal court title of Imperial Guards Right Corps (Ukon efu 右近衛府), but he was not a fighting man. Having stretched his material to its limits, the editor turns his attention to episodes on archery (*kyūsen*), remarking that "archery is not only facing an enemy and achieving victory. Even in smaller matters its potencies [*toku*] are many."[111] Thus he connects archery to the practice of *shī* and *waka*.[112]

After the second part, the clear, logical structure of lesson 10 breaks down. As shown in table 2.3, what follows is an amalgamation of isolated clusters and often even single episodes that evince no coherent pattern. Among them is an account related to *kemari*, in which a player sees the spirit of *kemari* (*mari no sei* 鞠の精) appear on the kickball field in the shape of a beautiful young man. The editor explains this event, once again, as arising from the potencies (*toku*) of *kemari*.[113] Other clusters of episodes return to the topic of music, with a focus on narratives from China, and there is also an episode about calligraphy. The rhetorical force obtained in the first two parts from the systematic arrangement of thematically related narratives is absent from these sections. The practice of appending somewhat related material to the end of a text when making a copy was widespread, so it is also possible that these last episodes were not part of the original design of *Jikkinshō*.[114]

In summary, the main rhetorical devices of *Jikkinshō* are organization and arrangement.[115] By structuring the work in thematic chapters and laying out the episodes in clusters within them, the editor indicated how each individual story was to be read. Now and then, episodes that could have been included in lesson 10 do appear in the other nine lessons. In lesson 4, "One Must Be Prudent with Other People," for example, a priest accused of lechery presents a poem at Kitano, and the god soon makes the accuser dance madly and confess that she had lied.[116] In lesson 8, "One Must Be Patient in All Situations," two women who have been abandoned by their husbands show no resentment toward them and ultimately win them back, thanks to their poems; the editor remarks about these episodes that "continuing to hold back one's emotions in this way is quite admirable!"[117] In none of these episodes, though, do we find editorial remarks connecting the events to the potencies of poems or even any general mention of the importance of developing skill in poetry, as we do in lesson 10.

Something similar occurs in *Kokonchomonjū*, both in chapter 6, "Classical Japanese Poetry," and throughout the other chapters in the collection, where we find many of the same episodes that appear in lesson 10 in *Jikkinshō*, but arranged chronologically and without any attempt to draw attention to the potencies of poems. There is, however, a cluster in chapter 6 of *Kokonchomonjū* that breaks the chronological order and includes episodes identical to those in *Jikkinshō*. These are mostly episodes from lesson 10, although some were taken from other lessons that can be read as instances of the potency of poems. The current understanding is that a later copyist borrowed these wholesale from *Jikkinshō* and intercalated them in *Kokonchomonjū*, for reasons that are not clear.[118]

The strict chronological order of *Kokonchomonjū* might offer a stark contrast to *Jikkinshō*'s systematic arrangement of episodes into nested clusters that suggest parallels between aristocratic courtiers and warriors, but Narisue does interpolate a handful of episodes on warriors into chapter 6.[119] One episode, for example, relates that the first shogun, Minamoto no Yoritomo, was once approached by a feeble Buddhist nun with a document claiming that land in Izumi that she had inherited was taken from her, and that a lawsuit she filed had been struck down. After examining the document and interviewing the nun, Yoritomo wrote a poem on a folding fan and gave it to her:

izuminaru	In Izumi Province,
shinoda no mori no	Shinoda Forest's
amasagi wa	herons

moto no furu-e ni shall return
tachikaerubeshi to their original old branches.[120]

いづみなる信太の杜のあまさぎはもとの古枝に立ちかへるべし

Later, when his son Sanetomo was shogun, the nun brought this fan to the attention of a judge, who recognized Yoritomo's hand and returned the land to her. Since the word *amasagi* (heron) contains *ama* (nun), the last two lines can also be read as meaning: "The nun should be able to return (*tachi-kaeru*) to the land she originally (*moto*) owned."[121] This episode presents Yoritomo as a wise ruler who follows the classical Sinitic model: he is mindful of the needs of his subjects and committed to fairness. It is related to the role of poems in ruler-subject relationships (such as the *jukkai* poems used to appeal for office), but takes it a step further by elevating poetry to the level of legal doocument.

Right after this episode, Narisue offers another story featuring Yoritomo:

The same commander of the Inner Palace Guards [Yoritomo] was hunting in Moruyama. Seeing that the strawberries were in full bloom, Hōjō Shirō Tokimasa, who was there with him, offered the first part of a poem:

moruyama no In Moruyama
ichigo sakashiku the strawberries
narinikeri have turned splendid.

The commander [Yoritomo] immediately responded:

mubara ika ni How happy
ureshikaruran must the briar be![122]

同じ大将守山にて狩せられけるにいちごのさかりになりたを見るて供に北条四郎時政が候ひけるが連歌をなんしける　もる山のいちごさかしくなりにけり　大将とりもあえず　むばらがいかにうれしかるらん

The previous passage had featured the use of *waka* in governance, and here Narisue seems to focus on the use of poetry in quotidian conversation among elite warriors. Hōjō Tokimasa 北条時政 (1138–1215) was the shogunal regent and the founding backer of the warrior government in Kamakura. Here Tokimasa and Yoritomo join in verse-capping, which became popular during the twelfth century, especially among warriors.[123] Tokimasa offers three lines, and Yoritomo caps them with two lines to form one full poem.[124] This verse-capping episode complements the presentation of Yoritomo as a legitimate ruler in the episode with the nun. Tokimasa was like a father to Yoritomo. In 1160, when Yoritomo was still a young man and the powerful Taira no Kiyomori forced him to leave the capital, Tokimasa sheltered him in Izu Province and married him to his teenage daughter, Hōjō Masako.[125] Tokimasa's three lines can also be read: "The child (*chigo*) I have raised and protected (*moru*) has turned smart and healthy (*sakashiku*)."[126] Yoritomo's capping lines similarly use puns to reply: "How happy must his nursemaid be!" offers the display of filial piety befitting a legitimate ruler.[127] Thus in chapter 6 of *Kokonchomonjū*, Narisue presents *waka*—the language of the classical court—as a language of governance and virtue for warriors, and, more generally, as a shared idiom of political, social, and cultural significance for social spaces outside the aristocracy.

Poetry and Truth

Jikkinshō provided a ready-made template that other editors could easily incorporate into their works.[128] In *Shasekishū*, Mujū repurposed—or, rather, *reafforded*—these materials and approach to construct a complex argument about the compatibility of *waka* and the monastic calling.[129] Table 2.6 offers an approximate sense of the contents and structure of the relevant passages.[130] Most of the narrative episodes in them are taken from *Jikkinshō*. Mujū complemented them with stories that are in every other way analogous to the episodes on courtiers and warriors in *Jikkinshō*, but set instead in a monastic environment.

The concerns about the compatibility of poetry and Buddhist truth (*shingon*) that Mujū addresses in *Shasekishū* has a long history. *Shī* on Buddhist teaching appear in *Kaifūsō*, the earliest anthology of *shī* in Japan, and in *Shōryōshū* 性霊集 (Collection of the spirit), a compendium of Sinitic prose and poetry by the founder of the Shingon school, Kūkai 空海 (774–835). Buddhist-themed *waka* are included in

Table 2.6. Structure of Passages in *Shasekishū* at the End of Book 5 (Upper) and the Beginning of Book 5 (Lower)

- Narrative episodes on humorous *waka* exchanges between monks
- Discussion of *waka* and truth

—End of book 5 (Upper, moto 本*) and beginning of book 5 (Lower,* sue 末*)—*

- Narrative episodes on the potency of *waka*
    - Involving gods and aristocrats
    - Involving people (aristocrats and monks)
- Brief discussion of *waka* and truth*
- Narrative episodes on aristocratic poets*
- Poems based on sutras and musical recitation (*rōei* [recitation] and *shirabyōshi* [song and dance])*
- Humorous narratives, including some on the potency of *waka**
- Verse-capping (elegant, Buddhist, and humorous) (more than 20 episodes)*
- Exchange of *waka* (*zōtōka*) (1 episode)*
- Discussion of potency of poems (aristocrats, monks, and commoners) (more than 10 episodes)
- Discussion of *waka* and truth
- *Waka* on the topic of laments (10 episodes)
- Discussion of *waka* and truth
- Narrative episodes on gods and buddhas composing *waka*
- Discussion of *waka* and truth in the Chan sect and in the traditional sects
- Narrative episode on the potency of *waka*
- Discussion of *waka* and truth

Note: Asterisks indicate passages found only in some manuscripts.

Man'yōshū and in all imperial anthologies from *Shūishū* onward.[131] The category of *Shakkyōka* 釈教歌 (*waka* on Buddhist teachings) became established with the inclusion of a marked-off subsection in *Goshūi wakashū* (*Goshūishū* 後拾遺集 [Later collection of gleanings]).[132] However, Mujū's main argument in support of the compatibility of poetry and Buddhist truth departs from these precedents in significant ways.

Mujū begins his argument in the opening passages of *Shasekishū* by establishing the identity of domestic gods (*kami* 神) and buddhas (*hotoke* 佛):

> When original beings [*honji*] take temporary manifestation [*suijaku*], their forms are diverse but their essence [*kokoro* 意] is unchanged. . . . In our land, [buddhas] softened their radiance [*wakō*] and manifested [*ato wo tare*] as godly brightness [*shinmei*], softening the rough hearts of people and working as expedient means [*hōben*] to assist the belief in the law of the Buddha.[133]
>
> 然れば本地垂跡のその御形異なれどもその意（こころ）かはらじかし。(...) 我が朝には和光の神明先づ跡を垂れて人の荒き心を和げて仏法を信ずる方便とし給へり。本地の深き心を仰ぎ和光の近き方便を信ぜば現生には息災安穏の望みをとげ当来には無為常住の悟りを開くべし。我が国に生を受けん人この意を弁ふべきをや。

This system of equivalence is today commonly referred to as *honji-suijaku* (*ato wo tare* is a gloss of *suijaku*) and is understood as a case of syncretism (*shinbutsu shūgō* 神仏習合 or *shinbutsu konkō* 神仏混淆 in Japanese scholarship), a phenomenon that is widely discussed in modern research on other religious traditions.[134] As Helen Hardacre shows, this syncretism should not imply equilibrium, as in Japan the worship of *kami* and of *hotoke* developed differently.[135] In this passage, Mujū acknowledges these differences by establishing a hierarchy in which the *hotoke* are a transnational essence (*honji*) that the *kami* manifest (*suijaku*) locally as an expedient means (*hōben*; Skt. *upāya*). The notion of expedient means, which articulates and negotiates the connection between gods and buddhas, also plays a central role in Mujū's discussion of the potencies of poems. Mujū's serpentine style of exposition makes it difficult to summarize or excerpt without losing definition on his argument:

> When we consider the potencies [*toku*] of *waka* poems, they have the potency [*toku*] to preclude the disorder and distractions of the mind [*kokoro* 心] and to bring serenity and quiet. Also, their meaning [*kokoro*] is contained in few words [*kotoba* 詞]. They have the potency [*toku*] of

the all-retaining [*sōji*].[136] The all-retaining is *darani*.[137] The gods of our realm are local manifestations [*suijaku*] of buddhas and bodhisattvas, the greater form of the manifested body [*ōjin*].[138] The god Susa-no-o was the first, with his poem in thirty-one syllables, "Izumo where eight clouds rise . . ." This was not different from the words [*kotoba*] of the Buddha. The *darani* of India are in the language of that country. The Buddha used it to expound on *darani*. For this reason, in Yì Xíng's *Commentary on the Mahavairocana Sutra* we read, "The languages of all lands are *darani*."[139] Had the Buddha come to our land, he surely would have considered that the language of our land is *darani*. *Sōji* were originally without writing [*monji nashi*]. Writing expresses *sōji*. In the writing of which country are the powers [*toku*] of *sōji* absent? What is more, the meaning [*kokoro*] contained in the Siddhaṃ script can be put into the five great characters [*gotai*] to great effect [*hibiki*].[140] The six defiling senses are all writing. Other than the five tones, there are no sounds [*koe*]. There are no words [*kotoba*] away from the Sanskrit character "A" [阿]. "A" is the foundation for the true words [*shingon*] of a buddha.[141] For this reason, the sutra reads, "The words uttered by the long-tongued one [the Buddha] are all true words."[142]

The thirty-one chapters of the *Mahāvairocana Sutra* correspond naturally to the thirty-one characters [*ji*] [of *waka*]. Because the principles of worldly and religious life are contained in these thirty-one characters [*ji*], they provoke a response [ō 応] from buddhas and bodhisattvas, and they move [*kan*] gods and humans. Even though *darani* employ secular [*sezoku*] Indian words, when they are given the name *darani* they have the virtue of eliminating sin. The *waka* of Japan use everyday words, too, but when called *waka* they can express feelings and therefore certainly provoke a response. And if they also contain the meaning [*kokoro*] of the Buddhist Law, they are definitely *darani*.

India, China, and Japan have different languages, but their essence [*kokoro* 意] is the same, so the teachings of the Buddha have spread not without benefits [*riyaku*]. Regardless of the language [*kotoba* 言], if one grasps the meaning [*kokoro* 心] and expresses feelings, without fail it will be moving [*kan*].[143]

和歌の徳を思ふに散乱麁動の心をやめ寂然静閑なる徳あり。また詞は少くして心を含めり。惣持の徳あり。惣持は即ち陀羅尼なり。我が朝の神には仏菩薩の垂迹応身の随一なり。素盞雄尊すでに出雲八重垣の三拾一字の詠をはじめ給へり。仏の詞に異なるべからず。天竺の陀羅尼もその国の人の詞なり。仏これを以て陀羅尼を説き給へり。この故に一行禅師の大日経の疏にも随方の詞みな陀羅尼といへり。仏若し我が国に出で給はばただ和国の詞を以て陀羅尼とし給ふべし。

惣持は本文字なし。文学は惣持をあらはす。何れの国の文字か惣持の徳なからむ。況や悉曇の心は五大にして響きあり。六塵悉く文字なり。五音に出でたる音なし。阿字を離れたる詞なし。阿字は即ち密教の真言の根本なり。されば経にも舌相言語皆是真言」といへり。

大日経の三十一品も自ら三十一字に当たれり。世間出世の道理を三十一字の中に包みたれば、仏菩薩の応もあり神明人類の感もあり。かの陀羅尼も天竺の世俗の詞なれども陀羅尼と名づけて此を以てば滅罪の徳あり。日本の和歌も世の常の詞なれども和歌と云ひて思ひも述ぶれば必ず感あり。まして仏法の心を含めらむは疑ひなく陀羅尼なるべし。天竺漢朝和国その言異なれどもその意同じき故に仏の教へ広まりて利益の空しからず。言に定まれる事なし。ただ心を得て思ひを述べば必ず感あるべし。

Mujū's argument interlaces three main notions. One stems from the widespread practice of ritual recitation of the Sanskrit or Pali phrases known as *darani*, which are said to contain unmediated truth (*shingon*). The other two, *kotoba* and *kokoro*, have a long history in writing about *waka*, as they appear prominently in the opening of Tsurayuki's kana preface to *Kokinshū*.[144] In exploring the significance of these concepts, Mujū draws attention to some of the disconnects between oral transmission (the words of a buddha) and written transmission (the sutras), as well as between truth (*shingon*, equated with *kokoro*) and its expression (*kotoba*, equated with sound). Related to this last distinction is the question of whether *waka* should be considered an indirect but efficient means (*hōben*) or a straight expression of truth (*shingon*). This is sophisticated theorizing, but Mujū ultimately bulldozes all these distinctions by establishing a fundamental identity between *waka* and *darani*.[145] This identity is modeled after that between the gods and the buddhas. It is this expression of truth, argues Mujū, that ultimately moves (*kan*) gods and humans, and prompts a response (*ō*) from buddhas.

Soon after this passage, Mujū includes many of the narrative episodes that he borrowed from *Jikkinshō* and later additions to *Kokonchomonjū*. But before that, he offers as an illustration of his argument one poem in particular, which he follows with his own commentary:

The Buddha appeared in our land and soon recited [*ju su* 誦す] *waka*. This is a composition by [the Kannon at] Kiyomizu:

tada tanome	Rely on me!
shimeji ga hara no	So should all sentient beings, numerous
sashi-mogusa	like the mugwort in the fields of Shimeji,
wa re yo no naka ni	as long as I am
aramu kagiri wa	in this world.

This must surely be a *darani*. There is no doubt about it. The gods [*shinmei*] are moved [*kan-ji*] by *waka* and realize people's wishes. The potency [*toku*] of *waka* and the teachings of the all-retaining [*sōji*] are to be understood as essentially one and the same.[146]

大聖我が国に現れて既に和歌を誦し給ふ。清水の御詠にも ただ頼めしめぢが原のさしも草我れ世の中にあらむ限りは とあり。これ必ず陀羅尼なるべし。疑ふべからず。神明また多く歌を感じて人の望みを叶へ給ふ。旁々和歌の徳惣持の義陀羅尼と一つに心を得べし。

In the poem, *sashi-mogusa* can mean both "mugwort" and "all sentient beings." Neither *ShinKokin wakashū* (*ShinKokinshū* 新古今集 [New collection of poems ancient and modern]) nor *Fukurozōshi*, in which the poem also appears, mentions *darani*, but Mujū's theoretical reading can retrofit any poem that refers to Buddhist truth (and even many poems completely unrelated to it) as a *darani*, and thus as a poem capable of moving the gods and buddhas.[147] The narrative episodes that follow this remark, and that were taken largely from *Jikkinshō*, appear in *Shasekishū* similarly sorted into nested clusters. Under the title "Gods That Are Moved [*kan-ji* 感じ] by Poems and Help People," Mujū includes episodes in which gods heal dangerous illnesses or clear the names of the falsely accused.[148] Under "Poems That Move [*kan aru* 感有る] People" are episodes in which criminals are pardoned, the poor marry up, and subjects are exempted from taxation.[149] Following this cluster, under "Poems That Appear in Dreams," episodes recount how the spirits of dead people use *waka* to communicate with the living.[150]

The stories unique to *Shasekishū* simply extend this logic to a monastic context. A court official's appeal to the emperor for appointment to rank and office—an episode that appears in *Fukurozōshi* and *Jikkinshō*—is transmuted into a story in which a Buddhist monk is granted higher ecclesiastical rank.[151] Narratives in which poems help lovers unite or reunite are replaced by an episode about a monk who falls out with a disciple and persuades him to return by sending him a *waka*.[152] Mujū's argument for identifying *waka* with *darani* offers an innovative explanation for the powers behind the potencies of *waka*. Even so, the narrative evidence he provides, as well as the language he uses to indicate the actual workings of these potencies, refer back to the capacity of poems to move (*kan-ji*, *kan ari*), which connects *Shasekishū*, by way of *Jikkinshō* (and the additions to *Kokonchomonjū*), to *Fukurozōshi* and *Toshiyori zuinō* and, through them, to the prefaces to *Kokinshū* and their model in the "Great Preface" to the *Shījīng*. As Mujū's work shows, when harnessing previous writings about poetry to speak to the place of *waka* in society, early medieval collections emphasize the centrality of the affective dimension of poetic practice. This calls for an approach informed by the tools of performance studies and affect theory.

A Theory of *Waka*

The emergence of a comprehensive and detailed discourse on the potencies of *waka* in early medieval collections has spurred a series of attempts to provide a theoretical system to make it intelligible. Moriyama Shigeru, for example, referred to these narratives as *katoku setsuwa* 歌徳説話 (brief narratives on the powers of *waka*) and theorized an underlying "awareness" of the potencies of poetry (*katoku ishiki* 歌徳意識).[153] Moriyama conceptualized *katoku* as a transhistorical phenomenon and attempted to explain it in linguistic terms. He identified analogous narratives from other historical periods, sorted them into categories according to the types of potencies displayed, and inspected the poems for distinctive linguistic structures.[154] In this approach, narrative episodes that appear isolated in earlier works, where there is no reference to the potencies of *waka*, can still retroactively be considered proof of a belief in *katoku*.

Moriyama's research agenda is representative of a historical moment in modern scholarship driven by the interest in identifying unique aspects of the Japanese language. Like another influential postwar scholar of *waka*, Watanabe Shōichi, Moriyama relied on the folklore studies of Yanagita Kunio and Orikuchi Shinobu, who posited a popular belief in the power of voiced words.[155] The expressions that became shorthand for this notion—*kotodama* 言霊 (spirit of words) and *kotoage* 言挙げ (offering of words)—appeared in ancient texts, but the notion itself only gained theoretical traction in the work of early modern thinkers such as Keichū 契沖 (1640–1701), Moto'ori Norinaga 本居宣長 (1730–1801), and Hirata Atsutane 平田篤胤 (1776–1843).[156] Reproduced in English by scholars such as Herbert Plutschow, this so-called *kotodama* theory has received much critical review and is now considered inapplicable to the study of medieval Japan.[157]

An alternative approach has been offered by Keller Kimbrough. His argument begins by highlighting that the recurring references to Sinitic *shī* (in *Jikkinshō*) and Sanskrit *darani* (in *Shasekishū*) invalidate any effort to investigate *katoku* as unique to Japan. Kimbrough has described Mujū's argument for the potency of *waka* as depicting a "magico-religious technology" that is able to condense in a few sounds (thanks to poetry's "semantic superabundance") a logical truth that can force a deity to grant a poet's wish. *Katoku*, in this view, would work analogously to the "Truth Acts" (Skt. *saccakiriyā*, *satyakriyā*) in the Pali and Sanskrit canon.[158] As evidence, Kimbrough cites a rainmaking poem by Priest Nōin, in which the last three lines are

sekikudase	divert to our rice paddies
ama kudarimasu	if, like rain, you descend from heaven
kami naraba kami	God, oh God!

Kimbrough argues, "Through linking the truth of the deity's origins (that it is a god come down from heaven) with the conjecture that it is a deity who bestows rain, Nōin creates a situation in which the deity cannot deny Nōin's one statement without denying the other."[159]

Mujū, however, makes no mention of Truth Acts or even of this poem.[160] Even if we assume that logic alone can force a divine being into action, it is impossible to identify other episodes in any of these works with poems that display similar adversarial logic traps.

A feature that the diverse narratives on the potencies of poems have in common is that a poem always is communicated, not just composed or written down. Ogawa Toyō connects these narratives with dialogues in which subjects make a request of the ruler, which often involves a poem, known as *jukkai*.[161] Ogawa explains the growth in relevance of *jukkai* during the twelfth century as a response to the destabilization of traditional power structures that led to the founding of the warrior government in Kamakura.[162] In this context, *jukkai* should be regarded not as simple expressions of grievance and frustration, but as performances of order and stability: as desperate attempts to construct a mighty ruler who will still act as a patron and grant requests. In summary, Ogawa argues that the discourse on the potencies of *waka* that emerged in early medieval Japan was a reaction to the weakening of channels of patronage that had supported the practice of *waka* until then.[163]

Most narrative episodes in early medieval collections, however, do not work analogously to Truth Acts or to *jukkai*. Only a few of these narratives are open to this interpretation. By contrast, the pervasive emphasis on dialogues and appeals enables us to reconsider the entirety of this corpus from a new perspective. Almost all the episodes present a poem as an act of communication that elicits a response. Often this reaction is explicitly described in affective terms—as sympathy, with an expression such as *aware to omohite* あはれと思ひて (thinking sympathetically), or, more commonly, as general emotion (*kan ari* 感あり [this elicited an affective response]). In the rest of the stories, this reaction can be inferred from the response itself: a miracle, a pardon, a gesture of kindness. In none of these narratives is it made clear, or even mentioned, which specific aspect of the poem made it effective—be it its language, its lexical choices, its more general meaning, or its technical skill. Finally, and vitally, the benefit is always granted by a figure of greater social or cultural status to a figure of lower status: a god to a human, a judge to a prisoner, a male courtier to a female courtier, or a courtier to a peasant. In *Shasekishū*, as noted, the same logic is extrapolated to interactions between monastics. The switch from the secular to the sacred leaves the narrative structure intact: regardless of the social spaces in which they are employed, poems remain effective in bridging power differences.[164]

This connects with a more general aspect of the practice of *waka*, that poems are always intended for someone else: the very word we translate as "to compose (a poem)" (*yomu* 詠む) is significantly close to "to read aloud" (*yomu* 読む, to recite). In this context, to versify is to say. This function is most visible in the role of *waka* at court, and in provincial aristocratic circles throughout the classical period, as a vehicle for communication in elegant dialogue. What, then, distinguishes the use of *waka* in dialogue more generally from the specific use of a poem for its potency?

Poems that bring practical, concrete results relate to what J. L. Austin called "performative sentences." These are situations in which the issuing of an utterance is equivalent to the performance of an action.[165] Austin cautions that for a sentence to be performative, it has to be uttered under appropriate circumstances. For example, saying "I do" is equivalent to getting married only in a very specific circumstance that has a social as well as a ritual dimension. In the strict sense defined by Austin, the poems in narratives about the potencies of poems do not constitute performative utterances. But the recognition that utterances are never an exclusively linguistic phenomenon is of great importance.[166] And the concept of "appropriate circumstances" is particularly useful, as it brings attention to the set of conditions that define the operative parameters for the practical uses of language.

The conditions in which *waka* brings beneficial outcomes can be gleaned from the narratives themselves. First, the poet is always beneath the addressee in terms of rank, social class, gender, or age. Emperors do not use poems to persuade subjects; judges do not use poems to reform the behavior of offenders. It is always the other way around. Second, the poem must be uttered, offered, or otherwise communicated. *Waka* are never depicted as magical charms that can operate from a distance.[167] Third, the appeal communicated in the poem has to be in proportion to the power of the addressee. Poems requesting rain are never addressed to emperors or estranged lovers. Fourth, and finally, the language of the poem has to match the linguistic ability of the addressee. Men and women tend to exchange *waka* rather than *shī*. In short, in these narratives, poems are powerful in situations where they can be employed as an effective means of communication across social, cultural, and physical divides. Unless these appropriate conditions are met, a poem will not hold any potency.

If these appropriate conditions are met, a poem will provoke an emotional response. Thus it is possible to consider the narratives about the potencies of *waka* in connection with affect theory. A fundamental characteristic of human affect is that a mere display of it by one person can provoke the same affect in other people. Sigmund Freud referred to this as "identification" (*Identifizierung*) and posited it as the "earliest expression of an emotional tie with another person" in the development of the psyche.[168] The notion of identification allowed Freud to postulate an underlying mechanism for the so-called hysterical physical symptom, by which a person (in this historical and discursive context, usually a woman) developed a symptom through unconscious imitation and without physiological etiology. Silvan Tomkins expanded the scope and valence of this insight through the notion of "affective resonance." This refers to the feedback loop in which, for example, a person's positive feelings radiate "out to others so transparently that he evoke[s] from them the positive feelings which he need[s], so that these positive feelings of his own [can] be nurtured and grow."[169] The key is that affective resonance allows us to move away from the unidirectional model in which a request leads to the granting of a reward, and toward an understanding of how in these narratives granter and grantee come together in a community of affect.

In this respect, it is helpful to understand affect as unfolding at the level of the relationship.[170] Brian Massumi defines affect not as the interior emotional response of a particular subject, but as a transsubjective capacity to be affected and to affect.[171] Melissa Gregg and Gregory Seigworth similarly postulate that "affect arises in the midst of in-between-ness: in the capacities to act and be acted upon" of bodies defined "by their potential to reciprocate or co-participate in the passages of affect."[172] The crucial role of reciprocity in the narratives about the benefits of *waka* is revealed by instances when the benefit granted by a deity is simply a reply in the form of another *waka* poem. In these cases, the poems follow the established pattern of poetic exchanges (*zōtōka* 贈答歌). The response can be delivered as an oracle through a medium (a practice known as *takusen* 託宣) or, more directly, by the god's appearance in a dream.[173] In this context, *waka* serves as a channel through which affect can emerge reciprocally between an affective *appeal* or *expression* on the side of the grantee, and an affective *response* (*kan*) on the side of the granter. Thus, the stories in which a poem elicits only sympathy are not lesser or forced examples; they represent the essence of this phenomenon.

An analysis centered on the relational and affective dimensions of narratives about the potencies of *waka* can reframe our understanding of the narratives themselves. It can shift attention away from Moriyama's transhistorical notion of the inherent power of poetic language to focus instead on the specific social and cultural contexts of these narratives. It also offers an alternative interpretation of the adversarial logic traps identified by Kimbrough, situating them within a broader framework of reciprocal affective resonance between granter and grantee. Similarly, Ogawa's analysis of *waka* as a tool for appealing to higher authorities at times of political and social unrest can be complemented by an examination of *waka*'s capacity not only to reassert social order but also to bridge divides and articulate communities of shared affect. In other words, what the discourses about the potencies of poems underscore is that the figures of authority or power—human or divine, aristocrat or elite warrior—actually *care*; that they care in a language originally exclusive to the aristocracy but now universally intelligible and accessible to all members of society; and, more fundamentally, that there is such a thing as an integrated society to which all now can belong.

The Future of *Waka* Pedagogy

As this chapter argues, there is a subset of texts within the early medieval writings on *waka* that targeted readers who fell within the category of midlevel warriors. When we consider how these texts present themselves—how their aims are framed in prefaces, how their thematic chapters are organized—they seem to be irreconcilably different: one is an encyclopedia of the world, another is a guide to career success, and yet another is a treatise on Buddhist doctrine. Nevertheless, when they discuss *waka* they invoke a strikingly similar corpus of material, predominantly derived from twelfth-century poetic treatises but newly framed and adapted for their respective contexts (through a process theorized in this book as diffusion and reaffordance). An analysis of how these materials are combined, juxtaposed, and organized in each case shows us a changing landscape: as interest in poetry expanded into nonaristocratic social spaces in early medieval Japan, *waka* gained in significance over all other classical courtly practices, for which it came to serve as the model and the index.

These three massive collections of brief narratives offered the kinds of cultural knowledge that non-elite warriors needed, among which was knowledge about *waka*. They also advanced a template for an integrated society in which emergent social groups could coalesce with more established ones. *Kokonchomonjū*, produced by a *zuryō*-level aristocrat in the service of a figure connected to both the court and warrior camps, offered knowledge about the lore, history, and preferences of the aristocracy, with an emphasis on the role of *waka* as an agent of social and cultural integration. *Jikkinshō* organized narratives around the notion of the potency of *waka* and extended its scope to other disciplines, including those favored by warriors. In *Shasekishū*, compiled by a priest of non-elite warrior background, the logic of integration was augmented to include the social space of the monastery. Across these three works, the rhetorical techniques, lexical choices, and conventional imagery of *waka* served as a shared emotional language that could overcome differences in power and reconcile a society strained by political and cultural strife.

As we move into late medieval Japan, we find that learning about *waka* continued to serve as a gateway to cultural education and social integration. At the same time, the practice of *waka* itself experienced significant change. In early medieval Japan it was still possible to draw a distinction between elite pedagogy—elite warriors learned from aristocratic *waka* specialists and saw their poems included in imperially sanctioned anthologies—and non-elite pedagogy, for midlevel warriors who saw in writings about *waka* a means to acquire knowledge of the culture of the court. That is why we find two distinct bodies of writing on *waka*: poetry treatises offer advice on composition, and collections of brief narratives contain knowledge about the court. In late medieval Japan, these two groups of practitioners began to merge, as did the styles of writing about *waka* that they had supported. As the elite *waka* salons opened up to more diverse practitioners in the fourteenth and fifteenth centuries, works about *waka* written by professional families such as the Nijō, the Kyōgoku, and the Reizei began to combine technical and cultural knowledge.

What this convergence of elite and non-elite pedagogical apparatuses looked like can be gleaned from the treatise *Shōtetsu monogatari* 正徹物語 (The tales of Shōtetsu, 1448–50). It combines the commentarial tradition and the scholarly elucidation of exemplary poems that were the hallmarks of elite treatises, with narrative accounts of poets, their poems, and poetic practice more generally. This work both continues and complements the collections that were compiled in the thirteenth century. It favors stories about the poets of the thirteenth and fourteenth centuries, thus supplementing and serving as a continuation for the narrative material in *Kokonchomonjū* and other earlier collections. And, as in *Jikkinshō*, *waka* is deployed in *Shōtetsu monogatari* as the yardstick to measure other cultural practices, as we see in this discussion of the nascent practice of the tea ceremony:

> There are many enthusiasts of poetry (*uta no suki*). Also of enthusiasts of tea (*cha no suki*) there is quite a variety. First, there are those we call "tea enthusiasts." They take deep pleasure in utensils such as tea bowls, kettles, and freshwater containers. If we draw a parallel to *waka*, these would be the enthusiasts who take deep pleasure in utensils such as inkstones, low desks, paper slips, pocket paper, and are at all times reciting poems and attending poetry gatherings.[174]

歌の数奇につきてあまたあり。茶の数奇にも品々あり。先づ茶の数奇といふ者は茶の具足を綺麗にして健盞天目茶釜水差などの色々の茶の具足を心の及ぶ程たしなみもちたる人は茶数奇なり。これを歌にていはば硯文台短冊懐紙などうつくしくたしなみて何時も一続など詠み会所などしかるべき人は茶数奇のたぐひなり。

Shōtetsu monogatari models its analysis of the new tea enthusiasts after the figure of the *waka* enthusiast (*sukimono*) that emerged in the late twelfth century in works such as *Fukurozōshi*.[175] The appreciation of tea was particularly popular in warrior circles. The author of *Shōtetsu monogatari*, Priest Shōtetsu 正徹 (1381–1459), like Narisue before him, had access to both aristocratic and warrior salons, and, like Mujū, was descended from a non-elite warrior family. Shōtetsu's father, Komatsu Hidekiyo 小松秀清 (n.d.), served as castle keeper for a local lord in Oda, in Bitchū Province (Okayama Prefecture today). In his teenage years, Shōtetsu was active in the elite poetry circles in the capital that included warrior magistrates and aristocrats. He trained in *waka* under Imagawa Ryōshun 今川了俊 (1326–1420), an elite warrior who had close ties to the Ashikaga shogunate and had been a patron-student of the aristocratic *waka* specialist Reizei Tamehide 冷泉為秀 (d. 1372). This affiliation with the Reizei brought Shōtetsu the animosity of the rival Nijō poets, who shut him out of the last imperial anthology, *Shin-shoku kokin wakashū* (*Shin-shoku Kokinshū* 新続古今集 [New collection of poems ancient and modern, continued], 1439), which was commissioned by the shogun Ashikaga Yoshinori 足利義教 (1394–1441, r. 1429–41) in 1433. Shōtetsu trained the next generation of notable poets, among them Shinkei 心敬 (1406–75), Senjun 専順 (1411–76), and Takayama Sōzei 高山宗砌 (d. 1455), who in turn served as teachers to Sōgi 宗祇 (1421–1502).[176]

Sōgi was the first commoner of nonwarrior extraction to rise to the spot of foremost poet of his time and secure the patronage of the warrior and aristocratic elite. Sōgi's disciple Sōchō 宗長 (1448–1532) was also a commoner, having been born to a family of firewood wholesalers in Suruga Province (present-day Shizuoka Prefecture). All of these poets were trained scholars and *waka* specialists, but they were active as practitioners of what was becoming the main poetic practice—the performative, collective composition of linked stanzas known as *renga* 連歌. *Renga* had its roots in the practice of verse-capping and was more open to diverse social spaces than *waka* proper. *Waka* and *renga* coexisted as mutually reinforcing but practically separate practices, although to most practitioners outside the aristocracy and the warrior groups, they were almost indistinguishable. In the long-form narratives written for urban commoners in the fourteenth and fifteenth centuries, including many commonly grouped under the umbrella term *otogizōshi* 御伽草子 (companion tales), *waka* and *renga* often became interchangeable indicators of aristocratic cultural practices, which the emerging merchant class approached not only with interest but also with a healthy dose of flippant skepticism.

CHAPTER THREE

The Pleasures of *Waka*

New genres develop inseparably from the emergence of new audiences. The expansion of the practice of *waka* during the Muromachi period (1392–1573) to commoners' social spaces, particularly the world of urban merchants, involved new venues and new forms of engagement. The key genre in this new development is a group of anonymous long-form narratives that first surfaced in fifteenth- and sixteenth-century manuscripts and thus are known as "Muromachi tales." This chapter focuses on a subgroup of these tales that deals with the sensibilities, interests, and customs of the rising townsfolk (*machishū* 町衆) in the century that followed the destruction of Kyoto, the capital, in the Ōnin War (1467–77). Their distinctive feature is not that they depict townsfolk but that they clearly were written predominantly *for townsfolk* readers. For this reason, we can conceptualize them as a genre of their own, and for lack of a better term call them "*machishū* tales."

These tales offer a fresh form of engagement with *waka* poetry and the culture of the court through their use of parody, satire, and compression.[1] They represent a rupture with the elite pedagogic approach based on the pairing of hereditary aristocratic *waka* professionals with patron-students, the origins of which are discussed in chapter 1. And they differ as well from the activity of early medieval cultural experts who had mediated non-elite warriors' access to the court and the aristocracy, in a process theorized in chapter 2 through the notions of *diffusion* and *reaffordance*.

Machishū tales belong in a broader category that comprises the approximately four hundred extant Muromachi tales, known since the nineteenth century as *otogizōshi* 御伽草子 (companion tales). Although it is now standard in Japanese scholarship, the term *otogizōshi* can create confusion. First, the word *otogi* originates from a woodblock edition published by the Osaka printing house of Shibukawa Seiemon 渋川清右衛門 during the period 1716–29. This work, titled *Shūgen otogi bunko* 祝言御伽文庫 (The felicitous wedding companion library), consisted of twenty-three tales presented in a sparsely illustrated horizontal format that imitated the style of the manuscript booklets known as *Nara ehon* 奈良絵本 (Nara illustrated books).[2] Shibukawa was not the first to commercialize Muromachi tales—that practice had begun as soon as commercial woodblock printing became widespread during the Kan'ei era (1624–44). It was the use of the term *otogi* (companion) in Shibukawa's title that ultimately led to the retroactive application of this label to the broader group of Muromachi manuscripts from which he drew his material. To acknowledge this problem, scholars today will often use the expression *muromachi no otogizōshi* 室町の御伽草子 (Muromachi-period companion tales) when they refer specifically to the manuscripts and not the later printed versions. In English, "Muromachi tales" can achieve this same objective.[3]

Second, as the title of Shibukawa's edition makes clear, the publisher marketed this set of texts as part of a trousseau. In early modern usage, the term *shūgen*—literally, "felicitous words"—could also mean "wedding." This edition targeted a specific group in terms of age and gender as well as, inevitably, class, since the texts promote cultural literacy.[4] Branding printed editions of old tales as part of a wider offer of didactic and practical guides for women was a savvy commercial strategy in the eighteenth century, but this marketing approach provides little insight into how we might interpret the earlier manuscripts.[5] We must avoid projecting the characteristics of Shibukawa's intended early modern readership back onto the readership of the late medieval period.[6] This point is particularly significant because some of the Muromachi tales analyzed in this chapter are specifically aimed at young women, and others depict relationships between men and women, exploring themes of courtship and marriage. Moreover, across all of them we can discern a pedagogic dimension, often tied to the cultivation of cultural literacy. The discussion of age, class, and gender in these Muromachi-period texts must be grounded in the social and historical context of the late Muromachi period, which the next section explores in detail.

The *Machishū* of Late Medieval Japan

Nonmilitary commoners had always played a key role in the cultural and artistic life of the realm. The artistic mastery and material sophistication of aristocratic life in the Heian period, for example, depended intimately on the technical expertise, trade, and highly skilled labor of commoners.[7] Yet their toil remained largely undocumented. The efforts of the cultural elites to shut themselves off from other social classes had the effect that little information remains about the values, prejudices, and anxieties of nonwarrior commoners. [8] Late medieval *machishū* tales are the earliest works meant for such an audience.[9] At the same time, the category of nonmilitary commoner is broad and vague—the *machishū* would have rejected it flatly. A first step toward analyzing the contexts in which *machishū* tales were used is gaining a precise understanding of the origins and place of this new social group in late medieval society. Of particular interest are their relationships with aristocrats and warriors, as well as with powerful religious institutions.

The emergence of an audience for literary works within nonwarrior circles connects to a fracture within the commoner class. The rise in the cultural, social, and political power of a very small group of commoners skilled in finance and trade does not imply the enfranchisement of the whole class. As Miura Kei'ichi argues, the advancement of urban merchants in the late medieval period has to be understood as a product of their differentiation from rural agricultural producers within the context of an integrated system for the circulation of goods.[10] It can be argued as well that something analogous occurred with the rise of a warrior elite in the late Heian period and the creation of a class of literate clerks from among those warriors in the Kamakura period, which left the lives of the numberless foot soldiers unchanged.

The tales analyzed in this chapter reflect the tensions between the new culture of merchant commoners and the established culture of impoverished aristocrats, as much as they do the anxieties of wealthy urbanites toward other commoner groups, such as provincial traders, farmers, and artisans. They also reveal a novel societal ambivalence, as more commoners attempted to understand and incorporate the perceived cultural preferences and habits of the aristocracy while simultaneously experimenting with taking pride in the cultural values and inclinations connected with their own lives, such as thrift and industriousness.[11]

The social stratification of the commoner class produced a group of wealthy owners of trading and manufacturing concerns. These were the urbanites who came to be known as *machishū*. The standard term used in aristocratic and warrior sources to mean "commoner," *jige* 地下, referred to any person without official courtly rank or office, particularly those who did not reside in the capital.[12] None of the *machishū* (except for a handful at the very top) were granted rank or office, but their financial power gave them access to the aristocracy, the warrior rulers, and the administrators of religious organizations—elite overlord institutions (*kenmon* 権門) that collected money and resources, in the form of taxes, in exchange for patronage and protection. The rise of the *machishū* is illustrated by a group of brewers of sake (rice wine) who became active in the fourteenth century and reached the peak of their social significance before the turn of the seventeenth century. The wealth they accumulated in the sake trade allowed them to serve as moneylenders, a role that had been played until then almost exclusively by powerful religious institutions. They served as well as "tax farmers," collecting and retaining future tax revenues owed to an overlord institution in exchange for an advance sum.[13] Even though these *machishū* shared some of the fundamental attitudes of other commoners, such as their regard for sound business and accounting practices, their wider interests and cultural prospects changed as they inched closer to the elites.[14]

The rise of *machishū* guilds—such as that of the brewers and moneylenders and those of investors in manufacturing, trade, transportation, and estate management—was the product not only of entrepreneurship and industry but also of wider historical changes. At the root of these transformations was a marked growth in population and prosperity across the board, brought about by a combination of enhanced immunity to disease and the associated increased stability of farming communities.[15] In an economy that remained predominantly agricultural, technological advances such as the waterwheel, more resilient strains of rice, and multiple cropping increased yields significantly. Yet the attendant prosperity was unevenly distributed, favoring nonaristocratic landowners and the traders who supplied them over laborers and farmhands.[16] This translated into chronic indebtedness, as the introduction of monetary exchanges and promissory notes, which became widespread by the middle of the fifteenth century, extended lending practices to all social classes.[17] Manual workers were constantly pushed into steep debt, and in the fifteenth century they organized into peasant leagues and carried out uprisings in demand of amnesty.[18] By the end of the century, the affluent *machishū* had as much in common with their elite aristocratic and warrior clients as with the less affluent nonaristocratic, nonwarrior social groups.

A distinctive characteristic of the *machishū* was their stake in international and transregional domestic trade. The economic fate of aristocrats and warriors was intimately connected to gaining and preserving control over land for military and economic purposes. Trade, by contrast, was more resilient amid the mayhem caused by the constant military and political upheavals during the Muromachi period. The increase in agricultural yields stimulated trade across domestic regions. Increasingly, commodified goods were traded for cash along routes that had been established centuries earlier for the payment in kind of rents and dues from provincial estates to the capital.[19] International trade was also accelerating. Steady trade routes with China and Korea during the Ming 明 (1368–1644) and Joseon 朝鮮 (1392–1897) dynasties were initiated by the third Ashikaga shogun, Yoshimitsu 足利義満 (1358–1408, r. 1368–94), and lasted until the middle of the sixteenth century. In addition to copper coins, the main commodities imported from the continent included porcelain, medicine, and cotton; the chief exports from Japan were sulfur; raw metals, such as copper; swords; folding fans; and folding screens. European traders, first Portuguese and then Dutch, established long-distance trade routes beginning in the middle of the sixteenth century. Two centers of commerce that grew during this period were the port cities of Hakata in Kyūshū and Sakai in present-day Osaka. Sakai, in particular, achieved a measure of autonomy, thanks to its significance as a purveyor of imported military supplies—such as muskets, bullets, and gunpowder—to the warring *daimyō* of the sixteenth century.[20] The *machishū* of the capital also enjoyed a brief period of autonomy in the 1530s, when townsmen representatives (*sōdai* 総代) governed the city.

The economic and political significance of a few commoner households was unprecedented. One way to understand their rise is to consider the commonalities among these households. Hayashiya Tatsusaburō has pointed out three salient characteristics that helped empower the *machishū*.[21] The first was their establishment of marriage ties with families of warrior officials. This can be seen, for example, in the case of the Hon'ami 本阿弥 household of specialists in sword appraisal, polishing, and burnishing. Around the middle of the fifteenth century, the Hon'ami married a daughter to a descendant of the Matsuda 松田 household, a hereditary line of *bakufu* officials, thus adopting their heir, Matsuda Uemon Kiyonobu 松田右衛門清信 (n.d.), as a son-in-law under the name Hon'ami Honkō 本阿弥本光.[22] This bond facilitated the Hon'ami family's access to warrior leaders such as the *daimyō* Oda Nobunaga 織田信長 (1534–82) and the shogun Tokugawa Ieyasu 徳川家康 (1543–1616, r. 1603–5), whose patronage led them to great financial and cultural power. As Hayashiya points out, family lore traced their lineage back to a sword appraiser called Hon'ami Myōhon 本阿弥妙本 (active fourteenth century), who had served the first Ashikaga shogun, Takauji 足利尊氏 (1305–58, r. 1338–58), as a retained consultant (*dōbōshū* 同朋衆). In fact, the recorded family history starts only at the time of the marriage alliance with the Matsuda.

The patronage of powerful institutions could be turned into commercial advantage. The second factor in the rise of the *machishū* is that many received monopolistic rights over the trade of specific commodities or the control of critical routes. The Chaya 茶屋, for example, were merchants who were engaged in the domestic wholesaling of textiles and the importing of raw silk and other commodities from Southeast Asia, from ports in Macao, Luzon, Siam (present-day Thailand), and Java. The transportation over water was conducted from the port of Nagasaki on ships that eventually came to be known as red-seal ships (*goshu'in-sen* 御朱印船) because in the first decades of the seventeenth century they operated under letters patent issued by the Tokugawa shogunate for the so-called Nanban 南蛮 trade routes.[23] A system of trade permits guaranteed that the Chaya, among a few other families, were the only traders allowed to import and wholesale textiles. A portion of the family's income from overseas trade stemmed from steep interest rates on loans made to ship captains by the family that held such a permit. As with the Hon'ami, the family history of the Chaya starts with an alliance with a warrior family. The earliest recorded Chaya was Shirōjirō Kiyonobu 茶屋四郎次郎清延 (1545–96), the scion of a warrior household from Mikawa (or perhaps Yamashiro) Province, who married into the Chaya. The bonds that the family eventually established with Tokugawa Ieyasu, whom they supplied with goods and information, continued through the Edo period as the Chaya served as the main purveyor of textiles to the Tokugawa shogunate.

Another *machishū* who amassed a fortune thanks to the protective international trade policy of Ieyasu, and of his predecessor Toyotomi Hideyoshi 豊臣秀吉 (1536–98), was Suminokura Ryōi 角倉了以 (1554–1614). The son of a physician, he married into the main branch of the Suminokura, who were moneylenders to warrior leaders. Thanks to his father-in-law's introduction, Ryōi became close to Hideyoshi's officials and, later, to Ieyasu's. In the first years of the seventeenth century, Ryōi sent a red-seal ship to Vietnam carrying weapons and sulfur, in order to acquire medicine and texts. He then invested the considerable profits into a project to open to navigation several rivers around the capital, Kyoto, for the transportation of grain, salt, and lumber. This integrated the city with the countryside, further boosting domestic commerce.

The third component of the sociocultural identity and success of the *machishū* was their religious affiliation. Merchants in the capital generally belonged to the Lotus (Hokke 法華) sect of Buddhism, which had been founded by the Kamakura-period priest Nichiren 日蓮 (1222–82). This set them apart from their warrior overlords, who tended toward the Zen 禅 sects, as well as from the agricultural workers in areas surrounding the capital, who were for the most part attached to Pure Land temples.[24] Their affiliation with the Lotus sect afforded the *machishū* an opportunity to organize and act on their interests. This became apparent, for example, in 1532 when a military conflict erupted between the *machishū*-backed Hokke temples and the peasant-supported Ikkō Pure Land temples. Through an alliance with the warrior leader Hosokawa Harumoto 細川晴元 (1514–63), the Hokke side was able to gain control of the city, which they enjoyed for four years until they were, in turn, defeated by a new alliance among Harumoto, the Ikkō sect, and the powerful Tendai-sect Enryakuji Temple 延暦寺 on Mount Hiei. In other words, as the *machishū* moved away from (and often against) other commoner groups, and developed cultural interests and political ambitions similar to those of their overlords, their shared religious affiliation offered not only vertical segmentation from other classes but also horizontal ties of solidarity and a sense of cultural and political commonality.

The military defeat notwithstanding, the Hokke-Ikkō conflagration marked the beginning of formal associations among urban merchant neighbors (*machigumi* 町組). Organized by area—West (Nishi gumi 西組), Center (Naka gumi 中組), Southeast (Tatsumi gumi 巽組), and so on—these neighborhood leagues played a progressively more significant role in the cultural life of the capital. As the *machishū* consolidated their commercial and political ties to the warrior leaders, their scions developed an interest in the cultural pursuits that were favored by military and aristocratic elites, such as calligraphy, poetry, painting, and ceramics. A salient illustration of this trend is evident in the career of a grandson of Hon'ami Honkō, the gifted Kōetsu 光悦 (1558–1637). Kōetsu continued in the family business, acting as sword connoisseur, finisher, and polisher for powerful warrior leaders such as the Kanazawa-based Maeda 前田 household. In parallel, he engaged in the cultural activities that warriors prized, creating an artist colony where *machishū* mingled with warriors. Among Kōestu's associates were *machishū* such as the Raku 楽 household of potters, and the dealer and painter Tawaraya Sōtatsu 俵屋宗達 (n.d.), as well as warrior leaders such as the tea masters and craftsmen Furuta Oribe 古田織部 (1544–1615) and Kobori Enshū 小堀遠州 (1579–1647). One of the financial backers of this colony was the third-generation Chaya Shirōjirō Kiyotsugu 茶屋四郎次郎清次 (1584–1622). Another patron was

Suminokura Ryōi's son Sōan 素庵 (1571–1632), who continued the household's trading and engineering business. Sōan learned calligraphy from Kōetsu and went on to found the Suminokura school of calligraphy. He was also a famous Noh performer and a leading force in a project to edit and print an anthology of courtly classics that had until then circulated only as manuscripts, such as *Ise monogatari* 伊勢物語 (The tales of Ise, mid-tenth century) and *Genji monogatari* 源氏物語 (The tale of Genji, early eleventh century), together with Noh librettos of the Kanze 観世 household.[25]

From all these instances of financially successful, socially mobile *machishū*, we learn that regardless of their business acumen and industriousness, the closer a family's ties were to the warrior administration, the higher were their chances of attaining commercial and social success. Key to building a lasting household was the descendants' ability to secure continued patronage from a roster of warrior leaders that changed continually, often several times within a generation. This can be seen in the case of the Gotō 後藤 metalworking household, which initially ran a workshop that supplied the Ashikaga shogunate with small metal objects, such as knives, guards and hilts for swords, and hairpins, in gold, gold-copper alloys, and silver—but never, as a rule, in iron. Their high-relief designs followed elite warriors' preference for lions, dragons, and elegant flora and fauna. The founding figure of the household, Gotō Yūjō 後藤祐乗 (Shirōbē I 四郎兵衛初代, 1440–1512), served the eighth Ashikaga shogun, Yoshimasa 足利義政 (1435–90, r. 1449–73), who had him appointed to the fifth rank. After Yūjō took the tonsure, Emperor GoHanazono 後花園 (1419–1471, r. 1428–64) granted him the highest rank in the priesthood, Hōin 法印. His descendants, chief among them the fifth-generation household head Gotō Tokujō 後藤徳乗 (1550–1631), received the protection and patronage of Oda Nobunaga, Toyotomi Hideyoshi, and the Tokugawa family. In the Edo period, the Gotō family's work (known as Gotōke 後藤家 or *iebori* 家彫り) became synonymous with elegant warrior attire for formal occasions, as distinct from the highly elaborate but less formal metalwork (known as *machibori* 町彫り) of craftsmen such as Yokoya Sōmin 横谷宗珉 (1670–1733). The Gotō trajectory illustrates that even in the rare instances when *machishū* household heads were granted courtly rank and office (which, in any case, was an imposing but largely symbolic achievement), their material prosperity ultimately remained contingent on securing warriors' patronage through the provision of goods and services.[26]

At the root of the rare success of a handful of *machishū* households, we find a combination of financial power and cultural expertise.[27] The financial services that the *machishū* offered their patrons had its precedent in the figure of the *dosō* 土倉 (literally, "earthen-walled warehouse").[28] The literal meaning of *dosō* stems from the practice of Heian-period moneylenders (*kashiage* 借上) of storing in these buildings the goods left by borrowers as security. Known as *dosō* since at least the Kamakura period, by the fourteenth century there were more than three hundred of these moneylenders in the capital, the large majority of whom were operating under the protection and authority of the Tendai temples on Mount Hiei. Powerful shrines such as Kasuga in Nara also offered protection to local *dosō*. During the Muromachi period, Zen temples entered the lending business, as well as the *machishū* makers of sake and miso (soybean paste). Aside from lending money at steep interest rates against securities such as personal property and real estate, the *dosō* allowed their clients to store cash and valuable goods in their safe warehouses. Among these clients were members of the imperial household, the aristocracy, and the *bakufu* administration, who seldom had their own safe warehouses and thus engaged the *dosō* as both property keepers and administrators.

The cultural and technical expertise that distinguished successful *machishū* households can be traced to a particular historical development. Starting with the Ashikaga shogunate, warrior leaders had begun to engage experts in arts and crafts as their close attendants.[29] These experts, collectively known as *dōbōshū* 同朋衆, usually were men of either commoner or low-level warrior origin who had taken the tonsure and traditionally adopted the name *-ami* 阿弥 (a reference to Amida Buddha). Among them were the experts in Chinese painting Nōami 能阿弥 (1397–1471), with his son Geiami 芸阿弥 (1431–1485) and grandson Sōami 相阿弥 (d. 1525). They were responsible for handling, curating, and generally managing the inventory of imported artworks that the Ashikaga displayed in their reception rooms when entertaining guests. Much like a twelfth-century *waka* or *kanbun* household, they preserved their knowledge in a treatise, which is known as *Kundai kan sōchō ki* 君台観左右帳記 (Records of the decorative art on the left and on the right in the shogun's residence). Begun by Nōami and continued by Sōami, the treatise is a catalog of paintings, ceramics, lacquerware, and metalware that covers the ways in which the works should be handled and displayed through their descriptions and illustrations. To some extent, the early Noh performers and writers Kan'ami 観阿弥 (1333–84) and his son Zeami 世阿弥 (ca. 1363–ca. 1443) were part of this wave of commoners who gained access to powerful officials thanks to their craft. As with the provision of financial services by the *dosō*, the work of the *dōbōshū* required the kind of practical knowledge, professional experience, and material resources that could be passed down a family line.

Most *machishū* did not enjoy the worldly success of the few households discussed so far. The access to power that the Hon'ami attained, the wealth of the Chaya and the Suminokura, the courtly rank of the Gotō—all were extraordinary achievements that made those families outliers rather than representatives of the average experience of the thousands of *machishū* in the capital and in provincial urban centers such as Nara and Sakai. For the majority, the less successful *machishū*—the small-time moneylenders, the artisans, the haulers, the retail merchants—the handful of wildly successful *machishū* households defined the parameters of what it was possible to achieve and offered guidelines for what had to be done to achieve it: namely, accumulate wealth and acquire cultural literacy.

The epitome of one who followed this aspirational arc was Haiya Shōeki 灰屋紹益 (also known as Jōeki 丞益; 1607–91). He was the son of Hon'ami Kōeki 本阿弥光益—who was Kōetsu's nephew—and became a son-in-law of Haiya Shōyū 灰屋紹由 (d. 1622).[30] The Haiya (literally, "ash merchants"), whose actual family name was Sano 佐野, had amassed a fortune through their monopolistic control of the ash that served as a catalyst in the production of indigo dye. Shōeki continued the family trade, but diverted the proceeds into funding a life of cultural sophistication. He studied *waka* with two aristocratic professional instructors, Karasumaro Mitsuhiro 烏丸光広 (1579–1638)

and Asukai Masa'aki 飛鳥井雅章 (1611–79); *haikai* with the leading master, Matsunaga Teitoku 松永貞徳 (1571–1653); calligraphy with Kōetsu; and the tea ceremony with the warrior leaders Kanamori Sōwa 金森宗和 (1584–1656) and Fujibayashi Sōgen 藤林宗源 (1608–95). Through the game of kickball (*kemari* 蹴鞠), he befriended Prince Toshitada 智忠 (1619–62), the nephew of Emperor GoMizuno'o 後水尾 (1596–1680, r. 1611–29). Shōeki joined GoMizuno'o's cultural salon, taking part in the design and construction of the Katsura Imperial Villa, completed in 1645. In an episode that captured the interest of the whole capital, Shōeki fought off his rival, the regent Konoe Nobuhiro 近衛信尋 (1599–1649), to win the right to buy the contract of a famous entertainer known as Yoshino Tayū 吉野太夫 (b. 1606), whom he married.[31] The wealth, artistic achievements, and romantic adventures of Haiya Shōeki proved that social mobility beyond one's wildest dreams was possible, even if only remotely, and that the means required were money and cultural expertise.

We do not know as much about the less wealthy *machishū* of the capital. Their aggregated economic activity and political impact are documented, but their individual trajectories remain, for the most part, obscure. Their cultural life, however—particularly the ways in which they engaged with the cultural legacy of the aristocratic and warrior classes—lives on in a number of narratives referred to here as *machishū* tales, a subgroup of the Muromachi tales.

Machishū Tales and Poetry

Efforts to systematize *machishū* tales—narratives written for townsfolk—into subcategories according to main themes, authorship, readership, or social function (pedagogic, religious, entertainment) have proved difficult.[32] For every useful generalization, there are a handful of consequential exceptions. And the same applies to the functions of poetry in these tales.

To contextualize a discussion focused on *machishū* tales, it is useful to take a look at the place of *waka* more generally in the constellation of hundreds of Muromachi tales. *Waka* and *waka*-related genres such as *renga* (collective linked stanzas) and *haikai* (a popular version of *renga*) not only are present in most of the tales but also play a key role in a remarkable number of them. As expected, other traditional aristocratic practices are also represented in these narratives. *Shī*, calligraphy, court music (in particular the *koto* 琴, a thirteen-string zither), archery, kickball, and the like appear in many tales, alongside newer pastimes popular among warriors, such as the tea ceremony. In terms of numbers, the representations of *waka* far exceed those of any other courtly practice. As Sawai Taizō has shown, *waka* and its related genres appear extensively.[33] Tales incorporate old poems taken from imperial anthologies and private collections, quoted in full or alluded to, as well as new compositions. Many of the *waka* appear as part of wooing exchanges, both between men and women and between older men and younger men. We also find poems used for pedagogic effect, a practice related to the inclusion of Buddhist poems in the imperial anthologies, as well as detailed depictions of *renga* and *haikai* gatherings. Some tales quote knowledge from medieval poetry treatises. And all of them depict *waka* as a practice that is no longer limited to the elites, but is accessible to and enjoyed by all social classes. These general findings apply, naturally, to the *machishū* tales as well.

What makes *machishū* tales particularly alluring for a study of the practice of *waka* among late medieval urban commoners is that poetry is revealed in these narratives as a gateway into a wider process of cultural production and transmission. The *machishū* tale *Monokusa Tarō* 物くさ太郎 (Lazy Tarō), for example, draws from early medieval narratives about the potencies of *waka* to offer a parody of improbable social mobility in which knowledge about aristocratic culture is humorously eroticized. The tale *Saru Genji sōshi* 猿源氏草子 (The tale of monkey Genji, sixteenth century) provides a glimpse of the role of cultural literacy in interactions between commoners, as a wealthy *machishū* uses his poetic and cultural literacy to impersonate an elite warrior and marry a high-ranking courtesan. By contrast, *Nakagoro no koto* 中ころの事 (Not too long ago), known today as *Menoto no sōshi* 乳母草子 (The nursemaid's book), is a compressed tale about the illusions of social mobility through cultural education, openly pitting *waka* and aristocratic values against the nascent culture of the urban merchant classes. In these *machishū* tales, *waka* are measured against humorous, witty variations known today as *kyōka* (absurd poetry). Close scrutiny reveals, however, that *kyōka* is not the bumpkin distant relative of *waka*; instead, it is the leading means by which the practice of *waka* proper was embraced by the *machishū*. Parody, satire, and cultural pedagogy come together in these texts to articulate the joint embracing of both *waka* and court culture in the emergent social space of sophisticated urban commoners.

The humor that is a distinctive feature of poems in *machishū* tales has its precursor in the comical passages and poems in the earlier collections of brief narratives. Humor was present, in fact, in the practice of *waka* since its very beginning, but its growth was systematically stunted by commentarial, editorial, and critical biases. Enforcing a distinction between proper and improper styles of composition had, from the start, been one of the central concerns of the editors of poetry anthologies.[34] Book 16 of *Man'yōshū* 万葉集 (Collection of myriad leaves, after 759), for example, contains a section of poems that are introduced by headnotes indicating that they are to be read as "making fun" poems (*warau uta* 嗤哥). The compliers of *Kokin wakashū* (*Kokinshū* Collection of poems ancient and modern], 905) marked off nonconforming poems by grouping them in a separate book titled *Zattei* 雑体 (Miscellaneous forms; book 19). This book contains archaic long poems (*nagauta* 長歌), metrically symmetric poems (*sedōka* 旋頭歌; literally, "poems in which the first half is repeated"), and humorous poems (*haikaika* 誹諧歌).[35] The diction and themes of the poems quarantined in book 19 of *Kokinshū* and book 16 of *Man'yōshū* do not appear in the rest of either collection. For centuries after the compilation of these anthologies, what constituted proper *waka* was epitomized by the poems in *Kokinshū*, with the exclusion of those in book 19.

This distinction perdured, but the term *haikai* itself, in its *Kokinshū* sense of "unorthodox poems," would not become part of the active critical lexicon. In fact, the expression fell into disuse after the tenth century. For example, the scholar Minamoto no Toshiyori stated in his poetry treatise *Toshiyori zuinō* 俊頼髄脳 (Toshiyori's essentials of poetry, 1111–14) that nobody understood the term anymore and suggested that, judging from its use in *Kokinshū*, *haikai* should be read as *zaregoto* ざれごと (to joke around) and similar to *zare-tawaburu* 戯れたはぶる (to jest).[36] The category *haikai* reemerged later as a subheading in book 18 of Fujiwara no Shunzei's imperial anthology *Senzai wakashū* (*Senzaishū* 千載集 [Collection of a thousand years]). In the treatise *Korai fūteishō* 古来風躰抄 (Poetic styles from the past, 1197–1201), Shunzei connected *haikai* to the poetry of the distant past, applying the category retroactively to humorous poems in books 3 and 16 of *Man'yōshū*.[37]

This does not imply that humorous poems ceased to be exchanged and recorded. They appeared, beginning in the twelfth century, in the practice of verse-capping (*renga*, known today as *tan-renga*). One person would offer the upper section of a *waka* for another to cap with a matching, often humorous lower section. Toshiyori included many passages in his poetry treatise depicting such humorous exchanges, as well as several instances of verse-capping in his imperial collection *Kin'yō wakashū* (*Kin'yōshū* 金葉集 [Collection of Golden Leaves]), under the heading *renga*. So did Tachibana no Narisue in *Kokonchomonjū* 古今著聞集 (Collection of tales written and heard in the past and present, 1254) and Mujū Dōgyō in *Shasekishū* 沙石集 (Collection of sand and pebbles, 1283).

If *Kokinshū* determined for posterity the parameters of "proper" *waka*—the accepted diction, themes, treatments, rhetorical techniques, social circumstances of practice, and so on—something analogous happened with unorthodox poems. There are, in fact, striking commonalities among tenth-century *haikai*, the later verse-capping, and the *kyōka* in *machishū* tales. In formal terms, all display a double movement, what a comedian today would call the setup and punch line. The poet sets up the listener or reader to expect one thing, and then breaks away from that expectation, often provoking amused surprise. The model for this form is found in poems as early as those in book 19 of *Kokinshū*, such as the following by Yoshimine no Harutoshi 良岑玄利 (Priest Sosei 素性法師; ca. 844–910):

yamabuki no	Dyed the yellow of kerria in bloom
hana iro koromo	this robe
nushi ya tare	but who might be its owner?
toedo kotaezu	I ask but get no answer
kuchinashi ni shite	from this mouthless gardenia.[38]

山吹の花色衣ぬしやたれ問へど答へずくちなしにして

The first part of the poem (*kami no ku* 上の句 [first three lines]) is indistinguishable from that of poems in the other books of the collection. Breaking away from the expectation that this will be another proper poem, the second part (*shimo no ku* 下の句 [last two lines]) introduces a play on words with *kuchinashi*, which can mean not only "gardenia" (梔子), the fruit of which is useful as a dye, but also "no mouth" (口無し) and, by extension, "silent." It is credibly this second meaning of *kuchinashi* that was not considered a proper poetic expression and thus was what placed the poem in book 19. The poems in the *haikai* section are diverse and impossible to systematize, but this basic structure, with an orthodox or proper first part and an unorthodox, improper second part, is representative of the style of humor they introduced. Some of the poems deploy fewer orthodox lines and shift more quickly into unorthodoxy, or even start with unorthodox expressions.[39] Still, the interest and humor in these poems stems from the contrast between a more proper reading and an alternative, less proper one.

The distinction between orthodox/proper and unorthodox/improper practices was inherited by the medieval collaborative linked verse known today as *renga*. Poetic sequences that abided by the diction, imagery, and techniques of orthodox *waka* were referred to as *kaki no moto* 柿の本 (under the persimmon tree) or *ushin renga* 有心連歌 (serious), while playful or lighter sequences were known as *kuri no moto* 栗の本 (under the chestnut tree) or *mushin renga* 無心連歌 (unserious).[40] The latter, unorthodox linked verse eventually evolved into *haikai no renga* 俳諧の連歌 (known today as *haikai*), which was the predominant form in the late medieval period. The common trait of the poems in book 16 of *Man'yōshū*, the *haikai* in *Kokinshū*, *tan-renga*, *mushin renga*, and *haikai no renga* is that they initially seem orthodox, and they work by upending the expectation—which they themselves create—that they will be orthodox throughout. Even when practitioners explicitly create humorous compositions, the humor comes from breaking the rules of *waka*.

The *kyōka* in *machishū* tales combine "straight" language with tropes that are in some way absurd or outrageous, so that their incongruity produces an effect of humor. The ostensible aim of this juxtaposition is comedic, but it also affords readers who do not usually practice *waka* a chance to learn by comparison what proper *waka* look like. *Machishū* tales are rich in *kyōka* poems, and they incorporate the logic of *kyōka* to shape their form, rhetoric, and narrative arcs. This extension of the juxtaposition of straight and absurd beyond the realm of poetry is what I call a "*kyōka*-esque" approach.[41] It is a parody that packs the target of parody within the parodic text, achieving the double effect of entertainment and education. In contrast to the *haikai* in *Kokinshū*, which are marked off for their unorthodoxy—their lack of compliance with the rules of proper *waka*—in *kyōka* poems and *kyōka*-esque prose, flippancy and impertinence take center stage, and parody, satire, and compression become the dominant form representing the *waka* tradition.

There is a *kyōka*-esque logic behind *Monokusa Tarō*'s parody of the social utility of *waka* and other forms of cultural literacy, *Saru Genji sōshi*'s satire of the associated hopes of social mobility, and *Nakagoro no koto*'s ridiculing of attempts to keep *waka* and *kyōka* separate and distinct from each other. The *kyōka*-esque—the coming together of orthodox and unorthodox, proper and improper, court culture and commoner culture—harnesses the *haikai* spirit to invert the affordances of *waka* that are extolled in such works as *Toshiyori zuinō* and *Jikkinshō*.[42]

Parody and Transformation

In *machishū* tales, *waka* appears as a gateway to cultural literacy, as it does in the poetry treatises and collections of brief narratives of classical and early medieval Japan. Yet in these stories, *waka* has become *kyōka*, and cultural literacy is transmitted through *kyōka*'s parodic, inverted form. *Monokusa Tarō* is ostensibly a tale about the transformation of a countrified person into a sophisticated aristocrat. The story it actually tells is about the transformation of court culture as it became available to the new social space of the urban commoners.

This is not a case of ontogeny recapitulates phylogeny, but of ontogeny *parodies* phylogeny. The cultural literacy that powers the social ascent of the main character would have been unrecognizable to the original readership of *Toshiyori zuinō* or *Jikkinshō*. Yet it is meaningless without the springboard of aristocratic culture. Thus *Monokusa Tarō* is the story of how, at the heart of the *kyōka*-esque, we find preserved—even honored—the culture of the court.

The transformation of the street beggar from a remote village in Shinano Province into a sophisticated aristocrat living in the capital was first told in anonymous Muromachi-period illustrated manuscripts. One is a scroll titled *Monokusa Tarō emaki* 物臭太郎繪巻 (Illustrated scroll of lazy Tarō), in which the text is interspersed with images.[43] Another is a set of two horizontal booklets in the *Nara ehon* format, titled *Monokusa Tarō*, in which each illustration occupies an entire page.[44] More than a century later, the tale surged in popularity after Shibukawa published it as part of his trousseau set in the early eighteenth century, leading to adaptations to other genres throughout the early modern period.[45] The publisher Urokogataya Magobē 鱗形屋孫兵衛 (active late eighteenth century) put out a condensed, heavily illustrated version in the style of the eighteenth-century *kusa zōshi* 草双紙 (text-picture book) graphic narratives; other identically titled works in the same style had more varied content.[46] A radically free adaptation for the *jōruri* 浄瑠璃 (puppet theater) stage, cowritten by Asada Icchō 浅田一鳥 (d. 1780) and Yasuda Akei 安田蛙桂 (n.d.), was performed around the same time under the title *Jūjō genji monokusa Tarō* 十帖源氏物ぐさ太郎 (Monokusa Tarō of the abridged tale of Genji).[47] By the late seventeenth century, the name Monokusa Tarō evoked a popular image of a lazy provincial, rather than a specific narrative. In the analysis that follows, however, I will focus exclusively on the narrative arc that circulated in manuscripts during the late medieval period, and that spoke to the social fractures and cultural dialogues that structured late medieval society.

The nature of the transformation depicted in the late medieval text (hereafter referred to simply as *Monokusa Tarō*) has received various interpretations. As Satake Akihiro has argued, one way to understand the tale is as a metamorphosis of the personality and character of the protagonist.[48] The story opens with Monokusa Tarō Hijikasu, a resident of Shinano Province, who lives in a makeshift hut. He wishes for wealth and comfort but, being slothful and unwilling to work, relies on charity to subsist. When the villagers receive a request to select and send a laborer to the capital, they use the opportunity to get rid of him. He agrees to go, after he is told that in the capital he will soon find a wife. Once there, his transformation is immediate and is described very succinctly by the narrator: "He did not show even the slightest laziness [*monokusa*]. There was nobody this industrious [*mame*]."[49] In Satake's argument, this seemingly abrupt incongruence belies a continuity. The protagonist is not simply industrious but full of vitality, as seen when he applies the same zeal to the pursuit of a wife. What looked like sloth was actually the individualistic, high-handed (*nosa*) stance of a person who has broken free from social expectations. As Satake points out, this was the personality type needed at a time when people's own resources and efforts allowed them to rise financially and socially.

Another way in which we can read the story is as a transformation of previous texts and genres. As noted by Ichiko Teiji, the foremost modern scholar of *otogizōshi*, at the end of many versions of the tale (including that in Shibukawa's edition), the protagonist is revealed to be a god called Otaga. This revelation brings the narrative closer to the many medieval accounts of the origins (*honji* 本地) of gods and buddhas associated with the founding of specific shrines and temples, texts known as *engi* 縁起.[50] As Shinoda Jun'ichi has suggested, *Monokusa Tarō* may also be a parody of that genre, especially since the tale's humor contrasts with the earnestness of the hagiographic *engi*.[51] Two other possible sources of parody were proposed by Virginia Skord, who has described the tale as a general "attempt to deflate generic conventions," with a substitution of "verbal agility for depth."[52] In her reading, the rags of the protagonist can be interpreted as a parody of the lavish battle dress depicted in warrior tales (*gunkimono* 軍記物), and his use of poetry to woo his future wife as a parody of courting practices portrayed in Heian-period aristocratic narrative texts (*monogatari* 物語). All these sources of parody were established and widely known genres among the elites of the late medieval period, and thus were likely part of the literary competence of the author of *Monokusa Tarō*. How familiar *machishū* readers would have been with this textual heritage is hard to determine; most likely it would have varied over a wide spectrum of cultural literacy levels.

Unlike the quick shift from sloth to industry succinctly described on Monokusa Tarō's arrival in the capital, his metamorphosis from a rustic provincial into a sophisticated aristocrat is depicted as a gradual, detailed process that takes up about three-quarters of the tale. The account unfolds as a series of witty courtship dialogues between the protagonist and the woman who would become his wife. These highly erotic exchanges are meant to serve as measures of the protagonist's cultural literacy and social advancement. But the quips they exchange are blatantly surreal and clearly not meant to be taken as realistic depictions of natural conversation. Rather than earnest, straightforward tests of a person's cultural literacy, like those explored in previous chapters of this book, these exchanges present a *kyōka*-esque parody of such tests of sociocultural status, combined with a satire of the person who willingly subjects himself to them.

The first exchange is a good illustration of this point, as it consists in a display of stock knowledge about the capital that seems, on its face, pointless. In this passage Monokusa Tarō, still wearing the rags from his village, approaches an elegant woman who is praying at the monthly festival of Kiyomizu Temple. He claims that they have met before:

> Hey, lady! I remember you from way back! Haven't we met before at the villages of Ōhara, Shizuhara, and Seryō; at Kōdō, Kawasaki, and Nakayama; at Chōrakuji and Kiyomizu; at Rokuhara and Rokkakudō; at Saga, Hōrinji, Daigo, Uzumasa, Kurusu, and Kohata; at Yodo, Yahata, Sumiyoshi, Kurumadera; at Gojō Tenjin and Kibune Myōjin; at Hiyoshi Sannō, Gion and Kitano, Kasuga and Kamo? How about it?[53]
>
> いかにや女房はるかにこそおぼえて候へ、小原、静原、芹生の里、革堂、河崎、中山、長楽寺、清水、六波羅、六角堂、嵯峨法輪寺、太秦、醍醐、栗栖、木幡山、淀八、幡、住吉、鞍馬寺、五条の天神、貴船の明神、日吉山王、祇園、北野、賀茂、春日、所々にて参りあひて候ひしはいかにと申しける。

This seemingly asinine list is ostensibly meant to impress the lady with the protagonist's knowledge of the city, but it is clear that something else is going on. Ichiko has argued that the enumeration follows the style of a genre known as *michiyuki* 道行, a passage of prose describing a journey that is embellished by the kind of sound play and association common in *waka*. The list does rely on sound, pairing Ōhara and Shizuhara; Rokuhara and Rokkakudō; Kohata and Yahata; Gojō Tenjin and Kibune Myōjin. The genre of *michiyuki* is all about linear movement, though, and thus by definition must name places in the geographic order in which they come up during the journey. What we find here, instead, is a list of culturally celebrated places organized in a way that facilitates memorization. For example, Ōhara, Shizuhara, and Seryō are mountain villages north of the capital; Chōrakuji, Kiyomizu, Rokkakudō, and Hōrinji are temples; and Gion, Kitano, Kasuga (in Nara), and Kamo are shrines, all of them deeply connected with the Heian aristocracy. The sound pairings that Ichiko points out are actually a common mnemonic featured in pedagogic genres such as the late medieval and early modern didactic *waka* known as *kyōkunka* 教訓歌. This list actually aims to provide the reader with a compressed, easy-to-remember catalog of high-culture landmarks. The *kyōka*-esque is not a mere parody of a classical source—knowledge of which is assumed in the reader—but carries within itself the bare minimum cultural knowledge to secure the enjoyment of the joke by a reader of emergent cultural literacy.

The next step in the dialogue between the protagonist and the lady has the same double structure. On the surface, on realizing that she is dealing with an unsophisticated provincial (*inaka no mono* 田舎の者), the woman grows confident that she can easily confound him and escape. Meanwhile, as only the reader is aware, she is generally circumscribing her lexicon to that of *waka*, and stringing her challenges in a way reminiscent of linked verse. This passage is hard to discuss without quoting it in full:

> Is that so? Here there are too many people. Please come by my home, she said.
>
> Where is it? he asked.

Thinking that she would confuse him with her words and use the opportunity to escape, she replied,
I live at a place called "Under the Pine" [*matsu no moto*].
Monokusa Tarō heard this and said,
I get what you meant by "Under the Pine." That would be Akashi Bay [*akashi no ura* (Bay of Light)].
She thought there could be nothing stranger than this, but thinking that he couldn't guess one more, she continued:
Actually, it's in a village where the sun sets [*hi-kururu sato*].
I get what you meant by "Sunset Village." How deep into Kurama [*kurama no oku* (deep into a dark place)]?
That is also where I live: Look for the street of lamps [*tomoshibi no kōji*].
How far down Oil Street [*abura no kōji*]?
This is also where I live: the town of shame [*hazukaji no sato*].
Where in Tucked-Away Town [*shinobu no sato*]?
This is also where I live: the town of *Aster yomena* flowers [*uwagi no sato*].
How far down Brocade Street [*nishiki no kōji*]?
In the province of consolation [*nagusamu kuni*].
How far into Ōmi Province, where lovers meet [*koishite ahumi no kuni*]?
In the village of cloudless cosmetics [*keshō suru kumori naki sato*], she said.
Where in Mirror Traveler's Lodge [*kagami no shuku*]?
In the province of autumn [*aki suru kuni*].
Where in Rice-Leaf Inaba Province [*inaba no kuni*]?
This is also where I live: in the province of farmlands [*hatachi no kuni* (*hatachi* also can mean "twenty years old")].
Where in Wakasa Province [*wakasa no kuni* (*wakasa* means "youth")]?
He spoke in this way, giving her no chances to escape.[54]

それはさる事も候はん。今はこれにては人目もしげしわらはがさぶらふ所へとふて入らせ給へとありければ、いづくにて候ぞと問いければ調子のことばをかけそれをふくせんその内に逃げばやと思召、わらはが候所をば、松のもとゝいふ所にて候。物くさ太郎是を聞き、松のもとゝは心得たり、明石の浦の事。かゝる希代の事はなし是一つをこそ聞き知るとも餘の事は知らじと思ひて、たゞし日暮るゝ里に候ぞ。日暮るゝ里も心得たり、鞍馬の奥はどの程ぞ。これもわらはがふる里よ、ともし火の小路をたづねよや。油の小路はどの程ぞ。是もわらはがふる里よ、はづかしの里に候よ。しのぶの里とはどの程ぞ。これもわらはが故里よ、うはぎの里に候。錦の小路はどの程ぞ。是もわらはがふる里よ、なぐさむ國に候は。それは戀してあふみの國はどの程ぞ。けしやうするくもりなき里とのたまへば、鏡の宿はどの程ぞ。秋する國に候よ。因幡國にはどの程ぞ。これもわらはがふる里よ、はたちの國に候よ。若狹國にはどの程ぞ。かやうにとかくいふ程に此上はわが身のがるべきやうなし。

The shape of this conversation is a series of independent whimsical riddles that have as solutions the names of real places, found by means of plays on words. In some cases, it is clear how the puzzle works. For example, to *uwagi no sato* (literally, "town of the *Aster yomena* flower"), the protagonist responds *nishiki no kōji* (Brocade Street), since *uwagi* can also mean "top robe," a garment that was likely to be made of brocade. In other cases, the connection is less clear, such as with *matsu* 松 *no moto* (under the pine) and *akashi* 明石 *no ura* (Akashi Bay). Ichiko speculates, for example, that since *matsu* was short for *taimatsu* 松明 (pine torch), it would be bright under the torch. This type of wordplay riddle appears in other late medieval texts.[55] It is connected to the poetic challenges of the Heian period, in which an aristocrat would quote or allude to a poem—it could be a *shī* or a *waka*—as part of a dialogue, for others to identify.[56] What the woman's test measures, then, is cultural literacy—which is to say, social class.[57]

The measure of cultural literacy is *waka*, and the associated practice of *renga*. The riddles are linked by carefully structured transitions. Some are thematic—the traveler's lodge (*shuku*) on Mount Kagami was located in Ōmi Province, which is mentioned in the previous riddle—while others are lexical: *shinobu*, *nagusamu*, and *aki* (from *aku*, "to lose interest") together suggest the theme of love, and all come together to structure a sequence of *renga*-style links (*tsukeai* 付合): pine (torch) and light; light and dark; darkness and a dark place; a dark place and a lamp; a lamp and its oil; oil and shame; shame and hiding; hiding and outerwear; and so on. The gratifying rhythm and flow of this passage rests on these links. There is nothing in the text that marks explicitly for the reader that such linkages are there. Along with that of the protagonist, what is being tested—and, to some extent, grown—is the reader's own cultural literacy.

Having established a baseline of rudimentary familiarity with *waka* diction and *renga* links, the lady then transitions to a more complex riddle. She offers a full *waka*, in the tradition of the classical poetry exchange (*zōtōka* 贈答歌).

In the hope of being able to escape while he was still thinking how to respond to a poem, and because he had a walking stick made of Chinese bamboo, she offered this:

karatake wo	Because the walking stick
tsue ni tsukitaru	is made of Chinese bamboo
mono nareba	it looks like it would be hard
fushi soi-gataki	for you to add
hito wo miru kana	another node.

When Lazy Tarō heard this, he was mortified, as he realized that she did not want to sleep with him. He replied:

yorozu yo no	There are myriad sections,
take no yo goto ni	and to each section of bamboo
sou fushi no	a node is attached;
nado karatake ni	so how come one can't add nodes
fushi nakaru beki	to Chinese bamboo?

"What a frightening man," she thought. "He says he wants to sleep with me, and although he does not look the part, it is quite nice how much he knows about *waka*."[58]

いやいや此者に歌をよみかけそれを案ぜぬ折ふしに逃げ去らばやと思ひて男の持ちたる唐竹の杖によそへてかくなん 唐竹を杖につきたる物なればふしそひがたき人を見るかな 物くさ太郎これを聞 あな口惜しやさてわれと寝じとごさんなれと思ひ御返事 よろづ世の竹のよごとにそふふしのなど唐竹にふしなかるべき あな恐ろしや此男は我と寝んといふまた姿には似ずかゝる道を知りたることやさしさよと思召て

This is a parody of a classical poetry exchange. The first poem follows the custom of using conventionally associated images (*engo* 縁語): *take* (bamboo) and *fushi* (node). And the reply, as expected, recombines these images to refute the point made in the first poem. Another common traditional technique is wordplay (*kakekotoba* 掛詞), which is used in this exchange in a novel way. In the first poem, the expression *fushi* can mean not only "bamboo node," but also "to lie down" and, by extension and in the context of this poem, "to sleep together." In the second poem, *yo* refers to the section between nodes of bamboo, but can also mean "night"—a traditional usage that, in light of the second meaning of *fushi*, takes a more explicit overtone. This, then, would be another way to read the poetry exchange:

Because you carry
a walking stick
made of Chinese bamboo,
it looks like it would be hard
to sleep with you.

For myriad nights,
every night you have
slept with bamboo.
So how come you can't sleep
with this Chinese bamboo?

This explicitly sexual reading moves the poems away from the constraints of orthodox *waka* diction and into the realm of the *kyōka*. One way in which this is funny is that the logic of the exchange is still analogous to that of the traditional aristocratic *zōtōka*. The contrast between the propriety of the form and the flippancy of the content produces the humor. The joke might work better for a reader who already is aware of the rules and expectations of classical aristocratic wooing customs. Even so, the exchange, through wordplay, stands as both target (orthodox reading) and parody (erotic reading), offering a less knowledgeable reader enough material to access its humor. A reader who has not read or heard a *zōtōka* obtains from this passage in *Monokusa Tarō* knowledge about classical poetry exchanges as well as how they can be upended in parody.

The story continues in the same vein. The protagonist and the woman exchange many other poems and once engage in verse-capping, where she offers the first part of a poem and he produces the rest. For the purposes of this analysis, though, their first exchange at Kiyomizu Temple completes the parodic transformation of an illiterate beggar into an accomplished poet, and, by extension, a rural commoner into an urban aristocrat. Because the key to this transmogrification is his poetic skill, his new father-in-law, an aristocratic provincial governor, bestows on him the aristocratic-sounding but fictional title Uta no Saemon うたの左衛門 (Left Guard of the Poetry Bureau). By the end of the tale, we have learned that the protagonist becomes known as an expert in linked verse (*renga no jōzu* 連歌の上手). Other habits associated with the aristocracy, such as hygiene and attire, are succinctly taken care of by the lady and her maids. Besides skill in *waka* (and *tan-renga* and *renga*), the narration suggests, all the attributes that served as class markers are to be considered secondary, as they can be swiftly acquired or learned.

What is the nature of the humor in *Monokusa Tarō*? Shinoda has suggested that the comedic effect is achieved by bathos, a descent from the sublime to the ridiculous.[59] He identifies this effect in passages such as one near the beginning of the tale, in which a detailed, lavish description of the kind of regal estate the protagonist would want to build for himself is followed by a brief description of his current state of poverty. Since the notion of bathos refers to a failed attempt at sublimity that results in an unintentional, shameful lapse into triviality, Skord offers instead anticlimax—an intentional drop that aims for comic effect—as a better way to explain the switch from a gorgeous mansion to a beggar's makeshift hut.[60] Bathos and anticlimax have in common their reference to a switch in tone or content within the narrative sections. This anticlimactic shift in the narrative from the high to the low is analogous to the comedic shift discussed earlier. In the lady's poem, the appearance of orthodoxy in the first three lines—*karatake o / tsue ni tsukitaru / mono nareba*—is upended in the last two lines—*fushi soi-gataki / hito wo miru kana*—by the wordplay on *fushi* (node / have sex). The same is true for the protagonist's poem, as the first three lines—*yorozu yo no / take no yo goto ni / sou fushi no*—could be part of a perfectly orthodox poem, while the last two—*nado karatake ni / fushi nakaru beki*—hinge on the same bawdy play on *fushi*. The basic structure for this shift is cognate with Priest Sosei's poem in book 19 of *Kokinshū*, in which an orthodox first part contrasts with a second part that hinges on a play on words, *kuchinashi*, conflating an orthodox meaning (gardenia) and a mischievous meaning (no mouth).

The poems in *Monokusa Tarō* are to any reader unmistakably *kyōka*, yet they are not signified as unorthodox by either narrator or characters. All who interact with the protagonist react as if he were composing proper *waka*. That, on its own, suffices to create a comedic effect—once again, through the break with expectations—but the tale ends on a more ambitious note, suggesting that it is in *kyōka*, not *waka*, where cultural literacy is to be found. This takes place in the last exchange, between Monokusa Tarō and the emperor:

> Summoning him to the main hall, the emperor said, "If you really are an expert in linked verse [*renga no jōzu*], compose two poems." Since it was the time when the warblers fly around the plum blossom and one can hear their twitter, he composed this:

uguisu no	The warbler's
nuretaru koe no	wet tweets
kikoyuru wa	can be heard.
ume no hanagasa	Is it the plum's umbrella-like flowers
moru ya harusame	that let the spring showers through?

> The emperor saw this and asked him, "Where you come from, do they also call it 'plum' [*ume*]?" Even before the emperor was done speaking, he replied,

shinano ni wa	In Shinano Province
baika to iu mo	flowering *Prunus* are called
ume no hana	plum blossoms.
miyako no koto wa	And in the capital,
ikaga aru-ramu	I wonder how it is.

The emperor heard this and was moved [*gyo-kan ni iri-te*] . . .[61]

大極殿に召し、なんぢはまことに連歌の上手にて侍るなる、歌二首つかまつれと宣旨なり。折ふし梅花に鴬の飛びちりてさへづるを聞きかくなん 鴬のぬれたる聲のきこゆるは梅の花笠もるや春雨 みかど是を叡覽有て、なんぢが方にも梅といふかと宣旨也ければ承りもあへず信濃には梅花といふも梅の花都の事はいかゞあるらんみかど是をきこしめし御感に入て

In this passage, Monokusa Tarō exhibits his familiarity with the culture of the court in three different but related ways. First, while both poems are compositions by the protagonist, they relate to each other as do the two poems in a *zōtōka*, with the second poem using images from the first poem in a novel and discrepant way. The emperor seems to assume that the images in the first poem—the warbler's tweets, the plum's blossoms, the spring showers—are a celebration of court culture, and thus he is curious about them in provincial culture. The second poem responds with the typical *zōtōka* playful inversion, saying that those images belong to the provinces and wondering how it is in the capital.

Second, the relationship of these two complete poems is analogous to that of the two parts of a *kyōka*. The first poem hinges on the image of plum blossoms on a tree being an umbrella made with flowers. This is an established, time-honored metaphor.[62] The second poem, by contrast, uses the expression *baika* (*baikuwa* in traditional orthography), a loanword that usually is glossed *ume no hana* and that while ubiquitous in *shī*, is not part of the orthodox *waka* lexicon. Third, the protagonist's second poem suggests that the language of *waka* is to be found first and foremost in the provinces, and that the diction of the court vernacular might not follow this common usage.

Something similar is at work in the emperor's emotional reaction at the end of the passage. As discussed in chapter 2, medieval narratives about the potencies of *waka* feature poems presented by a person with less power to a person with more power—a god, an emperor, a provincial governor, a husband in the case of a female poet, a woman of higher class in the case of a male poet—to elicit a favorable emotional reaction. These narratives stress the expectation that *waka* can serve as a language of affect shared across social spaces. The expression that these narratives use to refer to the affect elicited by a poem is *kan ari* 感あり ("there was an emotional reaction"). In *Monokusa Tarō*, the expression is, similarly, *gyo-kan* 御感 (*gyo* is an honorific prefix appropriate for an emperor). Here, the shared language of affect has been expanded to embrace the variety of lexical and thematic choices with which *kyōka* complements *waka*. Medieval warriors had to learn, through *waka*, the sociolect of the court. Here, the emperor and his court are beginning to learn, via *kyōka*, the sociolect of the commoners.

Medieval narratives about the potencies of poetry tended to be very short and focused on one incident—a man seduces a high-ranking lady with a single poem, or a poet receives material rewards after composing a poem in front of his social superiors, or a person gains the favor of the emperor thanks to an impromptu composition. In *Monokusa Tarō*, these separate brief anecdotes are combined to create one integrated narrative arc, with two seemingly contradictory effects. One is a parody in which *kyōka* subverts the cultural authority of courtly *waka* and stories about the potencies of *waka*. By treating *kyōka* as if they were *waka*, the emperor and the other aristocratic characters validate a form of poetry that is ultimately indecorous and undignified. The other effect, which is much more interesting, is the inscription of playful *kyōka* within the established narratives that supported for centuries the sacrality and social usefulness of *waka*. The protagonist does not come to the court to debase the cultural supremacy of the aristocracy, but to suggest that within the high culture of the court exists a language and a space that can be shared by provincial commoners. This was an ideal that had been expressed centuries earlier in the prefaces to the *Shījīng* 詩經 (Book of songs) and *Kokinshū*, but it is in *machishū* tales that this formulation takes its first steps toward concrete realization. By appropriating and bringing to the surface the long-suppressed aristocratic flair for humorous poems, *Monokusa Tarō* extends the expressive range of *waka* and begins to realize in practice the idea that *waka*, once expanded by *kyōka*, can express what matters to all.

Satire and Love

The intimate connection between poetic and cultural literacy and the hope for upward mobility among commoners in the sixteenth century appears as well in *Saru Genji sōshi*.[63] This tale was also known as *Iwashi uri no monogatari* 鰯ウリの物語 (The tale of the sardine peddler), as it centers on a man who marries into a household of fish merchants from Akogi Bay 阿漕の浦 in Ise Province. The son-in-law eventually takes over the family business with great success, travels to the capital, falls in love with a high-ranking courtesan, poses as a powerful *bakufu* official, and captivates her with his poetic talent. If the prince in *Genji monogatari* is the embodiment of courtly romance, this is the story of an uncouth—another meaning, besides "monkey," of *saru*—provincial merchant posing as Genji.

While *Monokusa Tarō* features a beggar as a protagonist, *Saru Genji sōshi* focuses on a merchant household. The former tale offers a hyperbolic version of linear social ascent, in which success follows success, often with no cogency, while the latter evinces a more historical and nuanced appreciation of the anxieties and pitfalls that befall people who move across social spaces. The protagonists of *Saru Genji sōshi*, for example, display two of the three elements identified by Hayashiya as the salient characteristics of successful *machishū*—marrying into a warrior household to secure the patronage of overlords and gaining control over a given industry or market—as well as the quick switch of focus from the accumulation of wealth to the development of cultural literacy, in which poetry plays the central role. This movement can be seen at once in the opening of the tale.

> Not long ago in Akogi Bay, Ise Province, there was a sardine peddler [*iwashi uri*]. His former name was Ebina no Rokurō-saemon, and he was a warrior in the eastern provinces. After his wife passed away, he married his daughter to a man he had recently taken into his service, called Saru Genji. He handed down to his son-in-law the sardine-peddling business [*shoku*], and traveled to the capital and shaved his head. There he became well known as the recluse Ebina no Na'amida-butsu. He got close to provincial warrior leaders [*daimyō*] and powerful families. In the meantime, his son-in-law Saru Genji brought his sardines to sell in

the capital, and he went around saying, “Buy sardines from Saru Genji from Akogi Bay in Ise Province!” When people heard him, they were curious about this sardine peddler, and many purchased from him, so that soon Saru Genji became wealthy [*utoku*]. As he went around peddling sardines, Saru Genji was crossing the bridge on Fifth Avenue just when a palanquin covered in wickerwork [*ajiro*] was coming from the opposite direction. The strong river wind suddenly blew the bamboo blinds open, and through the gap [*hima*] he saw inside the palanquin an elegant lady, with whom he fell in love [*koi*] at first sight [*hitome*]. Agonizing day and night and with his heart in complete distress, during the day he went to Fifth Avenue, [and] at night he went to the bridge, without a thought for his trade [*shōbai*]. Lying down [*uchi-fushi*], he thought of this old poem [*furu uta*],

ware bakari
mono omou hito wa
mata mo araji
omoeba mizu no
shita ni mo arikeri

Only me
yearning for a person,
nobody else,
I thought, yet under the water
there was someone else.

and thus he composed his own:

inochi araba
mata mo ya meguri
mi mo ya sen
musubu no kami no
aranu kagiri wa[64]

As long as I am alive
we will meet,
we will see each other,
the god who ties the knot
has vowed so.[65]

He looked so miserable it wasn’t clear he would live much longer.

中ごろの事にや有けん、伊勢國阿漕が浦に鰯賣一人あり。もとは海老名の六郎左衞門とて關東ざぶらひにてぞ有ける。妻にをくれて娘を一人もちたりしを日頃召し使ひける猿源氏といふものに取らせてすなはち鰯賣の職をゆづりわが身は都へ上りもとゆひ切り海老名の南阿彌陀佛とて隱れなき遁世者にてぞ有ける。大名高家近づけ給へり。さるほどに聟の猿源氏、鰯賣、都へ上りて洛中を、伊勢國に阿漕が浦の猿源氏が、鰯かふゑいといひて、商ひければ人々これを聞ておもしろき鰯賣哉とて人々買ひとる間猿源氏程なく有徳の身となりにけり。猿源氏鰯賣るとて五條の橋を渡りしが、折ふし網代の輿に行きあひしが川風はげしくて下簾をばつと吹きあげたる其隙より輿の内の上臈を一目見しより戀となり明け暮れ思ひわづらひて心もそぞろになりはてゝ明くれば五條、暮るれば橋へ出で商賣さらに身にしまず。うちふし一首　われ計物思ふ人は又もあらじ思へば水の下にも有けり　と古哥など思出し又かくなん　命あらば又もやめぐり見もやせん結ぶの神のあらぬ限りは　とよみ淺ましき有様、在命不定に見えにけり。

The characters of Ebina no Rokurō-saemon and Saru Genji were constructed by fusing the general traits of successful *machishū*—such as marriage ties to warriors, and thus patronage and commercial advantages—with specific historical fact. The Ebina family was an actual warrior household from the eastern provinces that claimed descent from the ninth-century Seiwa Genji 清和源氏.[66] Ebina Na'ami 海老名南阿弥 (Rokurō-saemon 六郎左衛門, d. 1381) was a retainer of the shogun Ashikaga Yoshimitsu who specialized in musical chanting. The character in the tale is, similarly, an eastern warrior who travels to the capital and secures the patronage of an overlord. Saru Genji marries into the Ebina, inherits the family trade and his father-in-law's connections, and becomes wealthy. In the tale, he is a sardine peddler (*iwashi uri*), but the means and personnel he commands later in the story in his efforts to seduce the elegant woman in the litter suggest that, rather than a simple street hawker, Saru Genji represents a wealthy merchant based in the capital and invested in provincial fisheries and regional transportation. Moreover, the mention of Akogi Bay, in which fishing was restricted to ritual harvesting for the Ise Shrine (Ise jingu 伊勢神宮) and all commercial fishing was forbidden, hints at the illegitimacy (in the eyes of more established households in the capital) of Saru Genji's newly acquired fortune. Finally, like many wealthy *machishū*, Saru Genji soon moves away from the source of his wealth and turns his attention to elegant pursuits—represented by two *waka*, one quoted from the tenth-century *Ise monogatari* and the other an original composition.

In these two poems, *Saru Genji sōshi* displays the same penchant for parody as in *Monokusa Tarō*. They are orthodox *waka*, but they are included in the tale with a *kyōka*-esque intention. The poem from *Ise monogatari* suggests a parodic parallel between its putative hero, Ariwara no Narihira 在原業平 (825–80), and Saru Genji. Moreover, the habit of recalling old poems to match a situation of heightened emotion is associated with his namesake, the hero of *Genji monogatari*, suggesting another parodic match. Even the act of lying down before composing a poem probably was taken from an episode in *Ise monogatari* in which Narihira, just like Saru Genji, wants to see his beloved but does not know where she lives. Through this warp of elegant classical associations there is a weft of tongue-in-cheek reminders of Saru Genji's investment in the fisheries. The image of "under the water" (*mizu no shita*) in the first poem is the most blatant hint; in the second poem, "ties the knot" (*musubu*) suggests fishing nets; and the wickerwork of the palanquin evokes the wickerwork (*ajiro*) of fish traps. The warp-and-weft structure of this passage is reminiscent of the technique of word association (*engo*) in orthodox *waka*, where images that connect with one another are interspersed throughout a poem. Yet while orthodox *engo* serve to deepen the gist of the poem, in this *kyōka*-esque version, they work against it for comedic contrast.

The tale of Saru Genji is satirical. It openly thematizes the incongruity of a merchant commoner posing as an elegant man steeped in aristocratic culture. In the quoted passage, the manner in which Saru Genji falls for the lady evokes the many episodes in Heian-period works in which stealing a peek through a gap (*suki* or *hima*) in a fence arouses in an aristocratic man the affect known as *koi* 戀, which is customarily translated as "love." Later in the tale, when Saru Genji confesses his feelings to Na'ami, saying, "I was unexpectedly assailed by the ailment [*yamai*] we call love [*koi*]," his father-in-law retorts, "I had never heard of a precedent [*tameshi*] for a fish peddler who had fallen in love [*koi*]. Under no circumstance should you let anybody know."[67] What Na'ami suggests is that the affect of *koi* was exclusive to the aristocracy, not a universal emotion that was experienced across social spaces. By falling in love like an aristocrat, Saru Genji completes the upwardly mobile transformation that started when he married into a warrior household and expanded his commercial enterprise.

The key to this passage, and arguably to the rest of *Saru Genji sōshi*, is the notion of *tameshi* (usually written 例), which I translate as "precedent." The belief that earlier events or actions should offer a guide to future behavior, and that they can be leveraged when criticizing other people, had been crucial to the aristocracy's sense of propriety since at least the Heian period. An instance of this outlook can be seen, for example, in connection with the establishment in the twelfth century of households of professional poetry specialists. As discussed in chapter 1, attacking rivals by suggesting that their poems were in breach of linguistic or thematic precedents was common practice among the poets of aristocratic and elite warrior circles. Professional poets had to commit to memory thousands of poems from canonical works, such as the imperially commissioned anthologies (*chokusenshū*), to be used as proof poems (*shōka*)—that is, as evidence for the existence of precedent in defenses against attacks of this type. The criticism sometimes referred to a specific use of a poem—for example, whether it was appropriate for a congratulatory setting—and professional experts had to study the historical criteria of court practice, through the examination of evidence in the form of brief narratives.

In this tale, Saru Genji similarly responds to Na'ami by relating an anecdote in which a fish peddler (*uo uri*) delivered his wares to the imperial palace, caught a glimpse of a lady, and fell in love. Saru Genji even ends this account with a *waka*. This anecdote is far-fetched and fabricated, parodic in spirit, but it faithfully mirrors the mechanics of precedent challenges among aristocrats.[68]

The rest of *Saru Genji sōshi* is similarly structured as a series of comedic challenges and responses. The anecdotes that Saru Genji produces also are similarly implausible and loosely connected to fact, and often are associated with Heian-period classical narratives. The climax of the whole tale, and the point at which its *kyōka*-esque anatomy is more patently revealed, is reached when Saru Genji, who is now impersonating the eastern *bakufu* official Utsu no Miya, spends his first night with the lady, whose name is Keiga and who is successfully employed as a distinguished entertainer (*yūgun*).[69]

That night, as Saru Genji is falling asleep, he involuntarily says the line that he used to shout in the street: "Buy sardines from Saru Genji from Akogi Bay!"[70] Keiga reacts with dismay:

> Keiga heard this, and realized with sadness that exactly as she had gathered from all that had looked suspicious, she had now in fact exchanged vows with a sardine peddler. She wondered what could be done.

> There was no way to hide it, and with the filth [*kitanasa*] and the fishy smell [*namagusa*], nobody would want her services anymore. Wishing to take the tonsure and get away wherever her feet took her, she sobbed quietly.[71]
>
> 螢火是を聞きされぱこそはじめより何とやらんをかしげに見えしが違はず鰯賣に契りし事の悲しさよ。さてこれは何となりゆくべきぞ。此事隱れ有まじければ鰯賣に契をこめし心の程きたなさよなまぐさやとて召さるゝ人も有まじければ髪おろし是よりいづくへも足にまかせて行かばやと思ひつゝさめざめと泣く涙

Upon realizing that she has been lied to and tricked, Keiga's concern is directed immediately to how this betrayal will affect her ability to attract clients and conduct business. What this highlights is that *Saru Genji sōshi* tells the story of a con by commoners of commoners—Saru Genji is aided by Na'ami in tricking Keiga, her coworkers, and her employers. Whereas *Monokusa Tarō* celebrates an unthinkable match between a peasant and the daughter of an aristocratic provincial governor, in *Saru Genji sōshi*, Keiga and Saru Genji are much closer to each other in terms of social class, and both make a living by competing with their peers for economic benefits by offering goods (fish) and services (sexualized entertainment). Unlike in *Monokusa Tarō*, at the end of this tale there is no revelation about Saru Genji's aristocratic pedigree or divine origin. He remains a commoner who has used his cultural literacy to exploit a fellow commoner.

The issue is what kind of cultural literacy is at stake. After Keiga confronts him, Saru Genji explains that he said "Akogi Bay" in his sleep because that famous place had recently come up during a linked-verse (*renga*) session that he was invited to attend, since the shogun knew that he liked *waka* (*uta no michi*). And he had said "Saru Genji" because he had been thinking about an episode in *Genji monogatari* in which the hero recites a poem on Saru-sawa Pond.[72] The last challenge that Saru Genji has to overcome, on which hinges the success of his whole enterprise, is the peddler's cry, "Buy sardines!" (*iwashi kō ei*), which is much harder to justify than the other two. Saru Genji tells Keiga that the last link in a poem at the shogun's party mentioned the expression *iwashi*:

otoko yama	On Manly Mountain
nani wo inori no	what to pray for?
iwashimizu	The pure waters of Iwashimizu Shrine.

This link can be read in two ways. The first is celebratory: Iwashimizu Hachimangū 石清水八幡宮 is the name of a famous shrine located south of the capital, in an area called Otoko-yama 男山. It was founded in the ninth century and enjoyed the patronage of the imperial household. The link can be read in a *kyōka*-esque way as well, since the name of the shrine, Iwashimizu (literally, "rock-spring water"), contains the sounds in *iwashi* (sardine). Saru Genji says that this link made him think of an anecdote involving Izumi Shikibu 和泉式部 (turn of the eleventh century), a famous Heian-period poet. He recounts how she was once caught by her lover eating a sardine and, in her embarrassment, composed this poem:

hi no moto ni	In our country
iwaware tamau	so widely celebrated, coming out of the rocks:
iwashimizu	The pure waters of Iwashimizu Shrine.
mairanu hito wa	There is no one who has not
araji to zo omou	paid pilgrimage to it.[73]

日の本にいははれ給ふいはしみづ参らぬ人はあらじとぞ思ふ

As before, this is apocryphal.[74] The poem probably was taken from a primer for children.[75] By framing the poem in this new narrative context, *Saru Genji sōshi* suggests that we read it in a *kyōka*-esque way: in the elegant register, *iwa ware* (literally, "split rock") in the second line refers to a spring of freshwater that gushes forth from between rocks, as well as puns on *iwau* (to celebrate); in the *kyōka*-esque register, *iwa / shimizu* can be parsed as *iwashi / mizu* (sardine water) and *mairu* (to go on a pilgrimage) can be read as an honorific expression meaning "to eat." This would be the alternative rendering:

In our country
so widely celebrated:

Sardines in fresh water,
there is no one who has not
ever eaten them.

In Saru Genji's telling, when Izumi Shikibu's lover heard this poem, he decided that eating sardines was good for a lady after all, and his affection for her only deepened. Keiga reacts similarly, thinking that if Saru Genji "were really a sardine peddler, then he would not know in this way the various aspects of the way of poetry [*uta no michi*] at all."[76] As she reassures herself that he is really a *bakufu* official on a visit to the capital, they undress, have sex, and spend the rest of the night together.

The tale concludes with two editorial comments that connect with the discourse on the potencies of poems discussed earlier, in the section "Parody and Transformation." The first is that "because Saru Genji had always dedicated himself to the way of poetry [*uta no michi*], he could conceal his disgrace on the spot, and furthermore accomplish an unattainable [*oyobanu*] true love [*koi no hon'i*]."[77] The second, with which *Saru Genji sōshi* closes, is an injunction that transforms the statement on the potencies of attaining cultural literacy in the specific case of Saru Genji into a universal prescription: "Since the way of poetry [*uta no michi*] is not trivial, what every person needs to study constantly is the way of poetry [*uta no michi*]."[78] Together, these two statements link the acquisition of knowledge about the culture of the aristocracy with participation in the social institution of *koi* (love), which the narrative presents as exclusive to the aristocracy and thus, in theory, unattainable for a person like Saru Genji.

Saru Genji sōshi is the story of a wealthy self-made merchant who seduces a successful professional entertainer by posing as a *bakufu* official. The man is conversant with the culture of the aristocracy but justifies his gaffes with the most preposterous anecdotes and poems. What can this tell us about the cultural and economic moment in which this story first circulated and about how and why cultural literacy was practiced and displayed, particularly regarding the roles of *waka* and *kyōka* in that process? And how can we theorize the absurdity and humor in the tale?

One possible way to understand *Saru Genji sōshi* is, as Michele Marra has argued, in the context of the accelerated and unpredictable opportunities for political and social mobility in the late fifteenth and sixteen centuries, when society experienced a process known as *gekokujō* 下克上 (*shimo ue ni katsu* [roughly, "the low topples the high"]). Marra defines the low and the high in simple economic terms—tax-paying commoners versus tax-charging elites—and posits a parallel with the emergence of the bourgeoisie in Europe and its creation of cultural patterns of "binary extremism." From this perspective, Marra understands the mix of low and high culture in late medieval texts as the product of ambiguity: "While laughing at the values of a social structure that they were turning upside-down, they also felt reverence for the providers of a tradition that, however dwarfed by the loss of economic legitimation, was extremely valuable to the formation of cultural capital."[79] In the specific case of *Saru Genji*, Marra believes that "the merchant's victory goes well beyond the gain of sexual gratification. He conquers the entire tradition, showing that the victims of domination can play a dominant role by appropriating the means of production—economic, cultural, and status capital—that legitimize the act of subjugation."[80] Pierre Bourdieu's notion of cultural capital is central to this idea because, by positing that cultural processes are analogous to economic ones, Marra argues, it enables us to see the merchants' interest in *waka* as a thinly veiled attempt to seize the means of production—and their investment in *kyōka* as class warfare.[81]

Marra's approach is helpful in that it brings to the fore the role of class differences in the production, circulation, and consumption of cultural artifacts. Yet this conceptualization of an uncomplicated class struggle, in which the underclass appropriates the means of cultural production to topple the overlords, does not apply to *Saru Genji sōshi*, mainly because Keiga is herself commoner. As part of her professional activity, Keiga may have access to more powerful individuals than does Saru Genji, but seeing the tension between her and Saru Genji as class struggle may be a case of "ethnographic dazzle," a term coined by anthropologist Robin Fox to refer to the blindness to underlying similarities between human groups that can occur when one is distracted by more visible superficial differences.[82] The status of Keiga as a non-elite worker is openly thematized in the tale. For example, when Saru Genji reveals that he has fallen in love with an entertainer, his father-in-law reacts in this way:

> All the same, if she were the daughter of an aristocratic family it would be possible for you to get her consent, but since she comes from a line [*nagare*] of professional entertainers [*yūjo*] upstanding like the mighty bamboo [*tatsuru kawatake*], she will not meet with any but the greatest families or the provincial lords.[83]
>
> ただし公家門跡などの御娘ならばいかなる料簡も及ぶべかりしがこれは流れをたつる川竹の遊女なれば大名高家よりほかへは出でず

This statement reflects both historical fact (the economic struggles of the aristocratic families of the capital in the aftermath of the Ōnin War) and narrative precedent. The deployment of poems by men of lower status for aristocratic addressees is a direct reference to medieval narratives about the potencies of poems. In Kubota Jun's analysis, this reference is window dressing, added almost as an afterthought in a tale that is purportedly invested instead in producing an effect of strangeness (*okashimi*).[84] Class difference, however, is key to this tale. In saying that had Keiga been an aristocrat, Saru Genji would have had a chance with her, Na'ami is setting up the punch line of his joke, that it is precisely because Keiga is an entertainer for hire that Saru Genji has no chance. What works against him is the importance of perceived differences among commoners.

The obstacle that Saru Genji is attempting to remove with his con is what the anthropologist Kate Fox has conceptualized as the "adjacent classes problem." In her ethnographic study of class in contemporary England, Fox found that each class "particularly despises the one immediately below it, and the prospect of being mistaken for a member of this adjacent class is therefore especially abhorrent."[85] From the perspective of powerful overlords, both Saru Genji and Keiga are commoners. But as a first-generation wealthy trader from the provinces who deals with the supply chain of food, Saru Genji can seem lower in social class and cultural status than the heir to a lineage of professional entertainers who are established in the capital and successful with elite warrior patrons. Thus Saru Genji's display of mastery of the *waka* lexicon and lore (however *kyōka*-esque and apocryphal to the reader) can be interpreted as an attempt by a commoner to harness the perceived language of the upper class to impress another commoner.

If the hyperbole and exaggeration in *Monokusa Tarō* confine it to the realm of parody, the depiction of economic, cultural, and aesthetic struggles within the urban commoner class in *Saru Genji sōshi* feels closer to the bone, too realistic for parody, more intimately laced with the sharpness of social satire. In both works, *waka* is absorbed into the more spacious *kyōka*-esque paradigm, yet *Saru Genji sōshi* offers a wider glimpse of what lies beyond the top-down process of cultural transmission—the trickling down of cultural capital produced by the impoverishment of aristocrats and the enrichment of warriors such as the Ashikaga: this is the production and circulation of culture horizontally, within *machishū* circles.

This can be seen, for example, in the choice of location for the origin of the tale. Akogi, as Ichiko Teiji points out, appears in classical poems and, as Marra emphasizes, is the title of a Noh play about the spiritual salvation of a fisherman. By the late medieval period, the term *akogi* had also come to take on the meanings "importunate" and "greedy," descriptions that could apply to the protagonists of both *Saru Genji sōshi* and *Monokusa Tarō*.[86] In economic and cultural terms, both are upstarts. Analogously, they practice a form of seduction that involves more accosting and pestering than cajoling. There is dishonesty and illegitimacy in both characters, a spirit of moving fast and breaking things—perhaps more so in Saru Genji. Despite this, *Saru Genji sōshi* is not a condemnation from the perspective of the overlords, but a sympathetic put-down by a peer who shares in the protagonist's folly.

Can we know for sure that this is how we should read the term *akogi* in this story? It is hard to say, since *Saru Genji sōshi* is a noncanonical text for which there are no contemporary commentaries to tell us how it was read at the time. But within the new *kyōka*-esque paradigm, it does not really matter, because the emphasis had moved away from textual authority and commentary, and poetry was now in the public domain and up for grabs.

Pedagogy and Compression

The hallmark of the *kyōka*-esque in *machishū* tales is the imbrication of aristocratic and popular cultures, not the erasure of the boundaries between them. The comedic punch line of a *kyōka* relies on *waka* to set it up. Conversely, for an audience initiated into poetic practice through comedic *kyōka*, it is impossible to conceive of *waka* in isolation. The effect of the *kyōka*-esque is that *waka* proper, orthodox, as wished by the editors of *Kokinshū*, is now but a subgenre, one of many positions on a continuum that covers not only *kyōka* but also orthodox and humorous *tan-renga* and *renga*. The consequences of this symbiotic integration of the low and the high are explored at length in the tale *Nakagoro no koto*.[87] Unlike in *Monokusa Tarō* and *Saru Genji sōshi*, where flippant *kyōka* are treated by characters other than the protagonists as sober *waka*, in *Nakagoro no koto* the formal, thematic, and rhetorical differences between *waka* and *kyōka* epitomize the wider cultural differences between the established elites and the emerging *machishū*.

Nakagoro no koto is about an aristocratic couple who spend their days practicing *waka*, *renga*, and *kemari*. Wholly uninterested in the day-to-day education of their two daughters, they entrust them to two different governesses. One is "proper" or "aristocratic," while the other is "vulgar," a "commoner." The former shows gentleness and patience, while the latter, given the derogatory nickname Dragon King (Ryūō 竜王) of the Sea, is gluttonous, ill-tempered, arrogant, and greedy.[88] While one governess teaches the daughters the aristocratic koto, the other teaches the popular biwa in the style of itinerant blind minstrels; one expounds on the elegant *Genji monogatari*, and the other on the bloody battle accounts in *Heike monogatari* 平家物語 (Tales of the Heike, mid-thirteenth century). The two governesses offer exaggerated, caricatural versions of two sets of cultural choices that are presented as irreconcilable. The humor of the tale arises from the tension between these two modes, with the vulgar governess's folly exaggerated and ridiculed for comedic effect.

To all intents and purposes, the Dragon King serves as a humorous foil in a cautionary tale that emphasizes the benefits of a proper education. *Nakagoro no koto*, in fact, draws heavily from *Menoto no fumi*

乳母の文 (The nursemaid's letter, 1264), a primer in epistolary form that was written by the early medieval aristocrat Nun Abutsu for her daughter Ki no Naishi 紀内侍 (b. 1251), who was preparing to enter the court. Abutsu wrote *Menoto no fumi* as part of a broader effort to help her daughter marry the crown prince and become the mother of a future emperor. Shaped as a letter, *Menoto no fumi* focuses on the behaviors and abilities that can secure the patronage of a powerful male courtier: refinement in sensibility, reserve in manner, skill in playing stringed instruments, mixing incense, calligraphy, sketching, and so on. Nun Abutsu's letter was later abridged and circulated in a condensed form titled *Niwa no oshie* 庭の訓 (Household teachings, n.d.), which by the late medieval period had become a standard reference in the education of young women. Today, the tale *Nakagoro no koto* is more commonly known as *Menoto no sōshi* 乳母草子 (The Nursemaid's Book). Abutsu's letter, though addressed from a mother to a daughter and making no mention of nursemaids, came retrospectively to be known as *Menoto no fumi*—likely due to its perceived connection to the fictional tale it inspired, *Nakagoro no koto/Menoto no sōshi*.

Abutsu's work offers a unique glimpse into what a gendered education in the medieval period looked like.[89] Of the Chinese literacy that accounted for most of the education of elite boys and young men, Abutsu recommends a very superficial knowledge, just enough to deal with the topics of poems in poetry collections. In terms of poetry, the bare minimum meant committing to memory all the poems in *Kokinshū* as well as in *Shin Kokin wakashū* (*ShinKokinshū*), the seventh imperial anthology. In the case of *Genji monogatari*, Abutsu demands not only memorization of the tale but also familiarity with works of reference, including catalogs of concordances and commentaries on passages that were particularly difficult to interpret.[90] She even mentions having collated manuscripts especially for her daughter's consultation. This emphasis on scholarship, commentary, and exegesis marks the main historical difference from the accounts of learning grounded solely in memorization that marked most of the Heian period.[91] In Abutsu's experience, in the context of a gendered scheme that restricted access to the forums of Sinitic learning, the scholarly study of, editing of, and commentary on domestic classics, such as imperial poetry anthologies and classical court narrative prose, could provide an avenue for women's intellectual exploration and worldly success.

The appeal of *Menoto no fumi* no doubt arose from its clear prose and its focus on practical, actionable advice. Its sustained circulation was fueled as well by the author's rare combination of firsthand experience of the female salons of the imperial court and involvement in the male-centric scholarly activities of professional households of *waka* specialists. Abutsu was born into an aristocratic household and as a young woman served at the court of Princess Hōshi 邦子内親王 (1209–83), who after the Jōkyū Disturbance became honorary empress mother (*junbo* 准母) to her maternal younger brother, Emperor GoHorikawa.[92] At court, Abutsu gained distinction for her knowledge of Heian-period poetry and prose works, to the point that the head of the Mikohidari school, Fujiwara no Tameie, commissioned from her a copy of *Genji monogatari* for his daughter Tameko 為子 (b. 1233), who was preparing to enter the court. Thereafter, Abutsu continued to assist Tameie with scholarly matters, and eventually she married him.[93] After Tameie died, Abutsu moved from the capital to Kamakura to litigate his legacy before the shogunal courts on behalf of their eldest son and against Tameie's children from a previous relationship. In Kamakura, Abutsu also engaged with patron-students who were interested in learning about the culture of the classical court through the study of *waka* and classical prose. (This was most likely the practice in the context of which she produced copies of her primer for her patrons.) It is from this combination of experience and scholarship that *Menoto no fumi* and *Niwa no oshie* drew their cultural authority.

The "good" governess in the *machishū* tale *Nakagoro no koto* represents the set of values and attitudes that Abutsu described in *Menoto no fumi* and *Niwa no oshie*. That Abutsu provided the model is further suggested by a letter that this governess writes toward the end of the tale, which borrows extensively from *Niwa no oshie*.[94] For this reason, Christina Laffin has argued that *Nakagoro no koto* is a popularized version of Abutsu's work "with the didactic elements presented in an entertaining and humorous manner."[95] In this reading, the *machishū* tale simultaneously documents and parodies the role of the female educator.[96] Noriko Reider has similarly suggested that it offers a representation of "what was expected of upper-class women during the medieval period and what, consequently, comprised the education for young women of high society, and possibly for young women who aspired to join the aristocracy as well."[97] Virginia Skord has taken this point further:

> The modern reader is likely to sympathize with the eccentric nurse and her charge and see in the narrative feminist themes quite alien to medieval Japan. The medieval reader would have been amused by the incongruity of an aristocratic young lady learning mathematics or strumming a lute like a blind minstrel. For the original audience, the lighthearted manner with which the story treated a serious subject by no means detracted from the weight of its message; this is a story that reaffirmed rather than disrupted traditional values.[98]

Yet this interpretation requires that we reduce the role of *kyōka* and humor in the tale to that of a comedic foil, a set of elements external to elite culture that is introduced only to amuse and to highlight the value of aristocratic upbringings. It assumes, moreover, that in late medieval Japan, there was still an undiluted aristocratic elite.

The role of *kyōka* in *Nakagoro no koto* challenges the assumption that there can be two distinct, diametrically opposed cultures representing two distinct, mutually impermeable social spaces. The *kyōka*-esque in this tale is not an alternative to traditional values, but a reformulation of those values within a wider and more comprehensive framework. This can be seen, for example, in the climactic passage of the tale, when the parents finally become aware of the ways of the Dragon King and dismiss her. This happens as the whole family gathers one autumn to compose poems under the harvest moon:

> The younger daughter composed,
>
> | | |
> |---|---|
> | *hana sakite* | There's the moon of spring, |
> | *haru ni kasumeru* | shining among the blossoms, |
> | *tsuki wa aredo* | and yet |
> | *aki no koyoi no* | nothing can compare to |
> | *sora ni kotonaru* | tonight's autumn sky. |

The elder sister composed,

tsukuzuku to	However intently I look,
nagamuru kai mo	this is useless.
na nomi nite	In name only
kuchi ni wa irazu	is this a rice cake in the sky
mochizuki no kage	that won't go into my mouth.

This last poem shocked all in attendance.[99]

妹君 花咲きて春にかすめる月はあれど秋の今宵の空に異なる 姉君 つくづくと眺むるかひも名のみにて口には入らず望月の影 かように読み給へば、皆呆きれたる様にて候に

The first poem, by the younger sister trained by the aristocratic governess, imitates the aesthetic that was fresh and appealing during the time of *Kokinshū*. By the late medieval period, though, a poem like the younger sister's would have sounded correct to the point of tired cliché, a cartoonish version of classical *waka*. By contrast, the second poem, by the elder sister trained by the commoner governess, attempts and achieves comedy.[100] *Mochizuki* (full moon) is a witty pun on *mochi-tsuki* (to pound glutinous rice to make sweet cakes). Through wordplay, the poet feigns disappointment at having been given an inedible rice cake. The poem is presented in this crucial passage of the tale as epitomizing the contrast between two cultural choices: *waka* is aristocratic and *kyōka* is *machishū*. The parents are *waka* practitioners, and from the poem composed by the elder daughter, they can tell that she is not being given a proper education.

The sweeping, shared shock with which this passage closes is meant to dramatize the conflict between the cultures the two sisters embody. The problem is, as much as *waka* and *kyōka* are different, they are not really mutually exclusive. The comedy in the elder sister's poem relies on a sudden break from the constraints of *waka*. The first three lines are perfectly orthodox; the humorous twist comes only in the last two lines, with the puns and the culinary image. More than half of her poem is an orthodox *waka*; it is funny only if one has a basic knowledge of *waka*'s boundaries and expectations. Still, one can get an intuitive sense of those boundaries and expectations just from the contrast between the two parts of the poem. In its specific form of transgression, *kyōka* contains the rule it breaks.

This undermines the claim that aristocratic culture and popular culture were incompatible, disconnected, contrasting social spaces. What *Nakagoro no koto* ultimately reveals is that at the root of the emerging urban commoner culture of the late medieval period, and despite its utilitarian outlook and satirical inclination, a space was reserved for the aristocratic culture that had been constructed in such works as *Kokinshū* and *Genji monogatari*. The parody of classical texts and the satire of contemporary social types in *Nakagoro no koto* and other tales are neither a straight reproduction nor an indication of the medieval court poetics that Abutsu embodied. They tap into a different affordance of *waka*, its potential for comedy, to round out what it meant to receive an education in poetry and high culture.

How, then, can we theorize the relationship of *Nakagaro no koto* to Abutsu's work, and, by extension, of *waka* to *kyōka* in late medieval culture? Christina Laffin's argument that *Nakagoro no koto* is a parodic version of Abutsu's letter can be complemented by Michael Emmerich's notion of replacement.[101] As discussed in the introduction, replacement refers to the emergence of a new work that enables the consumption of an old and canonical work that is not available, owing to lack of access (to physical manuscripts), lack of linguistic competence (to read cursive manuscripts or to decipher archaic lexical and grammatical forms), or even lack of physical extant copies (of the putative original created by the putative author, or of a later copy). A key feature of replacement is that the new work mediates the relationship of consumers to the old work, even when both works circulate side by side.

It is possible to regard *Nakagoro no koto* as a parodic replacement of Abutsu's texts. The epistolary primer by Abutsu that we know today as *Menoto no fumi* has been known for centuries by a series of different names, which indicates that it most likely circulated initially without a title. It is not clear by what process it came to be associated with the figure of a nursemaid (*menoto*), since its prestige came initially from having been written by an experienced mother for her promising daughter. Its connection to governesses likely began in the late Edo period. A series of lavishly illustrated woodblock editions published yearly between 1844 and 1854, written by the *kyōka* poet and illustrator Santō Kyōzan 山東京山 (1769–1858) and illustrated by Utagawa Toyokuni II 歌川二代目豊国 (1777–1835), were titled *Kyōkun menoto no sōshi* 教訓乳母草子 (The Nursemaid's Book: A Moral Instruction). In the introduction to the first volume, Kyōzan offers a rare explicit articulation of the logic behind the fundamentals of replacement:

> In the series *Corpus Organized* [*Gunsho ruijū*, 1819], vol. 4, no. 77, there is a work titled *The Nursemaid's Book* [*Menoto no sōshi*] by Nun Abutsu. According to *The Tales of Shōtetsu* [*Shōtetsu monogatari*, 1448–50], this Nun Abutsu was a lady-in-waiting known as Lady Fourth Avenue, in the service of Ankamon-in.[102] Abutsu's *The Nursemaid's Book* [*Menoto no sōshi*] was created as a letter, with teachings for ladies-in-waiting at the imperial court. Kyōzan's *The Nursemaid's Book* [*Menoto no sōshi*] is an illustrated book to instruct the children of city-dwelling commoners [*machikata*]. These are the sayings of a lowly nurse, but if you take them to heart, they can become a part of your education [*kyōkun*].[103]
>
> 群書類従（ぐんしよるゐじゅ）四百七十七巻目に阿仏尼（あぶつに）が作りたる乳母草紙（めのとのさうし）といふ物あり此阿仏尼（あぶつに）は、安嘉門院（あんかもんゐん）に仕（つか）えたる四条（しでう）といひし官女（かんぢよ）なりしよし徹書記（てつしよき）物語（ものがたり）に見えたり阿仏尼（あぶつに）が乳母（めのと）の草紙（さうし）は雲井（くもゐ）の宮女（きうぢよ）に示（しめ）したる教（をしえ）の文（ふみ）京山が乳母（めのと）の草紙（さうし）は街戸（まちかた）の童（わらべ）に諭（さと）す繪（ゑ）さうしなり此賤（いや）しき乳母（めのと）がいふ事なれど、心して聴（きゝ）たまはゞ教訓（けうくん）の一端（はし）ともなさばなりなんかし

In this passage, Kyōzan presents his didactic guidebook as the counterpart of Abutsu's for a different social class. Kyōzan states that while Abutsu's instruction was appropriate for women serving at court, other social spaces require different specific advice. This is reflected in the way the text is laid out on the printed page, since in this edition characters are frequently glossed with syllabic kana readings. This system of reading aids enabled and facilitated the reading process for a readership that was less proficient than Abutsu's original intended audience. Another interesting feature of this passage is that it refers to Abutsu's text as *Menoto no sōshi*, even though in the monumental anthology *Gunsho ruijū* 群書類従, cited here by Kyōzan, the title is actually *Menoto no fumi*, the name by which the text is widely known today. In other words, the way we refer to Abutsu's letter is mediated by the characters in *Nakagoro no koto*. Something similar happened later to *Nakagoro no koto* itself. The scholar Ichiko Teiji—assuming that *Nakagoro no koto* was the title given to the tale well after it was written (which is likely, since those are the first few words of the manuscript), acknowledging that we have no information about the original title of the tale, and citing reasons of expedience—decided to close the circle; in his seminal edition, he gave the text the title *Menoto no sōshi*.[104] Today, the tale *Nakagoro no koto* is known as *Menoto no sōshi* and Abutsu's letter as *Menoto no fumi*.

Ichiko's decision has led to confusion, though, since another text in *Gunsho ruijū* is titled *Menoto no sōshi*. It was found, unsigned, among the papers of the poet Hagiwara Munekata 萩原宗固 (Hyakka'an 百花庵, 1703–84), the author of many commentaries on classical texts and an active member of the *kyōka* circles in the Edo period. The text titled *Menoto no sōshi* in *Gunsho ruijū* is a sober, level-headed work on the proper training of young women that in spirit is much closer to *Niwa no oshie* than to *Nakagoro no koto*. This stance is made clear in the opening passage:

> The attitudes and comportment of women have existed since the distant past in both China and Japan, but more recently [*nakagoro*] the temperament of women, even to the most quotidian actions such as being on one's feet or sitting down, have thoroughly deteriorated in quality. That is the reason writers of great standing—tall as a pine—such as Murasaki Shikibu and the like have written down that those who are high should pity those below, those who are below should serve those on high, and households should be run peacefully and successfully. By consulting the items listed here, you should be able to temper your heart.[105]

むかしより女の心づかひ身もちなどのこと。もろこし日のもとにも侍りつれども。中比は女のこゝろばせ。おきふしたちゐまで。むげにしなくだり侍りしにより。たか松のにようゐん。紫式部などふかくなげきたまひて。上たるひとは下をあはれみ。下たるものはかみにつかへ。家をおさめ。身をたて侍るべきことをこまごまとかきとゞめたまひしなり。このことがきを御らんじて。御心をたしなみ給ふべし。

This text marks a shift away from the annotation and exegesis of Murasaki Shikibu's eleventh-century *Genji monogatari*, a handbook of poetry and an object of scholarly interest that Abutsu embraced in *Menoto no fumi*. In terms of theme and treatment, however, this work is still part of the *Menoto* universe, a cluster of texts variously related to Abutsu (even if only through the interest in *Genji monogatari*) and loosely connected with the figure of the "good" governess in *Nakagoro no koto*, all intimately committed to the education of young women by means of the acquisition of classical aristocratic skills and customs.

Since many readers first (and possibly only) accessed Abutsu's pedagogy through the teachings of the "aristocratic" governess (*menoto*) in *Nakagoro no koto*, it makes sense that Abutsu's letter was later retroactively given the title *Menoto no fumi* in *Gunsho ruijū* and *Menoto no sōshi* in Kyōzan's work. It is also understandable that new works related to the education of young women were patterned after Abutsu's text or titled in connection with the education provided by governesses, even when ostensibly written by male authors with a Confucian agenda—seeking the stability and overall prosperity of the whole of society—that is conspicuously absent from Abutsu's injunctions.

By analogy, works such as *Nakagoro no koto*, as well as *Monokusa Tarō* and *Saru Genji sōshi*, offered exposure to the world of *waka*, by way of parodic *kyōka*, to a readership that was at least partially—or, one would guess, mostly—composed of persons who did not have a working knowledge of *Kokinshū* and did not compose *waka* in their everyday lives. It is in this sense that, in these tales, *kyōka* came to "replace" *waka*—not by superseding its study or practice, but by offering a new frame of reference for those approaching it for the first time.

Kyōka and Self-Supported Cultural Transmission

The notion of tertiary circulation, or diffusion, introduced earlier in this book, is key to the transmission of ideas and narratives across social and cultural boundaries. Narrative material from Heian-period poetry treatises, which had been intended for specific individual readers (their primary circulation, or inception) and later circulated among contemporaneous readers with a similar socioeconomic background and linguistic competence (this was their secondary circulation, or dissemination), eventually resurfaced in early medieval collections of brief narratives meant for a significantly different readership. This tertiary stage of circulation is set apart from the intended and other immediate readers by the loss of explicit reference to the source texts. A reader encountering an anecdote about a classical poet in any of these collections would rarely find with it an explicit discussion of its source, the title of the text being consulted, or the place to find more information about it. Often, individual passages were "reborrowed" from another collection of brief narratives, further extending the distance from the classical source. The iteration of unattributed borrowings effectively incorporated these anecdotal narratives into a wider ecology of information about the culture of the aristocratic court, in which their value and relevance had less to do with their specific involvement with the composition of poetry than with a more general interest in the ways of the aristocratic and warrior elites who practiced poetry, among other things.

The late medieval tales considered in this chapter—*Monokusa Tarō*, *Saru Genji sōshi*, and *Nakagoro no koto*—display a similar commitment to making aspects of aristocratic culture available to wider audiences. They differ, though, in their relationship to the genres and texts of the aristocratic canon, because they incorporate three new gestures that distinguish them from instances of tertiary circulation. The first is their parodic approach. Parody is a key feature of many genres of narrative, visual, and material culture of the early modern period, of which these *machishū* tales stand as a forerunners. The issue of whether parody is an attempt to ridicule a social group or class connected with the established text it targets is still a matter under debate. Jeffrey Johnson, for example, has argued for reading early modern parody in the light of Mikhail Bakhtin's "carnivalesque" inversions of power and hierarchy, which expose the arbitrary nature of all social contracts and cultural expectations.[106] David Gundry has shown that, conversely, parody can be regarded as an effort by subaltern groups (merchants) to emulate elites (warriors) by taking part in the classical literary tradition of the aristocracy and the imperial court.[107] Eiko Ikegami has similarly shown that cultural practices (such as early modern *haikai*) that rely on knowledge and parody of classical culture can offer an opportunity for practitioners from different social and class spaces to mingle and network.[108] These connections among parody, openness, and horizontality are apparent in the *machishū* tales discussed in this chapter.

The second dimension of late medieval narratives that separates them from the tertiary circulation of classical material relates to the ways in which they compress the complexity of aristocratic culture into nuggets of information. These tales offer the reader lists and synopses for a wide range of cultural references, thus serving as guides to a vast network of texts and practices associated with the court. In a tale titled *Hachikazuki* 鉢かづき (The bowl girl), the protagonists of aristocratic pedigree list their cultural preferences in two separate instances. In the first passage, a man is described as a practitioner of *shī*, *waka*, and *kangen* (music) and as being fond of spending time under the blossoms while lamenting their falling, looking at the sky longingly, and composing *waka*. His wife is depicted as an avid reader of *Man'yōshū*, *Kokinshū*, and *Ise monogatari*, among other books, and as being fond of looking at the moon and lamenting its setting at dawn.[109] In the second passage, their daughter is queried about her skills (*nō* 能) and replies that her mother taught her to play the koto, biwa, *wagon* (six- or seven-string zither), *shō* (pipes), and *hichiriki* (flute), as well as to read *Man'yōshū*, *Kokinshū*, *Ise monogatari*, the Lotus Sutra in eight volumes, and several other sutras.[110] These two lists present succinct guides to the main themes of an aristocratic education for young women. They are so rudimentary, though, that they would be helpful only to a reader without any access to or training in aristocratic practices and texts. Compression is a device designed for an audience of outsiders, to give them a peek into the heritage of the court.

The radical compression of court culture in *Hachikazuki* is analogous to passages in the three main tales discussed in this chapter. In *Monokusa Tarō*, the protagonist enumerates the names of cultural landmarks in the capital in a sequence purposefully designed to aid memorization. In a later passage, he and an elegant woman exchange quips using basic poetic diction in a way that aids comprehension for the uninitiated. And compression need not be only mnemonic. In *Saru Genji sōshi*, the constant efforts of the protagonist to provide convincing (but hilarious) precedents for his strange behavior are condensed versions of the practice of recording and citing historical precedent (*tameshi*) in classical society and scholarship. In *Nakagoro no koto*, the entire system of class markers and cultural sensibilities that classical aristocrats developed and refined over centuries is crammed into simple, polar, and schematic distinctions between aristocratic and commoner cultures that pit koto against biwa, *Genji* against *Heike*, and so on. In all of these examples, a mere expression or word—often a text's title—substitutes for a whole complex array of cultural and textual information; this is starkly different from the borrowing of narrative material in the tertiary circulation in early medieval works.

The third dimension of late medieval narratives that separates them from earlier instances of tertiary circulation is satire. Some readers of *Monokusa Tarō*, *Saru Genji sōshi*, and *Nakagoro no koto* may not have been thoroughly conversant with the targets of parody or the aristocratic culture referenced in these tales, but they were all decidedly familiar with the scandals and social types of their world. A paradigm of the capital merchant with an interest in aristocratic skills and warrior pastimes was Haiya Shōeki, who inherited a successful business in the production and commercialization of fabric dyes, but devoted his time to learning not only *waka*, calligraphy, and kickball, but also *haikai* and the tea ceremony. By the time Shōeki succeeded in buying off the contract of a famous entertainment-district performer and marrying her, in the first half of the seventeenth century, the *machishū* tales considered here had been in circulation for some time. Nevertheless, it is likely that his example had precedents that resonated in the minds of earlier readers who enjoyed the escapades of Monokusa Tarō and Saru Genji. A related social type, the wealthy merchant in the capital who sought a governess conversant with aristocratic culture to bring up his daughter, seems to be behind *Nakagoro no koto*. Just as with parody, it is unclear whether the satire in these texts was meant to ridicule or to affectionately poke fun at the attempts by commoners to mingle with elites and take part in the wider cultural conversation.

Parody, compression, and satire can come together to offer caricatures of both elite and non-elite cultures that are enjoyable for readers who have the bare minimum of cultural literacy. In Linda Hutcheon's much-cited formula, a parodic text relies on the competence of a reader to inscribe continuity with a literary precedent or model while simultaneously creating the critical distance embodied in a double encoding.[111] This model of parody does not compute for a readership that lacks that competence, but Hutcheon introduces two qualifications that can illuminate the role of parody in *machishū* tales. First, even a text that assumes a sophisticated reader can be directive enough to instruct less sophisticated readers so they can "get" some of the parody.[112] And second, a parody of a work of the past often is meant to support the satirical ridicule of contemporary practices or groups.[113] Hutcheon illustrates this maneuver by noting how *Don Quixote* can work as a parody of the conventions of the genre of epic romance and, in the figure of the protagonist, as a satire of those readers who try to embody in their life the adventures depicted in that genre. It is possible to combine these two insights and extend Hutcheon's model to theorize a self-supportive parody in which knowledge of the target of satire compensates for insufficient knowledge of the target of parody. In this reversed scheme, it is the readers' understanding of who is being made fun of that allows them to intuit or approximate the kind of old text the tale is inverting.

A model to theorize the workings of this self-standing parody can be found in the many *kyōka* at the core of *Monokusa Tarō*, *Saru Genji sōshi*, and *Nakagoro no koto*. *Kyōka* have a double structure. The first part of a *kyōka* is usually indistinguishable from that of an orthodox *waka*. The second part breaks off by introducing lexical and thematic elements that are incompatible with the rules and expectations of orthodox *waka*. As much as a *kyōka* is a parody of *waka*, it is as well a parody of itself—of the bit of *waka* that it contains in its first part. The ostensible effect is comedic, but the humorous response masks a subtle process of learning and cultural transmission. To "get" a *kyōka*, it is not necessary to have mastered the poetic canon or the rich commentarial tradition. After reading many *kyōka*, any reader can pick up their general pattern and thrust, and glean from their first halves the preferences and limitations that the second halves upset.

Kyōka are both a parody and a drastically compressed version of the practice of *waka*. In *Nakagoro no koto*, this tight mechanism of cultural transmission is unfurled and made explicit when the *kyōka* composed by the elder daughter follows the traditional *waka* composed by her younger sister. Analogously, the tale includes excerpts from Abutsu's *Niwa no oshie* next to their comedic versions. In *Monokusa Tarō*, *waka* and *kyōka* sit side by side, underscoring the parodic power that arises from their juxtaposition. In *Saru Genji sōshi*, by contrast, we find no orthodox *waka* but only *kyōka*, and the fact that the other characters react as if the protagonist were composing orthodox *waka* heightens the satiric effect created by the outsize ambitions of a parvenu. Packing the target of parody within the parodic text is the hallmark of the *kyōka*-esque; it opens a pathway to high culture that short-circuits the medieval institutions and practices that had controlled and negotiated access to the world of *waka*, from the oligopolistic professional households of hereditary *waka* specialists who guarded access to manuscripts, to the preeminence of the poetry treatises they created for patrons and students as the means to produce and transmit knowledge about poetic practice.

EPILOGUE

The Future of *Waka*

In this study I argue that a body of discourse originally developed by professional instructors of *waka* for aristocrats and elite warriors in the late classical period came to be appreciated as an aspirational cultural literacy by midlevel warriors in the early medieval period and by sophisticated urban commoners in the late medieval era. I have also made the case that this body of discourse must be understood as an integral part of social and cultural practices structured around relationships between professionals and patrons, instructors and students, authors and audiences. Further, I have proposed that the key to unearthing how discourse and practice come together can often be found in the form that knowledge takes—as much as its content—as it traverses social spaces.

My references in the introduction to both a guide to contemporary urban design and a mid-twentieth-century story about postclassical Europe signaled my commitment to move the analysis beyond the poetic production, criticism, and commentarial traditions of the elites to focus on the activities that constituted the majority of medieval poetic practice in Japan: the process of learning about classical poetry, legendary poets, and the high culture of the aristocracy, as practiced by individuals who were not urgently concerned with the composition of poems, who had no contact with professional instruction, and who had no access to the life of the court.[1] To reveal the larger scope for this study of medieval Japan, I wish to address two outstanding questions. First, until when was this pedagogic apparatus for cultural transmission prevalent, and when did people begin to regard poems as the literary artifacts they are today? And second, as *waka* lost its cultural centrality, did any other cultural practice arise to occupy its spot as the fulcrum of shared cultural memory and knowledge transmission across social spaces? As a point of arrival for the rise of *waka* as the shared culture of the premodern period, we find the reformulation (or *reaffordance*) of the field of literary production in the late nineteenth century. As a point of departure, I posit the rise of the tea ceremony in the twentieth century as a vehicle for the preservation, transmission, and production of cultural knowledge about the past of Japan (that is, as a *replacement* of the role previously occupied by *waka*).

Points of Arrival: Masaoka Shiki's Reform of Poetry

In the summer of 1892, the critic and poet Masaoka Shiki 正岡子規 (1867–1902) launched a project to reform poetry that would have a deep impact on the field of literary production in Japan. In a series of articles published in the newspaper *Nihon* 日本 (Japan) throughout the 1890s, Shiki argued a thesis that would have startled the poets of previous centuries. He stated, with confidence, that *waka* was a part of literature, and literature a part of the arts. As such, *waka* were now to be appraised and criticized under the same criteria that regulated music and sculpture, painting and drama, and the prose of the modern novel, rather than according to the time-honored standards that had buttressed the practice of *waka* until then.

What *waka* ceased to be, under Shiki's reconfiguration, and how it got there, is the main subject of this book: thanks to its capacity for cultural synthesis, *waka* was an entry point into a complex cultural experience, that of the aristocracy and the court, to which few people enjoyed direct access, but which remained relevant to anybody who was engaging in cultural and social dialogues. This was the notion that even though *waka* could never encompass the entire complexity of classical court culture, it could still be conceived as a signpost for those venturing into the deeper recesses of contemporary high culture, as well as a necessary reference for anyone consuming popular culture in the form of narratives, drama, music, and material objects.

During the early modern period, more and more commoners composed not only *waka*, but also *kyōka*, *renga*, and *haikai*; commoner-owned publishers circulated commoner-authored narratives that alluded to and parodied *waka* and other forms of classical culture for a readership of ever-widening sociocultural diversity; visual artists brought to life poems and lore about poets in privately commissioned and mass-market woodblock prints; ceramicists wrote poems on their wares, as did lacquerers, dyers, woodworkers, blacksmiths, and every other craftsperson. Yet none of these practices modified the *kyōka*-esque relationship of *waka* to other forms of poetic practice, to the juxtapositions of high and low cultures, and to the cultural transmission that we identified in the *machishū* tales of the late medieval period. Not even the Genroku-era poet and storyteller Ihara Saikaku 井原西鶴 (1642–93) could do this; nor could the narrator who so influenced early Meiji-period authors, Kyokutei Bakin 曲亭馬琴 (1767–1848). The cultural life of *waka* throughout the Edo period remained firmly *kyōka*-esque. *Waka* continued to exist as part of a broader ecosystem in which different elements got their meaning chiefly from the way they differed from one another in form, themes, diction, and social circumstances of practice, but in which all circulated and existed conjointly.

What about the activity of the scholars of the so-called National Learning movement? They were a network of early modern intellectuals inspired by the turn toward philological rigor in the field of Chinese studies led by Ogyū Sōrai 荻生徂徠 (1666–1728). Writers such as Kada no Arimaro 荷田在満 (1706–51), Kamo no Mabuchi 賀茂真淵 (1697–1769), and Moto'ori Norinaga 本居宣長 (1730–1801) undertook a monumental revision of the forms of medieval scholarship, to present the study of *waka* as the key to an idealized ancient native oral practice that putatively preceded the introduction of continental traditions, such as Confucianism and Buddhism.[2] This intellectual movement was internally diverse. The interest in recovering the *Man'yōshū* as a source to understand the poetic past by scholars such as Keichū 契沖 (1640–1701), for example, was met by the criticism of Kagawa Kageki 香川景樹 (1768–1843) and his disciples of the Keien

桂園 school, Kinoshita Takafumi 木下幸文 (1779–1821) and Kumagai Naoyoshi 熊谷直好 (1782–1862), who emphasized the technical accomplishments of the *Kokin wakashū* (*Kokinshū*). Yet the heated arguments of these thinkers—regardless of the fact that there were commoners among them—were confined to poetry treatises and commentaries, and had relatively little impact on the life of poems as artifacts of practice in wider society, much like the intricate exchanges between Jorge Luis Borges's theologians Aureliano and Juan de Panonia.[3] As important as these debates would prove from the perspective of intellectual and political history, these writers framed their arguments against a cultural background that continued to be unyieldingly *kyōka*-esque.

In this context, it is helpful to lay out Shiki's argument, because in many ways it articulates our own understanding of what poetry is, what roles it can play in a society, and what effects it can have on a culture. It is possible to understand Shiki's project of reform as part of two wider, interconnected intellectual developments: the debates and experiments about the unification of spoken and literary languages, and the disputes over the reconfiguration of Japan's literary genres in response to the introduction of European critical discourses in the late nineteenth century.[4] Shiki saw *waka* essentially as a writerly pursuit, part of a field that he referred to as *bungaku* 文学, an expression that in the late nineteenth century came to be used as a translation for the European notion of "literature." According to this notion, *bungaku* could be subdivided into poetry (*shi* 詩), prose (*sanbun* 散文), and drama (*geki* 劇).

Shiki's drive to reform poetry was a response to the trials that the existing modes of cultural production faced during the Meiji period (1868–1911) as they attempted to find a place within the new ideology of modern literature and the modern nation-state. In the 1880s, it would not have been unthinkable to expect that such tried-and-true genres as *waka*, *shī*, and *haikai* would lose ground to new forms modeled after European poetry. The possibility had been discussed at length in *Shintaishi-shō* 新体詩抄 (A collection of new poetic forms, 1882). This anthology of poems in a new style included critical prefaces by the three compilers: Toyama Masakazu 外山正一 (1848–1900), Yatabe Ryōkichi 矢田部良吉 (1851–1899), and Inoue Tetsujirō 井上哲次

郎 (1855–1944). As the title of the collection announced, the editors brought together a series of poems that broke with precedent: fourteen translations of British and French poems into Japanese, followed by five original poems that the compilers explored to determine what a "new style" of Japanese poetry could look like.

The main question that *Shintaishi-shō* raised was about the place of *waka* and other traditional poetic practices in the future of the Japanese nation. In his critical preface, Inoue argued that *waka* was not worthy of the attention of modern poets and that a new form of poetry had to be found to match the times.[5] Yatabe contended that all judgments of value were culturally determined and thus relative, and that, consequently, it was very acceptable to compose poetry in "Western" styles.[6] And Toyama suggested that the "new style" of poetry would become as successful as poetry of the Tang dynasty (618–907), the most revered Chinese poetry of all time.[7] As part of this project, the editors chose the character *shi* 詩, which traditionally had been used to mean specifically poetry in Chinese (*kanshi* 漢詩), to refer more generally to the new style of verse they wanted to explore.

Another way in which *Shintaishi-shō* documents the contemporary anxieties about the future of literary production has to do with language. The editors' lexical choices reveal the state of flux in which literary and critical language existed in the early 1880s. For example, one of their prefaces was written in a style close to *kanbun* (classical Chinese); another, in a style based on the historical practice of glossing Chinese text into Japanese, often called Sino-Japanese (*kanbun-kundoku* 漢文訓読); and the last, in *wabun* 和文, a sort of neoclassical language of the early modern period inspired by the vernacular narratives of classical Japan.

The eagerness with which the editors of *Shintaishi-shō* dismissed centuries of *waka* and *shī* practice may have had to do with the fact that none of them had been exposed to the pedagogic apparatus for poetry. Toyama was a specialist in sociology and education. Yatabe had traveled to the United States to study botany at Cornell University. Inoue was a professor of philosophy at Tokyo Imperial University. They had not received proper, extensive training as poets, let alone served as mentors to aspiring poets. The publication of their collection suggests a nascent awareness among the Meiji intelligentsia that the rising debate about the Japanese nation and its language would not spare traditionally minded poets or their craft. It was evident that there was a problem, but *Shintaishi-shō*'s experimental, stilted translations were unable to offer much in the way of a solution.

Against this background, Shiki started his reform by turning to *haikai*, which was much more open than *waka* to vernacular and Sinitic expressions, as it fully embraced the lexical, thematic, and stylistic spectrum of the *kyōka*-esque. Shiki launched his project of reform on June 6, 1892. On that day, the newspaper *Nihon* carried the first installment of a serialized essay titled "Dassai sho'oku haiwa" 獺祭書屋俳話 (*Haiku* talks from the otter's den).[8] The first two installments offered a digest of the historical development of *haikai*. It was in the third installment, of July 18, that Shiki began to discuss the wider fate of poetic production in modern Japan:

> Since the great transformation of the Meiji period, literature [*bungaku*] also suffered a radical change, as translation [*honyaku*], new-style poetry [*shintaishi*], and the colloquial style [*genbun-icchi*] shook the literary world; there is no way back, and we have reached a situation of confusion [*takibōyō*]. But looked at from the perspective of the people who inhabit this land, this is just a step forward in the advancement of Literature. The great authors of Literature will emerge to combine the essence of traditional Literature and the virtues of modern Literature. Isn't this what happened already during the transformation of *haikai* in the Genroku period?[9]

> 明治の大改革ありてより文學も亦過劇の變遷を生じ飜譯文、新體詩、言文一致等の諸體を唱ふるものありて大に文學界を騒がし其極世人をして其歸着する所を知らず、竟に多岐亡羊の感を起さしむるに至れり。然れども天下の大勢より觀察し來れば是等も亦文學進歩の一段落に過ぎずして、後來大文學者として現出する者は必ず古文學の粋を抜き併せて今日の新文學の長所をも採取する者なるべく、而して是等は皆元祿時代に俳諧の變遷したると同じことならんと思はるヽなり。

Shiki begins by identifying the main sources of transformative influence, all of which can be traced back to Toyama, Yatabe, and Inoue's *Shintaishi-shō*: the efforts to translate into Japanese works coming from Europe, the exploration of new styles of verse influenced by these translations, and the consequent expansion of poetic diction to include expressions commonly used in colloquial conversation. Shiki describes the current state of the field as *takibōyō* 多岐亡羊, a situation in which there are so many possible roads to choose that one is confused about which road to take. Shiki also says that a similar situation of confusion was experienced before, during the Genroku era (1688–1704), a time marked by schism and rivalry, and from which emerged such heavyweight poets as Ihara Saikaku and Matsuo Bashō 松尾芭蕉 (1644–94).

There had been many other times of flux and innovation, but the Genroku era is particularly meaningful for Shiki's argument in the third installment of "Dassai-sho'oku haiwa." As he pointed out in the first two installments of the series, *haikai* had originated in medieval linked verse (*renga*), a collective practice in which a group of poets trained in the *waka* tradition got together to create long series of linked verses. During Genroku, the verse that would have served as the first link in a series came to be circulated as a stand-alone poem. This brief, seventeen-syllable poem, traditionally called *hokku* 発句 (opening verse), Shiki calls *haiku* 俳句 (originally a Genroku-era coinage), as we do today. The emergence of interest in the first link of a poetry series as a complete, independent work did not mean the end of *haikai* as a collective practice. *Haikai* practitioners continued to produce collective series of linked verses in great numbers throughout the Edo period. Yet in this shift of attention from the collective creation of a series to the output of an individual poet, Shiki probably saw a form of composition that more closely resembled the emphasis on the individual author in the European model that inspired his understanding of the new notion of *bungaku*.[10] In the fourth installment of "Dassai-sho'oku haiwa," published in *Nihon* on July 25, Shiki went on to anticipate that the program of reform he had just laid out for *haikai* would eventually have to be applied to *waka* as well.

The following year, Shiki resumed his reform project in a new series of articles in *Nihon* under the title "Bashō zōdan" 芭蕉雑談 (A conversation on Matsuo Bashō), which were published between November 13, 1893, and January 22, 1894. While in "Dassai-sho'oku haiwa" Shiki had paired *haikai* with *waka* as equivalent elements of the new field of *bungaku*, in "Bashō zōdan" he paired *haikai* with painting. Shiki suggests that the literary artist (*bungakusha* 文学者) and the plastic artist (*gijutsuka* 技術家), together with the products of their work—prose and poetry (*shibun* 詩文) and art objects (*bijutsuhin* 美術品)—share an artistic process and are shaped by similar constraints.

In "Bashō zōdan," Shiki stopped short of conceptualizing poetry and painting as subcategories of *bijutsu* 美術 (art). This he would do two years later in another series of articles in *Nihon*, titled "Haikai taiyō" 俳諧大要 (An outline of *haikai*), which were published between October 1 and December 27, 1895. The first installment of "Haikai taiyō" opens with a forceful statement that recapitulates in explicit language what Shiki had been implying until then:

> *Haiku* is a part of Literature. Literature is a part of the Arts [*bijutsu*]. Therefore, the criteria of artistic beauty [*bi*] are those of Literature. The criteria of Literature are those of the *haiku*. That is, only one set of critical criteria should be applied to all Painting, Sculpture, Music, Drama, Poetry, and Fiction.[11]
>
> 俳句は文學の一部なり。文學は美術の一部なり。故に美の標準は文學の標準なり。文學の標準は俳句の標準なり。即ち繪畫も彫刻も音楽も演劇も詩歌小説も皆同一の標準を以て論評し得べし。

The project of reconfiguration that Shiki had been building from the bottom up since "Dassai sho'oku haiwa," found in "Bashō zōdan" its definitive top-down formulation. By arguing that art encompasses literature, and thus poetry, of which *haikai* and *waka* are but two subgenres, Shiki finalized the flattening of partially overlapping but significantly heterogeneous early modern practices. Some of the corollaries of this formulation—such as the conflation of Noh with Kabuki and *jōruri*—would have puzzled anybody during the late Edo period, while others would have fit current practice well. For example, as Mark Morris has argued, the Sino-Japanese tradition of the *bunjin* 文人 (Ch. *wenjen*, "literati"), with which men like Bashō had identified, recognized no unavoidable discontinuity among poetry, calligraphy, and painting.[12] In the specific case of *waka*, for centuries poems had been combined with images on decorative folding screens (*byōbu*) and in later woodblock-printed illustrated editions, as well as inscribed on ceramic, lacquer, and metal objects; poems were a central feature of Noh drama and even more important in narrative fiction. Yet nobody would have regarded the presence of *waka* in other media as an indication that all shared a set of aesthetic and critical criteria. They all abided under the umbrella of the *kyōka*-esque but remained separate artifacts in terms of rules, techniques, and practice. Within this *kyōka*-esque structure, *waka* enjoyed preeminence as the practice against which all others were compared.

Where, then, would Shiki's efforts to reform the field of literary production leave *waka*? Shiki had begun composing *shī* in middle school, at the age of thirteen, when he and his friends put out a small literary magazine. He started training in *waka* under Ide Masao 井手真棹 (1837–1909) at the age of eighteen and in *haikai* under Ōhara Kijū 大原其戎 (1812–89) two years later.[13] As Robert Brower shows, Shiki's thinking about *waka* seems to have changed drastically around 1894—when he was in his late twenties—when he moved from the unexamined admiration for *Kokinshū* displayed by adherents of Kagawa's Keien school to an informed, militant endorsement of *Man'yōshū*. Brower connects this shift to the influence of contemporary thinkers such as the poet Yosano Tekkan 与謝野鉄幹 (1873–1935) and the editor of *Nihon*, Kuga Katsunan 陸羯南 (1857–1907), who were themselves inspired, in turn, by scholars such as Mabuchi.[14]

The new system of classification, with art at the top, had opened a fluid passage between *haikai* and *waka*. Between February 2 and March 4, 1898, Shiki published a series of essays on *waka* in epistolary form in *Nihon*, under the title "Utayomi ni atauru sho" 歌よみに与ふる書 (Letters to *waka* poets), which launched an attack on the contemporary schools of *waka* composition.[15] For example, Shiki opens "Letter 3" with this invective:

> There is hardly anybody as foolish and reckless as a *waka* poet. When they hear the words "composing *waka* poems" [*uta yomi*], they always believe that there's nothing better than *waka*; but *waka* poets do not know anything other than *waka*, and that is the reason they proudly believe it to be the best. They do not understand even the closest form to *waka*, the *haiku*, and assume that as both *haiku* and *senryū* [informal *haiku*] have seventeen syllables they must be identical; they are so

> reckless that they do not study Chinese poetry [*shina no shi*] and have only an illiterate and superficial knowledge of Western poetry, if they have any at all; all the more, how shocked and surprised will they be upon hearing that novels [*shōsetsu*] and the texts of dramatic plays [*inpon*] are part of Literature [*bungaku*] as much as *waka* is![16]

> 歌よみの如く馬鹿な、のんきなものは、またと無之候。歌よみのいふ事を聞き候へば和歌程善き者は他に無き由いつでも誇り申候へども歌よみは歌より外の者は何も知らぬ故に歌が一番善きやうに自惚候次第に有之候。彼等は歌に尤も近き俳句すら少しも解せず十七字でさへあれば川柳も俳句も同じと思ふ程の、のんきさ加減なれば、況して支那の詩を研究するでも無く西洋には詩といふものが有るやら無いやらそれも分らぬ文盲淺學、況して小説や院本も和歌と同じく文學といふ者に屬すと聞かば定めて目を剥いて驚き可申候。

Shiki enumerates the different elements in the *kyōka*-esque ecosystem—*waka*, *kyōka*, *haiku*, *senryū*, *shī* (and the implied *kyōshi*)—as part of a gesture meant to dismantle and reconfigure it. His suggestion that composing *waka* now requires knowledge of Chinese and Western poetry, as well as drama and prose narrative, is a step toward loosening the legacy differences in vocabulary, themes, tropes, and rhetorical devices that structured the *kyōka*-esque field. Shiki made this last point explicit in a comparatively short essay, "*Man'yōshū* maki jūroku" 万葉集巻十六 (*Man'yōshū*, book sixteen), serialized in *Nihon* between February 2 and March 1, 1899, in which he argues that Mabuchi and his followers overlooked the most consequential section of the *Man'yōshū*, in book 16.[17] Shiki offers book 16 as the site of a refreshing poetic conception (*shukō* 趣向), different from the rest of this collection.

The advantage that Shiki finds in book 16 of *Man'yōshū* lies in its incorporation of humor (*kokkei* 滑稽) and its use of poetic materials not allowed in orthodox *waka* (but permitted in *haikai*)—for example, Chinese loanwords and vulgar terms such as *fun* 糞 (shit). Shiki argues his point in this way:

> Humor is part of the interest of Literature. However, the people of our country, *waka* poets, painters, and *kanshi* poets, as a matter of fact, despise humor in general. They attempt to eliminate humor, whether the

> humor of the *Man'yōshū*, of *haiku*, of *kyōka* [humorous *waka*], or of *kyōku* [humorous *haikai*], as if it lay outside the sphere of Art and Literature, and in this way put themselves in a position where they can't understand the part that humor plays in Beauty. It is not that there is nothing literary in the humor of *kyōka* and *kyōku*. However, *kyōku* tends to veer toward logical riddles, and *kyōka* rushes into frivolous puns (the poems labeled as *haikai* in *Kokinshū* do this, too).[18] To compare them with the sophisticated humor of *Man'yōshū* or of *haiku* is to mix up miso paste and shit.[19]
>
> 滑稽は文學的趣味の一なり。然るに我邦の人、歌よみたると繪師たると漢詩家たるとに論なく一般に滑稽を排斥し、萬葉の滑稽も俳句の滑稽も狂歌狂句の滑稽も苟も滑稽とだにいへば一網に打蓋して美術文學の範囲外に投げ出さんとする、是れ滑稽的美の趣味を解せざるの致す所なり。狂歌狂句の滑稽も文學的なる者なきに非ず、然れども狂句は理窟(謎)に傾き狂歌は佗洒落に走る。(古今集の誹諧歌も佗洒落なり)これを以て萬葉及び俳句の如く趣味を備へたる滑稽に比するは味噌と糞を混同する者なり。

The formal, expositional language of most of this passage contrasts with the colloquial, vulgar turn in the last sentence. This deft visual juxtaposition of food and feces embodies the interest in juxtaposition that lies at the core of *kyōka* and the *kyōka*-esque as an ecosystem in which *waka*, *kyōka*, and *haiku* coexist. Yet that system is precisely what Shiki aims to tear down in the name of literature and art. This passage presents Shiki's position as a fine-tuning of the levels and types of humor that can elevate poetry to the realm of art, but the effect on the place of *waka* in society and culture could not be more consequential. The incorporation of humor into *waka*, the effacement of the boundaries between *waka* and *kyōka*, and the removal of lexical constraints—all point in the direction that the *waka* form would take in the twentieth century. That form is what we today know as *tanka*, a poem following the *waka* pattern (*chōshi* 調子 in Shiki's terminology) of rhythmic units distributed as 5-7-5-7-7, but otherwise completely free to explore any and all expressive opportunities, as befits a modern art form.

Tanka, delivered from the thematic and lexical divisions between *waka* and *kyōka*, gains in latitude and scope, but in exchange loses one of the main affordances of *waka*: the provision of the elegant, time-honored, but stilted backdrop against which—and only against which—the irreverence of *haikai* and *kyōka* can attain meaning and significance. Without the stiff upper lip of *waka*, there can be no shock in bringing versification close to defecation. If Shiki's reform threw the baby out with the bathwater—a justified instinct at the time, given a baby's propensity to versify in the bath—this book has aimed to understand what was lost, how it had gotten there in the first place, and why it endured for so long.

Tanka has been a lasting, successful literary genre. Salient examples range from the work of Yosano Akiko 与謝野晶子 (1878–1942), who deployed the *waka* form to engage the most pressing issues of the time, such as the role of women in the modern nation and Japan's project of imperial expansion, to Tawara Machi 俵万智 (b. 1962), whose collection *Sarada kinenbi* サラダ記念日 (Salad anniversary, 1987) has sold consistently since its publication. Yet it is unquestionable that the long-lasting practice of *tanka* does not in any way represent the reinstatement of *waka* as the vigorous force that shaped the social body and created cultural community, that represented all that was good (and bad) in the upper classes, and that for this very reason was so easy—and so much fun—to parody and ridicule.

This is not to mean that Shiki single-handedly took down the *kyōka*-esque edifice. His writing belonged to a cultural and intellectual moment in which the affordances of poetry were changing because social practices were changing. The role assigned to *waka* within that edifice—witness to the cultural achievements of the elite, benchmark of high culture, and entrance into the upper levels of precious and rarefied social practice—was already being reassigned to a different historical practice: the early modern tea ceremony.

Points of Departure: The Tea Ceremony and the Notion of a Synthetic Culture

If the Ministry of Foreign Affairs were to rename its Japan Foundation in the prevailing fashion—following the models of the Instituto Cervantes, Goethe-Institut, Confucius Institute, Instituto Dante Alighieri, and so on—a likely candidate would be Rikyū Foundation, a much better fit than the more immediately obvious Murasaki Shikibu. Sen no Rikyū 千利休 (1522–91), the so-called father of the tea ceremony, is a historical figure associated with the early stages of national unification and the emergence of an enduring aesthetic system. The tea ceremony, for which he often serves as a synecdoche, came to be presented throughout the twentieth century as a synthesis of Japanese culture, a portal for both domestic and international students who were eager to learn about and preserve the traditional arts, crafts, and social practices of the Japanese cultural past. A reexamination of the origins of this idea can throw light on the cultural place that *waka* enjoyed throughout the premodern period.

Tea, Waka, *and Cultural Pedagogy*

The tea ceremony, known in Japanese as *chanoyu* 茶湯 (literally, "hot tea") or *sadō* 茶道 (the way of tea), is a late medieval phenomenon. It was initially shaped by the *dōbōshū* 同朋衆, retainers of commoner origins who served the Ashikaga shogunal house as catalogers and curators of fine objects, such as Chinese ceramics.[20] In the sixteenth century, a group of wealthy merchants from the city of Sakai, striving to dignify the act of drinking tea from such precious vessels, incorporated elements from the poetry tradition of the court into the ceremony. The tea master Takeno Jōō 武野紹鴎 (1502–55), for example, sought training in *waka* from Sanjōnishi Sanetaka 三条西実隆 (1455–1537), a high-ranking aristocrat who had been a disciple of the eminent poet Sōgi and of Asukai Masachika 飛鳥井雅親 (1417–90). As a young man, Jōō had also practiced *renga* under Shinkei, who was himself trained by the Reizei-school poet Priest Shōtetsu.

The discourses about *waka* provided early tea masters with a critical framework for elevating the nascent culture of tea. As Dennis Hirota shows, Murata Jukō 村田珠光 (ca. 1423–ca. 1502) discussed the introduction of traditional, domestically crafted, rough and uneven ceramic styles, such as Bizen and Shigaraki, to social spaces dominated by smooth-textured Song dynasty imports by borrowing the critical notion of *hiekaruru* (chill and withered), which Shinkei had used in a letter of instruction for a patron-student.[21] This eventually became the conceptual point of departure for Jōō's influential notion of *wabi* (rough).[22] Similarly, these late medieval merchant tea masters embraced the pedagogic apparatus built during the medieval period around direct oral transmission, the stewardship of authoritative manuscripts and commentaries, and the production of pedagogic treatises for patron-students.

The next generation of merchant tea masters in the service of powerful lords continued this approach to *waka* and aristocratic culture. Jōō's disciples Imai Sōkyū 今井宗久 (1520–1593) and Sen no Rikyū, together with another Sakai merchant, Tsuda Sōkyu 津田宗及 (d. 1591), served the warrior leader Oda Nobunaga as *cha-dōbō* 茶同朋 (or *chadō* 茶頭, Head of Tea), a position that merged curatorship and cultural consultancy with diplomacy and logistics.[23] With the death of Nobunaga and the rise of Toyotomi Hideyoshi 豊臣秀吉 (1536–1598) as the dominant military leader, Rikyū established himself as the chief *cha-dōbō* in charge of orchestrating the tea gathering hosted by Hideyoshi for Emperor Ōgimachi 正親町 (1517–93, r. 1560–86) at the imperial palace. This connection with *waka* and the culture of the court became a staple of tea practice during the early modern period. As Rebecca Corbett has shown in her study of the tea practitioners and craftswomen Tagami Kikusha 田上菊舎(1753–1826) and Ōtagaki Rengetsu 太田垣蓮月(1791–1875), both of whom fashioned tea utensils, even toward the end of the period the main cultural point of reference for makers of tea implements was still *waka*.[24]

The changes in the social circulation of *waka* during the late medieval period are apparent as well in the emergence of a pedagogic apparatus (or, rather, apparatuses) for *chanoyu* in the first decades of the early modern period. As Tsutsui Hiroichi shows, soon after the beginning of the early modern period a number of extant manuscripts surfaced, and new works created for the nascent woodblock-printing industry appeared, that include poems on the practice of tea.[25] For example, a series of poems about the different utensils necessary for a tea gathering was printed in a movable-type edition of a kana booklet (*kanazōshi*), *Ocha monogatari* 御茶物かたり(Tales of tea, 1630), published in Kyoto. Among more than forty poems is the following on the topic of the tea whisk (*chasen*):

chasen dake	The bamboo of the whisk
hito yo wo komeshi	bound into one knot
chigiri sae	should it come undone
en usukereba	for lack of fastening strength
furare koso sure	will become wobbly.[26]

ちゃせんだけ一よをこめしちぎりさへゑんうすければふられこそすれ

As is the rule with *kyōka*, a coordinated series of wordplays enable a double reading of the poem. The expression *dake* means not only "bamboo" but also "only"; *yo* means not only "knot" but also "lifetime"; *en* can mean "connection" in the physical sense and also in the sense of a karmic bond; *furu* can mean "to whisk" but also "to let go" and "to repeat." This allows one to read the poem as meaning "The tea whisk is like the vow to attain enlightenment after just one life: if the karmic bond is not deep enough, one is reborn again in this world." A similar tongue-in-cheek juxtaposition of the lofty and the everyday appears in a series of poems in *Takuan oshō chaki eikashū* 澤菴和尚茶器詠歌集 (Priest Takuan's collection of poems on tea vessels, 1659), a posthumously published, illustrated edition attributed to the calligrapher, painter, and Rinzai Zen priest Takuan Sōhō 澤菴宗彭 (沢菴, 1573–1645).[27] And in a similar work, *Chagu shiika* 茶具詩歌 (Poems in Chinese and Japanese about tea utensils, n.d.), Takuan offers a sequence of linked, alternating *waka* and *kanshi*. The following poem is representative:

imasara ni	Even if right now
omohisutemu mo	I give up my attachments
kurushikute	how painful!
uki ni makasete	At the mercy of suffering
yo wo sugosu nari	I will be in this world.[28]

今更に思ひすてむもくるしくておきにまかせて世を過す也

This poem uses a form of wordplay that dates back to the subgenre *mono no na* 者の名 (names of things) featured in book 10 of *Kokinshū*. Those poems worked as a puzzle, in which the reader must find a hidden key. In the *mono no na* of *Kokinshū*, the hidden images are taken from the flora and fauna that are part of well-known, sanctioned poetic diction, such as *uguisu* (bush warbler), *hototogisu* (lesser cuckoo), and *ustusemi* (cicada shell). But the topic of Takuan's *kyōka*-esque *mono no na* is instead *tenmoku* 天目, the Jian ware tea bowls imported from China and cherished by tea connoisseurs. In the poem, the expression *te-mu-mo-ku* is hidden across the end of the second line and the beginning of the third. Like the *kyōka* in *Ocha monogatari*, Takuan's poems are clever and humorous.

Poems in other works about *chanoyu* are straightforward and practical. A series of practical poems about *chanoyu* can be found in *Usoshū hyakushu* 烏鼠集百首 (Collection of crows and mice of one hundred poems, 1642).[29] The seventy-four poems in this compilation use the 5-7-5-7-7 form to list the main types and standard variants of utensils that *chanoyu* practitioners had to be familiar with. Since the poems follow the order of the utensils listed in a textbook titled *Chagu bitōshū* 茶具備討集 (A guide to the props and implements of tea, 1554), compiled by Ichiōken Sōkin 一漚軒宗金 (n.d.), Tsutsui suggests that *Usoshū hyakushu* most likely was composed as an aid to memorizing the information collected in *Chagu bitōshū*.[30] A similar use of the poetic form for teaching about *chanoyu*, but one in which the focus is not on technical information but on wider issues such as the appropriate attitudes to learning and practicing, can be found in *Chōka chanoyu monogatari* 長歌茶湯物語 (A tale in a long *waka* poem on the way of tea, possibly ca. 1515), variously attributed to the painter Sōami 相阿弥 (d. 1525) and to Sen no Rikyū's son Dōan 道安 (1546–1607).[31] *Chōka chanoyu monogatari* is a 139-line *waka* (*chōka*), followed by an envoy poem (*hanka*) in the style reminiscent of the poems in *Man'yōshū*. The poem remonstrates with young practitioners of *chanoyu* who lack manners and display debased attitudes.

The most influential work on *chanoyu* in *waka* form, and one that combines the practical and the ethical dimensions of the practice, was preserved in a cluster of texts that emerged in the late seventeenth century, now known collectively as *Chanoyu hyakushu* 茶湯百首 (One hundred poems on the way of tea). The poems vary from text to text in their number, content, and wording, but a significant portion of them appears in most of the works, sometimes with minor variations.[32]

The poems in *Chanoyu hyakushu*, like *kyōka*, preserve the *waka* form but incorporate themes, images, and diction that lie outside the orthodox parameters of the form. Unlike most *kyōka*, though, they do not display an interest in wordplay or double readings. For example, this poem opens the collection:

so no michi ni	In that path
iramu to omohu	one wishes to enter
kokoro koso	with all one's heart,
waga mi nagara no	it is within oneself
shishō narikere	that the teacher lies.[33]

其道にいらむとおもふ心こそわが身ながらの師匠なりけれ

This poem connects *chanoyu* with the history of *waka* in several ways. In the first place, the term *shishō* 師匠 (teacher) has a long history of attestation in prose works connected with pedagogy, particularly the pedagogy of Chinese literacy and *waka*. Second, the notion that a discipline (*michi*) is better learned through one's own powers of observation than through external instruction comes from the *waka* pedagogy pioneered by Fujiwara no Teika, common ancestor of the main households of medieval *waka* specialists. In contrast to the investment by other professional instructors in the production of detailed and comprehensive treatises, Teika preferred to send his patron-students lists of poems chosen by him for their excellence. He justified his method by arguing, in the preface to *Eiga no taigai*, "In *waka* poetry, there are no instructors; we simply make old poems into our teachers."[34]

The third way in which the opening poem in *Chanoyu hyakushu* connects with the practice of *waka* is related to a subgenre known in modern scholarship as *kyōkunka* 教訓歌.[35] These poems are pedagogic in their aims and incorporate diction and grammar that lie outside the orthodox *waka* form, such as imperative constructions. They have a precedent in the *shakkyōka* 釈教歌 (*waka* on Buddhist teachings) of the late classical period (see chapter 2) but do not share their ritual or votive functions. More immediate models are the poems in the collection by Minamoto no Mitsuyuki 源光行 (1163–1244),

Mōgyu waka 蒙求和歌 (Poems on the child's treasury, 1204), which gloss historical anecdotes from the Tang-period history primer *Méng qiú* 蒙求 (Jp. *Mōgyu*; Child's treasury).[36] Some medieval collections of *kyōkunka* are works of moral education, such as *Yo no naka hyakushu* 世中百首 (One hundred poems on worldly life, 1515) by the *renga* and *haikai* master Arakida Moritake 荒木田守武 (1473–1549).[37] Others are devoted to specific disciplines, such as *GoKyōgoku-dono taka sanbyakushu* 後京極殿鷹三百首 (Three hundred poems on hawking, early Kamakura period) by the powerful poet and scholar Fujiwara no Yoshitsune, and *Kemari hyakushu* 蹴鞠百首 (One hundred poems on kickball, 1506) by the poet and kickball master Asukai Masayasu 飛鳥井雅康 (1436–1509).[38] As do the collections on hawking and kickball, *Chanoyu hyakushu* combines in a mnemonic form injunctions about the attitudes expected of students and technical specifications about the spaces and objects particular to the cultural practice of *chanoyu*.

There is a fourth parallel between *waka* and *chanoyu* that has to be highlighted. It has to do with the incorporation of knowledge from other fields into the pedagogy of *waka* in the late classical period, and the progressive repositioning of *waka* practice as an entryway to the aristocratic culture that peaked in the late medieval period. The practice of *chanoyu* retraced this trajectory in a much shorter time span. As Corbett shows in her analysis of early modern *chanoyu* treatises for elites and handbooks for commoners, "Tea was used historically to teach aspirational women and men how to comport themselves in the manner of their social superiors, and to teach women how to be feminine and refined."[39] Corbett concludes that, by the middle of the period, knowledge of *chanoyu* was considered indispensable for any woman who aspired to be seen as "cultured, well-bred and up-to-date."[40] Like the role of *waka* in medieval Japan, the function of *chanoyu* pedagogy in early modern society expanded beyond its immediate scope of applicability (cultured hospitality among the elites) to reach sweeping relevance in the construction of a high culture that was recognized as such across the board. Similarly, it was offered as a means for the transmission of cultural knowledge across diverse social spaces.

Tea Culture as the Synthetic Culture of the Japanese Nation

The early modern conception of *chanoyu* as a vehicle for the transmission of other kinds of knowledge and other practices unfolded during the modern period through two related but distinct discourses. One was the expectation that the study of *chanoyu* could also teach *sahō* 作法 (gendered manners and morality). As Etsuko Katō and Kristin Surak show, starting in the Meiji period, standardized techniques for the preparation of tea (*temae* 点前) were taught in practice and through textbooks as a vehicle for imparting *sahō* to schoolgirls within the new system of imperially sanctioned educational institutions.[41] The other discourse emphasized the potential of *chanoyu* to produce good political subjects in the context of the imperial expansion of Japan. The cosmopolitan art historian Okakura Kakuzō 岡倉覚三 (Tenshin 天心, 1862–1913), for example, described *chanoyu* as an amalgam of ethics, religion, hygiene, economics, and morals that represented the modern democratic values that he hoped Japan would spread throughout Asia to counter European imperialism.[42] The art critic and philosopher Yanagi Sōetsu 柳宗悦 (1889–1961) wrote glowingly of the tea masters of the late sixteenth century that "the things that they loved are what all people wish to love . . . in the utensils they selected they presented us with the final criterion of ideal beauty."[43] In summary, these modern discourses extolled *chanoyu* as a proscriptive, universal criterion of civilized life that was applicable at the everyday and public levels, both within Japan and abroad throughout its expanding empire.

The notion of *chanoyu* as a repository of cultural knowledge was taken to its most radical formulation during the postwar period. The modern scholar and tea master Hisamatsu Shin'ichi 久松慎一 (1889–1980), for example, argued as follows in a best-selling collection of essays published in 1948:

> The culture of the way of tea [*sadō*], put simply, leverages the act of having tea—that is, leverages the act of drinking a bowl of powdered tea—to create a synthetic culture system. Since it is synthetic, or perhaps since it is unified, it has a comprehensive quality. The Noh theater, for

> example, is representative of Japanese culture, but lacks the form of a synthetic culture. The way of tea, on the other hand, is a synthetic culture system. Its synthetic quality cannot be found elsewhere. It embraces the Arts, Ethics, Philosophy, and on top of that Religion, absorbing every facet of culture and producing a unified cultural system.[44]

> 茶道文化とは、ひとくちにいうならば、喫茶を契機として、すなわち抹茶を服することを契機として創造せられた、綜合的文化体系であるといえると思う。茶道文化は綜合的な点で、しかも統一された点で、包括性をもっている。たとえば能楽というものは、やはり日本文化の代表的なものであるが、綜合的な文化形態をもっていない。しかし茶道は綜合的文化体系である。他に類をみないほど綜合的なものである。その中には芸術も、道徳も、哲学も、のみならず宗教でも含まれていて、文化のあらゆる部面において、茶道はすべてを吸収して、一つの文化体系をつくりあげている。

The notion of a "synthetic [compound] culture system" (*sōgo teki bunka taikei* 綜合的文化体系) allows Hisamatsu to argue that *chanoyu* not only represents the best of Japanese culture but also literally contains it thoroughly and comprehensively. This has proved an enduring notion that still provides the ideological foundation for many present-day practitioners of *chanoyu*. For example, a website owned by the Urasenke household of *chanoyu* specialists explains the cultural significance of the practice: "The way of tea is based on deep spirituality and independent thinking; it has been passed down for many years as the archetypal traditional culture of Japan. Furthermore, it is a cultural synthesis, made up of several fields of practice, such as arts and crafts, architecture, garden design, and so on."[45]

Similar wording has been discussed by Surak in connection with materials that promote the Urasenke Professional College (Urasenke Gakuen, Kyoto) as well as Urasenke's International Chado Culture Foundation. Urasenke's dominant position within tea circles in contemporary Japan and abroad, built through programs such as the Urasenke Midorikai fellowship for non-Japanese students—who are expected to return to their countries of origin upon graduation—has transformed the notion of synthetic culture into the prevailing ideological foundation for *chanoyu* as a contemporary practice.

It is possible to analyze this ideological construct as several related but discrete components. In the first place, it postulates the habits and preferences of practitioners of the tea ceremony as a set of criteria of beauty with validity across social spaces and regions. Yanagi, for example, regarded the collecting of premodern Korean, Japanese, and Ryūkyū craftworks as a way to express a prescriptive aesthetic ideal. Second, it assumes that these criteria apply to all other disciplines, regardless of medium or technique. As we see clearly in the works of Okakura and Hisamatsu, this premise is accompanied by claims that fundamental knowledge about these other disciplines can be obtained through the practice of *chanoyu*. Third, the aesthetic criteria of *chanoyu* and the other disciplines have in common that they are posited as high culture, in the sense of the habits and sensibilities of the social elites. Finally, the status of *chanoyu* as a gateway into high culture makes it an ideal means for the acquisition of ideologically prescribed and heavily gendered habits and expectations. These habits are immediately relevant to practitioners in terms of their public personae as imperial subjects, but also in their private lives in the shape of what scholars have called "genteel femininity" and modern writers refer to as *sahō*. In summary, the notion of synthetic culture makes claims of universality and representation expressed in heavily classed and gendered modes.

It is possible to draw parallels between the totalizing modern discourse on *chanoyu* and the status of *waka* in the medieval period. The postwar claim of cultural synthesis is a magnification of *chanoyu*'s actual representational qualities: the historical fact that many disciplines did come into play in the staging of tea gatherings, and that those tea gatherings historically played an important political, social, and cultural role. This book has traced the trajectory by which the practice of *waka* became a portal to other fields of knowledge, a model for other disciplines, and a means of acquiring and transmitting high culture across social spaces. Key to widening the base of stakeholders—consumers, producers, practitioners, learners across society—was the stretching of *waka*'s lexical and thematic boundaries through the practice of *kyōka*. By parodying *waka*, *kyōka* expanded its expressive potential and, simultaneously, confirmed *waka*'s status as a canonical genre of the elite class. As commoners became more culturally visible and significant, *waka* became representative of the culture of the elite, both an aspirational practice and a suitable target of parody—the very definition of high culture.

Regardless of whether *waka* was understood as *aspirational* high culture *for* all (an elite practice that everybody could learn about) or as the *representative* culture *of* all (a shared language that connected practitioners across diverse social spaces) its undisputed centrality had been its hallmark for most of the premodern period.[46] Throughout the twentieth century, though, international dignitaries who visited Japan were not treated to a *waka* recital, they were offered a cup of powdered green tea. The symbolic appropriation of *chanoyu* by modern cultural nationalists can be traced to the specifics of the practice during its early modern history and to the imperial expansionist project of the first half of the twentieth century. Yet the template for this came from *waka*. The underlying assumption—even the very possibility—that a social practice could rise to represent a whole group, class, or nation stems from the arc that *waka* had traced over more than a millennium of complex, rich, contradictory, and fertile cultural production and transmission.

Notes

Notes to Introduction

1 Today, the Chinese *shi* poems are known as *kanshi* 漢詩 (poetry of the Han). In classical Japan, the characters 漢詩 were often read as *kara uta* (poems of China), such as, for example, in Ki no Tsurayuki's *Tosa Nikki* (Tosa diary), 10th c.

2 *Waka* poets remain active at the official and popular levels. Every New Year, the imperial household hosts a televised public reading of poems in which selected compositions submitted by the general public are recited for the emperor. This event is known as *Utakai hajime* (first poetic gathering of the year). As is common in other contemporary societies, poetry is not as widely practiced as prose narrative, but a collection of *waka* poems by the poet Tawara Machi 俵万智 (b. 1962) has sold more than 2.5 million copies since the late 1980s.

3 Ogawa Takeo, *Bushi wa naze uta wo yomu ka*.

4 "Shi to setsuwa" constitutes the second half of a volume that also includes a discussion of *Heike monogatari* (Tales of the Heike), in Gomi, *Heike monogatari*. See also Komine, "Setsuwa no ba to katari"; Ogawa Toyō, "Katoku ron josetsu."

5 Jorge Luis Borges, "Los teólogos," in Borges, *El Aleph*, 45 (my translation).

6 The foundational English monograph on this dimension of poetic practice is the flawed but deeply stimulating Brower and Miner, *Japanese Court Poetry*, which provoked scores of excellent scholarly responses. See, for example, Huey, "Medievalization of Poetic Practice," *Making of Shinkokinshū*, and *Kyōgoku Tamekane*; Atkins, *Teika* and "Nijō v. Reizei"; Carter, *Householders*, *Regent Redux*, and *Literary Patronage*; Royston, "*Utaawase* Judgments"; McAuley, "Fine Thing for the Way"; and Horton, "Portrait of a Medieval Japanese Marriage."

7 Mars and Kohlstedt, *The 99% Invisible City*, ix.

8 This is what Sigmund Freud called the "narcissism of minor differences." Freud and Strachey, *Civilization and Its Discontents*, 114.

9 While the heads of the hereditary households of professional poets were by and large male, we do have research on the scholarly and poetic activity of a number of medieval female aristocrats. See Laffin, *Rewriting Medieval Japanese Women*; Kimura, "Regenerating Narratives"; and Tonomura, "Coercive Sex in the Medieval Japanese Court."

10 On the connections between the earliest *waka* anthology, *Man'yōshū* 万葉集 (Collection of myriad leaves, after 759), and the political and ideological positioning of the eighth-century court, see Duthie, "*Man'yōshū*." For an annotated translation of selections from the *Man'yōshū*, see Cranston, *Gem-Glistening Cup*. On the roles that *waka* poetry played in response to political divisions during the ninth and tenth centuries, see Heldt, *Pursuit of Harmony*.

11 This specific enumeration of the standard functions of *waka* is in Morris, "*Waka* and Form, *Waka* and History." According to Morris, "*Waka* were useful things to know how to make," 554.

12 Kuboki, *Ori no bungaku*.

13 See, for example, Shirane, *Bridge of Dreams*; Kamens, Utamakura, *Allusion, and Intertextuality*; and Okada, *Figures of Resistance*.

14 Poems 277 and 278 in Katagiri, *Gosen wakashū*, 85.

15 One of the contests was *Ōmi no miyasudokoro no utaawase* 近江御息所歌合 (Poetry Contest of the Concubine from Ōmi, n.d.).

16 In her book *Forms: Whole, Rhythm, Hierarchy, Network*, Caroline Levine's notion of form offers a particularly versatile way for literary scholars to discuss what in other scholarly traditions has been called a "social institution," which can range from conventional social expectations (connected with genres of written and oral performance) to ingrained habits and inclinations (overlapping with Pierre Bourdieu's notion of *habitus*) to more abstract social configurations (stemming from Claude Lévi-Strauss's notion of structure).

17 Levine, *Forms*, 16.

18 Hashimoto, *Inseiki no kadanshi* and *Ōchō wakashi no kenkyū*. For an analysis of mid-classical poetry contests and their connections with the first two imperially sponsored anthologies, see Satō, "Gosenshū no utaawase uta."

19 Kubota, *Heian shūka zenki* and *Kokin wakashū hyōshaku*.

20 Inoue, *Chūsei kadan to kajinden no kenkyū*, 361–64.

21 Kuboki, *Ori no bungaku*.

22 Kamens, *Waka and Things*, 5. Working from a similar perspective but on a later period, Tomoko Sakomura has examined "*waka* artifacts" as the convergence of verbal (poetry), visual (illustrations and calligraphed scripts), and material objects (folding screens, handscrolls, fans). Sakomura, *Poetry as Image*, 8–11.

23 Relatedly, while the social uses of poetry could still be learned during the processes of enculturation and socialization into aristocratic society—the more or less coordinated practices that gradually assimilated a person into the community and initiated them in the particular forms of subjectivity and cultural memory that were part of the fabric of life at the imperial court and the network of provincial administrative seats—composing successful works on poetic topics required specialized training.

24 Levine, *Forms*, 6.

25 The process of diffusion will be discussed in detail in chapter 2.
26 Haruo Shirane, "*The Tale of Genji* and the Dynamics of Cultural Production: Canonization and Popularization," in *Envisioning "The Tale of Genji."*
27 Bowring, "*Ise monogatari*," 477. These studies by Bowring and Shirane are inscribed within the field of reception studies and theory pioneered by the work of Konstanz School scholars such as Hans Robert Jauss and Wolfgang Iser on how readers construct meaning. Later they were expanded by others to highlight the entanglement of interpretation with issues of authority, value, and legitimacy—i.e., sociopolitical phenomena. For a recent and detailed overview of the field (with an emphasis on European texts), see Willis, "Reception Theory."
28 Bowring, "*Ise monogatari*," 405.
29 Emmerich, "*Tale of Genji.*"
30 Poem 564, in Komachiya, *Shūi wakashū*, 162. The poem relies on wordplay (*shimo* 霜 is frost; *shimoto* 笞 is a punishment stick) and metaphor, as frost conventionally suggests the white hair of an old man. See chapter 2 for a discussion of this poem's rhetorical and narrative contexts.
31 The poem is framed analogously, but without mention of a pardon, in *Shūishō* 拾遺抄 (Abridged collection of gleanings, 996–99), an anthology compiled by Fujiwara no Kintō 藤原公任 (966–1041) that served as a draft for *Shūishū* and enjoyed similarly high cultural prestige.
32 In *Uji shūi monogatari*, the poem is given a slightly different opening line.
33 Levine, *Forms*, 16.
34 Levine, *Forms*, 152n.15.
35 Levine, *Forms*, 12.
36 Norman, *Design of Everyday Things*, 10.
37 Gibson, *Ecological Approach to Visual Perception*, 127. In *The Senses Considered as Perceptual Systems*, Gibson brings up the notion of affordances but offers no explicit definition or clarifications.
38 Gibson, *Ecological Approach to Visual Perception*, 128.
39 Gibson, *Ecological Approach to Visual Perception*, 128–29.
40 A significant difference between environment and object is that environments are a given from the point of view of the animal, whereas objects are crafted by a maker after a careful consideration of the intended user.
41 Norman uses the word "signifier" in a different way than it is used in the field of semiotics, in *Design of Everyday Things*, 10–23.
42 I discuss the concept that poems and treatises have not only literary but also specific practical uses in chapter 1, through the notion of "artifacts of practice." I first heard the phrase "artifact of practice" from Steven Carter at the Waka Workshop 2014 at Stanford University and found it particularly concise and evocative.
43 Wimsatt and Beardsley, "The Intentional Fallacy," 469–70.
44 Mikahil Bakhtin, "Discourse in the Novel," in Bakhtin, *Dialogic Imagination*, 279.

45 For a transnational discussion of pedagogic practices, see Glomb, Gehlmann, and Lee, *Confucian Academies*. For a historical introduction to pedagogic practices in Japan, see Suzuki Hiro'o, *Genten kaisetsu Nihon kyōikushi*; Ishikawa, *Nihon kyōikushi*.

46 Tanaka Fumio, *Tōraijin to Kikajin*. For a discussion of the cultural and technological transfer from the Korean Peninsula to Japan up to the early seventh century, see Rhee, Aikens, and Barnes, *Archaeology and History of Toraijin*.

47 This section follows the work of Hisaki, *Nihon kodai gakkō no kenkyū*; Guest, "Primers, Commentaries, and Kanbun Literacy"; Steininger, *Chinese Literary Forms*, 129–38; and Ury, "Chinese Learning and Intellectual Life." For a detailed Daigakuryō curriculum from the mid-eighth century, see Bender and Lu, "Research Note"; and Hisaki, *Nihon kodai gakkō no kenkyū*.

48 On the emergence of writing in Japan, see Lurie, *Realms of Literacy*.

49 Steininger, *Chinese Literary Forms*, 161–63.

50 Minamoto no Tamenori, *Kuchizusami*, 68–91. For the manuscript, glosses, and careful annotation, see Minamoto no Tamenori, *Kuchizusami chūkai*. *Kuchizusami* includes more than three dozen *waka*, which are inscribed using the already archaizing/Sinicizing style that was common to the ancient chronicles and the *Man'yōshū*, instead of the more current phonetic system of inscription known today as *hentaigana* 変体仮名.

51 For a discussion of the preface to *Wamyō ruijūshō* in the context of other prefaces to works of lexicography, see Takahashi Tadahiko and Takahashi Hisako, *Nihon no kojisho*, 20–33. For a discussion of *Yōshi kangoshō* 楊氏漢語抄 (Notes on Chinese words by Master Yako, ca. 720), a Sinitic-Japanese dictionary that is no longer extant but is referenced in *Wamyō ruijūshō*, and the argument that it should be understood as a pedagogic tool for clerical training, see Manieri, "Technical Education in Nara Japan."

52 Significantly, in Minamoto no Shitagō's rendition of Kinshi's request we find a mention of a number of preexisting works that are described as *gyō no sho* 業書, an expression that when read in context seems to refer to works containing foundational or beginning knowledge. See Kariya, *Senchū wamyō ruiju shō*, 8. Steininger discusses, in this context, a recorded use of *Wamyō ruijūshō*, along with *Kuchizusami*, as a primer for a boy; see *Chinese Literary Forms*, 200.

53 *Wamyō ruijūshō* exists in two versions: one in ten volumes (with twenty-four headings) and one in twenty volumes (thirty-two headings). It is highly likely that *Kuchizusami* existed in disparate versions as well, with different levels of commentary, but its manuscript history is more obscure than that of *Wamyō ruijūshō*. In fact, the version most often quoted is from the series *Zoku gunsho ruijū*, which reproduces a woodblock version from 1807 based on the only extant manuscript. For a discussion of the history of the academic reception of *Wamyō ruijushō*, see Tsukishima, *Wamyō ruijushō*.

54 The authors of these works, like the authors of *waka* treatises in the following centuries, seem to have been clearly aware of these diverse practices of use, making moot the question of whether their works were originally intended to be used as primers or for reference.

55 For a discussion of alternative approaches, such as following sociopolitical power structures or varying degrees of centralization, as well as a methodical defense of the approach adopted in this book, see Friday, *Japan Emerging*, 16–20. For an assessment of the hazards and promises of constructing a global periodization, see Bentley, "Cross-Cultural Interaction."

56 All these historiographical terms have a long history of diverse usage in Japanese works, and in most cases—*nakagoro* being a salient exception—in Sinitic texts as well.

57 For a review of historiography in English and Japanese focusing on the sixth to twelfth centuries, see Piggott, "Defining 'Ancient' and 'Classical.'" Piggott's argument for defining the *kodai* era as the period in which the foundations of Japanese civilization were set is based on factual historical analysis, while I base my argument on how this period was perceived by later (in particular, medieval) writers.

58 Andrew Edmund Goble argues that the late twelfth to late sixteenth centuries should be categorized as medieval because of the central roles played by military activity, social mobility, and active engagement with the overseas world; see Goble, "Defining 'Medieval.'" He highlights these three characteristics as a means to differentiate the period from the previous classical period and the succeeding early modern period. For a comprehensive analysis of the new political and institutional practices of the Kamakura period, see Mass, *Development of Kamakura Rule*, and Adolphson, *Gates of Power.*

59 Mary Elizabeth Berry argues that the Edo period had in common with global early modernity the emergence of a strong state and the consolidation of a market economy; see Berry, "Defining 'Early Modern,'" in Friday, *Japan Emerging*, 42–52. For the early monetization of the economy during the medieval period, see Segal, "Awash with Coins" and *Coins, Trade, and the State.*

Notes to Chapter One

1 Modern scholars make a distinction between *karon-sho* 歌論書 and *kagakusho* 歌学書 to contrast the former's strict focus on composition with the latter's sweeping interest in poetic culture, etiquette, and lore. Writers of the eleventh century referred to works in both categories as *zuinō* 髄脳, a term that pertains literally to the spinal cord and the brain, and figuratively to an essence, or gist. In the context of *waka* practice, it was used in the sense of "treatise."

2 For leading research on twelfth-century poetry treatises, see Komine, *Insei-ki bungakuron*; Suzuki Norio, *Toshiyori zuinō no kenkyū*; and Inoue, *Chūsei kadan to kajinden no kenkyū.*
3 See, for example, Kuboki, *Ori no bungaku*; Huey, "Medievalization of Poetic Practice."
4 Huey, "Medievalization of Poetic Practice," 664–65.
5 Minamoto no Tsunenobu and Minamoto no Toshiyori were hardly the first father and son to reach the upper echelons of the poetic world. The first imperial anthology, *Kokinshū*, was compiled by Ki no Tsurayuki 紀貫之 (ca. 866–ca. 945), whose son, Ki no Tokibumi 紀時文 (n.d.), was among the compilers of the second imperial anthology, *Gosenshū.*
6 Suzuki Norio, *Toshiyori zuinō no kenkyū*, 3.
7 Komine, *Insei-ki bungakuron*, 466.
8 Toshiyori also left a collection of his own poems, *Sanboku kikashū* 散木奇歌集 (Useless wood: Collection of eccentric poems, ca. 1128); of the collection's 1,622 poems, more than 200 were subsequently included in imperial anthologies.
9 Although the Minamoto never really became a stable household of specialists, a few scholars treat the continuity between Tsunenobu and Toshiyori as constitutive of a household, which they refer to as the Rokujō Genke 六条源家 (Rokujō Minamoto house) to distinguish it from the later household known simply as the Rokujō, which they refer to as the Rokujō Tōke 六条藤家 (Rokujō Fujiwara house). See, for example, Kawakami, *Rokujō Tōke kagaku no kenkyū.* I consider the Rokujō Fujiwara house to be the first historical instance of a household of *waka* specialists.
10 For a discussion of gender in poetry circles during the twelfth century, see Bundy, "Gendering the Court Woman Poet." Bundy describes the place of women in the newly professionalized poetry houses as ambiguous; although the poetic production of women was regarded as different from that of their male counterparts, professional male poets at the same time admired, feared, and desired the female poets.
11 In this *utaawase*, instead of the customary one-time meeting, the host first commissioned a sequence of 100 poems from each participant on the topics of spring, summer, autumn, winter, and love. The resulting 1,200 poems were paired in 600 rounds, evaluated by each of the two sides, and finally submitted to the judge. The whole process took more than one year. For a discussion of this *utaawase*, see Royston, "*Utaawase* Judgments." For a comparative analysis of the arguments deployed in the judging, see McAuley, "Fine Thing for the Way."
12 Steven Carter beautifully describes the relationship between patron and poet: "The patron became a student of the artist he supported." See Carter, *Literary Patronage*, 16. Although Carter is writing about patronage in late medieval Japan, this trend started in late classical aristocratic circles.
13 Ogawa Takeo, *Bushi wa naze uta wo yomu ka*, 12–24.

14 Huey, "Medievalization of Poetic Practice," 651–52. After Fujiwara no Shunzei compiled the seventh imperial anthology, *Senzai wakashū* (*Senzaishū* 千載集 [Collection of a thousand years], 1187), Rokujō poets never again received a commission to compose an imperial anthology. All such assignments went to the consecutive heads of Shunzei's Mikohidari household, or to one of its three later branches.

15 Huey, "Medievalization of Poetic Practice," 652.

16 As also mentioned in the introduction, see Hashimoto, *Inseiki no kadanshi* and *Ōchō wakashi no kenkyū*; Kuboki, *Ori no bungaku.*

17 Brower and Miner, *Japanese Court Poetry.*

18 Katō, "*Mumyōshō* of Kamo no Chōmei," 336.

19 Shibayama, "Ōe no Masafusa," 311.

20 Research on *Toshiyori zuinō* can be found in Smits, "Teika and the Others," and Shibayama, "Ōe no Masafusa." See also Commons, "Japanese Poetic Thought." A discussion of Tsunenobu's work can be found in Smits, *Pursuit of Loneliness.* On Chōmei, see Katō, "*Mumyōshō* of Kamo no Chōmei."

21 *Kashiki* is also known by the title *Kakyō hyōshiki* 歌経標式 (Formulary for verse based on the canon of poetry). See Rabinovitch, "Wasp Waists and Monkey Tails."

22 For translations of the two texts by Fujiwara no Kintō, see Teele, "Rules for Poetic Elegance."

23 The sections of *Toshiyori zuinō* that deal specifically with poetic diction have aspects in common with the type of linguistic inquiry that Fujiwara no Nakazane displayed in *Kigoshō*, which was written roughly at the same time as *Toshiyori zuinō*, suggesting that the early part of the twelfth century was marked by a widening interest in linguistic inquiry. To clarify a series of poetic expressions, Nakazane quotes poems from *Man'yōshū* and the imperial anthologies and adds his commentary. Nakazane's eminently linguistic interest has led *Kigoshō* to be considered a precursor to attempts at compiling a dictionary of the Japanese language.

24 Suzuki Norio, *Toshiyori zuinō no kenkyū*, 279.

25 Verse-capping is commonly referred to today as *tan-renga* 短連歌 to distinguish it from the later linked-verse practice, also known as *renga*, in which three or more poets alternate to compose much longer chains.

26 Colophons often were inscribed at the end of a manuscript decades or even centuries after its initial circulation, so there is little certainty here. One of the two main lines of *Toshiyori zuinō* manuscripts includes a colophon stating that Toshiyori was commissioned to write the text by Fujiwara no Tadazane for his daughter Kunshi. A passage in the historical tale *Imakagami* 今鏡 (Mirror of the present, 1170) seems to support this claim. Kawakita, *Imakagami zenchūshaku*, 114. That Toshiyori uses honorific language in the few instances where he addresses his reader directly is compatible with this view. For example, after a long list of exemplary poems, Toshiyori writes, "Upon taking a look at these, you will come to

understand the gist" (*sorera o goranjite, kokoro o esasetamau beki nari* それらを御覧じて心を得させ給ふべきなり), in which *goran* and the auxiliary verb *tamau* are honorific. Minamoto no Toshiyori, *Toshiyori zuinō*, 64.

27 Hashimoto, "Kaidai," 14.

28 For example, in the poetry treatise *Yakumo mishō* 八雲御抄 (His majesty's eight-cloud treatise, 1242), by Emperor Juntoku 順徳 (1197–1242, r. 1210–21), *Toshiyori zuinō* is listed as one of the five treatises by renowned masters (*goka no zuinō* 五家髄脳).

29 Umeda, "Tsūdoku suru kagakusho." For a similar analysis of Kiyosuke's primer *Waka shogakushō* 和歌初学抄 (First studies in *waka*, 1169), see Umeda, "'Waka shogakushō' no shomen sen'i."

30 Diffusion to a third audience involves a degree of "reaffordance," as discussed in chapter 2.

31 Quoted in Minamoto no Toshiyori, *Toshiyori zuinō*, 110. The poem appears in *Man'yōshū* as *iwashiro no hamamatsu ga e wo hikimusubi masakiku araba mata kaerimimu* (磐白乃濱松之枝乎引結真幸有者亦還見武). Kojima, Kinoshita, and Tōno, *Man'yōshū*, 106–7.

32 Minamoto no Toshiyori, *Toshiyori zuinō*, 111–12.

33 The headnote reads, "During the time of the emperor ruling the realm from the Okamoto Palace (Emperor Kōgyoku, after her abdication, ascended to the throne at Okamoto Palace), Prince Arima, grieving over his lot, tied up the branch of a pine tree and composed these two poems" 後岡本宮御宇天皇代 [天豊財重日足姫天皇譲位後即後岡本宮] 有間皇子自傷結松枝歌二首 (*Man'yōshū*, book 2, poem 141, 106).

34 Kojima et al., *Nihon shoki*, 217–18.

35 This is not the only place where Toshiyori's retelling differs from the accounts in his sources. For an analysis of a few of these instances, see Komine, *Insei-ki bungakuron*, 418–28.

36 For a discussion of banishment and execution in the Heian period, see Stockdale, *Imagining Exile in Heian Japan*.

37 Minamoto no Toshiyori, *Toshiyori zuinō*, 131–32. This story appears in greater detail in Ikegami Jun'ichi, *Konjaku monogatari shū*, 288. The most obvious source for this very famous story is *Shiji* 史記 (Records of the Grand Historian, ca. 91 BCE), vol. 6, which Toshiyori does not mention. It is possible that Toshiyori is drawing from a digest version or liberally adapting the anecdote for his intended reader.

38 Minamoto no Toshiyori, *Toshiyori zuinō*, 105. Toshiyori may be referring here to the *Daijikkyō* 大集経 sutra, which contains a similar passage with only minor differences.

39 Other sources invoked by Toshiyori include the folk legend *Urashima Tarō* 浦島太郎, sections of sutras (for Buddhist *shakkyōka* poems), tales of Chinese historical events (such as the tragedy of Yang Guifei related in Bái Jūyì's *Cháng hèn gē* 長恨歌 (Jp. *Chōgonka* [Song of everlasting sorrow], 806), and passages from the Confucian classics.

40 At the time, Fujiwara no Sukenaka was middle controller (*chūben* 中弁) of the right.
41 Fujiwara no Akizane 藤原顕実 (d. 1110), eldest son of Sukenaka, would eventually rise to the office of counselor (*sangi* 参議).
42 Recounted in Minamoto no Toshiyori, *Toshiyori zuinō*, 112–13.
43 The first *ōraimono* was *Meigō ōrai* 明衡往来 (Akihira's letter copybook, 1040), by Fujiwara no Akihira 藤原明衡 (989–1066). Collections of written exchanges to be used as models emerged within the court; later in the medieval period, they became part of warrior culture. For example, *Teikin ōrai* 庭訓往来 (Letter copybook for use at home, mid-14th c.), a primer attributed to the Tendai priest Gen'e 玄慧 (1279–1350), is organized as letters for each month of the year that contain lessons in social interaction.
44 The connections between *Toshiyori zuinō* and *Konjaku monogatari shū* are unique in this context. Many similar stories appear in both, but it is not clear in which direction the borrowing took place. According to Suzuki Norio, a process of hybridization took place between the texts, and about two dozen passages in *Konjaku monogatari shū* have their source in *Toshiyori zuinō*; see Suzuki Norio, *Toshiyori zuinō no kenkyū*, chap. 9.
45 Komine, *Insei-ki bungakuron*, 460–65.
46 Komine, *Insei-ki bungakuron*, 460–65. A detailed discussion of gloss reading and textual commentary as fundamental aspects of literacy in Japan can be found in Guest, "Primers, Commentaries, and Kanbun Literacy."
47 Hashimoto, *Inseiki no kadanshi*; Hashimoto, *Ōchō wakashi no kenkyū*. Huey, "Medievalization of Poetic Practice."
48 Kubota Jun, "Critical Introduction," in Kamo no Chōmei, *Mumyōshō*, 283–84.
49 Katō, "*Mumyōshō* of Kamo no Chōmei," 340–41.
50 Kamo no Chōmei, *Mumyōshō*, 25 (*dan* 12). させる重代にもあらず詠みくちにもあらず。また時にとりて人に許されたる好士にもあらず。しかあるを一首にも入れるはいみじき面目なり.
51 Kamo no Chōmei, *Mumyōshō*, 87 (*dan* 68).
52 As noted, Toshiyori's treatise lacked a definitive title and was sometimes referred to as *Toshiyori mumyōshō* (Toshiyori's untitled notes). Chōmei, similarly, did not give his treatise a title. It was known as *Mumyōshō*, but also as *Mumyō hishō* 無名秘抄 (Untitled secret notes), *Chōmei waka monogatari* 長明和歌物語 (Chōmei's tales of poems), and *Chōmeishō* 鴨明抄 (Chōmei's notes).
53 Quoted in Kamo no Chōmei, *Mumyōshō*, 57 (*dan* 41).
54 Kamo no Chōmei, *Mumyōshō*, 58 (*dan* 42).
55 Kamo no Chōmei, *Mumyōshō*, 94 (*dan* 71). やや宗論のたぐひにてこときるべくもあらず. Chōmei structured this section as a conversation between an anonymous disciple and an anonymous master, but both parts are evidently the product of his own thinking. This could not have been a record of a conversation between Chōmei and his own teacher, Minamoto no

Shun'e, since the anonymous master mentions Shun'e among a list of current poets.

56 Quoted in Kamo no Chōmei, *Mumyōshō*, 104 (*dan* 72).

57 Quoted in Kamo no Chōmei, *Mumyōshō*, 105 (*dan* 72).

58 For a discussion of precedent guides and household diaries, see Ogawa Takeo, *Chūsei no shomotsu to gakumon*; Matsuzono, *Nikki no ie.*

59 *Hentai kanbun* was a mixed logographic writing system that combined the grammar of literary Chinese with elements of Japanese grammar, reflecting the intention that both would be successfully recuperated when the text was read according to the rules of glossing (*kundoku*). On the structure of *hentai kanbun*, see Schreiber, *Japanese Morphography.* On the development of *kundoku*, see Lurie, *Realms of Literacy.*

60 In *Fukurozōshi*, *hentai kanbun* serves as a sort of shorthand; even *waka*, which are customarily spelled out in kana, are presented in this compressed form. For example, the line *koromo utsu beki toki ya kinuramu* ("I wonder if the time has come when they beat clothes on the fulling block") is written 衣可打時ヤキヌラン, where the Chinese expression 可打 is to be rendered by means of *kundoku* as *utsu beki.* See Fujiwara no Kiyosuke, *Fukurozōshi*, 374. Accessibility, of course, is relative to the linguistic competence of the reader. Toshiyori wrote for a young female aristocrat, so he did not incorporate *kanbun* elements in which she would not have been trained. Toshiyori's regular juxtaposition of kanji and kana elements produced a style closer to that of later texts in what today is referred to as *wakan konkōbun* 和漢混交文 ("mixed style"). See Seeley, *History of Writing*; Habein, *History of the Japanese Written Language.*

61 Fujiwara no Kiyosuke, *Fukurozōshi*, 401–2.

62 Teeuwen, "Introduction: Japan's Culture of Secrecy from a Comparative Perspective" and "Knowing vs. Owning a Secret: Secrecy in Medieval Japan, as Seen through the *sokui kanjō* Enthronement Unction," in Scheid and Teeuwen, *Culture of Secrecy*, 1–34 and 172–203.

63 Klein, *Allegories of Desire.*

64 Fujiwara no Kiyosuke, *Fukurozōshi*, 401–2.

65 The unattributed diffusion of material from poetry treatises to other genres is analyzed in chapter 2.

66 Fujioka Tadaharu, "Kaisetsu," in Fujiwara no Kiyosuke, *Fukurozōshi*, 497–500. Fujioka is building on the research of Kawakami, "Yōmei bunko zō Kiyosuke Fukurozōshi kō," and Kawakami and Kanechiku, "Yōmei bunko Kiyosuke *Fukurozōshi.*"

67 Higuchi, "Fukurozōshi Mumyōzōshi."

68 Fujiwara no Kiyosuke, *Fukurozōshi*, 350.

69 Clothes customarily were beaten with a fulling block to make the fabric soft and glossy. Presumably, the painting on the folding screen depicted a person engaged in this task. The poem does not appear in Taira no Kanemori's personal collection (*Kanemori shū* 兼盛集, [Collection of Kanemori], n.d.) nor in any major anthology. This anecdote is retold in *Kokonchomonjū*

and in *Jikkinshō*, where the full poem is given as follows: "When I hear the sound of the wild geese deep in the autumn clouds, I wonder if the time has come when they beat the clothes on the fulling block" *aki fukami kumoi no kari no koe sunari koromo utsubeki toki ya kinuramu* 秋深み雲居の雁の声すなり衣うつべき時や来ぬらむ (episode 188 in Tachibana no Narisue, *Kokonchomonjū*, ed. Nishio and Kobayashi, 244; episode 4:11 in Asami, *Jikkinshō*, 168–69).

70 The Horse-Welcoming ceremony (*koma mukae* 駒迎え) was an annual event in the eighth month, when horses from the eastern provinces were sent to the capital and an emissary of the emperor went to meet them at Osaka Barrier, on the border of Yamashiro and Ōmi Provinces. *Mochizuki no koma* refers to the tribute horses brought from the Mochizuki (full moon) stables in Shinano Province. The poem quoted here is included in *Tsurayuki shū* 貫之集 (Collection of Tsurayuki, mid-10th c.) and the *Shūishū*: "At Osaka Barrier, a reflection on the pure waters: I wonder if right now they are pulling the horses of the full moon" (*Ōsaka no seki no shimizu ni kage miete ima ya hikuramu Mochizuki no koma* 逢坂の関の清水に影見えて今やひくらむ望月の駒). For a discussion of this poem in context, see Sorensen, *Optical Allusions*, 144.

71 Fujiwara no Kiyosuke, *Fukurozōshi*, 374.

72 Kanemori was active during the *Gosenshū* period; he was governor of Suruga and, according to some accounts, the father of the well-known poet Akazome Emon 赤染衛門 (n.d.). Tokibumi, the son of Ki no Tsurayuki, was a member of the *Nashitsubo no gonin* 梨壺の五人, a committee that compiled the *Gosenshū* and worked on an edition of the *Man'yōshū*.

73 Sei, *Makura no sōshi*, 54.

74 This well-known passage cannot, on its own, serve as conclusive evidence of a widespread culture of memorization; it is even possible that Sei Shōnagon presented it as an eccentric or exceptional incident. Nevertheless, memorization would emerge as a recurring theme in pedagogical texts of later centuries. For instance, as discussed in chapter 3, Nun Abutsu 阿仏尼 (1225–83) wrote to her daughter, who was soon to enter the court and compete for the crown prince's favor, about the need to memorize canonical poetic anthologies and works of narrative.

75 This form of enhanced memorization is connected to two other literary practices of the late Heian period: allusive variations on older poems (*honkadori*) and, in prose, allusions to poems (*hikiuta* 引歌).

76 Kamo no Chōmei, *Mumyōshō*, 21–22 (*dan* 10).

77 A poem by Fujiwara no Tomofusa 藤原知房 (n.d.) is included in *Kin'yōshū*, the imperial anthology compiled by Toshiyori, but otherwise not much is known about him. Fujiwara no Koreie 藤原伊家 (1041–84), however, was a successful court poet who took part in poetry contests and had poems included in several imperial anthologies, beginning with *Goshūishū* and including *Kin'yōshū*.

78 Fujiwara no Kiyosuke, *Fukurozōshi*, 379.

79 Fujiwara no Kiyosuke, *Fukurozōshi*, 375. 仰云重代者カタホナル事タニアリ尤有興之歌躰。(. . .) 雖不堪事依此道度々有面目。是多年稽古之所致歟。

80 The professionalization process had parallels in other times and regions. For the case of Renaissance Italy, see, for example, McClure, *Culture of Profession*.

81 Nagatō's father, also governor of Iga Province, achieved the senior fourth rank, lower grade, while Nagatō himself made it to only the junior fifth rank, upper grade. His older sister, known only as the Mother of Michitsuna, is the author of the personal diary *Kagerō nikki* 蜻蛉日記 (Gossamer diary, ca. 977).

82 Nōin was the son of the governor of Higo and a graduate of the Daigakuryō.

83 This poem appears as poem 264 in the Sansōbon 三奏本 manuscript line (the third and final draft) of the imperial anthology *Kin'yōshū*, compiled by Toshiyori, and as poem 144 in the imperial anthology *Shikashū*, compiled by Akisuke. In both compilations, the poem is attributed to Ōe no Yoshitoki 大江嘉言 (d. ca. 1009), a contemporary of Nagatō and Nōin. Since it was a cardinal rule to avoid selecting poems for one imperial anthology that had been included in an earlier one, apparently Akisuke did not consider the manuscript in the Sansōbon line to be the official version of *Kin'yōshū*.

84 *Gengenshū* 玄玄集 (Collection of great depths, ca. 1046) was compiled by Nōin and contains the works of poets in his circle. Nagatō, with ten poems, is the poet most represented in *Gengenshū*. Fujiwara no Kiyosuke, *Fukurozōshi*, 380.

85 Kamo no Chōmei, *Mumyōshō*, 68 (*dan* 50). 師弟の契り結び。

86 *Zuryō* were lower-level public officials who traveled to the provinces to oversee administrative activities in lieu of the slightly higher-level *yōnin* 遥任, holders of the office of provincial governor (*kami* 守), who often stayed in the capital. Nagatō, who served as governor of Iga, belonged to the latter group. For biographies of Nōin, see Mezaki, *Heian bunkashi ron*, and Forrest, *Model Life*. For the history of the *zuryō*, see Hérail, *Emperor and Aristocracy*, 233–64.

87 It is plausible that Nōin came to use the character 能, the second character in Nagatō's given name, to write his adopted Buddhist name as a symbol of the filial relationship that he developed with his *waka* instructor. During the Heian period, it was common for parents to name their children using one of the two characters in their own given names as a token of filiation.

88 The Clique of Six included Fujiwara no Norinaga 藤原範永 (n.d.), Taira no Munenaka 平棟仲 (n.d.), Minamoto no Yorizane 源頼実 (1015–44), Minamoto no Kanenaga 源兼長 (Shigenari 重成, n.d.), Fujiwara no Tsunehira 藤原経衡 (1015–72), and Minamoto no Yoriie 源頼家 (n.d.). For a discussion of their powerful patrons, see Forrest, *Model Life*, 37. On the relationship of high-ranking nobles with middle-ranking provincial governors, see Hurst, "*Kugyō* and *Zuryō*."

89 See, for example, Pandey, *Writing and Renunciation*, as well as Kamens review of *Writing and Renunciation*. See also Marra, "Semi-Recluses (*tonseisha*) and Impermanence (*mujō*)," and Hare, "Reading Kamo no Chōmei," 185.

90 Kamo no Chōmei, *Mumyōshō*, 25 (*dan* 12).

91 Fujiwara no Tokinobu 藤原節信 (Toshinobu; Kakuya no Sesshin 加久夜節信, n.d.) served as deputy governor (*gon no kami*) of Kōchi 河内 Province and as head of the *tachihaki no toneri* 帯刀舎人 ("sword-bearing retainers"), who were in charge of escorting the crown prince.

92 Fujiwara no Kiyosuke, *Fukurozōshi*, 369.

93 See, for example, *Kokinshū*, poems 826, 890, and 1051, for Nagara Bridge and poem 125 for Ide. The frogs common in Ide are known as *kajika* 河鹿 (*Buergeria buergeri*).

94 Fujiwara no Kiyosuke, *Fukurozōshi*, 369. スキ玉ヘスキヌレハ秀歌ハヨムトソ申ケレ.

95 The expression *suki*, related to *suku*, has been discussed similarly as "aesthetic self-indulgence," in Kamens, *Utamakura, Allusion, and Intertextuality*, 149–54. The term "zeal" used here aims to emphasize the excess *suku* involved in Kiyosuke's perspective.

96 Fujiwara no Kiyosuke, *Fukurozōshi*, 369.

97 The poem is recorded, for example, in Nōin's personal collection, *Nōin hōshi shū* 能因法師集 (Collection of Priest Nōin, after 1050).

98 Fujiwara no Kiyosuke, *Fukurozōshi*, 369. *Yaso shima no ki* 八十島記 is not extant. Kosobe nyūdō 古曾部入道 (the Lay Practitioner from Kosobe in Settsu Province) was an alternative appellation for Nōin.

99 Fujiwara no Kiyosuke, *Fukurozōshi*, 366–67.

100 Toshiyori, *Toshiyori zuinō*, 228. さればかばかり思ふばかりの人の歌などはおぼつかなき事ありとも難ずまじき料にしるし申すなり.

101 Fujiwara no Teika, *Maigetsushō*, 496. この道をたしなむ人は仮初にも執する心なくてなほざりによみ捨つる侍るべからず.

102 Hashimoto, *Ōchō wakashi no kenkyū*. As I discuss in the introduction, Hashimoto connects this decline with *waka*'s shift from a situational literature rooted in social occasions (until the mid-Heian period) to an individual-centered poetics (during the Insei period).

103 Exceptions to the focus on the Mikohidari are a few translations of some brief, very early treatises: Fujiwara no Hamanari's *Uta no shiki* 歌の式 (The code of poetry, 772) and, by Fujiwara no Kintō, *Shinsen zuinō* and *Waka kuhon*. See Rabinovitch, "Wasp Waists and Monkey Tails," and Teele, "Rules for Poetic Elegance," 145–64.

104 On the works referenced, see Bundy, "Poetic Apprenticeship"; Fujiwara no Teika, *Fujiwara Teika's "Superior Poems of Our Time"* and, for a discussion of its inception, Atkins, *Teika*, 92–93; Fujiwara no Teika, *Essentials of Poetic Composition*, 605–7, and *Outline for Composing Tanka*, 202–4; Huey, *Making of Shinkokinshū*; and Kamens, "Waking the Dead." *Maigetsushō* has an ambiguous status as a text that cannot be

attributed to Teika with certainty; for competing arguments, see Atkins, *Teika*; Brower, "Fujiwara Teika's *Maigetsushō*"; and Watanabe and Esteban, "Hearkening to the 'Voice' of Teika."

105 *Teika jittei* is translated in Cranston, "'Mystery and Depth.'"

106 On the works mentioned, see the following: Brower, "Foremost Style of Poetic Composition"; Laffin, *Rewriting Medieval Japanese Women*; Huey and Matisoff, "Lord Tamekane's Notes on Poetry"; Brower, *Conversations with Shōtetsu.*

107 Fujiwara no Shunzei, *Korai fūteishō*. For a partial translation, see Fujiwara no Shunzei, "Poetic Styles from the Past." In terms of comprehensiveness and detail, *Korai fūteishō* dwarfs other prose works by Shunzei, such as his commentary on the *Kokinshū*, *Kokin mondō* (A conversation on the *Kokinshū*, n.d.). See Kami, "Shunzei kokinmondō kō."

108 See, for example, LaFleur, *Karma of Words*; Stone, *Original Enlightenment*; Kimbrough, "Reading the Miraculous Powers," 4; and Fujiwara no Shunzei, "Poetic Styles from the Past," 587–88. For an analysis of the interests of compilers of imperial anthologies in Buddhist thought, see Stephen Miller, *Wind from Vulture Peak.*

109 In the introduction and colophon to extant manuscripts, Shunzei explains that *Korai fūteishō* was commissioned by a high-ranking personage. Internal evidence suggests that this person was, in fact, Princess Shokushi. See Matsuno, *Fujiwara Toshinari no kenkyū.*

110 Shunzei here incorporates poetic diction in the form of brief prefaces to the expressions "good" (*yoshi*) and "bad" (*ashi*; homonymous with "reeds").

111 Fujiwara no Shunzei, *Korai fūteishō*, 250.

112 For a discussion of *Móhē zhǐguān* in the context of Tendai soteriology, see Swanson, *Foundations of T'ien-T'ai Philosophy*. A number of interpretations for the reference to *Móhē zhǐguān* by Shunzei have been offered. One is that it was an attempt to reconcile the composition of poetry with Buddhist teachings and practices. See, for example, Fujihira, *Karon no kenkyū*; LaFleur, *Karma of Words*; and Ramirez-Christensen, *Emptiness and Temporality*. More recently, Ethan Bushelle has revised these interpretations: in Bushelle, "Joy of the Dharma," he argues that Shunzei incorporated *Maka shikan* discourse into his poetry treatise "as point of reference for emphasizing the importance of voice in *waka* poetry" (222) and as "an epistemological framework for recognizing the composition and oral recitation of all *waka* poetry, even the sinful form of love poetry, as a Buddhist activity" (223).

113 Shunzei uses the expression *fugen kigo* 浮言綺語, closely related to *kyōgen kigo* 狂言綺語 (crazy words and fancy expressions), a common expression that had its origins in a poem by the Chinese poet Bái Jūyì (772–846). In it, the poet, worrying about the incompatibility of poetry and the religious call, prays that the transgressions of his poetry be turned to good causes and lead him to enlightenment.

114 Fujiwara no Shunzei, *Korai fūteishō*, 251.

115 Fujiwara no Shunzei, *Korai fūteishō*, 252–53.
116 It is very likely that Kenjō consulted Prince Shukaku's library while preparing his treatise, *Shūchūshō*, according to Ikeda, "Shūchūshō to taikan honzō," 58.
117 On Shunzei's scholarship on the *Man'yōshū* in the context of his rivalry with the Rokujō, see Citko, "How to Establish a Poetic School."
118 The decision to place the poems from the *Man'yōshū* in the first part of *Korai fūteishō* suggests that Shunzei regarded this collection as a repository for poems that required careful study, but not necessarily as inspiration for further composition. Yet since this treatise was created for a specific individual rather than for wide circulation, we should be careful to qualify this speculation. In *Korai fūteishō*, Shunzei suggests to Shokushi that she should focus on the imperial anthologies.
119 For a translation, see Fujiwara no Teika, *Fujiwara Teika's "Superior Poems of Our Time."*
120 For translations, see Fujiwara no Teika, *Essentials of Poetic Composition*, 605–7, and *Outline for Composing Tanka*, 202–4.
121 Cranston, "'Mystery and Depth.'"
122 Brower, "Fujiwara Teika's *Maigetsushō*."
123 See, for example, Yashima, "*Maigetsushō* songi"; Tanaka Yutaka, *Teika karonshū*.
124 Fujiwara no Teika, *Maigetsushō*, 496. 或は難を負ひ果てて思ひ死にまかりしたぐひも聞こえ侍り.
125 Huey, *Making of Shinkokinshū*.
126 For a translation, see Brower, "Foremost Style of Poetic Composition."
127 Fujiwara no Teika, *Eiga no taigai*, 475. 和哥無師匠。只以旧歌為師。染心於古風。習詞於先達者。誰人不詠之哉。
128 For a schematic comparison of the use of narrative passages in *Fukurozōshi* and *Ōgishō*, see Moriyama, "Karon to setsuwa." For a comparison with Toshiyori's treatise, see Moriyama, "*Toshiyori zuinō* to ōgishō to."
129 Ikeda, "Shūchūsho to ruisho (*leishu*)."
130 On the philology associated with Rokujō-house poetry, see, for example, Brower and Miner, *Japanese Court Poetry*. For the argument that Teika adopted a similar focus, see Vieillard-Baron, "Issues at Stake in Poetic Commentary."

Notes to Chapter Two

1 These three collections of brief narratives are today grouped together in the genre of *setsuwa-shū* (usually translated as "anecdotal literature"), but if genre is connected with the affordances of a text and the expectations of its intended readership, I believe these works belong to three different

genres. Their common derivative approach could be conceptualized as a medium rather than a genre. The term "brief narratives" aims to highlight their connection with the recounting of events, the portrayal of characters, and the power of narrative action to seize the attention of a reader. The Japanese term *setsuwa* has been otherwise glossed as "explanatory tales," to emphasize how they can help an audience understand complex topics. See, for example, Eubanks, *Miracles of Book and Body*, 7.

2 This is, in other words, a formal analysis as understood by proponents of New Formalism such as David Atherton, who writes, "I understand literary works as proposing models of the world. The formal features of literary works—which, again, I define capaciously in terms of elements that reproduce or pull against recognizable patterns, at scales ranging from phrasing to character, trope, intertextual reference, and plot structure—create arrangements of order and relation that open and foreclose possibilities of perception. They suggest what the world contains and excludes; how it is connected, organized, and made to cohere (or not); what kinds of voices it amplifies or diminishes; and what dynamics of relation and antagonism animate it" (Atherton, *Writing Violence*, 4).

3 The Sinitic expression *dé* 徳/德 has a rich and varied textual history. For a *longue durée* study of this concept in the Chinese textual tradition, starting with inscriptions on bone and metal, and covering the works of Mengzi 孟子, Xunzi 荀子, Zhuangzi 莊子, Zhu Xi 朱熹, and Wang Yangming 王陽明, see Nivison, *Ways of Confucianism*. In the *Mengzi* (Jp. *Mōshi*; late 4th c. BCE), Mencius (ca. 372–ca. 289 BCE), for example, mentions *dé* as a moral quality that can make a good ruler, and thus the closest translation would be "virtue," but it seemingly involved something close to what we call "charisma." See Bloom, *Mencius*, 7.

4 The expression "Leafy green willows" is conventionally associated with spring. See, for example, Ki no Tsurayuki, in *Kokin wakashū*, book 1 ("Spring"), poem 26. A poem similar to the warrior's in this passage appears in *Shūishū*, book 5 ("Felicitous Poems"), poem 278, attributed to the poet and scholar Kiyohara no Motosuke 清原元輔 (908–90), the father of Sei Shōnagon.

5 Asami, *Jikkinshō*, 171–72.

6 The term used to describe the man is *saburai* 侍 (or *samurai* from the late medieval period onward). Originally meaning "retainer" or "attendant," and including those on guard duty at the imperial palace, in the early medieval period it referred more often to men serving powerful households as domestic security or in a military capacity. Elsewhere in *Jikkinshō*, the term appears in this last sense or refers directly to warriors more generally: e.g., in episode 7.24, "A *samurai* wearing an indigo robe, close-fitting trousers, and a sword walked in" (*Jikkinshō*, 321. 縹の襖に襖袴着て太刀はきたる侍の歩み入りて); and in episode 6.24, "Among the *samurai* of the Taira household there was one called Naniwa

Saburō Tsunefusa" (*Jikkinshō*, 252. 近くは平家の侍に難波三郎経房といふもの).

7 In *Jikkinshō*, the emphasis is on the ladies' mistake, as can be gleaned from its placement within a group of passages that similarly depicts events in which someone's rash words or deeds lead to mortification.

8 In the warrior's poem, *hataori* (a type of grasshopper) doubles as *hata ori* 機織 (loom weaving); *aoyagi* (green willows) is a standard prefatory expression (*makura kotoba*) for *midori* (verdant) and *ito* (yarn); *kurikae* can mean "to coil" (a string) and "to do something again"; and in the fourth line, *he-te* means "to pass" (time, *fu* 経) and "to stretch" (yarn vertically to act as warp on the loom, *fu* 綜). Through their connection with weaving, *ito* (yarn), *kuri* (to coil), and *he-te* (to warp) are conventionally associated expressions (*engo*).

9 In this changing context, elite religious institutions deployed strategies to retain their rights and privileges. For a discussion of this fascinating process, see Adolphson, *Gates of Power.*

10 For an examination of the transformation of elite warriors into culturally legitimate political actors, see Mass, *Court and Bakufu in Japan* and *Development of Kamakura Rule.*

11 Kuboki, *Ori no bungaku*; Huey, "Medievalization of Poetic Practice."

12 Ogawa Takeo, *Bushi wa naze uta wo yomu ka.*

13 The central provinces were known collectively as *kinai* 畿内 and were located to the south and west of the capital: Yamashiro 山背, Yamato 大和, Kōchi, Izumi 和泉, and Settsu 摂津.

14 The eastern provinces were located around Musashi 武蔵: Shimotsuke 下野 and Kōzuke 上野 to the north, Hitachi 常陸 to the east, Kai 甲斐 and Sagami 相模 to the south, and across the bay (known today as Tokyo Bay), Awa 安房, Kazusa 上総, and Shimōsa 下総.

15 Kyūsojin, *Date-bon Kokin waka shū*, poem 1098, 277.

16 This poem was included in the last section of *Kokinshū*, under the heading *azuma uta* 東歌 (Poems on the eastern provinces), together with other compositions on Kai, Michinoku, Sagami, and Hitachi that rely on poetic images such as waves, islands, bays, or the boiling of brine to make salt—none of which is applicable to poems about the landlocked capital. The two other poems from this collection that also include the expression *kotozute* (message), poems 152 and 742, make similar reference to faraway mountains, with the implied assumption that the point of reference to measure remoteness is the capital.

17 From *Keigyoku wakashū* 瓊玉和歌集 (Collection of precious gems, 1264), a manuscript in the collection of the Imperial Household Agency, quoted in *Shinpen Kokka Taikan*, vol. 7, entry no. 94. The poem also appears in *Ryūyō wakashū* 柳葉和歌集 (Collection of willow leaves, mid-13th c.), held in the archive of the Imperial Household Agency, and quoted in *Shinpen Kokka Taikan*, vol. 7, entry no. 95.

18 This is a traditional trope, stemming from the continental fivefold scheme

(五行; Ch. *wǔxíng*, Jp. *gogyō*) that assigned the season of spring to the east. The poem draws from it to present the east (*azuma*) not as a remote wasteland, but as the source of positive energy and creation.

19 In *Bushi wa naze uta wo yomu ka*, Ogawa Takeo analyzes the activity of the third Kamakura shogun, Minamoto no Sanetomo; the first Muromachi shogun, Ashikaga Takauji 足利尊氏 (1305–58, r. 1338–58); and the eastern *daimyō* Ōta Dōkan 太田道灌 (1432–86). These figures shared with other men in the warrior elite their direct access to the households of aristocratic *waka* specialists. Through the late medieval period, provincial *daimyō* would receive training from the likes of Reizei Tamekazu 冷泉為和 (1486–1549), a courtier of the highest rank who fled the war in the capital and established himself as a professional *waka* instructor in Suruga 駿河 Province, just south of Kai and west of Sagami; he served as the *waka* teacher of Imagawa Ujichika 今川氏親 (1471–1526), a local *daimyō* connected to the Ashikaga house.

20 In this section I follow the research in Kuroda Toshio, *Nihon chūsei no shakai to shūkyō*, and Ishii, *Miyako to hina no chūseishi*. The organization of the information is also adopted from these two sources. There are other possible approaches to organizing information on the social composition of early medieval society, but degree of power is particularly relevant for my analysis.

21 For the standard treatment of political and institutional practices in the Kamakura period, see Mass, *Development of Kamakura Rule*.

22 For the most recent examination of the Jōkyū Disturbance, see McCarty, "Divided Loyalties and Shifting Perceptions."

23 Ishii, *Miyako to hina no chūseishi*, 75.

24 Jeffrey P. Mass, "*Jitō* Land Possession in the Thirteenth Century: The Case of *Shitaji Chūbun*," in Hall and Mass, *Medieval Japan*, 157–83. Mass, *Warrior Government in Early Medieval Japan*.

25 Goble, *Kenmu*, xv–xvii.

26 Research shows that this diversity was not necessarily acknowledged in medieval sources. In his analysis of the language of medieval war tales (*gunkimono* 軍記物), many of which were written by courtiers, McCarty proposes a distinction between the term *hyōshi* 兵士 (or *heishi*), which for centuries had designated what we would call soldiers (in the sense of infantrymen), and the word *bushi* 武士, which in the late eleventh century came to refer to warriors as a social group (rather than an aggregate of individuals with a similar profession), emphasizing their origin in the eastern regions and attributing to them qualities of character such as loyalty. McCarty shows that by the late classical period, the people referred to either as *hyōshi* or *bushi* were essentially identical, and that the choice of one term over the other reflected the point of view of the speaker rather than actual differences in social activity or status. Moreover, McCarty teases out a textual link between the term *bushi* and the notion of *ban* 蛮 (usually translated as "barbarian"), quoting a series of writers who,

absorbing the continental discourse that placed civilization at the center and barbarians at the periphery, gave *bushi* the connotation of barbarians of the east who were far removed from the central provinces surrounding the capital. See McCarty, "Divided Loyalties and Shifting Perceptions," 183–85. (Interestingly, Karl F. Friday has argued against using the word *bushi*, which he describes as gaining prominence only in 1930s scholarship, and prefers the term *ikusa* 軍, which appears in historical documents throughout the Heian period; see Friday, *Hired Swords*, 93–94.)

27 Lorraine F. Harrington, "Social Control and the Significance of *Akutō*," in Mass, *Court and Bakufu in Japan*, 221–50.

28 Oxenboell, *Akutō and Rural Conflict in Medieval Japan*.

29 These military and police practices began in the tenth century with the establishment of the positions of *ōryōshi* 押領使 (envoy to subdue the territory) and *tsuibushi* 追捕使 (envoy to pursue and capture) among the provincial warriors who were fighting on behalf of the court. These two offices had different points of origin, but by the late tenth century the occupants of both positions were appointed on a standing basis, with jurisdiction over a single province and similar law-enforcement responsibilities. Another office of importance was that of *tsuitōshi* 追討使 (envoy to pursue and strike down), warrior members of *zuryō* houses who were appointed for the duration of a specific crisis. Friday, *Hired Swords*.

30 Friday, *Samurai, Warfare and the State*.

31 Friday, *Hired Swords*, 144–48.

32 Hongō, *Chūseijin no keizai kankaku*, 106–39. For an analysis of warrior-aristocrat relations in the Kamakura period with an eye to their later transformation in the Muromachi period, see Kaneko, *Chūsei buke seiken to seiji chitsujo*.

33 The expression is *chōsan daibu* 朝散大夫, in Tachibana no Narisue, *Kokonchomonjū*, ed. Nishio and Kobayashi, 414.

34 Narisue's study of the biwa (lute) is recorded in *Bunkidan* 文机談 (Literary table talk, late 13th c.), a text on the tradition of biwa performance by Bunkibō Ryūen 文机房隆円 (active 1248). Bunkibō mentions a Narisue who studied with Takatoki and then taught other courtiers, among them Grand Counselor Kazan-in Nagamasa 花山院政長. Bunkibō modeled *Bunkidan* after works of history (*kagami mono*). On the role of historiography in medieval Japan, see Brightwell, *Reflecting the Past*.

35 Sakurai Rika, "*Kokonchomonjū* no wakasetsuwa."

36 A good point of entry is the review of literature in the back matter of Tachibana no Narisue, *Kokonchomonjū*, ed. Nishio and Kobayashi. See also the editions edited by Nakajima, and by Nagazumi and Shimada.

37 His highest rank was junior fifth rank, upper grade, the title he signed with at the end of his collection. It is likely that most men in the Tachibana family were similarly stuck at the fifth rank. A historical chart included in the late Edo period collection of documents *Gunsho ruijū* 群書類従 (Corpus

organized, 1819) traces the family's genealogy back to the mid-Heian courtier Tachibana no Norimitsu 橘則光 (b. 965), who served as the provincial governor of Mutsu 陸奥 and was a descendent of the powerful eighth-century politician Tachibana no Moroe 橘諸兄 (684–757). See Hanawa and Kokusho, *Gunsho ruijū*, vol. 5, sec. 63 (Household genealogies), 277–84.

38 As suggested by Fujiwara no Teika in his diary *Meigetsuki*, covering the years 1180 to 1235. Teika writes that in 1230, the regent Kujō Michi'ie provided five retainers as attendants for the Kamo Shrine Festival, and one of them is listed as Captain of the Right Gate Guard Narisue. (Interestingly, in other entries Teika describes Narisue as a skilled horseman, which was a highly valued ability among militarized *zuryō* and non-elite warriors.) These references are widely accepted as referring to the author of *Kokonchomonjū*, but Gomi Fumihiko has argued that more research is necessary before identifying him as the Narisue mentioned in *Meigetsuki*; see Gomi, *Heike monogatari.*

39 This date comes from Bunkibō, who states that after Narisue's death, Nagamasa received a secret transmission from Hōshinbō's son. The son died soon after his father, on the ninth day of the fifth month of the ninth year of Bun'ei (1273); see Tachibana no Narisue, *Kokonchomonjū*, ed. Nagazumi and Shimada, 8. Thus if Nagamasa studied with Takatoki's son after Narisue's death, Narisue must have died before 1273.

40 For a discussion of Kujō Michi'ie's life, see Iikura, *Nihon chūsei no seiji to shiryō*, 7–21.

41 As was customary among powerful aristocrats, Kujō Michi'ie left behind a diary: *Gyokuzui* 玉蘂 (Jeweled stamen, first half of the 13th c.). See Kujō, *Gyokuzui.*

42 The family harked back to Fujiwara no Michinaga 藤原道長 (966–1027). Like his grandfather Kujō Kanezane and father, Kujō Yoshitsune 九条良経 (1169–1206), Michi'ie served as imperial regent (*sesshō* 摂政, infant emperor; *kanpaku* 関白, adult emperor). Michi'ie's mother was the niece of Minamoto no Yoritomo and the daughter of Ichijō Yoshiyasu 一条能保 (1147–97), a high-ranking courtier who served as a channel of communication for negotiations between the court and the *bakufu.*

43 Michi'ie's father-in-law was Saionji Kintsune 西園寺公経 (1171–1244), who emerged from the Jōkyū Disturbance as a powerful political player. He created for himself the office of *kantō mōshitsugi* 関東申次 (Liaison to the Eastern Provinces), which Michi'ie inherited.

44 Another aristocrat who would serve as a literary and cultural instructor to warriors from the eastern provinces was the scholar of *waka* and courtly narratives known as Abutsu. Having been adopted by a provincial governor, as a young woman she served the imperial princess and later empress Ankamon-in 安嘉門院 (1209–83). She enjoyed the prestige of her association with the head of the Mikohidari, Fujiwara no Tameie, but was legally unable to inherit the household after his death. In light of these constraints, there is evidence that Abutsu served as a tutor to warrior

families during her stay in the city of Kamakura, according to Morii, "Abtsu-ni to genji monogatari," 45. See also Laffin, *Rewriting Medieval Japanese Women.*

45 A facsimile of the manuscript at the Imperial Household Agency, known as *Goshobon* (Imperial Palace manuscript), is in *Goshobon Jikkinshō*, 2:145.

46 Nagai, "Jikkinshō no sakusha."

47 Inui, "Jikkinshō no sakusha wa Sugawara no Tamenaga ka"; Shimura, "Jikkinshō no hensha ni tsuite."

48 Gomi, "Setsuwa to ie."

49 Asami, *Jikkinshō*, 502. Gomi's and Asami's positions are discussed briefly in Brightwell, *Reflecting the Past*, 158–59.

50 Dykstra, "Notable Tales Old and New," 472

51 Ōsumi, *Jiten no kataru nihon no rekishi*, 63. 伝統的な貴族文化に強い憧れを抱くようになった時代の、貴族文化の百科事典であった。

52 Brownlee, "*Jikkinshō*," 129. For modern scholarship in English on this collection, see also John Brownlee, "*Jikkinshō*, the Continuity of Practicality," in Takeda, *Essays on Japanese Literature*, 54–65; and Geddes, "Partial Translation and Study" and "Buddhist Monk in the *Jikkinshō*."

53 Kimbrough, "Reading the Miraculous Powers," 6.

54 Throughout the Heian period, *shī*, *waka*, and music were performed together at banquets and other social functions. In an episode from the anonymous historical tale *Ōkagami* 大鏡 (The great mirror, ca. 1120) that is also recounted at the beginning of chapter 10 in *Jikkinshō*, boats were provided for performers of each of the three disciplines at a lavish outdoor party. It was understood that excellence in all three was a once-in-a-generation occurrence, so each participant was asked to choose one boat. But Fujiwara no Kintō was so skilled that he hesitated, finally choosing *waka* but later coming to regret his choice, in the belief that success at *shī* would have brought him more glory. See Tachibana and Katō, *Ōkagami*, 116.

55 This tally takes into account episodes that are believed to have been added to the text. The totals change if we do not count those, but not significantly, since the later poems include twenty-two *shī*, sixty-nine *waka*, and three *haikai.*

56 For a detailed discussion of the development of *haikai* and *kyōka*, see chapter 3. *Imayō* (literally, "in the contemporary style") were sung pieces that borrowed some of their rhythms, images, and diction from *waka*. Their standard form is four lines in the 7-5 pattern. Originally developed by female entertainers (*kugutsu* 傀儡) who worked at posting stations along main roads, they became more accepted at court thanks to the enthusiasm of GoShirakawa, who engaged female performers as instructors.

57 This calculation is based on an estimation of approximately seven hundred episodes in *Kokonchomonjū*. As with *Jikkinshō*, this number varies slightly, depending on how one parses the text.

58 This tally of episodes differs from that in modern annotated editions, which, for no reason, clump together several episodes as one, particularly toward the end of chapter 10. Premodern manuscripts and editions of *Jikkinshō* do not feature any such parsing, episode numbers, or episode titles.

59 The relative numbers of poems varies greatly from manuscript to manuscript. The tally for the *Yonezawa-bon* 米沢本 (the basis of Kojima's modern edition) is 111 *waka* and 5 *shī*; the *Bonshun-bon* 梵舜本 (the basis of Watanabe's modern edition, which nevertheless fuses it with the end of the *Yonezawa-bon*) includes even fewer *shī* poems. Putting together several different manuscripts, the *Shinpen Kokka Taikan* edition registers 5 *shī* and 206 *waka*.

60 Genette, *Paratexts*, 197.

61 Genette, *Paratexts*, 196–236.

62 A preface is where the author signifies some of the work's affordances and relegates others to the background.

63 Narisue writes *shunnōden* 春鶯囀, a standard metaphor for *gagaku* (court music). The pairs—spring and warbler, autumn and geese—are poetic conventions.

64 Tachibana no Narisue, *Kokonchomonjū*, ed. Nishio and Kobayashi, 27–28. Nishio and Kobayashi suggest that "Nan-En" 南袁 represents the first and last characters in a playful, Sinicized way of writing the name Narisue: 南理須袁.

65 For this reason they are referred to here as "collections of brief narratives" instead of the more common "anecdotal collections," with its undertones of unreliability.

66 Tachibana no Narisue, *Kokonchomonjū*, ed. Nishio and Kobayashi, 413.

67 Tachibana no Narisue, *Kokonchomonjū*, ed. Nishio and Kobayashi, 412. 終りの宴になずらへて. *Kokonchomonjū*'s preface in *kanbun* and postface in the *wakan konkōbun* register seem similarly inspired in the *kanbun* (*manajo* 真名序) and *wabun* (*kanajo* 仮名序) prefaces in *Kokinshū*. The choice of twenty as the number of scrolls further connects these two collections.

68 On the casting of Hitomaro as an ancestral teacher and the presentation of offerings to a portrait of him, a practice known as *Hitomaro eigu* 人丸影供 (Hitomaro-portrait offerings), see Commons, *Hitomaro*, 91; Klein, *Allegories of Desire*, 80.

69 Asami, *Jikkinshō*, 17. The three times of leisure were winter, evenings, and rainy days.

70 Hirao, "Katoku setsuwa no kenkyū," 32.

71 Mūjū, *Shasekishū*, 19.

72 For a discussion of the *kyōgen kigo* issue in late classical and medieval Japan, see Watanabe Yasuaki, "Kyōgen kigo kan wo megutte," in *Chūsei waka no seisei*; Kikuchi, *Shokunō to shite no waka*; Itō, "Bon-kan-wago"; Nishiki, "Waka no shisō eigin wo shiza to shite"; Misumi, "Iwayuru kyogen kigo kan ni tsuite"; Pandey, *Writing and Renunciation*; and

Bowring, "*Ise monogatari*," 441–42. Ethan Bushelle has argued that *kyōgen kigo* as a liturgical formula has been overemphasized in modern scholarly studies on the relationship between Buddhism and literature, which overlook the emergence of new liturgical uses for literary genres during the early medieval period; Bushelle, "Joy of the Dharma."

73 The expression *kigo* 綺語, when used on its own, displayed a similar uncertainty. It could have a positive connotation, as in the title of Fujiwara no Nakazane's dictionary of poetic terms, *Kigoshō* 綺語抄 (Digest of ornate expressions, 1107–16), or a negative one, as in the postface to *Kokonchomonjū*, where Narisue uses it to describe his collection self-deprecatingly as "crazily rough fancy phrases" (*kyōkan no kigo* 狂簡の綺語); Tachibana no Narisue, *Kokonchomonjū*, ed. Nishio and Kobayashi, 414. Similarly, Fujiwara no Shunzei mentions in his poetry treatise *Korai fūteisho* (Poetic styles from the past, 1197–1201) the fear that poems would be regarded as the "jesting of frivolous words and fancy expressions" (*fugen kigo* 浮言綺語). See, among others, LaFleur, *Karma of Words*.

74 *Yìwén lèijù* was commissioned by Emperor Gāozǔ 李淵 (566–635, r. 618–26), the founder of the Tang dynasty, and was compiled by a team of scholars led by Ōuyàng Xún 欧陽詢 (557–641).

75 Another important work in the *leishu* genre is the partially extant *Běitáng shūchāo* 北堂書鈔 (A selection of texts from the North Hall), compiled by the Tang court official and scholar Yú Shìnán 虞世南 (558–638). Also of note is *Chūxué jì* 初学記 (Jp. *Shogakuki* [Record for beginning study], 727), a more concise thirty-volume reference and primer compiled at the order of the sixth Tang emperor, Xuánzōng 玄宗 (685–762, r. 712–56), to help his children in their studies.

76 Duthie, "*Man'yōshū*," 107–11.

77 For a discussion of works in the *leishu* genre and their influence on Japanese writers, see Guest, "Primers, Commentaries, and Kanbun Literacy," 59. For a theoretical discussion of the transition from compilation to classification, see Ogawa Takeo, *Chūsei no shomotsu to gakumon*, 66–78.

78 Tachibana no Narisue, *Kokonchomonjū*, ed. Nishio and Kobayashi, 79. 盗賊は刑獄の法たり。辜を改め険を行ふの心絶ゆることなく暗かに浮雲の富を求め悕に深夜の悕きをなすなり。都鄙禁ぜざるべからず。

79 Tachibana no Narisue, *Kokonchomonjū*, ed. Nishio and Kobayashi, chap. 19, episode 442, 108.

80 The expression *toku* appears in the preface to lesson 10 in the *Katakana* manuscript, which is translated here, and in the *Rufu hanpon* early-modern standard woodblock version, but not in the *Kokkai toshokan* manuscript (previously known as the *Kunaichō* manuscript). Modern scholars tend to consider the *Katakana* manuscript the oldest version, but all are later copies of unknown provenance. As is true of many premodern texts, there are no extant versions of *Jikkinshō* that can be traced to the moment of its inception. Asami, *Jikkinshō*, 385.

81 The term *toku* can cover a wide semantic range. It appears in many different

contexts in *Jikkinshō*, always in connection with something both extraordinary and beneficial. As a stand-alone expression, it can mean "profit" or "benefit" (episode 1.29) and "wealth" or "success" (2.0); it can refer to magic, such as the ability to make bees stop flying (1.6) or to trigger a heavenly vision in another person (1.7); and it can allude to miracles and practical benefits (6.18). It can describe desirable personal qualities, such as the ability to keep a household peaceful, in particular in the relationship between wife and husband (5.14), and the effect of developing talent (*sainō* 才能 [6.34]) or patience (8.0). It also appears as one of the five Confucian virtues (8.0) and as the opposite of stupidity (*orokanaru* 愚かなる [3.12]). As part of a compound, it appears as *tokusei* 徳政 (virtuous government [2.5 and 10.76]); *kudoku* 功徳 (blessings bestowed by deities [gods and buddhas] to persons of merit [1.7]); *dōtoku* 道徳 (proper or correct conduct [3.16]), in the *Katakana*, but not the *Kokkai toshokan* manuscript; *ontoku* 恩徳 (care [6.20]); *gentoku* 験徳 (miracles produced by incantations or prayers [7.2]); *gyōtoku* 行徳 (incantatory miraculous practices [7.20]); *shintoku* 身徳 (one's own *toku* [10.73]); and *sekitoku* 碩徳 (an accomplished Buddhist priest [10.73]).

82 Komachiya, *Shūi wakashū*, book 9 ("Miscellaneous"), poem 564, 162. この歌によりて許され侍にけり.

83 Minamoto no Toshiyori, *Toshiyori zuinō*, 56. この歌の徳にゆるされにけりとぞ聞ゆる。

84 Fujiwara no Kiyosuke, *Ōgishō*, 223.

85 The poem is technically sophisticated. *Shimo* (frost) is, by convention, a metaphor for the white hair of an old man, common in poems begrudging old age and bad fortune (classified in imperial anthologies under the heading *jukkai* 述懐); *shimoto* was a stick used to inflict physical pain as a form of legal punishment.

86 Asami, *Jikkinshō*, 429–30.

87 Ki no Tsurayuki, kana preface to *Kokin wakashū*, 4. 力をも入れずして天地を動かし目に見えぬ鬼神をも哀れと思はせ男女の仲をも和らげ猛き武人の心をも慰むるは歌なり。

88 Ki no Yoshimochi, *mana* preface to *Kokin wakashū* by Ki no Tsurayuki, 342. 至有好色之家、以此為花鳥之使、乞食之客、以此為活計之謀。In the *mana* preface, Yoshimochi discusses the functions of poetry in three different passages: the one just quoted ("Persons of an amorous disposition . . ."); "Through [poems] one can express one's feelings [*jukkai*] and express one's anger [*happun*]. In driving heaven and earth, affecting the demons and gods, inculcating upright conduct, and softening the relationships between husband and wife, nothing is better than *waka* poems" 可以述懐、可以發憤。動天地、感鬼神、化人倫、和夫婦、莫宜於和歌 (338); and "The vulgar contend for profit and fame, and have no use for *waka* poems. How sad! How sad! Even if a person achieves honor—combining the offices of minister and general—and wealth—leaving no riches unpossessed—their

bones will still rot in the dirt and their name disappear from the world. Those known by posterity are rare, and all of them are *waka* poets" 俗人争事栄利、不用詠和歌。悲哉々々。雖貴兼相将、富余金銭、而骨未腐於土中、名先滅世上。適為後世被知者、唯和歌之人而巳 (346).

89 Tsurayuki and Yoshimochi borrowed selectively from the "Great Preface," as discussed in Wixted, "Chinese Influences," 217; Ki no Tsurayuki, *Kokin wakashū*, 342; Heldt, *Pursuit of Harmony*, 59–64; Persiani, "China as Self," 48.

90 Toshiyori was the first to mention a *toku* of poetry. No reference to a *shī toku* 詩德 (Ch. *shīdé*) can be found in the "Great Preface" or in commentarial works such as the influential *Máoshī zèngyì* 毛詩正義 (Jp. *Mōshi seigi* [Correct meanings in the *Book of Songs*]) by Kǒng Yǐngdá 孔穎達 (574–648). Kenjō later pointed out parallels in the potencies in the kana and *mana* prefaces, and offered illustrations of each benefit with poems from the *Kokinshū* and *Ise monogatari* in his treatise *Kokinshū jochū* 古今集序注 (Notes on the *Kokinshū* Preface, 1183) for his patron-student, the Shingon-sect priest Prince Shukaku.

91 Before *Toshiyori zuinō*, it is possible to find similar brief narrative episodes—without any mention of a *toku*—in the poem-tales (*uta monogatari* 歌物語) of the tenth century, such as *Ise monogatari* and *Yamato monogatari*; in imperial anthologies, such as *Shuishū* and *Goshūishū*; and in individual collections, such as *Tsurayuki-shū* 貫之集 (Collection of Tsurayuki) and *Akazome-emon-shū* 赤染衛門集 (Collection of Akazome-Emon).

92 Ishibashi Shōhō, among others, makes this argument. Ishibashi was the first modern scholar to attempt a comparative study of extant manuscripts, in Ishibashi, *Jikkinshō shōkai*, 1:5.

93 Separating the two, the editor remarks that "these are examples [*tagui*] of poems used by people to communicate their feelings" (Asami, *Jikkinshō*, 437). これら歌を人してつかはして心のうちをあらはせるたぐひなり。

94 This structure is not discussed by modern scholars. The issues outlined with episodes 39 and 47 appear in the *Katakana* line of the manuscript, which is considered the oldest (see the facsimile in *Goshobon Jikkinshō*), and in the *Kokkai toshokan* manuscript, which marks off episodes with line breaks but without any episode numbers (see the facsimile in *Jikkinshō*, Koten shiryō 10–11). They are reflected in the modern editions Asami, *Jikkinshō*; Ishibashi, *Jikkinshō shōkai*; and Nagazumi, *Jikkinshō*. Nishijima Masayuki, by contrast, follows the early modern standard woodblock version (*Rufu hanpon*), which merges episodes 35–39 and 40–51; see Nishijima, *Jikkinshō*.

95 Minamoto no Toshiyori, *Toshiyori zuinō*, 40. おほよそ歌は神仏みかどきさきよりはじめたてまつりてあやしの山賤にいたるまでその心あるものは皆詠まざるものなし。

96 The sorting of stories into divine and secular clusters may have been inspired

by—or, at the very least, related to—the roughly contemporary collection of brief narratives *Konjaku monogatari shū*, which separates episodes relating to the Buddhist truth from episodes dealing with lay events.

97 Toshiyori says, "They represent a digression, but I humbly recorded them here as a continuation to the poem by the god [at Kibune] as a way to bring to your gracious attention the fact that things like this happen. All the more, those who were born human shall be fond of it and practice it. Out of all living creatures, which does not know this? We read in an ancient text that it affects the invisible gods and demons, and that it calms the heart of fierce warriors, and yet, this is a thing of the past. In recent times we don't see this happen" (Minamoto no Toshiyori, *Toshiyori zuinō*, 50). これらよしなき事なれど神の御歌のつづきにさることありけりとも聞こし召さむ料に書きて候なり。まして人のかたちしたらむ者は好み習ふべきにや。生きとし生けらむもののなにものか知らざらむ。目に見えぬ鬼神をもあはれと思はせ猛きもののふの心をもなぐさむと古きものにも書けれど昔の事にや。この頃はさも見えず。The translation attempts to reflect Toshiyori's use of humble (e.g., *sōrō* 候) and honorific (e.g., *kikoshimesu* 聞こし召す) language in this passage. As discussed in chapter 1, *Toshiyori zuinō* was prepared for a high-ranking patron's daughter. Much has been made of Toshiyori's apparent skepticism about *waka*'s powers more recently. Kamioka Yūji has argued that we should regard it as an attempt to disagree with a putative unidentified rival who conceivably expressed his belief in the powers of *waka*; see Kamioka, *Wakasetsuwa no kenkyū*, 203–5. (Kamioka is admittedly projecting later conditions back onto Toshiyori's time.) It is also possible to interpret Toshiyori's comment in connection with analogous remarks about other topics—the composition of poems by old men (Minamoto no Toshiyori, *Toshiyori zuinō*, 51), by children (52), by rival lovers (54), and by thieves (55)—in which he similarly states that these were more common in the past.

98 The first story (Izumi Shikibu), for example, is presented as part of the cluster on divine poets, and the other two (Tsurayuki and Nōin) are part of the following cluster, in *Toshiyori zuinō*.

99 The poem is unattributed in *Toshiyori zuinō*, but most likely was borrowed from the imperial anthology *Goshūishū*.

100 The shrine of the deity Aridōshi myōjin 蟻通明神 in present-day Osaka. This story appears in *Tsurayuki-shū* after a long narrative headnote, and is referenced in passing in Sei Shōnagon, *Makura no sōshi*, 361.

101 Poems connected with rainmaking have a fascinating, long history. There is precedent for rainmaking poems in *Man'yōshū* in a passage that outlines how Ōtomo no Yakamochi 大伴家持 (718?–85) recited a long poem (*chōka* 長歌, book 18, poem 4122) and an envoy poem (*hanka* 反歌, poem 4123) after three weeks of drought. The long poem, describing the suffering brought by the drought, is an explicit appeal to the gods. The last line reads "please give us rain" (*ame mo tamawane* 安米母多麻波祢). A third poem (poem 4124), recited three days later, expresses gratitude for the

rain. This poem has received scholarly attention because it contains the word *kotoage* 言挙げ (offering of words), discussed later in this chapter. Rainmaking rituals (*amegoi* 雨請い) also appear repeatedly in *Nihon shoki* 日本書紀 (Chronicles of Japan; ca. 720), where they are called *shō-u* 請雨 (requesting rain). A related practice, the Shingon ritual of *shōukyō-hō* 請雨経法 (prayers and austerities to request rain) involves an appeal to the gods and buddhas to provide relief during a drought. Similar events would appear much later in the collection of brief narratives *Konjaku monogatari shū*, book 14, episode 41.

102 The servant's accuser was Toshiyori's paternal grandmother, Takakura no Ama'ue 高倉の尼上 (early 11th c.), after she noticed the disappearance of a gift of *wakame* seaweed that had been sent to her by the governor of Mikawa Province.

103 The preface is preserved in *Honchō zoku monzui* 本朝続文粋 (More literary masterpieces of our land, after 1140), book 8.

104 Kiyosuke writes, "*Waka* is a thing full of interest. When presenting a document to a ruler or someone of the highest standing, one can count on this way [*michi*]. Historical precedent indicates that one should compose a poem and include it in written applications for rank and office, as well as in official documents that certify the conferral of rank and office" (Fujiwara no Kiyosuke, *Fukurozōshi*, 375). 和歌ハ有興事也。無止事人及帝王ニモ達事ヲ其道也。所望申文若ハ名籍ニモ制之先蹤也.

105 For a general discussion of this anthology, see Kim, *Songs to Make the Dust Dance*. For the most recent discussion in English of GoShirakawa's engagement with *imayō*, see Morris, "*Imayō* as a Vocal Art Supreme."

106 For an introduction to and translation of lesson 10 of *Kuden shū* in the main manuscript line, see Kim, "Emperor's Songs." This reference to the notion of *toku* appears in only one branch of manuscripts (known unhelpfully as the *i'hon kudenshū* manuscript, or alternative manuscript line), as pointed out by Ogawa Toyō, "Karon ron josetsu," 59. See also Yamasaki, "I'hon *Ryōjin hishō kudenshū*," 42–45.

107 What is translated here as "music" is the term *kangen* 管弦 (literally, "pipes and strings"), which comprised the performance of several types of *fue* 笛 (flute), such as the *yamato-bue* 大和笛 and *shakuhachi* 笏拍子, as well as the *koto* 琴 (harp) and biwa. An ensemble of *kangen* musicians traditionally performed genres of *gagaku* 雅楽 (instrumental court music), such as *kagura* 神楽 (sacred music). The word *kangen* included, as well, the performance of *mai* 舞 (dance) that frequently accompanied the music.

108 Asami, *Jikkinshō*, 418.

109 Yǎng Yóujī 養由基 (Jp. Yō Yūki; d. 599 BCE), a military general during the Spring and Autumn period, was famous for his skill at archery; Lǐ Guǎnglì 李広利 (Jp. Ri Kōri; d. 88 BCE) was a military general of the Western Han dynasty. Asami, *Jikkinshō*, 444.

110 Asami, *Jikkinshō*, 446.

111 Asami, *Jikkinshō*, 447. 弓箭の道は敵に向ひて勝負をあらはすのみにあらず。うちまかせたることにもその徳多く聞ゆ。

112 The potency of archery is illustrated by a tale from the extended commentary to the Chinese classic *Chūnqiū* 春秋 (Spring and autumn annals) known as *Zuǒshì Zhuàn* 左氏伝 (Jp. *Sashiden*), in which an ugly man endears himself to his reluctant wife by capturing a pheasant with only one arrow. In another archery episode, the warrior Minamoto no Yorimasa 源頼政 (1104–80) engages in verse-capping, a practice related to *waka* and particularly popular with warriors.

113 Asami, *Jikkinshō*, 467. その徳やいたりにけむ.

114 The last cluster of episodes in lesson 10 (74–79) deals mostly with criminals and makes no mention of poetry, music, or any other courtly discipline. Incongruously, in episode 78 a court official loses a bid for higher office because he is spending too much time on poetry and neglecting his job.

115 It is possible for a collection of brief narratives to rely on clustering, without any nesting or hierarchical treelike structure. For example, clusters can be linked by word association to adjacent clusters, with the effect of movement without a sense of linear progression. Virginia Skord Waters shows, for example, that stories in *Konjaku monogatari shū* are arranged "according to associative links, such that the primary hermeneutical thrust—almost invariably didactic—of a tale is dependent upon that of adjacent texts in the collection" (Waters, "Sex, Lies, and the Illustrated Scroll," 59). Waters offers an example from a cluster of episodes about people who were saved by the Lotus Sutra: an episode about a woman who transforms into a snake and burns a monk inside a bell at Dōjōji Temple follows an episode about a snake and a mouse, and is followed in turn by an episode about another woman who transforms into a snake. All three stories depict animals that are saved from their fate by the Lotus Sutra. This style of sideways movement without progression creates an effect of constant topical change without thematic or historical progression, analogous to the mechanics of medieval *renga* (linked verse).

116 Asami, *Jikkinshō*, 162–63. Enshrined at Kitano is the spirit of Sugawara no Michizane, who was himself falsely accused (of treason, by political rivals) during his lifetime.

117 Asami, *Jikkinshō*, 364. かように忍び過ぐせるはまことにいみじくおぼゆかし.

118 Episodes 171–77 in *Kokonchomonjū* display the same content and arrangement as episodes 10.10–16 in *Jikkinshō*, and episodes 190–202 in *Kokonchomonjū* include many passages taken from episodes 4.14–15, 10.35–36, 10.42–47, and 10.50 in *Jikkinshō*. A third cluster (episodes 183–87) comes from episodes 3.1, 3.2, 3.4, 3.6, and 4.6 in *Jikkinshō*. For a discussion of later additions, see the critical introductions (*kaisetsu*) in Tachibana no Narisue, *Kokonchomonjū*, ed. Nagazumi and Shimada, 29–38, and in Tachibana no Narisue, *Kokonchomonjū*, ed. Nishio and Kobayashi, 489–99.

119 In the brief preface to chapter 6, however, Narisue states this about poems,

omitting the canonical line from *Kokinshū* about fierce warriors: "As it says in the preface to *Kokinshū*, they have the human heart as seed and myriad words as leaves. That is why gods and buddhas do not turn their back on them. Wise monarchs and discerning subjects certainly heap praise on them" (Tachibana no Narisue, *Kokonchomonjū*, ed. Nishio and Kobayashi, 195). 和歌は素戔嗚の古風より起りて久しく秋津洲の習俗たり。三十一字の麗篇をもて数千万端の心緒をのぶ。古今の序にいへるがごとく人の心をたねとしてよろづのことの葉とぞなりにける。これによりて神明仏陀もすて給はず。明主賢臣も必ず賞し給ふ。春の花の下秋の月の前これをもて豫遊のなかだちとしこれをもて賞楽の友とす。

120 Tachibana no Narisue, *Kokonchomonjū*, ed. Nishio and Kobayashi, chap. 6, episode 214, 272.

121 Herons are not a standard poetic image; the expression *amasagi* is not found in imperial anthologies. This is not a contrived pun, either; the word, in fact, could be written as 甘鷺 (sweet heron) or 尼鷺 (nun heron).

122 Tachibana no Narisue, *Kokonchomonjū*, ed. Nishio and Kobayashi, chap. 6, episode 215, 272.

123 Verse-capping received formal sanction as a subgenre of *waka* when it appeared as a separate subsection (*budate* 部立) in the imperial anthology *Kin'yō wakashū* (*Kin'yōshū* [Collection of golden leaves]) compiled by Minamoto no Toshiyori. During the twelfth and thirteenth centuries, verse-capping was known simply as *renga* (literally, "stringed poems"), but in modern scholarship, to distinguish it from the later practice of *renga*, or linked verse, it is referred to as *tan-renga*.

124 *Kokonchomonjū* records fifteen separate instances of verse-capping, distributed across a number of chapters—from "Classical Japanese Poetry" to "Witticism" to "Eating and Drinking." More than half of them involve humor.

125 Taira no Kiyomori has a mixed reputation in historical and semihistorical medieval narratives. *Jikkinshō* depicts him as a wise and compassionate leader. For a discussion of the portrayal of specific historical figures as models, see Geddes, "Courtly Model."

126 This reading is possible thanks to puns on Moruyama (in present-day Shiga Prefecture) and "to protect" (*moru*), as well as on "strawberry" (*ichigo*) and "child" (*chigo*). *Sakashiku*, similarly, can mean "splendid" but also "intelligent" and "healthy and robust." Since at least the compilation of *Kokinshū*, Moruyama had been connected with autumn images, such as dew (*tsuyu*) and cold rain showers (*shigure*). Yoritomo breaks with this precedent when mentioning strawberries, which are a summer fruit.

127 *Mubara* (thorny bush) contains *muba* (literally, "nursemaid"), which by extension includes anybody who looks after a child other than the parents.

128 *Jikkinshō* remained influential through the early modern period. The collection *Waka itoku monogatari* 和歌威徳物語 (Tales of the dignity and potency of *waka*, 1689), for example, contains episodes taken from

Jikkinshō and sorted into three clusters, under the headings *shinkan* 神感 (emotional responses of gods), *kun'on* 君恩 (patronage of the ruler), and *nin'ai* 人愛 (human affection). These sections contain, respectively, stories in which poets move gods to make miracles, poets persuade powerful people, and poets of relatively low status seduce people of higher status. The same material and approach appear in other early modern collections, such as *Waka kimyō-dan* 和歌奇妙談 (Conversations on strange *waka* poems), *Waka toku monogatari* 和歌徳物語 (Tales of the potencies of *waka* poems), and *Waka kitoku* 和歌奇徳 (The mysterious potencies of waka poems).

129 Narrative episodes about monks and nuns, as well as about their *waka*, abound in *Kokonchomonjū* and *Jikkinshō*. In *Kokonchomonjū*, Narisue devoted chapter 2, "Buddhism," to episodes about the teachings of the Buddha. Lesson 10 in *Jikkinshō* includes a cluster of stories about music, *shī*, and *waka* in connection with Buddhist deities. After the episode on archery already referred to, we find an account of an archer who receives the help of the god and bodhisattva enshrined at Hachiman, the tutelary shrine of the Minamoto household. This is followed by a succinct mention of the different abilities of Buddhist monks. These include mastering the teaching of the eight established sects (*hasshū* 八宗), practicing incantations (*darani* 陀羅尼), and reciting the Lotus Sutra (*hokke* 法華), and they lead to miracles (*reigen* 霊験) and benefits (*gyōtoku* 行徳). The editor notes them only in passing and explains that he finds it difficult to cover these topics in this collection. The gist of this brief episode is that being skilled (*nō* 能) in these pursuits might well be connected to the afterlife (*goze* 後世), but it can also help monks be summoned to court to receive honors and titles in this life.

130 Mujū Dōgyō's *Shasekishū* isn't nearly as comprehensively organized as *Jikkinshō* or *Kokonchomonjū*, so there is limited utility in offering a general table of contents. The sections that discuss poems appear in book 5, which is divided into an upper chapter (*hon*) and a lower chapter (*matsu*), and are loosely laid out.

131 For a survey of Buddhist poems in the imperial anthologies, see Ishihara, *Shakkyōka no kenkyū*; Morrell, "Buddhist Poetry"; Hori, "Shakkyōka seiritsu no katei ni tsuite"; and Hirano, "*Shakkyōka.*"

132 The term *shakkyō* refers literally to a pedagogic practice (the teaching of the Buddha), and a *shī* or *waka* that glosses a line from a sutra would fall under the sanctioned practice of *hōben* 方便 (Skt. *upāya*, expedient means), which Mujū discusses at length. This is the technique of using similes and metaphors—ultimately false, but nonetheless beneficial—with the expectation that students will revisit and discard this pedagogic scaffolding once they achieve higher understanding. The marked-off subsection "Shakkyō," introduced in *Goshūishū*, book 20 ("Miscellaneous"), was dropped in the next two imperial anthologies—Toshiyori's *Kin'yōshū*

and Fujiwara no Akisuke's *Shikashū* (Collection of verbal flowers)—but it returned in expanded form in Shunzei's *Senzaishū* (Collection of a thousand years) and Teika's *ShinKokinshū*.

133 Mujū, *Shasekishū*, ed. Kojima, 25.

134 This elucidation of the relationship between *kami* and *hotoke* would appear in other medieval collections of brief narratives, one of which, *Shintōshū* 神道集 (Collection of the way of the gods, 1352–61), is a compilation of the origin stories of *kami* shrines from different provinces.

135 By the time the rites for *kami* coalesced into a system in the seventh century, Buddhism had accumulated centuries of sophisticated doctrinal development and exchanges, from Tibet to the Korean kingdoms to Japan. Among these developments were the professionalized monastic institutions that trained and certified monks and nuns, which had no parallel in the worship of *kami*. See Hardacre, "Esotericization of Medieval Shinto," 144. For discussion of the larger East Asian contexts of this feature of Japanese religious history, see Yoshida, *Shinbutsu yūgō no Higashi Ajia-shi*.

136 *Sōji* 惣持 refers literally to the ability to retain in one's memory the teachings of Buddhism, but the word is widely used as a translation of the Sanskrit term *darani*.

137 The Japanese term *darani* is a transliteration of the Sanskrit word *dhāraṇī* धारणी by way of the Chinese *tuóluóní* 陀羅尼. For a discussion of the use of this concept in later medieval texts, see Yamada, "Chūsei kōki ni okeru waka soku darani no jissen," 290–92; Kikuchi Hitoshi, "Waka-darani kō," in Watanabe Yasuaki, *Higi to shite no waka*, 217–34.

138 *Ōjin* 応身 is the physical form adopted by buddhas and bodhisattvas to appear on Earth in order to save human beings.

139 *Dainichikyō-sho* 大日経疏 (A commentary on the Mahavairocana Sutra) was compiled by Yì Xíng 一行 (Jp. Ichigyō; 683–727) based on the lectures given by his Indian teacher on the sutra.

140 The Siddhaṃ script is used by esoteric sects in Japan to write out mantras and, on some occasions, sutras.

141 *Shingon* refers literally to the true words of a buddha, but is often used interchangeably with *darani* and *sōji*.

142 A long tongue is one of the thirty-two marks of the Buddha.

143 Mujū, *Shasekishū*, ed. Kojima, episode 5a14.4, 252–53.

144 Fujiwara no Shunzei later reformulated these notions to offer a theory of *waka* aesthetics in his treatise *Korai fūteishō*.

145 By contrast to Sanskrit, a Japanese poem can be noted down in myriad ways that depend on register, as discussed in connection with *Fukurozōshi* in chapter 1. Conversely, it is often not clear exactly how a poem that has been written down is supposed to be read aloud, a problem particularly common when reading older texts, such as the *Man'yōshū*.

146 Mujū, *Shasekishū*, ed. Kojima, episode 5a14.4, 253.

147 The poem (attributed to the Kannon Bodhisattva at Kiyomizu Temple)

is in *ShinKokinshū*, book 20 ("Buddhist Poems"), and in *Fukurozōshi*. Kiyosuke remarks only that Kannon offered it to a woman who was suffering (*mono omohi-keru*) and said that if she had nobody to rely on, she wanted to die, in *Fukurozōshi*, 392. 物思ケル女ノハカばかシカルマシクハシナント申ケルニ示ケル。(On the incongruity that this poem was composed by Kannon, not by the suffering woman, Mujū remains adamant.) In both works, the poem's first line reads *naho* (still, all the more) instead of *tada* (simply).

148 Mujū, *Shasekishū*, ed. Kojima, episodes 5b.1.1–4, 259. *Shinmei uta wo kanjite hito wo tasuketamau koto* 神明歌を感じて人を助け給ふ事.

149 Mujū, *Shasekishū*, episodes 5b.2.1–4 and 41–48, 261. *Hito no kan aru uta no koto* 人の感有る歌の事. Episodes 5b.2.5–40, which appear in only the *Yonezawa-bon* and the *Genō-bon* 元応本 manuscripts, form a later insertion, possibly by the editor himself, but this is still unclear. We will consider them separately.

150 Mujū, *Shasekishū*, ed. Kojima, episodes 5b.3.1–3, 287. *Yume no naka no uta no koto* 夢の中の歌の事. Some of the poems in these episodes are *shī*, but as in *Jikkinshō* and *Kokonchomonjū*, in Mujū's work *waka* vastly outnumber *shī*.

151 Mujū, *Shasekishū*, ed. Kojima, episode 5b.4.44, 285.

152 Mujū, *Shasekishū*, ed. Kojima, episode 5b.2.41, 262–63.

153 Moriyama, "Katoku setsuwa ron josetsu," 17. The term *katoku* 歌徳 is a modern coinage, created through a Sino-Japanese reading of Toshiyori's notion of an *uta no toku* 歌徳.

154 On identifying analogous narratives, see Moriyama, "Katoku setsuwa ron josetsu," 4–5. In sorting those narratives into categories, one could argue he adopted exactly the same approach as the editor of *Jikkinshō*; see Moriyama, "Katoku no shujusō," 8–9. The results of Moriyama's search for distinctive linguistic structures are underwhelming: he was able to conclude only that, compared with other *waka*, these *katoku* poems seem to favor unadorned language over rhetorical techniques; Moriyama, "Katoku setsuwa no waka ni tsuite," 22. He also analyzed the prose narratives, noting their tendency to lose detail even as they became more numerous over time; Moriyama, "Katokusetsuwa no denshō ni tsuite," 11 and 20.

155 Watanabe Shōichi, *Nihongo no kokoro*, 110; Moriyama, "Katoku setsuwa ron josetsu," 2. See also Orikuchi Shinobu, "Nihon bungaku keimō," in *Orikuchi Shinobu zenshū*, 23:326–50.

156 For a discussion of Keichū's *Man'yō daishōki* 万葉代匠記 (Record of a substitute teacher of the *Man'yōshū*, 1688–90), see Duthie, "*Man'yō daishōki*," 108–14. For a discussion of the linguistic and religious aspects of *kokugaku* nationalism, see Murphy, "Urgency of History," 65–66.

157 Plutschow, *Chaos and Cosmos*, 10. See Suzuki, *Tozasareta gengo nihongo no sekai*; Roy Miller, "'Spirit' of the Japanese Language"; Boot,

"*Kotodama* and the Ways of Reading," 41–52; Heldt, *Pursuit of Harmony*; and Joko, "Reassessing *Kotodama*." For a critique of Norinaga by Fujitani Mitsue 富士谷御杖 (1768–1823), see Marra, "Nativist Hermeneutics," 365–415. As Heldt has shown, even early Heian-period attestations of the expression *kotodama* can be better understood in connection with wider political rhetorics; as Joko has discussed, Toshiyori and Kiyosuke used the expression *kotodama* in at least one of their poems, but neither showed any critical or linguistic interest in it in their poetry treatises.

158 Kimbrough, "Reading the Miraculous Powers," 18.

159 Kimbrough, "Reading the Miraculous Powers," 17–18.

160 Mujū must have been aware of Priest Nōin's poem, since it appears in a number of works from which he borrowed material, such as *Toshiyori zuinō*, *Fukurozōshi*, and *Jikkinshō*. It also is in *Nōin hōshi shū* 能因法師集 (Priest Nōin's Poems, after 1050) and *Kin'yōshū*, and among the later additions to *Kokonchomonjū*.

161 Ogawa Toyō, "Katoku ron josetsu," 69–73. The expression *jukkai* can be glossed by way of *kundoku* as *omohi wo noberu* or *kai wo jutsu su*. Brian Steininger pithily conceptualizes *jukkai* as "an authorial stance of aggrieved misfortune" (Steininger, *Chinese Literary Forms*, 115).

162 While this notion has a long history (appearing in the earliest collection of *shī*, *Kaifūsō*, and in the *mana* preface to *Kokinshū*), neither *Kokinshū* nor any of its immediate successors gave *jukkai* official sanction as a subsection (*budate* 部立). It was officially established as a subgenre of *waka* only in the twelfth century in the imperial collections *Kin'yōshū*, *Shikashū*, and *Senzaishū*, all of which use it in editorial headnotes to poems. It is for this reason that Ogawa regards *jukkai* poems as expressing a fundamental characteristic of the twelfth century, in Ogawa Toyō, "Katoku ron josetsu."

163 In asserting that a discourse on potency stems from anxieties about that same potency, Ogawa is working within what has come to be known as the "school of suspicion" or the "hermeneutics of suspicion" (originating in Paul Ricœur's writings) and later as "paranoid reading" (in Eve Sedgwick's work). See Ricœur, *Conflict of Interpretations*; and Sedgwick, *Touching Feeling*, esp. 123–30.

164 The poems in these narratives are always written for an addressee, and are offered as a performance and as part of a wider, complex, and constantly unfolding social dialogue. A consequence of this historical practice is the leniency toward—even expectation of—proxy versifying. A poem is credited in poetry anthologies to the person who recited it, sent it, made it public, or circulated it as part of a social interaction—the tacit, unsignified, but operating assumption being that anybody who was in the room at the time of composition chipped in, from ladies-in-waiting to visiting relatives to particularly learned servants. On a specific case of this accepted practice of ghostwriting, see Takeshi Watanabe, "Versifying for

Others." For a theoretical exploration of authorship in medieval Japan through the notion of "authori(ali)ty" as the foundation of a literary persona, see Tommasi, "Neither Plagiarism nor Patchwork."

165 Austin, *How to Do Things with Words*, 6. (The book is the published version of Austin's William James Lectures, delivered at Harvard University in 1955.)

166 Later in his lectures, Austin generalized this realization by arguing that the technical distinction between performative and constative sentences should be qualified, because all utterances have a performative dimension and thus belong to "more general *families* of related and overlapping speech acts." (Austin, *How to Do Things with Words*, 150).

167 Some poems were considered to work as charms, but they are in a separate category from the narratives on the benefits of poems. In *Fukurozōshi*, at the very end of volume 1, Kiyosuke lists a few poems that were said to work as charms, under the heading *jūmon no uta* 誦文歌 (Poem spells). According to Kiyosuke, these poems were to be recited after having a bad dream, after seeing a corpse, when experiencing nausea, and so on. None of them appears in *Jikkinshō*, *Kokonchomonjū*, or *Shasekishū*. Similarly, a ritual about which the addressee had no knowledge would not be effective. There were no instances in which poems presented at poetry contests or simply included in anthologies brought any benefits.

168 Freud, *Group Psychology*, 105.

169 Tomkins, *Affect Imagery Consciousness*, 1:470.

170 This is another reason that, in the introduction, I explore affordances as relationships between a functional object and a user, rather than as simple properties of the object.

171 Massumi, "Autonomy of Affect," 92.

172 Seigworth and Gregg, "Inventory of Shimmers," 2.

173 The earliest poetic back-and-forth with a god appears in the fourth imperial anthology, *Goshūishū*, as an exchange between Izumi Shikibu and the god at Kibune Shrine.

174 Shōtetsu, *Shōtetsu monogatari*, 141–42.

175 See the epilogue for a detailed discussion of the tea ceremony and its connection with *waka* pedagogy.

176 The Nijō school contributed to Sōgi's training as well, since Takayama Sōzei had been a student of Asayama Bontō 朝山梵燈 (1349–ca. 1427), who had studied with Nijō Yoshimoto 二条良基 (1320–88).

Notes to Chapter Three

1 The word "parody" has been defined in starkly different ways and is sometimes treated as synonymous with "satire," "irony," or "sarcasm." I refer to satire when the target is a contemporary group, parody when the target

is a text or genre, and irony when what is said is the opposite of what is meant or, analogously, when what happens is the opposite of what was expected.

2 *Nara ehon* booklets emerged in the sixteenth century as a practical alternative to harder-to-handle illustrated scrolls. As with *otogizōshi*, the critical category *Nara ehon* seems to have been introduced by nineteenth-century literary scholars.

3 Despite the methodological problems it introduces, *otogizōshi* remains the standard term in Japanese. Even though in this chapter I use "Muromachi tales" instead, in the rest of the book I use *otogizōshi* to avoid distracting the casual reader.

4 For a discussion of Shibukawa's collection as part of a nuptial library, see McCormick, "Gilded Library." For a discussion of *otogizōshi* as a genre, see, among others, Kimbrough, *Preachers, Poets, Women*; Skord, *Tales of Tears and Laughter*, 1–11; Mulhern, "*Otogi-zōshi*."

5 The view that Muromachi tales are predominantly didactic works for women and children has continued to appear in the work of serious scholars; see, for example, Sawai, "Waka renga to otogizōshi," 283.

6 This idea is discussed in detail in Hayashiya, *Machishū*, 198. For an early discussion of the problems with projecting characteristics of Shibukawa's early modern readership onto the readership of the late medieval period, see Putzar, "Tale of Monkey Genji," 288, and 293.

7 For a study of tenth-century local craft and agriculture in Owari Province, from the point of view of the laborers and taxpayers, see Von Verschuer, "Life of Commoners in the Provinces."

8 For an analysis of how Heian-period aristocratic writers discussed commoners as a way to perform class differences, see Angles, "Watching Commoners, Performing Class." Also interesting is Thomas E. McAuley's discussion of the incorporation of plebeian reports into poetic judgments in "Fine Thing for the Way."

9 If texts are always *for* a specific intended user *in* a specific context of use, as discussed in chapter 1 in conceptualizing literary texts as "artifacts of practice," then *machishū* tales represent a new form of literary practice.

10 Miura, *Nihon chūsei no chiiki to shakai*, 176. For an analysis of the material aspects of commoner life during the medieval period, organized as a reconstruction of yearly and life cycles, see 328–78.

11 For a recent study of materiality and sociability in a specific locale, the castle town (*jōkamachi* 城下町) of Ichijōtani, see Pitelka, *Reading Medieval Ruins*, chap. 5.

12 By extension, the expression *jige no kugyō* 地下の公卿 referred to low-ranking aristocrats who had not been granted access to the court.

13 Gay, *Moneylenders*.

14 For comparison, see the economic and political study of a rural commoner community in late medieval Japan in Tonomura, *Community and Commerce*.

15 For a discussion of agriculture, commerce, and population growth in medieval Japan, see Farris, *Japan's Medieval Population.*

16 On the transfer of control of arable land from the aristocracy to provincial warrior elites during the Muromachi period, see Arnesen, *Medieval Japanese Daimyo.* On the creation on that land of castle towns, in which both warriors and merchants lived, see Matsuyama, *Chūsei jōkamachi no kenkyū.*

17 The monetary exchanges during the late medieval period originated in the circulation of copper coins imported from Song China during the late Heian period, according to Segal, "Awash with Coins." There had been coins earlier, but by the mid-Heian period, they had disappeared, and rice, silk, and other forms of cloth were the main forms of exchange and repositories of wealth. See also Segal, *Coins, Trade, and the State.*

18 For an analysis of the development of markets, guilds, and financial instruments, as well as of their effect on taxpayers and borrowers, see Yamamura, "Growth of Commerce." For an analysis of uprisings, see Hosaka, *Hyakushō ikki to sono sahō.* For a discussion of the development of guilds and other horizontal alliances, see Eiko Ikegami, *Bonds of Civility*, chap. 4.

19 For a study of how the deterioration of the estate system led to the repurposing of tribute routes as commodity trade routes in the late medieval period, see Damian, "As Estates Faded."

20 Among the Sakai merchants were also powerful tea ceremony masters, such as Imai Sōkyū 今井宗久 (1520–53) and Sen no Rikyū 千利休 (1522–91).

21 Hayashiya, *Machishū*, 176. Hayashiya lists the three characteristics as marriage ties, monopolistic business practices, and rapid growth during the Tenbun era (1532–55), but immediately connects them to the Buddhist Hokke (Lotus) sect. In the passages that follow I adapt his argument slightly, presenting religious affiliation as the third characteristic.

22 Hayashiya, "Hon'ami ke."

23 The Nanban ("southern barbarian") trade routes connected Nagasaki to China and Southeast Asia and provided Japan with a market for its commodities, such as copper and silver, and access to European goods. This policy of sanctioned trade was started by Toyotomi Hideyoshi in the 1590s and was discontinued in 1634 as part of enhanced restrictions on international trade.

24 Hayashiya with Elison, "Kyoto in the Muromachi Age," 32.

25 These editions were produced in the first decades of the seventeenth century, using wooden movable type for the kana syllabary and including woodblock illustrations. They are known as *Saga-bon* 嵯峨本 (Saga books) after their place of edition (the Saga area in the capital) and alternatively as *Kōetsu-bon* 光悦本 or *Suminokura-bon* 角倉本, after their chief editors.

26 This last assertion, while generally correct, deserves qualifying, as there is evidence that access to the court could be fundamental in establishing a manufacturing and trade network. See, for example, Paula Curtis's

analysis of the career of the metal caster Matsugi Hisanao 真継久直 (d. 1598), in Curtis, "Entrepreneurial Aristocrat."

27 The rise of a powerful group of commoners was enabled by changes in the structures of power that came to the fore in the last decades of the fourteenth century. As Arnesen has discussed in *The Medieval Japanese Daimyo*, the turn of the fifteenth century was marked by the collapse of the power of the surviving aristocratic bureaucracy at the imperial court and the transfer of land to provincial lords (*shugo daimyō* 守護大名), who then maneuvered successfully to impose limits on the power of the central warrior government, turning the Ashikaga shogunate into a loose confederacy and, during the latter part of the fifteenth century, leading to widespread strife and chaos. These circumstances created a space and a need for the services that merchant commoners could provide. Recently, Thomas Conlan has revisited the role of the Ōuchi in our understanding of this period, in Conlan, *Kings in All but Name*.

28 Wakita, *Muromachi jidai*.

29 For a detailed discussion of *dōbōshū* and their warrior patrons, see Murai, *Buke bunka to dōhōshū*. See also Hall, "Muromachi *Bakufu*," 223; Berry, *Culture of Civil War*.

30 Powerful *machishū* households tended to associate through bonds of friendship and marriage. For example, Hon'ami Kōetsu was close to the third-generation Chaya Shirōjirō Kiyotsugu 茶屋四郎次郎清次 (1584–1622). At one point, the Chaya and the Hon'ami intermarried.

31 Many entertainers went by the name Yoshino Tayū. This person was the most famous among them.

32 For details and critiques of these efforts, see Hayashiya, *Chūsei bunka no kichō*; Skord, *Tales of Tears and Laughter*, 9–11; Ruch, "Medieval Jongleurs."

33 Sawai, "Waka renga to otogizōshi," 282–97.

34 There is no standard historical term to refer to the resulting corpus of sanctioned poems. Inoue Muneo has suggested the term "proper style" (*shōfūtei*), which he defines by its orthodoxy (*seitō* 正統) and its investment in elegance and sophistication (*fūga* 風雅); see Inoue, "Waka no jitsuyōsei to bungeisei," in *Chūsei kadan to kajinden no kenkyū*, 361–405. The expression *shōfūtei* dates back to the title of an anthology of eighty-one poems compiled by the Nijō school and titled *Shōfūteishō* 正風体抄 (The proper style, 1601). In the Edo period, this term was used in *haikai* circles to describe proper, or orthodox, *haikai* poetry.

35 The *Kokinshū*-era *haikai* 誹諧 (humorous *waka*) should not be confused with the early modern *haikai* 俳諧 (popular linked verse). Katagiri Yōichi argues that the correct reading of 誹諧 should be *hikai*. See Katagiri, *Kokin wakashū*, 403n1011. The term *haikai* originally was used for humorous Chinese verse. See Kubukihara, "Haikai no uta kara waka he;" Kubukihara, "Zareuta no jidai Heian kōki waka no kadai."

36 Minamoto no Toshiyori, *Toshiyori zuinō*, 26.

37 Fujiwara no Shunzei, *Korai futeishō*, 334.

38 Ki no Tsurayuki, *Kokin wakashū*, book 19, poem 1012, 309.

39 The first part of poem 1026, for example, puns on *kuchinashi* and on *miminashi* (no ears). See Ki no Tsurayuki, *Kokin wakashū*, book 19, 312.

40 As a continuation of post-*Kokinshū* compiling practice for *waka*, the first imperially commissioned anthology of *renga* links, *Tsukubashū* 菟玖波集 (The Tsukuba anthology, 1356), compiled by Gusai 救済 (ca. 1284–ca. 1378) and his disciple Nijō Yoshimoto 二条良基 (1320–88), contains no humorous verses.

41 A related concept in early modern and modern critical approaches to textual and visual works is *gazoku* 雅俗 ("elegant and vulgar"). One key difference between the notions of *gazoku* and the *kyōka*-esque is that the former highlights the aesthetic effect produced by a juxtaposition of different paradigms (the high culture of the court legacy and the low popular culture of the urban centers), and the latter emphasizes the mutual imbrication by which the low can carry the high within itself.

42 The term *kyōka* would later be associated with humorous poems composed by members of elite literary circles of the early modern Tenmei era (1781–89), such as the Edo-based *bakufu* officials Akera Kankō 朱楽菅江 (1740–99), Karagoromo Kisshū 唐衣橘洲 (1744–1802), and Ōta Nanpo 大田南畝 (1749–1823). Ōta Nanpo edited and published the anthology *Manzai kyōka shū* 万載狂歌集 (Wild poems of ten thousand generations, 1783) and two sequels: *Toku waka go-manzaishū* 徳和歌後万載集 (Potent poems of ten thousand generations, 1785) and *Kyōka saizōshū* 狂歌才蔵集 (Ten thousand generations of wild poems, 1787). *Kyōka* of the Tenmei era explore neoclassical techniques, such as *honka-dori* (the allusive variation popular in the twelfth and thirteenth centuries), as well as productive tensions with *shī* and Sinitic prose. Ōta Nanpo, for example, published a successful collection of *kyōshi* 狂詩 and *kyōbun* 狂文 titled *Neboke sensei bunshū* 寝惚先生文集 (Literary works of Master Groggy, 1767). Also sparking new interest in *kyōka* was the narrative fiction of Jippensha Ikku 十返舎一九 (1765–1831), with such work as *Tōkaidō hizakurige* 東海道中膝栗毛 (Shank's mare, 1802–14).

43 *Monokusa Tarō emaki*, Nakamozu Library.

44 *Monokusa Tarō*, National Diet Library, 2 vols. The eighteenth-century edition from Shibukawa adopted this version, keeping the text intact for the most part, but supplying new illustrations. For a theoretical approach to the reading of medieval illustrated manuscripts versus early modern illustrated printed editions, see Kuroda Hideo, *Rekishi to shite no otogizōshi*, 53–144.

45 *Monokusa Tarō*, in Shibukawa, *Shūgen otogi bunko*, 341–78.

46 For a complete translation of the *kusa sōshi* version and an analysis of the publication and consumption of these adaptations, see Kimbrough, "Illustrating the Classics."

47 Takahashi Noriko, *Monokusa Tarō*.

48 What follows is a highly summarized account of the rich and nuanced philological examination of the linguistic associations of key terms in the tale, in Satake, "Taida to teikō." For a brief discussion of Satake's argument, see Skord, "*Monogusa Taro*," 172. An argument that illustrates the kind of reading that puts laziness at the center, and against which Satake reacts, can be found in Sakurai Yoshirō, "Gekokujō no kamigami *Monokusa Tarō*," 32–33. Sakurai regards the tale as an allegory in which Tarō's laziness marks him as a sacred person. For example, Tarō's initial lying around (*fusu* 伏す) could symbolize the supine position connected to the mystical practices of mountain ascetics (*yamabushi* 山伏).

49 *Monokusa Tarō*, National Diet Library, 1:11. すこしもものくさげなるけしきもなし是ほどにまめなりものあらじとて. The wording varies slightly but the gist is similar in *Monokusa Tarō emaki*, Nakamozu Library, 14. For the purposes of this discussion, I will quote from the National Diet Library manuscript.

50 Ichiko, *Chusei shōsetsu no kenkyu*, 179–80.

51 Shinoda, "Musō *Monokusa Tarō* ron," 199–228.

52 Skord, "*Monogusa Tarō*," 182.

53 *Monokusa Tarō*, 1:17. I have replaced kana for characters and added punctuation to improve legibility, in consultation with *Monokusa Tarō*, in Ichiko, *Otogizōshi*, Iwanami bunko, 1:212.

54 *Monokusa Tarō*, 2:2–3.

55 Sawai, "Waka renga to otogizōshi," 291.

56 A famous instance appears, for example, in *Makura no sōshi*, *dan* 280, where Sei Shōnagon reports that on a snowy day, on being asked by her patron how the snow on Mount Xianglu would look, she responded by raising the blinds, showing that she could identify the allusion to a line from a poem by Bái Jūyì : "Raising the blinds and contemplating the snow on Mount Xianglu" 香爐峰雪撥簾看 (*Kōrohō no yuki wa sudare wo kakagete miru*). A couplet extracted from Bái Jūyì 's poem that includes this line appears in *Wakan rōeishū* (Collection of Chinese and Japanese poems for singing, ca. 1013), no. 554. See Sei Shōnagon, *Makura no sōshi*, 433. For an annotated version of this anecdote, see Asami, *Jikkinshō*, 56.

57 The cultural literacy under scrutiny in this passage is not representative of the standards of literacy among the elites. For the political and bureaucratic elites, the mark of solid linguistic training was Sinitic literacy and the associated practice of reading and writing Japanese sentences by means of *kundoku* glossing. What the lady is testing here, by contrast, is the protagonist's familiarity with what Heian period aristocrats called *yamato kotoba* 大和言葉, a lexical classification defined by the exclusion of Chinese loan words and recently imported words. Most of the expressions in the dialogue are part of a subcategory of this lexicon, the strictly regulated diction of *waka*. Akashi, Inaba, and Ōmi, for example, are places with a long poetic tradition because they allow for punning. The specific type of cultural literacy being tested speaks to the ways in which

social class was constructed and measured. In this passage, knowledge about *waka* is presented as the preeminent marker of class.

58 *Monokusa Tarō*, 2:3–4.

59 Shinoda uses the English word "bathos" and glosses it as *zenkō* 漸降 and *tonkō* 頓降. See Shinoda, "Musō *Monokusa Tarō* ron," 201.

60 Skord, "*Monogusa Taro*," 180.

61 *Monokusa Tarō*, 2:16.

62 Whereas in *Kokinshū* the metaphor appears only in a poem included in book 20, presented as an informal song (*saibara* 催馬楽) from a banquet, in the next imperial anthology, *Gosen wakashū* (*Gosenshū*), it appears in a poem in book 1, together with other poems on plum blossoms.

63 *Saru Genji sōshi* is an anonymous story that had circulated in manuscript form since the sixteenth century. It is among the manuscripts that, like *Monokusa Tarō*, were adapted and published by Shibukawa in *Shūgen otogi bunko*. For the manuscript history of this tale, see Sawai Taizō, "Monokusa Tarō," in Tokuda, *Otogizōshi jiten*, 270. *Saru Genji sōshi* should not be confused with *Saru no sōshi* 猿の草子 (Tale of the monkeys), a lavishly illustrated late medieval manuscript in the *Nara ehon* style, whose only extant copy is in the British Museum and whose protagonists are literally monkeys. A transcript and a facsimile of *Saru no sōshi* are in Ichiko, *Muromachi monogatarishū*, 433–67.

64 Following Ichiko, I am reading *aranu* as *aran/aramu*. A literal reading would render the last two lines as "because the god who ties the knot has not made such a vow," which would jar with the preceding passage.

65 *Saru Genji sōshi*, in Ichiko, *Otogizōshi*, Iwanami bunko, 1:177–78.

66 The Seiwa Genji descended from princes who were born to Emperor Seiwa 清和 (850–80, r. 858–76) and who received the nonaristocratic surname Minamoto 源.

67 *Saru Genji sōshi*, in Ichiko, *Otogizōshi*, Iwanami bunko, 1:179. わたくし不慮に戀といふ病にをかされてこそ候へ。(. . .) 鰯売の戀をしたりといふためしいまだ聞かず。かまへてがまえて風聞すべからず。

68 Ichiko Teiji suggests that some details of the anecdote are similar to those in a passage in *Uji shūi monogatari* 宇治拾遺物語 (A collection of tales from Uji, early 13th c.). See Ichiko, *Saru Genji sōshi*, in *Otogizōshi*, Nihon koten bungaku taikei 38, 168n2.

69 This is written in kana in the text, probably standing for 遊君 (*yūgun*, distinguished entertainer). Ichiko suggests that this is a mistake and that the proper orthography should be *yūkun*. Ichiko, *Saru Genji sōshi*, in *Otogizōshi*, Nihon koten bungaku taikei 38, 174n.10.

70 阿漕が浦の猿源氏が鰯かふゑい。

71 *Saru Genji sōshi*, in Ichiko, *Otogizōshi*, Iwanami bunko, 1:194.

72 This passage of *Saru Genji sōshi* was actually freely adapted from a passage in the mid-Heian poem-tale *Yamato monogatari*.

73 *Saru Genji sōshi*, in Ichiko, *Otogizōshi*, Iwanami bunko, 1:200.

74 For a discussion of medieval narratives about Izumi Shikibu, see Pandey, *Perfumed Sleeves*, 82–118.

75 Ichiko identifies the poem as coming from *Hachimangū dōkun* 八幡愚童訓 (The story of Hachiman Shrine explained to children, early 14th c.), in Hanawa and Kokusho, *Gunsho ruijū*, vol. 1, sec. 13 (Divine Matters), 386–436.

76 *Saru Genji sōshi*, in Ichiko, *Otogizōshi*, Iwanami bunko, 1:200. 螢火其時思ふやうまことの鰯賣ならばかやうにさまざまの歌の道をばよも知らじ.

77 *Saru Genji sōshi*, in Ichiko, *Otogizōshi*, Iwanami bunko, 1:201. See also Ichiko, *Otogizōshi*, Nihon koten bungaku taikei 38, 185. つねに歌の道に心がけし故當座の恥を隠すのみならず及ばぬ戀の本意を遂げし事.

78 *Saru Genji sōshi*, in Ichiko, *Otogizōshi*, Iwanami bunko, 1:201. または歌の道浅からざりし故なればかへすがへす人ごとに學び給ふべきは歌の道なるべし.

79 Marra, *Representations of Power*, 139.

80 Marra, *Representations of Power*, 154.

81 Pierre Bourdieu developed this theory in connection with his circular notion of *habitus*: "a principle of division into logical classes which organizes the perception of the social world is itself the product of internalization of the division into social spaces" (Bourdieu, *Distinction*, 170).

82 Robin Fox, "The Cultural Animal," 19.

83 *Saru Genji sōshi*, in Ichiko, *Otogizōshi*, Iwanami bunko, 1:188.

84 As Kubota Jun rightly points out, this passage connects to the narratives on the potencies of poems, yet he interprets this reference to medieval discourses as an afterthought, in Kubota Jun, "Otogizōshi no waka," 313.

85 Kate Fox, *Watching the English*, 134. Fox says this phenomenon explains the drastic emphasis in upper-middle-class circles on saying "Sorry?" instead of "Pardon?" in order avoid a dialectal marker identified with the middle-class people just below them, while they remain oblivious to the custom in both upper- and lower-class circles of instead simply saying "What?" (76).

86 The Japanese dictionary *Nihon kokugo daijiten* registers attestation of this use of the term as early as the transition from the late medieval period to the early modern. Unlike the *Oxford English Dictionary*, *Nihon kokugo daijiten* does not attempt to offer the earliest attestation, so the term may have circulated even earlier.

87 At one point, *Nakagoro no koto* circulated as an illustrated manuscript, but the images eventually were lost in the process of reproduction. Only the text of the work is extant.

88 The nickname emphasizes the governess's fierce countenance and terrifying behavior. The Dragon King of the Sea is a figure traditionally associated with the protection of the Buddha's teachings and, in medieval practice, connected with prayers for rain. In *Genji monogatari*, the Dragon King appears to the protagonist in a dream during a fearful storm; in her letter,

Abutsu mentions the Dragon King as the epitome of the man she would not want her daughter to marry. For a discussion of this passage in *Genji monogatari* and Abutsu's letter, see Laffin, *Rewriting Medieval Japanese Women*, 32–33.

89 The passage discussed here appears in translation and with a critical introduction in Abutsu-ni, "The Nursemaid's Letter." For a discussion of aristocratic female readers and authors in the late medieval period, see Rowley, "Tale of Genji." For the most recent discussion of the reception of this text, see Tabuchi et al., *Abutsu no fumi*, 238–44.

90 Abutsu-ni, *Menoto no fumi*, 120; Hanawa and Kokusho, *Gunsho ruijū*, vol. 4, sec. 27 (Miscellanea), entry 32.

91 Sakomura Tomoko has argued that the references to *Genji monogatari* in late medieval educational texts go beyond its role as a poetic text and position it as a sourcebook on human behavior. Sakomura, *Poetry as Image*, 193.

92 Princess Hōshi took the name Ankamon-in 安嘉門院. For this reason, Abutsu was known more generally as Ankamon-in no Shijō 安嘉門院四条 (Lady Fourth Avenue at the Court of Ankamon-in). Abutsu enjoyed an intimate knowledge of the upper echelons of the aristocracy, on a par with that of more famous authors of the Heian period, such as Murasaki Shikibu, Sei Shōnagon, Izumi Shikibu, and Akazome-emon. However, Abutsu was the only one who left behind a primer on aristocratic culture.

93 Abutsu and Tameie had two sons, one of whom was Tamesuke , the founder of the Reizei poetry household. The other, Tamemori 為守 (1265–1328), aka Gyōgetsubō 暁月坊, compiled *Kyōka sake hyakushū* 狂歌酒百首 (One hundred wild poems on drinking alcohol) and went on to be recognized as the father of *kyōka*. Ki no Naishi was Abutsu's daughter from a previous marriage. Tameie also had children from an earlier relationship. His father, Teika, had married him into a powerful warrior family: Tameie's first wife was the daughter of Utsu-no-miya Yoritsuna 宇都宮頼綱 (1172–1259), an influential warrior commander from the eastern provinces, and the granddaughter of the most powerful warrior of the period, Hōjō Tokimasa, who led the military government in Kamakura.

94 For a discussion of letter writing and pedagogic texts in the first decades of the early modern period, see Moretti, *Pleasure in Profit*, chap. 5.

95 Laffin, *Rewriting Medieval Japanese Women*, 57.

96 Laffin, *Rewriting Medieval Japanese Women*, 47.

97 Reider, "'Menoto no sōshi,'" 62–63.

98 Virginia Skord, "A Tale of Two Nursemaids: *Menoto no sōshi*," in Skord, *Tales of Tears and Laughter*, 169.

99 "*Menoto no sōshi*," in Ichiko, *Muromachi monogatarishū*, 346–47.

100 Or, instead of funny, perhaps it would be more accurate to say pleasurable. But not in the sense that Moretti gives to it in her book on seventeenth-century pedagogic narratives: "pleasure [that] resides within profit, in particular in the profit gained from acquiring knowledge" (*Pleasure in Profit*, 20). The pleasures afforded by *Nakagoro no koto* are, instead, the

more embodied, reflexive, and culturally specific experiences that we associate with comedy and laughter.

101 Emmerich, "*Tale of Genji.*"

102 Shōtetsu, *Shōtetsu monogatari*, 17. *Shōtetsu monogatari* 正徹物語 (Conversations with Shōtetsu, 1448–50) is a poetry treatise written in the form of a collection of brief narratives. Shōtetsu studied *waka* under two aristocratic poets connected to the Reizei household of Abutsu's descendants: Reizei Tametada 冷泉為尹 (Tamemasa, 1361–1417) and Imagawa Ryōshun 今川了俊 (1326–1420).

103 Santō and Utagawa, *Kyōkun menoto no sōshi.*

104 See "*Menoto no sōshi*," in Ichiko, *Mikan chūsei shōsetsu*, 1:10–11.

105 See "*Menoto no sōshi*," in Hanawa and Kokusho, *Gunsho ruijū*, vol. 4, sec. 27 (Miscellanea), no. 477, 229.

106 Johnson, "Saikaku and the Narrative Turnabout," 326; see also 324–25.

107 Gundry, *Parody, Irony and Ideology*, 70.

108 Eiko Ikegami, *Bonds of Civility*, 8.

109 "*Hachikazuki*," in Shibukawa, *Shūgen otogi bunko*, 65–66.

110 "*Hachikazuki*," in Shibukawa, *Shūgen otogi bunko*, 79.

111 Hutcheon, *Theory of Parody*, 6.

112 Hutcheon, *Theory of Parody*, 90.

113 Hutcheon, *Theory of Parody*, 11.

Notes to Epilogue

1 The works I refer to in the introduction are Mars and Kohlstedt, *The 99% Invisible City*; Jorge Luis Borges, "Los teólogos," in Borges, *El Aleph.*

2 On the Kokugaku 国学 (National Learning) movement, see Burns, *Before the Nation*; Flueckiger, *Imagining Harmony*; and Thomas, *Way of Shikishima.*

3 See the story "Los teólogos," in Borges, *El Aleph.* One of the main interests of National Learning scholars was in reformulating *waka*'s relationship to governance and social virtue. This can be seen in the essay "Kokka hachiron" 國歌八論 (Eight points of Japanese poetry, 1742) by Kada no Arimaro, and the reactions of Tayasu Munetake 田安宗武 (1715–71) and Kamo no Mabuchi, as well as writers of the following generation, led by Norinaga and Ban Kōkei 伴蒿蹊 (1733–1806). Arimaro had spurred debate by arguing that *waka* had no practical value for the business of governance; Munetake replied that it used to, especially during the period of the *Man'yōshū*; Mabuchi agreed and specified that this value stemmed from its ability to express emotions without recourse to superfluous intellectualization and with more allure than equivalent prosaic statements of fact. Norinaga inverted Mabuchi's logic, arguing that the study of the ancients was not a means to become a better poet, but a way to become

more like ancient persons in sensibility and expression. See Flueckiger, *Imagining Harmony*, 151–62, 190–94.

4 For a discussion of these two intellectual and social trends in the historical formation of modern Japanese literature, see Tomi Suzuki, *Narrating the Self*. The notion of a "national literature" appeared first in *Meiji bungakushi* 明治文学史 (A literary history for the Meiji period, 1894) by Ōwada Tateki 大和田建樹 (1857–1910).

5 Inoue Tetsujirō, preface to *Shintaishi-shō*, by Toyama, Yatabe, and Inoue, 60.

6 Yatabe Ryōkichi, preface to *Shintaishi-shō*, Toyama, Yatabe, and Inoue, 61.

7 Toyama Masakazu, preface to *Shintaishi-shō*, Toyama, Yatabe, and Inoue, 63–64.

8 Masaoka, "Dassai-sho'oku haiwa," 138–43.

9 Masaoka, "Dassai-sho'oku haiwa," 140–41.

10 This shift from the collective to the personal was pioneered by Matsuo Bashō. The leader of a network of loosely connected literary circles across a dozen provinces, Bashō traveled extensively to teach his disciples and associates. He did not regard his new focus on the brief *hokku* link as a way to reinforce the importance of the individual poet—quite the opposite. He saw it as a means to bring the practice of *haikai* closer to that of *waka*, particularly its cultural and poetic associations built around natural phenomena, prominent locales, and cultural artifacts connected with the past of the imperial court. As reflected in his travel diaries, such as *Oi no kobumi* 笈の小文 (Notes from my knapsack, after 1687) and *Oku no hosomichi* おくのほそ道 (The narrow roads to Oku, 1694), Bashō's own project to reform *haikai* involved recasting these elements of collective high-cultural memory (*ga*) by placing them against the new commoner culture (*zoku*) that came to the fore in the Genroku period.

11 Masaoka, "Haikai taiyō," 220.

12 This is a central argument in an article published in two installments. See Mark Morris, "Buson and Shiki: Part One" and "Buson and Shiki: Part Two."

13 Kubota Masafumi, "Masaoka Shiki."

14 Brower, "Masaoka Shiki and Tanka Reform," 388.

15 A discussion of Shiki's "Utayomi ni atauru sho" in light of discourses on national identity and gender can be found in Tuck, *Idly Scribbling Rhymers*, chap. 5.

16 Masaoka, "Utayomi ni atauru sho," 294.

17 A translation of book 16 of *Man'yōshū* can be found in Vovin, *Man'yōshū (Book 16)*.

18 *Dajare* 佗洒落 (today usually written 駄洒落) refers to dull jokes in general but is historically associated more specifically with strained plays on words. For a discussion of *dajare* in late Edo and Meiji works, see Levy, *Sirens of the Western Shore*, 45–48.

19 Masaoka, "*Man'yōshū* maki jūroku," 7:133.

20 Berry, *Culture of Civil War*, 261.

21 See "Heart's Mastery: Murata Jukō's Letter to Furuichi Harima," in Hirota, *Wind in the Pines*, 196.
22 Early modern treatises such *Nanpōroku* 南方録 (Records of Priest Nanpō, 1690), by Tachibana Jitsusan 橘実山 (1655–1708), recount how Takeno Jōō and Sen no Rikyū quoted *waka* by early medieval poets Fujiwara no Teika and Fujiwara no Ietaka to explain their understanding of the notion of *wabi*. See Kumakura, *Nanpōroku wo yomu*, 76.
23 Plutschow, *Rediscovering Rikyu*.
24 Corbett, "Crafting Identity."
25 Tsutsui, *Chasho no kenkyū* and *Chanoyu kotohajime*.
26 I am quoting from a contemporaneous manuscript, for lack of access to the movable-print 古活字本 edition: *Ocha monogatari*, Tokyo National University, 9. This and the following poems on *chanoyu* quoted in this section are mentioned (but not discussed in full) in Tsutsui, *Chasho no kenkyū*.
27 Takuan Sōhō served as abbot of Daitokuji Temple 大徳寺 in Kyōto and had ties to the third Tokugawa shōgun, Iemitsu 家光 (1604–51, r. 1623–51).
28 Takuan, *Chagu shiika*, 3:3.
29 *Usoshū hyakushu* is dated 1642, but it is preserved in only two much later anthologies of pedagogic texts about *chanoyu*: *Chanoyu hishō* 茶湯秘抄 (Secret notes on the way of tea, 1783) and *Usoshū yon-kan sho* 烏鼠集四巻書 (Collection of crows and mice, book 4, 1802).
30 *Chagu bitōshū* also is preserved in *Usoshū yon-kan sho*. Tsutsui, *Chasho no kenkyū*, 395.
31 Tsutsui, *Chanoyu kotohajime*, 54–59.
32 This suggests that copyists and editors borrowed from a widely circulating aggregate of poems and arbitrarily stamped on them attributions to established tea masters of the past. In modern tea circles, *Chanoyu hyakushu* is casually assumed to be the work of Sen no Rikyū. This is partly because a version of the poems was inscribed with his name on a set of paper partitions in the Konnichian compound in Kyoto by Gengensai 玄々斎 (1810–77), the eleventh head of the Urasenke household of *chanoyu* specialists. This work was known as *Hogo fusuma* 法護普須磨 (Dharma-protector paper screens), but *hogo* can be taken to mean instead "discarded paper" (反故). A manuscript of *Chanoyu hyakushu* similarly attributes the poems to Rikyū and retroactively offers the year 1598 for their composition. And a printed edition titled *Rikyū kōji sadō waka hyakushu* 利休居士茶道和歌百首 (Layman Rikyū's one hundred *waka* poems on the way of tea, 1748) confirms this attribution in a brief preface. However, three extant manuscripts in the Konnichian collection are titled *Enshū hyakushu* 遠州百首 (Kobori Enshū's one hundred *waka* poems), after the powerful tea master Kobori Enshū 小堀遠州 (1579–1647). Similar poems appear as well in *Jōō chanoyu hyakushu* 紹鴎茶湯百 (Takeno Jōō's one hundred *waka* poems on the way of tea), included in Hanawa and Kokusho, *Zoku gunsho ruijū*, 19:447–53. And they also appear in a manuscript titled *Nanpō nihyakushu* 南方二百首 (Two hundred poems by

Nanpō), after Nanpō Sōkei 南坊宗啓, the Sakai merchant to whom the influential *chanoyu* treatise *Nanpōroku* 南方録 (Nanpō's record, late seventeenth century) was retroactively attributed.

33 "Hogo fusuma" [transcription of the text on the *Hogo fusuma* screens], in Sen, "Chadō kyōyu hyakushu ei," 10:133.

34 Fujiwara no Teika, *Eiga no taigai*, 475. 和哥無師匠。只以旧歌為師。

35 *Kyōkunka* is known alternatively as *dōka* 道歌 and *shodō kyōkunka* 諸道教訓歌. The expressions *kyōkunka* and *kyōkun no uta* are attested as early as the Kamakura period; *dōka* was coined in the late Muromachi period in connection with moral teachings. See Inoue, *Chūsei kadan to kajinden no kenkyū*, 369.

36 Minamoto no Mitsuyuki, *Mōgyu waka*. Relatedly, Fujiwara no Shunzei, Mitsuyuki's teacher, gave *shakkyōka* a more prominent place in the seventh imperial poetry collection, *Senzai wakashū* (Collection of a thousand years).

37 These works are discussed in Inoue, "Chūsei kyōkunka ryaku kaidai."

38 Fujiwara no Yoshitsune was also a student of Shunzei. The Asukai household of *waka* and *kemari* specialists is discussed in detail in Ratcliff, "Cultural Arts in Service."

39 Corbett, *Cultivating Femininity*, 15.

40 Corbett, "Learning to Be Graceful," 86.

41 Etsuko Kato, *Tea Ceremony and Women's Empowerment*, 67; Surak, *Making Tea, Making Japan*, 77.

42 Okakura, *Book of Tea*, 3. For a discussion of *The Book of Tea*, see Surak, *Making Tea, Making Japan*, 83.

43 Yanagi, *Unknown Craftsmen*, 183.

44 Hisamatsu, "Chadō bunka no seikaku," 58.

45 From the website Chado-Kentei.com; see www.chado-kentei.com/aboutus, retrieved January 2017; archival version at https://web.archive.org/web/20170309001346/http://www.chado-kentei.com/aboutus/. This website promoted an examination run by the Urasenke school that led to a formal certificate in *chanoyu* 茶道は、深い精神と独自の哲学のもと、長い年月をかけて受け継がれてきた日本を代表する伝統文化です。また、美術工芸、建築、庭園など様々な分野からなる総合文化でもあります。

46 Claims of the universality of *chanoyu* made by postwar writers extended beyond the high culture of the Japanese elites. Yanagi, for example, understood the ceramics from the Song dynasty (960–1279) that were venerated in Japanese *chanoyu* circles in these terms: "Sung craftsmen were not self-conscious artists, they were not learned men, they were mere craftsmen making articles for daily use; most of them were extremely poor and had to work hard from morning till night, most also were probably badly educated and uninformed" in Yanagi, *Unknown Craftsman*, 132). In line with this interest in the material production of a romanticized commoner class, the collection of East Asian craftworks that Yanagi amassed at his Mingei-kan (Japan Folk Crafts Museum) in Tokyo includes

many pieces that until then had been considered lowly and inartistic, such as the ceramics produced by anonymous Korean potters for the everyday use of subjects of the Joseon state ruled by the Yi dynasty (1392–1897), as well as the textiles and architectural styles of the commoner craftspeople of the Ryūkyū archipelago. Similarly, Okakura's claim in *The Book of Tea* that *chanoyu* embodies modern democratic values—in which the romanticized notion of a class-independent citizenry with equal rights and responsibilities is central—emphasizes its ability to embrace practitioners from all social spaces.

Bibliography

Abutsu-ni 阿仏尼. *Menoto no fumi* 乳母の文. In *Kōchū Abutsu-ni zenshū* 校註阿佛尼全集, edited by Yanase Kazuo 簗瀬一雄, 109–38. Tokyo: Kazama Shobō, 1958.

———. "The Nursemaid's Letter." Translated by Christina Laffin. In *Reading the Tale of Genji: Sources from the First Millennium*, edited by Thomas Harper and Haruo Shirane, 140–44. New York: Columbia University Press, 2015.

Adolphson, Mikael. *The Gates of Power: Monks, Courtiers, and Warriors in Premodern Japan*. Honolulu: University of Hawai'i Press, 2000.

Adolphson, Mikael, Edward Kamens, and Stacie Matsumoto, eds. *Heian Japan: Centers and Peripheries*. Honolulu: University of Hawai'i Press, 2007.

Angles, Jeffrey. "Watching Commoners, Performing Class: Images of the Common People in *The Pillow Book of Sei Shōnagon*." *Japan Review*, no. 13 (2001): 33–65.

Arnesen, Peter Judd. *The Medieval Japanese Daimyo: The Ōuchi Family's Rule of Suō and Nagato*. New Haven, CT: Yale University Press, 1979.

Asami Kazuhiko 浅見和彦, ed. *Jikkinshō* 十訓抄. Shinpen Nihon koten bungaku zenshū 51. Tokyo: Shōgakkan, 1997.

Atherton, David. *Writing Violence: The Politics of Form in Early Modern Japanese Literature*. New York: Columbia University Press, 2023.

Atkins, Paul S. "Nijō v. Reizei: Land Rights, Litigation, and Literary Authority in Medieval Japan." *Harvard Journal of Asiatic Studies* 66, no. 2 (2006): 495–529.

———. *Teika: The Life and Works of a Medieval Japanese Poet*. Honolulu: University of Hawai'i Press, 2017.

Austin, J. L. *How to Do Things with Words*. Cambridge, MA: Harvard University Press, 1975.

Bakhtin, Mikhail. *The Dialogic Imagination: Four Essays*. Edited by Michael Holquist. Translated by Caryl Emerson and Michael Holquist. Austin: University of Texas Press, 1981.

Bender, Ross, and Zhao Lu. "Research Note: A Japanese Curriculum of 757." *PMJS Papers*, 2010. https://www.pmjs.org/pmjs-papers/papers-index/bender-zhao-j-curriculum.

Bentley, Jerry H. "Cross-Cultural Interaction and Periodization in World History." *American Historical Review* 101, no. 3 (1996): 749–70.

Berry, Mary Elizabeth. *The Culture of Civil War in Kyoto*. Berkeley: University of California Press, 1994.

Bloom, Irene, trans. *Mencius*. Edited by Philip J. Ivanhoe. New York: Columbia University Press, 2009.

Boot, Willem Jan. "*Kotodama* and the Ways of Reading the *Man'yōshū*." In *Florilegium Japonicum: Studies Presented to Olof G. Lidin on the Occasion of His 70th Birthday*, edited by Bjarke Frellesvig, Christian Morimoto Hermansen, and Olof G. Lidin, 41–52. Copenhagen: Akademisk Forlag, 1996.

Borges, Jorge Luis. *El Aleph*. Buenos Aires: Emecé, 1957.

Bourdieu, Pierre. *Distinction: A Social Critique of the Judgement of Taste*. Translated by Richard Nice. Cambridge, MA: Harvard University Press, 1984.

Bowring, Richard. "The *Ise monogatari*: A Short Cultural History." *Harvard Journal of Asiatic Studies* 52, no. 2 (1992): 401–80.

Brightwell, Erin. *Reflecting the Past: Place, Language, and Principle in Japan's Medieval Mirror Genre*. Cambridge, MA: Harvard University Asia Center, 2020.

Brower, Robert H., trans. *Conversations with Shōtetsu (Shōtetsu Monogatari)*. Introduction and notes by Steven D. Carter. Ann Arbor: Center for Japanese Studies, University of Michigan, 1992.

———. "The Foremost Style of Poetic Composition: Fujiwara Tameie's *Eiga no Ittei*." *Monumenta Nipponica* 42, no. 4 (1987): 391–429.

———. "Fujiwara Teika's *Maigetsushō*." *Monumenta Nipponica* 40, no. 4 (1985): 399–425.

———. "Masaoka Shiki and Tanka Reform." In *Tradition and Modernization in Japanese Culture*, edited by Donald H. Shively, 379–418. Princeton, NJ: Princeton University Press, 1971.

Brower, Robert H., and Earl Roy Miner. *Japanese Court Poetry*. Stanford, CA: Stanford University Press, 1961.

Brownlee, John, trans. "*Jikkinshō*: A Miscellany of Ten Maxims." *Monumenta Nipponica* 29, no. 2 (1974): 121–61.

Bundy, Roselee. "Gendering the Court Woman Poet: Pedigree and Portrayal in 'Fukuro zōshi.'" *Monumenta Nipponica* 67, no. 2 (2012): 201–38.

———. "Poetic Apprenticeship: Fujiwara Teika's *Shogaku Hyakushu*." *Monumenta Nipponica* 45, no. 2 (1990): 157–88.

Burns, Susan. *Before the Nation: Kokugaku and the Imagining of Community in Early Modern Japan*. Durham, NC: Duke University Press, 2003.

Bushelle, Ethan. "The Joy of the Dharma: Esoteric Buddhism and the Early Medieval Transformation of Japanese Literature." PhD diss., Harvard University, 2015.

Carter, Steven D. *Householders: The Reizei Family in Japanese History.* Cambridge, MA: Harvard University Asia Center, 2007.

———, ed. *Literary Patronage in Late Medieval Japan.* Ann Arbor: Center for Japanese Studies, University of Michigan, 1993.

———. *Regent Redux: A Life of the Statesman-Scholar Ichijō Kaneyoshi.* Ann Arbor: Center for Japanese Studies, University of Michigan, 1996.

Citko, Malgorzata Karolina. "How to Establish a Poetic School in Early Medieval Japan: Fujiwara no Shunzei's *Man'yōshū Jidaikō.*" *Monumenta Nipponica* 74, no. 2 (2019): 173–209.

Commons, Anne. *Hitomaro: Poet as God.* Leiden: Brill, 2009.

———. "Japanese Poetic Thought, from Earliest Times to the Thirteenth Century." In *The Cambridge History of Japanese Literature*, edited by Haruo Shirane, Tomi Suzuki, and David Lurie, 218–29. Cambridge: Cambridge University Press, 2016.

Conlan, Thomas D. *Kings in All but Name: The Lost History of Ouchi Rule in Japan, 1350–1569.* Oxford: Oxford University Press, 2024.

Corbett, Rebecca. "Crafting Identity as a Tea Practitioner in Early Modern Japan: Ōtagaki Rengetsu and Tagami Kikusha." *U.S.-Japan Women's Journal* 47 (2015): 3–27.

———. *Cultivating Femininity: Women and Tea Culture in Edo and Meiji Japan.* Honolulu: University of Hawai'i Press, 2018.

———. "Learning to Be Graceful: Tea in Early Modern Guides for Women's Edification." *Japanese Studies* 29, no. 1 (2009): 81–94.

Cranston, Edwin. "'Mystery and Depth' in Japanese Court Poetry (Fifty-Eight *Yūgen* Style Poems Translated from *Teika jittei*)." In *The Distant Isle: Studies and Translations of Japanese Literature in Honor of Robert H. Brower*, edited by Thomas Hare, Robert Borgen, and Sharalyn Orbaugh, 65–104. Ann Arbor: Center for Japanese Studies, University of Michigan, 1996.

———, trans. and ed. *A Waka Anthology*, vol. 1, *The Gem-Glistening Cup.* Stanford, CA: Stanford University Press, 1998.

Curtis, Paula R. "An Entrepreneurial Aristocrat: Matsugi Hisanao and the Forging of Imperial Service in Late Medieval Japan." *Monumenta Nipponica* 75, no. 2 (2020): 241–79.

Damian, Michelle. "As Estates Faded: Late Medieval Maritime Shipping in the Seto Inland Sea." In *Land, Power, and the Sacred: The Estate System in Medieval Japan*, edited by Janet R. Goodwin and Joan R. Piggott, 351–74. Honolulu: University of Hawai'i Press, 2018.

Duthie, Torquil. "*Man'yō daishōki* no bunkengaku no rekishiteki igi omegutte" 「万葉代匠記」の文献学の歴史的意義をめぐって. *Anahorisshu kokubungaku*, no. 1 (2013): 108–14.

———. *"Man'yōshū" and the Imperial Imagination in Early Japan*. Leiden: Brill, 2014.

Dykstra, Yoshiko K. "Notable Tales Old and New: Tachibana Narisue's *Kokon Chomonjū*." *Monumenta Nipponica* 47, no. 4 (1992): 469–93.

Emmerich, Michael. *"The Tale of Genji": Translation, Canonization, and World Literature*. New York: Columbia University Press, 2013.

Eubanks, Charlotte. *Miracles of Book and Body: Buddhist Textual Culture and Medieval Japan*. Berkeley: University of California Press, 2011.

Farris, William Wayne. *Japan's Medieval Population: Famine, Fertility, and Warfare in a Transformative Age*. Honolulu: University of Hawai'i Press, 2006.

Flueckiger, Peter. *Imagining Harmony: Poetry, Empathy, and Community in Mid-Tokugawa Confucianism and Nativism*. Stanford, CA: Stanford University Press, 2011.

Forrest, Stephen Michael. *The Model Life of an Eccentric Poet: Nōin Hōshi and Nōin Shū*. Cambridge, MA: Harvard University Press, 2005.

Fox, Kate. *Watching the English: The Hidden Rules of English Behaviour*. London: Hodder & Stoughton, 2004.

Fox, Robin. "The Cultural Animal." In *Issues in Cultural Anthropology: Selected Readings*, edited by David W. McCurdy and James P. Spradley, 15–18. Boston: Little, Brown, 1979.

Freud, Sigmund. *Group Psychology and the Analysis of the Ego*. Translated by James Strachey. London: Hogarth Press and the Institute of Psycho-Analysis, 1966.

Freud, Sigmund, and James Strachey. *Civilization and Its Discontents* [1st American ed.]. New York: W. W. Norton, 1962.

Friday, Karl F. *Hired Swords: The Rise of Private Warrior Power in Early Japan*. Stanford, CA: Stanford University Press, 1996.

———, ed. *Japan Emerging: Premodern History to 1850*. New York: Routledge, 2018.

———. *Samurai, Warfare and the State in Early Medieval Japan*. New York: Routledge, 2004.

Fujihira Haruo 藤平春男. *Karon no kenkyū* 歌論の研究. Tokyo: Perikansha, 1989.

Fujiwara no Kiyosuke 藤原清輔. *Fukurozōshi* 袋草子. Edited by Fujioka Tadaharu 藤岡忠美. Shin Nihon koten bungaku taikei 29. Tokyo: Iwanami Shoten, 1995.

———. *Ōgishō* 奥義抄. Edited by Sasaki Nobutsuna 佐佐木信綱, Kyūsojin Hitaku 久曾神昇, and Higuchi Yoshimaro 樋口芳麻呂. Nihon Kagaku taikei 1. Tokyo: Mazama Shobō, 1964.

Fujiwara no Shunzei 藤原俊成. *Korai fūteishō* 古来風躰抄. In Hashimoto, Ariyoshi, and Fujihira, *Karonshū*, 247–446.

———. "Poetic Styles from the Past (*Korai fūteishō*, 1197)." In *Traditional Japanese Literature: An Anthology, Beginnings to 1600,* edited by Haruo Shirane, 587–91. New York: Columbia University Press, 2007.

Fujiwara no Teika 藤原定家. *Eiga no taigai* 詠歌大概. In Hashimoto, Ariyoshi, and Fujihira, *Karonshū*, 473–90.

———. *Essentials of Poetic Composition* (*Eiga no taigai*). Translated by Lewis Cook. In *Traditional Japanese Literature: An Anthology, Beginnings to 1600*, edited by Haruo Shirane, 605–7 New York: Columbia University Press, 2008.

———. *Fujiwara Teika's "Superior Poems of Our Time": A Thirteenth-Century Poetic Treatise and Sequence.* Translated by Robert H. Brower and Earl Miner. Stanford, CA: Stanford University Press, 1967.

———. *Maigetsushō* 毎月抄. In Hashimoto, Ariyoshi, and Fujihira, *Karonshū*, 491–510.

———. *An Outline for Composing Tanka* (*Eiga no taigai*). Translated by Hiroaki Satō. In *From the Country of Eight Islands: An Anthology of Japanese Poetry*, edited by Hiroaki Satō and Burton Watson, 202–4. Seattle: University of Washington Press, 1981.

Gay, Suzanne. *The Moneylenders of Late Medieval Kyoto.* Honolulu: University of Hawai'i Press, 2001.

Geddes, Ward. "The Buddhist Monk in the *Jikkinshō*." *Japanese Journal of Religious Studies* 9, nos. 2–3 (1982): 199–212.

———. "The Courtly Model: Chōmei and Kiyomori in *Jikkinshō*." *Monumenta Nipponica* 42, no. 2 (1987): 157–66.

———. "A Partial Translation and Study of the *Jikkinshō*." PhD diss., Washington University, 1976.

Genette, Gérard. *Paratexts: Thresholds of Interpretation.* Translated by Jane E. Lewin. Cambridge: Cambridge University Press, 1997.

Gibson, James J. *The Ecological Approach to Visual Perception.* Boston: Houghton Mifflin, 1979.

———. *The Senses Considered as Perceptual Systems.* Boston: Houghton Mifflin, 1966.

Glomb, Vladimir, Martin Gehlmann, and Eun-Jeung Lee, eds. *Confucian Academies in East Asia*. Leiden: Brill, 2020.

Goble, Andrew Edmund. "Defining 'Medieval.'" In Friday, *Japan Emerging*, 32–41.

———. *Kenmu: Go-Daigo's Revolution*. Cambridge, MA: Council on East Asian Studies, Harvard University, 1996.

Gomi Fumihiko 五味文彦. *Heike monogatari, shi to setsuwa* 平家物語、史と説話. Tokyo: Heibonsha, 2011.

———. "Setsuwa to ie: *Jikkinshō* kara *Kokonchomonjū* he" 説話と家「十訓抄」から「古今著聞集」へ. In *Shomotsu no Chūseishi* 書物の中世史, 384–99. Tokyo: Misuzu Shobō, 2003.

Goshobon Jikkinshō: Kunaichō Shoryōbu Zō 御所本十訓抄：宮内庁書陵部蔵. Edited by Izumi Motohiro 者泉基博. 3 vols. Tokyo: Kasama Shoin, 1983.

Guest, Jennifer Lindsay. "Primers, Commentaries, and Kanbun Literacy in Japanese Literary Culture, 950–1250 CE." PhD diss., Columbia University, 2013.

Gundry, David J. *Parody, Irony and Ideology in the Fiction of Ihara Saikaku*. Leiden: Brill, 2017.

Habein, Yaeko Sato. *The History of the Japanese Written Language*. Tokyo: University of Tokyo Press, 1984.

Hall, John W. "The Muromachi *Bakufu*." In *The Cambridge History of Japan*, vol. 3, *Medieval Japan*, edited by Yamamura Kōzō, 175–230. Cambridge: Cambridge University Press, 1990.

Hall, John W., and Jeffrey P. Mass. *Medieval Japan: Essays in Institutional History*. Stanford, CA: Stanford University Press, 1974.

Hanawa Hokinoichi 塙保己一 and Kokusho Kankōkai 国書刊行会 , eds. *Gunsho ruijū* 群書類從. 30 vols. Tokyo: NetAdvance, 2014.

———. *Zoku gunsho ruijū* 続群書類従. 37 vols. Tokyo: NetAdvance, 2014.

———. *Zoku zoku gunsho ruijū* 続々群書類従. 17 vols. Tokyo: NetAdvance, 2014.

Hardacre, Helen. "The Esotericization of Medieval Shinto." In *Shinto: A History*, 147–76. New York: Oxford University Press, 2017.

Hare, Thomas Blenman. "Reading Kamo no Chōmei." *Harvard Journal of Asiatic Studies* 49, no. 1 (1989): 173–228.

Hashimoto Fumio 橋本不美男. *Inseiki no kadanshi: Horikawa–in kadan wo keisei shita hitobito* 院政期の歌壇史研究：堀河院歌壇を形成した人々. Tokyo: Musashino Shoin, 1966.

———. "Kaidai." In Hashimoto, Ariyoshi, and Fujihira, *Karonshū*, 14.

———. *Ōchō wakashi no kenkyū* 王朝和歌史の研究. Tokyo: Kasama shoin, 1972.

Hashimoto Fumio 橋本不美男, Ariyoshi Tamotsu 有吉保, and Fujihira Haruo 藤平春男, eds. *Karonshū*. Shinpen Nihon koten bungaku zenshū 87. Tokyo: Shōgakkan, 2002.

Hayashiya Tatsusaburō 林屋辰三郎. *Chūsei bunka no kichō* 中世文化の基調. Tokyo: Tōkyō Daigaku Shuppankai, 1963.

———. "Hon'ami ke" 本阿弥家. In *Kokushi Daijiten* 國史大辭典. Tokyo: Yoshikawa Kōbunkan, 1997.

———. *Machishū: Kyōto ni okeru "shimin" keiseishi* 町衆：京都における「市民」形成史. Chūkō shinsho 59. Tokyo: Chūō Kōronsha, 1964.

Hayashiya Tatsusaburō, with George Elison. "Kyoto in the Muromachi Age." In *Japan in the Muromachi Age*, edited by John Whitney Hall and Toyoda Takeshi. Berkeley: University of California Press, 1977.

Heldt, Gustav. *The Pursuit of Harmony: Poetry and Power in Early Heian Japan*. Ithaca, NY: Cornell University Press, 2008.

Hérail, Francine. *Emperor and Aristocracy in Heian Japan: 10th and 11th Centuries*. Translated by Wendy Cobcroft. Self-published, CreateSpace, 2013.

Higuchi Yoshimaro 樋口芳麻呂. "Fukurozōshi Mumyōzōshi no seiritsu jiki ni tuite" 袋草子・無名草子の成立時期について. *Kokugo to kokubungaku* 47, no. 4 (1970): 81–96.

Hirano, Tae. "*Shakkyōka* of the Late Medieval Imperial *Waka* Anthologies" 中世後期の勅撰和歌集における釈教歌. In *Waka Workshop: Shakkyōka*, edited by Edward Kamens. Materials from *Waka* Workshop 2013, Yale University, https://elischolar.library.yale.edu/waka2013.

Hirao Yūko 平尾裕子. "Katoku setsuwa no kenkyū: So no teigi wo megutte" 歌徳説話の研究—その定義をめぐって. *Kokugo kokubungaku kenkyū* 40 (2005): 31–48.

Hirota, Dennis. *Wind in the Pines: Classic Writings of the Way of Tea as a Buddhist Path*. Fremont, CA: Asian Humanities Press, 1995.

Hisaki Yukio 久木幸男. *Nihon kodai gakkō no kenkyū* 日本古代学校の研究. Tokyo: Tamagawa Daigaku Shuppanbu, 1990.

Hisamatsu Shin'ichi 久松真一. "Chadō bunka no seikaku" 茶道文化の性格. In *Wabi no chadō* わびの茶道, 57–69. Tōei sensho 10. Kyoto: Ittōen Tōeisha, 1987.

Hongō Keiko 本郷恵子. *Chūseijin no keizai kankaku* 中世人の経済感覚. Tokyo: Nihon Hōsō Shuppan Kyōkai, 2004.

Hori Ichirō 堀一郎. "Shakkyōka seiritsu no katei ni tsuite" 釈教歌成立の過程について. *Indogaku bukkyogaku kenkyu* 3, no. 2 (1955): 393–97.

Horton, H. Mack. "Portrait of a Medieval Japanese Marriage: The Domestic Life of Sanjōnishi Sanetaka and His Wife." *Japanese Language and Literature* 37, no. 2 (2003): 130–54.

Hosaka Satoru 保坂智. *Hyakushō ikki to sono sahō* 百姓一揆とその作法. Rekishi bunka raiburarī 137. Tokyo: Yoshikawa Kōbunkan, 2002.

Huey, Robert N. *Kyōgoku Tamekane: Poetry and Politics in Late Kamakura Japan.* Stanford, CA: Stanford University Press, 1989.

———. *The Making of Shinkokinshū.* Cambridge, MA: Harvard University Asia Center, 2002.

———. "The Medievalization of Poetic Practice." *Harvard Journal of Asiatic Studies* 50, no. 2 (1990): 651–68.

Huey, Robert N., and Susan Matisoff, trans. "Lord Tamekane's Notes on Poetry: *Tamekanekyō Wakashō.*" *Monumenta Nipponica* 40, no. 2 (1985): 127–46.

Hurst, G. Cameron III. "*Kugyō* and *Zuryō*: Center and Periphery in the Era of Fujiwara no Michinaga," in Adolphson, Kamens, and Matsumoto, *Heian Japan*, 66–102.

Hutcheon, Linda. *A Theory of Parody: The Teachings of Twentieth-Century Art Forms.* New York: Methuen, 1985.

Ichiko Teiji 市古貞次. *Chūsei shōsetsu no kenkyu* 中世小説の研究. Tokyo: Tokyo Daigaku Shuppankai, 1955.

———, ed. *Mikan chūsei shōsetsu* 未刊中世小説. Koten bunko 18. Tokyo: Koten Bunko, 1942.

———, ed. *Muromachi monogatarishū* 室町物語集. Shin Nihon koten bungaku taikei 54. Tokyo: Iwanami Shoten, 1989.

———, ed. *Otogizōshi* 御伽草子. 2 vols. Iwanami bunko. Tokyo: Iwanami Shoten, 1985.

———, ed. *Otogizōshi.* Nihon koten bungaku taikei 38. Tokyo: Iwanami Shoten, 1958.

Iikura Harutake 飯倉晴武. *Nihon chūsei no seiji to shiryō* 日本中世の政治と史料. Tokyo: Yoshikawa Kōbunkan, 2003.

Ikeda Masahiro 池田昌広. "Shūchūsho to ruisho (*leishu*)" 『袖中抄』と類書. *Kyōto Sangyō Daigaku Nihon Bunka Kenkyūsho kiyō* 27 (2022): 1–19.

———. "Shūchūshō to taikan honzō" 袖中抄と大観本草. *Wakan hikaku bungaku* 68 (2022): 58–72.

Ikegami, Eiko. *Bonds of Civility: Aesthetic Networks and the Political Origins of Japanese Culture.* Cambridge: Cambridge University Press, 2005.

Ikegami Jun'ichi 池上洵一. *Konjaku monogatari shū* 今昔物語集, vol 10. Shin nihon koten bungaku taikei 34. Tokyo: Iwanami Shoten, 1999.

Inoue Muneo 井上宗雄. *Chūsei kadanshi no kenkyū* 中世歌壇史の研究. Tokyo: Meiji shoin, 1987.

———. *Chūsei kadan to kajinden no kenkyū* 中世歌壇と歌人伝の研究. Tokyo: Kasama Shoin, 2007.

———. "Chūsei kyōkunka ryaku kaidai" 中世教訓歌略解題. *Rikkyō daigaku Nihon bungaku* 24 (1970): 100–119.

Inseiki Bunka Kenkyūkai 院政期文化研究会編, ed. *Kenryoku to bunka* 権力と文化. Tokyo: Shinwasha, 2001.

Inui Katsumi 乾克己. "Jikkinshō no sakusha wa Sugawara no Tamenaga ka" 十訓抄の作者は菅原為長か. *Kokugakuin zasshi* 68, no. 5 (1967): 20–33.

Ishibashi Shōhō 石橋尚宝, ed. *Jikkinshō shōkai* 十訓抄詳解. 3 vols. Tokyo: Meiji shoin, 1901.

Ishihara Kiyoshi 石原清志. *Shakkyōka no kenkyū* 釈教歌の研究. Kyoto: Dōhōsha, 1980.

Ishii Susumu 石井進. *Miyako to hina no chūseishi* 都と鄙の中世史. Tokyo: Yoshikawa Kōbunkan, 1992.

Ishikawa Matsutarō 石川松太郎. *Nihon kyōikushi* 日本教育史. Tokyo: Tamagawa Daigaku Shuppanbu, 1987.

Itō Satoshi 伊藤聡. "Bon-kan-wago dōitsu kan no seiritsu kiso" 梵・漢・和語同一観の成立基礎. In Inseiki Bunka Kenkyūkai, *Kenryoku to bunka*, 203–28.

Jikkinshō 十訓抄. 2 vols. Koten shiryō 10–11. Tokyo : Sumiya Shobō, 1970.

Johnson, Jeffrey. "Saikaku and the Narrative Turnabout." *Journal of Japanese Studies* 27, no. 2 (2001): 323–45.

Joko, Iori. "Reassessing *Kotodama* Usages and Interpretations." Master's thesis, Columbia University, 1993.

Kamens, Edward. Review of *Writing and Renunciation in Medieval Japan: The Works of the Poet-Priest Kamo no Chōmei*, by Rajyashree Pandey. *Harvard Journal of Asiatic Studies* 60, no. 1 (2000): 318–23.

———. Utamakura, *Allusion, and Intertextuality in Traditional Japanese Poetry*. New Haven, CT: Yale University Press, 1997.

———. *Waka and Things, Waka as Things*. New Haven, CT: Yale University Press, 2017.

———. "Waking the Dead: Fujiwara no Teika's *Sotoba kuyō* Poems." *Journal of Japanese Studies* 28, no. 2 (2002): 379–406.

Kami Hiroyuki 紙宏行. "Shunzei kokinmondō kō" 俊成『古今問答』考. *Waka bungaku no kenkyū*, no. 93 (2006): 1–11.

Kamioka Yūji 上岡勇司. *Wakasetsuwa no kenkyū* 和歌説話の研究. Tokyo: Kasama shoin, 1986.

Kamo no Chōmei 鴨長明. *Mumyōshō* 無名抄. Edited by Kubota Jun 久保田淳. Tokyo: Kadokawa Bunko, 2013.

Kaneko Hiraku 金子拓. *Chūsei buke seiken to seiji chitsujo* 中世武家政権と政治秩序. Tokyo: Yoshikawa Kōbunkan, 1998.

Kariya Ekisai 狩谷棭齋. *Senchū wamyō ruiju shō* 箋注倭名類聚抄. Osaka: Zenkoku Shobō, 1943.

Katagiri Yōichi 片桐洋一, ed. *Gosen wakashū* 後撰和歌集. Tokyo: Iwanami Shoten, 1990.

———, ed. *Kokin wakashū* 古今和歌集. Zen taiyaku Nihon koten shinsho. Tokyo: Kasama Shoin, 2005.

Katō, Etsuko. *Tea Ceremony and Women's Empowerment in Modern Japan: Bodies Re-Presenting the Past*. New York: Routledge, 2004.

Katō, Hilda. "The *Mumyōshō* of Kamo no Chōmei and Its Significance in Japanese Literature." *Monumenta Nipponica* 23, nos. 3–4 (1968): 321–49.

Kawakami Shin'ichirō 川上新一郎. *Rokujō Tōke kagaku no kenkyū* 六条藤家歌学の研究. Tokyo: Kyūkoshoin, 1999.

———. "Yōmei bunko Kiyosuke Fukurozōshi shinshutsu kanmatsu bubun honkoku" 陽明文庫蔵「清輔袋双紙」—新出巻末部分翻刻. *Waka bungaku kenkyū* 和歌文学研究, no. 54, (April 1987): 45–60.

———. "Yōmei bunko zō Kiyosuke Fukurozōshi kō" 陽明文庫蔵「清輔袋双紙」考. *Waka bungaku kenkyū*, no. 50 (1985): 36–45.

Kawakami Shin'ichirō and Kanechiku Nobuyuki 兼築信行. "Yōmei bunko Kiyosuke Fukurozōshi shinshutsu kanmatsu bubun honkoku" 陽明文庫「清輔袋双紙」—新出巻末部分翻刻. *Waka bungaku kenkyū*, no. 54 (1987): 45–60.

Kawakita Noboru 河北騰. *Imakagami zenchūshaku* 今鏡全注釈. Tokyo: Kasama Shoin, 2013.

Kikuchi Hitoshi 菊地仁. *Shokunō to shite no waka* 職能としての和歌. Tokyo: Wakakusa Shobō, 2005.

Kim, Yung-Hee. "The Emperor's Songs: Go-Shirakawa and *Ryōjin Hishō Kudenshū*." *Monumenta Nipponica* 41, no. 3 (1986): 261–98.

———. *Songs to Make the Dust Dance: The "Ryojin hisho" of Twelfth-Century Japan*. Berkeley: University of California Press, 1994.

Kimbrough, R. Keller. "Illustrating the Classics: The *Otogizōshi Lazy Tarō* in Edo Pictorial Fiction." *Japanese Language and Literature* 42, no. 1 (2008): 257–304.

———. *Preachers, Poets, Women, and the Way: Izumi Shikibu and the Buddhist Literature of Medieval Japan*. Ann Arbor: Center for Japanese Studies, University of Michigan, 2008.

———. "Reading the Miraculous Powers of Japanese Poetry: Spells, Truth Acts, and a Medieval Buddhist Poetics of the Supernatural." *Japanese Journal of Religious Studies* 32, no. 1 (2005): 1–33.

Kimura, Saeko. "Regenerating Narratives: The Confessions of Lady Nijō as a Story for Women's Salvation." *Review of Japanese Culture and Society* 19 (2007): 87–102.

Ki no Tsurayuki 紀貫之 et al., comp. *Kokin wakashū* 古今和歌集, edited by Kojima Noriyuki 小島憲行 and Arai Eizō 新井栄蔵. Shin Nihon koten bungaku taikei 5. Tokyo: Iwanami Shoten, 1989.

Klein, Susan Blakeley. *Allegories of Desire: Esoteric Literary Commentaries of Medieval Japan*. Cambridge, MA: Harvard University Press, 2003.

Kojima Noriyuki 小島憲之, Kinoshita Masatoshi 木下正俊, and Tōno Haruyuki 東野治之, eds. *Man'yōshū* 萬葉集. Shinpen Nihon koten bungaku zenshū 6. Tokyo: Shōgakkan, 1994.

Kojima Noriyuki, Naoki Kōjirō 直木孝次郎, Nishimiya Kazutami 西宮一民, Kuranaka Susumu 蔵中進, and Mōri Masamori 毛利正守, eds. *Nihon shoki* 日本書紀. Shinpen Nihon koten bungaku zenshū 4. Tokyo: Shōgakkan, 1994.

Komachiya Teruhiko 小町谷照彦, ed. *Shūi wakashū* 拾遺和歌集. Shin Nihon koten bungaku taikei 7. Tokyo: Iwanami Shoten, 1990.

Komine Kazuaki 小峯和明. *Insei-ki bungakuron* 院政期文学論. Tokyo: Kasama shoin, 2006.

———. "Setsuwa no ba to katari" 説話の場と語り. In *Setsuwa to wa nani ka* 説話とは何か, edited by Honda Giken 本田義憲, 101–21. Tokyo: Benseisha, 1991.

Kuboki Tetsuo 久保木哲夫. *Ori no bungaku: Heian waka bungakuron* 折の文学 平安和歌文学論. Tokyo: Kasama shoin, 2007.

Kubota Jun 久保田淳. "Otogizōshi no waka" 御伽草子の和歌. In *Otogi-zōshi, kana-zōshi* 御伽草子 仮名草子, edited by Ichiko Teiji 市古貞次 and Noma Kōshin 野間光辰. Kanshō Nihon koten bungaku, *dai 26-kan*. Tokyo: Kadokawa Shoten, 1976.

Kubota Masafumi 久保田正文. "Masaoka Shiki." In *Kokushi Daijiten* 国史大辞典. Tokyo: Yoshikawa Kobunkan, 1997.

Kubota Utsubo 窪田空穂. *Heian shūka zenki* 平安秀歌前期. Tokyo: Shunjūsha, 1957.

———. *Kokin wakashū hyōshaku* 古今和歌集評釋. Tokyo: Tōkyōdō, 1960.

Kubukihara Rei 久富木原玲. "Haikai no uta kara waka he" 誹諧の歌から和歌へ. *Kokugo to kokubungaku* 60, no. 1 (1983): 14–31.

———. "Zareuta no jidai Heian kōki waka no kadai" 戯れ歌の時代—平安後期和歌の課題. *Kokugo to kokubungaku* 63, no. 7 (1986): 43–57.

Kujō Michi'ie 九条道家. *Gyokuzui* 玉蘂. Edited by Imagawa Fumio 今川文雄. Kyoto: Shibunkaku Shuppan, 1984.

Kumakura Isao 熊倉功夫. *Nanpōroku wo yomu* 南方録を読む. Kyoto: Kōdansha, 1983.

Kuroda Hideo 黒田日出男. *Rekishi to shite no otogizōshi* 歴史としての御伽草子. Tokyo: Perikansha, 1996.

Kuroda Toshio 黒田俊雄. *Nihon chūsei no shakai to shūkyō* 日本中世の社会と宗教. Tokyo: Iwanami Shoten, 1990.

Kyūsojin Hitaku 久曽神昇, ed. *Date-bon Kokin waka shū Fujiwara Teika hitsu* 伊達本古今和歌集藤原定家筆. Tokyo: Kasama Shoin, 2005.

Laffin, Christina. *Rewriting Medieval Japanese Women: Politics, Personality, and Literary Production in the Life of Nun Abutsu*. Honolulu: University of Hawai'i Press, 2013.

LaFleur, William R. *The Karma of Words: Buddhism and the Literary Arts in Medieval Japan*. Los Angeles: University of California Press, 1983.

Levine, Caroline. *Forms: Whole, Rhythm, Hierarchy, Network*. Princeton, NJ: Princeton University Press, 2015.

Levy, Indra A. *Sirens of the Western Shore: The Westernesque Femme Fatale, Translation, and Vernacular Style in Modern Japanese Literature*. New York: Columbia University Press, 2006.

Lurie, David. *Realms of Literacy: Early Japan and the History of Writing*. Cambridge, MA: Harvard University Asia Center, 2011.

Mabuchi Kazuo 馬渕和夫, Kunisaki Fumimaro 国東文麿, and Inagaki Taiichi 稲垣泰一, eds. *Konjaku monogatari shū* 今昔物語集. 4 vols. Shinpen Nihon koten bungaku zenshū 35–38. Tokyo: Shōgakkan, 1999.

Manieri, Antonio. "Technical Education in Nara Japan: Text and Context of the *Yōshi Kangoshō* (ca. 720)." *Annali Sezione Orientale* 82, nos. 1–2 (2022): 172–210.

Marra, Michele. "Nativist Hermeneutics: The Interpretative Strategies of Motoori Norinaga and Fujitani Mitsue." In *Essays on Japan: Between Aesthetics and Literature*, 365–415. Boston: Brill, 2010.

———. *Representations of Power: The Literary Politics of Medieval Japan*. Honolulu: University of Hawai'i Press, 1993.

———. "Semi-Recluses (*tonseisha*) and Impermanence (*mujō*): Kamo no Chōmei and Urabe Kenkō." *Japanese Journal of Religious Studies* 11, no. 4 (1984): 313–50.

Mars, Roman, and Kurt Kohlstedt. *The 99% Invisible City: A Field Guide to the Hidden World of Everyday Design*. New York: Dey Street Books, 2020.

Masaoka Shiki 正岡子規. "Dassai-sho'oku haiwa" 獺祭書屋俳話. In *Masaoka Shiki shū*, 137–43.

———. "Haikai taiyō" 俳諧大要. In *Masaoka Shiki shū*, 219–87.

———. "*Man'yōshū* maki jūroku" 万葉集巻十六. In *Shiki zenshū* 子規全集, vol. 7, 133. Tokyo: Kōdansha, 1975.

———. *Masaoka Shiki shū* 正岡子規集. Edited by Matsui Toshihiko 松井利彦. Nihon koten bungaku taikei 16. Tokyo: Kadokawa shoten, 1969.

———. "Utayomi ni atauru sho" 歌よみに与ふる書. In *Masaoka Shiki shū*, 289–344.

Mass, Jeffrey, ed. *Court and Bakufu in Japan: Essays in Kamakura History*. New Haven, CT: Yale University Press, 1982.

———. *The Development of Kamakura Rule, 1180–1250: A History with Documents*. Stanford, CA: Stanford University Press, 1979.

———. *Warrior Government in Early Medieval Japan: A Study of the Kamakura Bakufu, Shugo, and Jitō*. New Haven, CT: Yale University Press, 1974.

Massumi, Brian. "The Autonomy of Affect." *Cultural Critique* 31, pt. 2 (Autumn 1995): 83–109.

Matsuno Yōichi 松野陽一. *Fujiwara Toshinari no kenkyū* 藤原俊成の研究. Tokyo: Kasama Shoin, 1973.

Matsuyama Hiroshi 松山宏. *Chūsei jōkamachi no kenkyū* 中世城下町の研究. Tokyo: Kindai Bungeisha, 1991.

Matsuzono Hitoshi 松薗斉. *Nikki no ie: Chūsei kokka no kiroku soshiki* 日記の家: 中世国家の記録組織. Tokyo: Yoshikawa Kōbunkan, 1997.

McAuley, Thomas E. "A Fine Thing for the Way: Evidence, Counter-Evidence and Argument in the *Poetry Contest in Six Hundred Rounds*." *Japan Forum* 33, no. 4 (2021): 704–30.

McCarty, Michael. "Divided Loyalties and Shifting Perceptions: The Jōkyū Disturbance and Courtier-Warrior Relations in Medieval Japan." PhD diss., Columbia University, 2013.

McClure, George W. *The Culture of Profession in Late Renaissance Italy*. Toronto: University of Toronto Press, 2004.

McCormick, Melissa. "The Gilded Library: Bridal Treasuries, Illustrated Manuscripts and the Song of Everlasting Sorrow." In *Splendours of Japan: Highlights from the Bodleian Library*, edited by the Bodleian Library, 50–89. Chicago: University of Chicago Press, 2025.

Mezaki Tokue 目崎徳衛. *Heian bunkashi ron* 平安文化史論. Tokyo: Ōfūsha, 1968.

Miller, Roy. "The 'Spirit' of the Japanese Language." *Journal of Japanese Studies* 3, no. 2 (1977): 251–98.

Miller, Stephen D. *The Wind from Vulture Peak: The Buddhification of Japanese Waka in the Heian Period*. Ithaca, NY: Cornell University East Asia Program, 2013.

Minamoto no Mitsuyuki 源光行. *Mōgyu waka* 蒙求和歌. In *Zoku gunsho ruijū* 続群書類従, vol. 15 (upper), 74–150.

Minamoto no Tamenori 源為憲. *Kuchizusami* 口遊. In *Zoku gunsho ruijū* 続群書類従, vol. 32, 61–85.

———. *Kuchizusami chūkai* 口遊注解. Edited by Yōgaku no Kai 幼学の会. Tokyo: Benseisha, 1997.

Minamoto no Toshiyori 源俊頼. *Toshiyori zuinō* 俊頼髄脳. In Hashimoto, Ariyoshi, and Fujihira, *Karonshū*, 15–254.

Misumi Yōichi 三角洋一. "Iwayuru kyōgen kigo kan ni tsuite" いわゆる狂言綺語観について. In Wakan hikaku bungakukai, 和漢比較文学会, ed. *Shinkokinshū to kanbungaku* 新古今集と漢文学, 23–40. Tokyo: Kyūko Shoin, 1992.

Miura Kei'ichi 三浦圭一. *Nihon chūsei no chiiki to shakai* 日本中世の地域と社会. Tokyo: Shibunkaku Shuppan, 1993.

Monokusa Tarō 物くさ太郎. NDL Digital Collections, 7325469, 午-66, 2 vols. National Diet Library. https://dl.ndl.go.jp/pid/2574839.

Monokusa Tarō emaki 物臭太郎繪巻. Nakamozu Library, Ōsaka Metropolitan University, 913.49M2, 244.0018.007, 36B. National Institute of Japanese Literature. https://kokusho.nijl.ac.jp/biblio/100074954.

Moretti, Laura. *Pleasure in Profit: Popular Prose in Seventeenth-Century Japan*. New York: Columbia University Press, 2020.

Morii Nobuko 森井信子. "Abtsu-ni to genji monogatari" 阿仏尼と『源氏物語』. *Tsurumi nihon bungaku* 5 (2001): 39–48.

Moriyama Shigeru 森山茂. "Karon to setsuwa Ōgishō to *Fukurozōshi* to taishō ni" 歌論と説話：『奥義抄』と『袋草紙』とを対象に. *Onomichi daigaku geijutsu bunka gakubu kiyō*, no. 1 (2002): 12–22.

———. "Katoku no shujusō" 歌徳の種々相. *Onomichi tanki daigaku kenkyū kiyō* 26 (1977): 1–22.

———. "Katoku setsuwa no denshō ni tsuite" 歌徳伝承について. *Onomichi tanki daigaku kenkyū kiyō* 24 (1975): 1–20.

———. "Katoku setsuwa no waka ni tsuite" 歌徳説話の和歌について. *Onomichi tanki daigaku kenkyū kiyō* 25 (1976): 1–22.

———. "Katoku setsuwa ron josetsu" 歌徳説話論序説. *Onomichi tanki daigaku kenkyū kiyō* 23 (1974): 1–20.

———. "*Toshiyori zuinō* to ōgishō to no sōi kyōtsū suru jikō no kentō wo tōshite"『俊頼髄脳』と『奥義抄』との相違—共通する事項の検討を通して. *Onomichi tanki daigaku kenkyū kiyō* 48, no. 3 (1999): 27–56.

Morrell, Robert. "The Buddhist Poetry in the *Goshuishu*." *Monumenta Nipponica* 28, no. 1 (1973): 87–100.

Morris, Julie. "*Imayō* as a Vocal Art Supreme: Transformation of the Body in *Ryōjin hishō*." Master's thesis, University of California, Los Angeles, 2023.

Morris, Mark. "Buson and Shiki: Part One." *Harvard Journal of Asiatic Studies* 44, no. 2 (1984): 381–425.

———. "Buson and Shiki: Part Two." *Harvard Journal of Asiatic Studies* 45, no. 1 (1985): 255–321.

———. "*Waka* and Form, *Waka* and History." *Harvard Journal of Asiatic Studies* 46, no. 2 (1986): 551–610.

Mujū Ichien 無住一円. *Shasekishū* 沙石集. Edited by Kojima Takayuki 小島孝之. Shinpen Nihon koten bungaku zenshū 52. Tokyo: Shōgakkan, 2001.

———. *Shasekishū* 沙石集. Edited by Watanabe Tsunaya 渡邊綱也. Tokyo: Nihon Shobō, 1943.

Mulhern, Chieko Irie. "*Otogi-zōshi*: Short Stories of the Muromachi Period." *Monumenta Nipponica* 29, no. 2 (1974): 181–98.

Murai Yasuhiko 村井康彦. *Buke bunka to dōhōshū: seikatsu bunka shiron* 武家文化と同朋衆: 生活文化史論. Tokyo: San'ichi Shobō, 1991.

Murphy, Regan E. "The Urgency of History: Language and Ritual in Japanese Buddhism and Kokugaku." PhD diss., Harvard University, 2010.

Nagai Yoshinori 永井義憲. "*Jikkinshō* no sakusha (Yuasa Munenori)" 十訓抄の作者(湯浅宗業). *Kokugo to kokubungaku* 9 (1952): 34–36.

Nagazumi Yasuaki 永積安明, ed. *Jikkinshō* 十訓抄. Iwanami bunko. Tokyo: Iwanami Shoten, 1957.

Nihon kokugo daijiten 日本国語大辞典. Tokyo: Shōgakkan, 2003.

Nishijima Masayuki 西島政之, ed. *Jikkinshō* 十訓抄. Kokushi taikei 15. Tokyo: Keizai Zasshisha, 1901.

Nishiki Hitoshi 錦仁. "Waka no shisō eigin wo shiza to shite" 和歌の思想—詠吟を視座として. In Inseiki Bunka Kenkyūkai, *Kenryoku to bunka*, 233–73.

Nivison, David. *The Ways of Confucianism: Investigations in Chinese Philosophy*. Chicago: Open Court, 1996.

Norman, Donald. *The Design of Everyday Things*. Rev. ed. New York: Basic Books, 2013.

Ocha monogatari 御茶物語. Tokyo National University, microfilm 4-3-7. https://kotenseki.nijl.ac.jp/biblio/100000174.

Ogawa Takeo 小川剛生. *Bushi wa naze uta wo yomu ka: Kamakura shōgun kara sengoku daimyō made* 武士はなぜ歌を詠むか：鎌倉将軍から戦国大名まで. Tokyo: Kadokawa Gakugei Shuppan, 2008.

———. *Chūsei no shomotsu to gakumon* 中世の書物と学問. Tokyo: Yamakawa Shuppansha, 2009.

Ogawa Toyō 小川豊生. "Katoku ron josetsu" 歌徳論序説. In Watanabe Yasuaki, *Higi to shite no waka*, 55–74.

———. "Katoku ron josetsu (ni)" 歌徳論序説(二). In *Uta monogatari to waka setsuwa* 歌物語と和歌説話. Osaka: Seibundō Shuppan, 1999, 239–73.

Okada, Richard. *Figures of Resistance: Language, Poetry, and Narrating in "The Tale of Genji" and Other Mid-Heian Texts*. Durham, NC: Duke University Press, 1991.

Okakura, Kakuzō. *The Book of Tea*. New York: Putman, 1906.

Orikuchi Shinobu 折口信夫. *Orikuchi Shinobu zenshū* 折口信夫全集, vol. 23. Tokyo: Chūō Kōronsha, 1997.

Ōsumi Kazuo 大隅和雄. *Jiten no kataru nihon no rekishi* 事典の語る日本の歴史. Tokyo: Kōdansha gakujutsu bunko, 2008.

Ōwada Tateki 大和田建樹. *Meiji bungakushi* 明治文学史. Edited by Hiraoka Toshio 平岡敏夫. Tokyo: Nihon Tosho Sentā, 1982.

Oxenboell, Morten. *Akutō and Rural Conflict in Medieval Japan*. Honolulu: University of Hawai'i Press, 2018.

Pandey, Rajyashree. *Perfumed Sleeves and Tangled Hair: Body, Woman, and Desire in Medieval Japanese Narratives*. Honolulu: University of Hawai'i Press, 2016.

———. *Writing and Renunciation in Medieval Japan: The Works of the Poet-Priest Kamo no Chōmei*. Ann Arbor: Center for Japanese Studies, University of Michigan, 1998.

Persiani, Gian-Piero. "China as Self, China as Other: On Ki no Tsurayuki's Use of the *wa-kan* Dichotomy." *Sino-Japanese Studies* 23 (2016): 31–58.

Piggott, Joan R. "Defining 'Ancient' and 'Classical.'" In Friday, *Japan Emerging*, 21–31.

Pitelka, Morgan. *Reading Medieval Ruins: Urban Life and Destruction in Sixteenth-Century Japan*. Cambridge: Cambridge University Press, 2022.

Plutschow, Herbert E. *Chaos and Cosmos: Ritual in Early and Medieval Japanese Literature*. Leiden: Brill, 1990.

———. *Rediscovering Rikyu and the Beginnings of the Japanese Tea Ceremony*. Folkestone, UK: Global Oriental, 2003.

Putzar, Edward D., trans. "The Tale of Monkey Genji: *Sarugenji-Zōshi*." *Monumenta Nipponica* 18, nos. 1–4 (1963): 286–312.

Rabinovitch, Judith. "Wasp Waists and Monkey Tails: A Study and Translation of Hamanari's *Uta No Shiki* (*The Code of Poetry*, 772), Also Known as *Kakyō Hyōshiki (A Formulary for Verse Based on the Canons of Poetry).*" *Harvard Journal of Asiatic Studies* 51, no.2 (1991): 471–560.

Ramirez-Christensen, Esperanza. *Emptiness and Temporality: Buddhism and Medieval Japanese Poetry*. Stanford, CA: Stanford University Press, 2008.

Ratcliff, Christian. "The Cultural Arts in Service: The Careers of Asukai Masaari and His Lineage." PhD diss., Yale University, 2007.

Reider, Noriko T. "'Menoto no sōshi' (A Tale of Two Nursemaids): Teaching for the Women of High Society in the Medieval Period." *U.S.-Japan Women's Journal*, no. 42 (2012): 62–83.

Rhee, Song Nai, and C. Melvin Aikens, with Gina L. Barnes. *Archaeology and History of Toraijin: Human, Technological, and Cultural Flow from the Korean Peninsula to the Japanese Archipelago c. 800 BC–AD 600*. Oxford: Archaeopress Archaeology, 2021.

Ricœur, Paul. *The Conflict of Interpretations: Essays in Hermeneutics*. Edited by Don Ihde. Evanston, IL: Northwestern University Press, 1974.

Rowley, G. G. "The Tale of Genji: Required Reading for Aristocratic Women." In *The Female as Subject: Reading and Writing in Early Modern Japan*, edited by P. F. Kornicki, Mara Patessio, and G. G. Rowley, 39–57. Ann Arbor: Center for Japanese Studies, University of Michigan, 2010.

Royston, Clifton W. "*Utaawase* Judgments as Poetry Criticism." *Journal of Asian Studies* 34, no. 1 (1974): 99–108.

Ruch, Barbara. "Medieval Jongleurs and the Making of a National Literature." In *Japan in the Muromachi Age*, edited by John Whitney Hall and Toyoda Takeshi, 279–309. Berkeley: University of California Press, 1977.

Sakomura, Tomoko. *Poetry as Image: The Visual Culture of Waka in Sixteenth-Century Japan*. Leiden: Brill, 2016.

Sakurai Rika 桜井利佳. "*Kokonchomonjū* no wakasetsuwa: Ietaka Teika setsuwa ni miru setsuwa saitaku no hōhō" 古今著聞集の和歌説話―家隆・定家説話にみる説話採択の方法. *Tōyō daigaku daigakuin kiyō* 42 (2005): 55–71.

Sakurai Yoshirō 桜井好郎. "Gekokujō to kamigami *Monokusa Tarō kō*" 下剋上と神々—物くさ太郎考. In *Chūsei Nihon no seishinshiteki keikan* 中世日本の精神史的景観, 314–343. Tokyo: Hanawa Shobō, 1974.

Santō Kyōzan 山東京山 and Utagawa Toyokuni II 歌川二代目豊国. *Kyōkun menoto no sōshi* 教訓乳母草子. 10 vols. Kikakudo 喜鶴堂 [Sanoya Kihei 佐野屋喜兵衛], 1844.

Satake Akihiro 佐竹昭広. "Taida to teikō: *Monokusa Tarō*" 怠惰と抵抗物くさ太郎. In *Gekokujō no bungaku* 下剋上の文学, 5–36. Tokyo: Chikuma shobō, 1967.

Satō Kōmei 佐藤高明. "Gosenshū no utaawase uta no itsudatsu ni tsuite" 後撰集の歌合歌の逸脱について. *Gengo to bungei* 1, no. 5 (1959): 21–29.

Sawai Taizō 沢井耐三. "Waka renga to otogizōshi" 和歌・連歌と御伽草子. In *Otogizōshi hyakka ryōran* お伽草子百花繚乱, edited by Tokuda Kazuo 徳田和夫, 282–97. Tokyo: Kasama Shoin, 2008.

Scheid, Bernhard, and Mark Teeuwen, eds. *The Culture of Secrecy in Japanese Religion*. New York: Routledge, 2006.

Schreiber, Gordian. *Japanese Morphography*. Leiden: Brill, 2023.

Sedgwick, Eve Kosofsky. *Touching Feeling: Affect, Pedagogy, Performativity*. Durham, NC: Duke University Press, 2003.

Seeley, Christopher. *A History of Writing in Japan*. Leiden: Brill, 1991.

Segal, Ethan. "Awash with Coins: The Spread of Money in Early Medieval Japan." In *Currents in Medieval Japanese History: Essays in Honor of Jeffrey P. Mass*, edited by Gordon Mark Berger, Andrew Edmund Goble, Lorraine F. Harrington, and G. Cameron Hurst III, 331–61. Los Angeles: Figueroa Press, 2009.

———. *Coins, Trade, and the State: Economic Growth in Early Medieval Japan*. Cambridge, MA: Harvard University Asia Center, 2011.

Sei Shōnagon 清少納言. *Makura no sōshi* 枕草子. Edited by Matsuo Satoshi 松尾聰 and Nagai Kazuko 永井和子. Shinpen Nihon koten bungaku zenshū 18. Tokyo: Shōgakukan, 1997.

Seigworth, Gregory J., and Melissa Gregg. "An Inventory of Shimmers." In *The Affect Theory Reader*, edited by Melissa Gregg and Gregory J. Seigworth, 1–25. Durham, NC: Duke University Press, 2010.

Sen Sōshitsu 千宗室, ed. "Chadō kyōyu hyakushu ei." In *Chadō koten zenshū*, 133–47. Kyoto: Tankō shinsha, 1961.

Shibayama, Saeko. "Ōe no Masafusa and the Convergence of the 'Ways': The Twilight of Early Chinese Literary Studies and the Rise of *Waka* Studies in the Long Twelfth Century in Japan." PhD diss., Columbia University, 2012.

Shibukawa Seiemon 渋川清右衛門, ed. *Shūgen otogi bunko* 祝言御伽文庫. 23 vols. Osaka: Shibukawa Seiemon, ca. 1716–29.

Shimura Kunihiro 志村有弘. "Jikkinshō no hensha ni tsuite: Sugawara no Tamenaga setsu saikō" 「十訓抄」の編者について: 菅原為長説再考. *Baikō jogakuin daigaku kokugo kokubungaku kai* 9 (1973): 59–70.

Shinoda Jun'ichi. "Musō *Monokusa Taro* ron" 夢想「物くさ太郎」論. In *Kokugo kokubungaku ronshū: Taniyama Shigeru Kyōju taishoku kinen* 国語国文学論集：谷山茂教授退職記念, 199–228. Tokyo: Hanawa Shobō, 1972.

Shinpen Kokka Taikan 新編国歌大観. Edited by Shinpen Kokka Taikan Henshū Iinkai「新編国歌大観」編集委員会. Tokyo: Kadokawa Shoten, 1983–1992.

Shirane, Haruo. *The Bridge of Dreams: A Poetics of "The Tale of Genji."* Stanford, CA: Stanford University Press, 1987.

———, ed. *Envisioning "The Tale of Genji": Media, Gender, and Cultural Production*. New York: Columbia University Press, 2008.

Shōtetsu 正徹. *Shōtetsu monogatari* 正徹物語. Edited by Ogawa Takeo 小川剛生. Kadokawa Sophia bunko 317-1. Tokyo: Kadokawa Gakugei Shuppan, 2011.

Skord, Virginia. "*Monogusa Taro*: From Rags to Riches and Beyond." *Monumenta Nipponica* 44, no. 2 (1989): 171–98.

———, trans. *Tales of Tears and Laughter: Short Fiction of Medieval Japan*. Honolulu: University of Hawai'i Press, 1991.

Smits, Ivo. *The Pursuit of Loneliness: Chinese and Japanese Nature Poetry in Medieval Japan, ca. 1050 –1150*. Stuttgart: Steiner, 1995.

———. "Teika and the Others: Poetics, Poetry, and Politics in Early Medieval Japan," review of *The Making of Shinkokinshū* by Robert N. Huey and *Fujiwara no Teika (1162-1241) et la notion d'excellence en poésie* by Michel Vieillard-Baron.

Sorensen, Joseph T. *Optical Allusions: Screens, Paintings, and Poetry in Classical Japan (ca. 800–1200)*. Leiden: Brill, 2012.

Steininger, Brian. *Chinese Literary Forms in Heian Japan: Poetics and Practice*. Cambridge, MA: Harvard University Asia Center, 2017.

Stockdale, Jonathan. *Imagining Exile in Heian Japan: Banishment in Law, Literature, and Cult*. Honolulu: University of Hawai'i Press, 2015.

Stone, Jacqueline. *Original Enlightenment and the Transformation of Medieval Japanese Buddhism*. Honolulu: University of Hawai'i Press, 2003.

Surak, Kristin. *Making Tea, Making Japan: Cultural Nationalism in Practice*. Stanford, CA: Stanford University Press, 2012.

Suzuki Hiro'o 鈴木博雄. *Genten kaisetsu Nihon kyōikushi* 原典・解説日本教育史. Tokyo: Nihon Tosho Bunka Kyōkai, 1985.

Suzuki Norio 鈴木徳男. *Toshiyori zuinō no kenkyū* 俊頼髄脳の研究. Tokyo: Shibunkaku shuppan, 2006.

Suzuki Takao 鈴木孝夫. *Tozasareta gengo nihongo no sekai* 閉された言語・日本語の世界. Tokyo: Shinchōsha, 1975.

Suzuki, Tomi. *Narrating the Self: Fictions of Japanese Modernity*. Stanford, CA: Stanford University Press, 1996.

Swanson, Paul L. *Foundations of T'ien-T'ai Philosophy: The Flowering of the Two Truths Theory in Chinese Buddhism*. Berkeley, CA: Asian Humanities Press, 1989.

Tabuchi Kumiko 田淵句美子, Komeda Yuri 米田有里, Ikuura Hiroyuki 幾浦裕之, and Saitō Ruka 斉藤瑠花, eds. *Abutsu no fumi menoto no fumi niwa no oshie chūshaku* 阿仏の文乳母の文庭の訓注釈. Tokyo: Seikansha, 2023.

Tachibana Kenji 橘健二 and Katō Shizuko 加藤静子, eds. *Ōkagami* 大鏡. Shinpen Nihon koten bungaku zenshū 34. Tokyo: Shōgakkan, 1996.

Tachibana no Narisue 橘成季. *Kokonchomonjū* 古今著聞集. Edited by Nagazumi Yasuaki 永積安明 and Shimada Isao 島田勇雄. Nihon koten bungaku taikei 84. Tokyo: Iwanami shoten, 1966.

———. *Kokonchomonjū*. Edited by Nakajima Etsuji 中島悦次. Tokyo: Kadokawa, 1975.

———. *Kokonchomonjū*. Edited by Nishio Kōichi 西尾光一 and Kobayashi Yasuharu 小林保治. Shinchō Nihon koten shūsei 76. Tokyo: Shinchōsha, 1986.

Takahashi Noriko 高橋則子. *Monokusa Tarō*. In *Nihon kakū denshō jinmei jiten* 日本架空伝承人名事典, edited by Ōsumi Kazuo. Tokyo: Heibonsha, 2000. Accessed August 7, 2025. https://japanknowledge.com/lib/display/?lid=52510KK0062800.

Takahashi Tadahiko 高橋忠彦 and Takahashi Hisako 高橋久子. *Nihon no kojisho: Jobun batsubun wo yomu* 日本の古辞書: 序文・跋文を読む. Tokyo: Taishūkan Shoten, 2006.

Takeda, Katsuhiko 武田勝彦, ed. *Essays on Japanese Literature*. Tokyo: Waseda University Press, 1977.

Takuan Sōhō 澤庵宗彭. *Chagu shiika* 茶具詩歌. In *Takuan oshō zenshū* 沢庵和尚全集, edited by Takuan Oshō Zenshū Kankōkai, 1–7. Tokyo: Nihon Tosho Sentā, 2001.

Tanaka Fumio 田中史生. *Tōraijin to Kikajin* 渡来人と帰化人. Tokyo: Kadokawa, 2021.

Tanaka Yutaka 田中裕. *Teika karonshū* 定家歌論集. Tokyo: Shintensha, 1969.

Teele, Nicholas J. "Rules for Poetic Elegance: Fujiwara no Kintō's *Shinsen Zuinō* and *Waka Kuhon*." *Monumenta Nipponica* 31, no. 2 (1976): 154–64.

Thomas, Roger K. *The Way of Shikishima: Waka Theory and Practice in Early Modern Japan*. Lanham, MD: University Press of America, 2008.

Tokuda Kazuo 徳田和夫, ed. *Otogizōshi jiten* お伽草子事典. Tokyo: Tōkyōdō Shuppan, 2002.

Tomkins, Silvan S. *Affect Imagery Consciousness: The Complete Edition*. New York: Springer, 2008.

Tommasi, Pier Carlo. "Neither Plagiarism nor Patchwork: The Culture of Citation and the Making of Authorship in Medieval Japanese Poetry." *Monumenta Nipponica* 77, no. 2 (2022): 207–58.

Tonomura, Hitomi. "Coercive Sex in the Medieval Japanese Court: Lady Nijō's Memoir." *Monumenta Nipponica* 61, no. 3 (2006): 283–338.

———. *Community and Commerce in Late Medieval Japan: The Corporate Villages of Tokuchin-ho*. Stanford, CA: Stanford University Press, 1992.

Toyama Masakazu 外山正一, Yatabe Ryōkichi 矢田部良吉, and Inoue Tetsujirō 井上哲次郎, eds. *Shintaishi-shō* 新体詩抄. In *Meiji Taishō yakushishū* 明治大正訳詩集, edited by Yoshida Seiichi 吉田精一 and Mori Ryō 森亮. Nihon kindai bungaku taikei 52, 59–103. Tokyo: Kadokawa Shoten, 1971.

Tsukishima Hiroshi 築島裕. *Wamyō ruijushō* 和名類聚抄. In *Kokushi Daijiten* 国史大辞典. Tokyo: Yoshikawa Kōbunkan 吉川弘文館, 1997.

Tsutsui Hiroichi 筒井紘一. *Chanoyu kotohajime: Shoki chadōshi ronkō* 茶の湯事始: 初期茶道史論考. Tokyo: Kōdansha, 1992.

———. *Chasho no kenkyū: Suki furyū no seiritsu to tenkai* 茶書の研究 : 数寄風流の成立と展開. Kyoto: Tankōsha, 2003.

Tuck, Robert. *Idly Scribbling Rhymers: Poetry, Print, and Community in Nineteenth-Century Japan*. New York: Columbia University Press, 2018.

Umeda Kei 梅田径. "Tsūdoku suru kagakusho, kensaku suru kagakusho" 通読する歌学書、検索する歌学書. *Waseda RILAS* [Research Institute for Letters, Arts, and Sciences] *Journal* 2 (2014): 15–25.

———. "'Waka shogakushō' no shomen sen'i: Kōmoku haichi to kyōju" 『和歌初学抄』の書面遷移: 項目配置と享受. *Jinbungaku no shōgo* 4 (2013): 39–56.

Ury, Marion. "Chinese Learning and Intellectual Life." In *The Cambridge History of Japan,* vol. 2, *Heian Japan*, edited by Donald H. Shively and William H. McCullough, 341–89. Cambridge: Cambridge University Press, 1999.

Vieillard-Baron, Michel. "Issues at Stake in Poetic Commentary in Medieval Japan: Fujiwara no Teika's *Secret Investigations of Kenshō's Commentary [on Kokin waka shū], Kenchū mikkan* (1221)." *Journal of the European Association for Chinese Studies* 5 (2024): 225–44.

Von Verschuer, Charlotte. "Life of Commoners in the Provinces: The Owari no Gebumi of 988." In Adolphson, Kamens, and Matsumoto, *Heian Japan*, 305–28.

Vovin, Alexander, ed. and trans. *Man'yōshū (Book 16): A New English Translation Containing the Original Text, Kana Transliteration, Romanization, Glossing and Commentary*. Leiden: Brill, 2021.

Wakita Haruko 脇田晴子. *Muromachi jidai* 室町時代. Chūkō shinsho 776. Tokyo: Chūō Kōronsha, 1985.

Watanabe Shōichi 渡部昇一. *Nihongo no kokoro* 日本語のこころ. Tokyo: Kōdansha, 1974.

Watanabe, Takeshi. "Versifying for Others: Akazome Emon's Proxy Poems." *Monumenta Nipponica* 77, no. 1 (2022): 1–26.

Watanabe Yasuaki 渡部泰明. "Kyōgen kigo kan wo megutte" 狂言綺語観をめぐって. In *Chūsei waka no seisei* 中世和歌の生成. Tokyo: Wakakusa shōbō, 1999.

———, ed. *Higi to shite no waka: Kōi to ba* 秘儀としての和歌: 行為と場. Tokyo: Yūseidō, 1995.

Watanabe, Yumiko, and Eric Esteban. "Hearkening to the 'Voice' of Teika: Authors and Readers of Poetry Treatise Forgeries in Medieval Japan." *Postmedieval* 15 (2024): 461–85.

Waters, Virginia Skord. "Sex, Lies, and the Illustrated Scroll: The *Dōjōji Engi Emaki*." *Monumenta Nipponica* 52, no. 1 (1997): 59–84.

Willis, Ika. "Reception Theory, Reception History, Reception Studies." *Oxford Research Encyclopedia of Literature*. Oxford: Oxford University Press, 2021.

Wimsatt, W. K., and M. C. Beardsley. "The Intentional Fallacy." *Sewanee Review* 54, no. 3 (1946): 468–88.

Wixted, John Timothy. "Chinese Influences on the *Kokinshū* Prefaces." In *Kokinshū: A Collection of Poems Ancient and Modern*. Translated by Laurel Rasplica Rodd, with Mary Catherine Henkenius, 387–400. Princeton, NJ: Princeton University Press, 1984.

Yamada Shōzen 山田昭全. "Chūsei kōki ni okeru waka soku darani no jissen" 中世後期における和歌即陀羅尼の実践. *Indogaku bukkyōgaku kenkyū* 16, no. 1 (1967): 290–92.

Yamamura, Kōzō. "The Growth of Commerce in Medieval Japan." In *The Cambridge History of Japan*, vol. 3, *Medieval Japan*, edited by Yamamura Kōzō, 344–95. Cambridge: Cambridge University Press, 1990.

Yamasaki Kaoru 山崎薫. "I'hon *Ryōjin hishō kudenshū* no denpon: Maki dai-jū ichi wo chūshin ni"『異本梁塵秘抄口伝集』の伝本—巻第十一を中心に. *Heian-chō bungaku kenkyū* 28 (2019): 42–45.

Yanagi, Sōetsu. *The Unknown Craftsman: A Japanese Insight into Beauty.* Adapted by Bernard Leach. Tokyo: Kodansha International, 1972.

Yashima Chōjū 八島長寿. "*Maigetsushō* songi" 毎月抄存疑. *Kokugo* 2, no. 1 (1953): 1–21.

Yoshida Kazuhiko 吉田一彦, ed. *Shinbutsu yūgō no Higashi Ajia-shi* 神仏融合の東アジア史. Nagoya: Nagoya Daigaku Shuppankai, 2021.

Index

Page numbers for figures and tables are in italics.

Harvard East Asian Monographs
(most recent titles)

443. Adam J. Lyons, *Karma and Punishment: Prison Chaplaincy in Japan*
444. Craig A. Smith, *Chinese Asianism, 1894–1945*
445. Sachiko Kawai, *Uncertain Powers: Sen'yōmon-in and Landownership by Royal Women in Early Medieval Japan*
446. Juliane Noth, *Transmedial Landscapes and Modern Chinese Painting*
447. Susan Westhafer Furukawa, *The Afterlife of Toyotomi Hideyoshi: Historical Fiction and Popular Culture in Japan*
448. Nongji Zhang, *Legal Scholars and Scholarship in the People's Republic of China: The First Generation (1949–1992)*
449. Han Sang Kim, *Cine-Mobility: Twentieth-Century Transformations in Korea's Film and Transportation*
450. Brian Hurley, *Confluence and Conflict: Reading Transwar Japanese Literature and Thought*
451. Simon Avenell, *Asia and Postwar Japan: Deimperialization, Civic Activism, and National Identity*
452. Maura Dykstra, *Uncertainty in the Empire of Routine: The Administrative Revolution of the Eighteenth-Century Qing State*
453. Marnie S. Anderson, *In Close Association: Local Activist Networks in the Making of Japanese Modernity, 1868–1920*
454. John D. Wong, *Hong Kong Takes Flight: Commercial Aviation and the Making of a Global Hub, 1930s–1998*
455. Martin K. Whyte and Mary C. Brinton, compilers, *Remembering Ezra Vogel*
456. Lawrence Zhang, *Power for a Price: The Purchase of Appointments in Qing China*
457. J. Megan Greene, *Building a Nation at War: Transnational Knowledge Networks and the Development of China during and after World War II*
458. Miya Qiong Xie, *Territorializing Manchuria: The Transnational Frontier and Literatures of East Asia*
459. Dal Yong Jin, *Understanding Korean Webtoon Culture: Transmedia Storytelling, Digital Platforms, and Genres*
460. Takahiro Yamamoto, *Demarcating Japan: Imperialism, Islanders, and Mobility, 1855–1884*

461. Elad Alyagon, *Inked: Tattooed Soldiers and the Song Empire's Penal-Military Complex*
462. Börje Ljunggren and Dwight H. Perkins, eds., *Vietnam: Navigating a Rapidly Changing Economy, Society, and Political Order*
463. En Li, *Betting on the Civil Service Examinations: The Lottery in Late Qing China*
464. Matthieu Felt, *Meanings of Antiquity: Myth Interpretation in Premodern Japan*
465. William D. Fleming, *Strange Tales from Edo: Rewriting Chinese Fiction in Early Modern China*
466. Mark Baker, *Pivot of China: Spatial Politics and Inequality in Modern Zhengzhou*
467. Peter Banseok Kwon, *Cornerstone of the Nation: The Defense Industry and the Building of Modern Korea under Park Chung Hee*
468. Weipin Tsai, *The Making of China's Post Office: Sovereignty, Modernization, and the Connection of a Nation*
469. Michael A. Fuller, *An Introduction to Literary Chinese (Second Edition)*
470. Gustav Heldt, *Navigating Narratives: Tsurayuki's* Tosa Diary *as History and Fiction*
471. Xiaolu Ma, *Transpatial Modernity: Chinese Cultural Encounters with Russia via Japan (1880–1930)*
472. Yueduan Wang, *Experimentalist Constitutions: Subnational Policy Innovations in China, India, and the United States*
473. M. William Steele, *Rethinking Japan's Modernity: Stories and Translations*
474. Judith Vitale, *The Historical Writing of the Mongol Invasions in Japan*
475. Hang Tu, *Sentimental Republic: Chinese Intellectuals and the Maoist Past*
476. John D. Phan, *Lost Tongues of the Red River: Annamese Middle Chinese and the Origins of the Vietnamese Language*
477. Jungwon Kim, *Virtue That Matters: Chastity Culture and Social Power in Chosŏn Korea (1392–1910)*
478. Shiuon Chu, *Reinventing Examination and the State in Twentieth Century China and Taiwan*
479. Helen Hardacre, *Shinto Shrines in Prewar and Wartime Japan*
480. Wen-Chin Chang, *Echoes from the Sino-Burmese Borderlands: Untold Stories of Overland Chinese Migrants During the Cold War*
481. Talia Andrei, *Sacred Journeys and Institutional Rivalries: Pilgrimage Mandalas and the Art of Fundraising in Medieval Japan*
482. Ashton Lazarus, *Performing Transgression: Crowds and Bodies in Heian Japan*
483. Aihe Wang, *Painting into Being:Underground Art During China's Cultural Revolution*
484. Russell Burge, *The Promised Republic: Developmental Society and the Making of Modern Seoul, 1961–1979*
485. Ariel Stilerman, *Court Poetry and the Culture of Learning in Japan*